WOMEN WORKING
Theories and Facts in Perspective

WOMEN

WORKING

THEORIES AND FACTS IN PERSPECTIVE

EDITED BY

Ann H. Stromberg
PITZER COLLEGE

AND

Shirley Harkess
UNIVERSITY OF KANSAS

 Mayfield Publishing Company

Library of Congress Catalog Card Number: 77-089921
International Standard Book Number: 0-87484-301-4

The quotations on pages 363 and 365–6 are from *False
Promises* by Stanley Aronowitz. Copyright 1973 by
Stanley Aronowitz. Used with permission of McGraw-
Hill Book Company.

Manufactured in the United States of America
Mayfield Publishing Company
285 Hamilton Avenue, Palo Alto, California 94301

This book was set in TxT Baskerville by ATS and was
printed and bound by the R. R. Donnelley Company.
Sponsoring editor was Alden C. Paine, Carole Norton
supervised editing, and Zipporah Collins was manuscript editor. Michelle Hogan supervised production,
the book and cover were designed by Nancy Sears, and
photographs used on the cover are by Betty Medsger,
© Betty Medsger.

Ch 2 9 10   72pgs.

Contents

ONE

Women, Work, and the Labor Force

TWO

Sociological Perspectives on Women Working

THREE

Specific Occupational Experiences of Women

FOUR

Women's Work and Social Change

34
38

Preface and Acknowledgments

Until recently sociological studies of work devoted little attention to women. With a few notable exceptions, empirical investigations have concentrated on male-dominated occupations to the neglect of female-dominated occupations, such as retail sales work, clerical jobs, private household service, nursing, librarianship, social work, and elementary school teaching. Studies of occupations in which women are in the minority or are equally represented with men often view the women as deviants or ignore them entirely. Similarly, theoretical analyses of work processes and structures, supposedly sex-blind, have actually presented models of the work world of men. Women have figured primarily in sections treating the relationship between work and the family. With such empirical and theoretical bases, it is not surprising that leading sociological texts on work discuss women in special, usually short, subsections, or cover them only by implication. Differences in the labor force experience of men and women workers generally go unrecognized, and the work experience most common to women—household work—is rarely analyzed.

Recently, sociologists and economists have begun to devote more attention to women's work roles in the marketplace and in the home. This development is due in part to the growth in female labor force participation to the extent that the contributions and experiences of women workers can no longer be ignored. Today over half (53 percent) of the women eighteen to sixty-four years of age are employed and, according to the United States Women's Bureau, nine out of ten will participate in the labor force at some point in their lives. The growing attention to women's work may also be attributed to recent recognition and criticism of the biases implicit in numerous sociological studies. Now, by adapting old theories and methods and by developing new ones, many scholars—like the authors in this volume—are striving to describe and explain the work experiences of women more fully and accurately. From this intellectual and social ferment the present volume has emerged.

In 1973 each of us developed a course on women's work at our respective institutions, drawing on scattered sources in sociology and demography. We soon recognized that students needed a central reference. This volume attempts to provide an up-to-date description of women's market and nonmarket activities, their rewards, and their problems, in addition to original empirical and theoretical analyses of the work roles of women. It gives special emphasis to women workers frequently overlooked even in the study of female labor force participation, such as minority women, women in blue-collar and service jobs, private household workers, clerical workers, and women in the female-dominated professions. It also examines the work of housewives. Overall, the book underscores the differences between the work experiences of men and women: how their socialization and education prepare them for different work roles, how their life-cycles and careers interact in distinct ways, and how their positions and mobility in organizational hierarchies differ.

Most of the chapters are original materials commissioned especially for this volume, to cover areas of particular interest to us that had not been extensively researched in the past. While many of the contributions are exploratory rather than definitive, together they represent a significant foray into previously uncharted terrain. It is our hope that this venture will lead the way for further research.

The book is directed primarily to undergraduate students of sociology and women's studies who are enrolled in courses on sex roles, women in the economy, the sociology of occupations, and industrial sociology. It will also be useful to economics and business students in labor and management courses; and selected chapters are pertinent to sociology courses in social stratification, marriage and the family, social problems, and social theory. Although the articles were prepared with undergraduates in mind, more advanced students and professionals interested in the study of work may find that the readings enrich their background, and women and men in nonacademic settings may find them helpful in interpreting their own work experiences.

Many people have contributed to the development of this volume. Parker Marden introduced us to the study of women's labor force participation by way of demography. The work of Judith Blake, Alice Cook, Cynthia Fuchs Epstein, Jennie Farley, Helen Mayer Hacker, Juanita Kreps, Judith Long

Laws, Ann Oakley, Valerie Kincade Oppenheimer, and Constantina Safilios-Rothschild inspired us to pursue this topic.

Among the colleagues who encouraged us, we wish, in particular, to acknowledge the support of Rudi Volti, Jonathan Reader, Harvey Botwin, Jane Arnault, Mary Zimmerman, Jill Quadagno, Juanita Wehrle-Einhorn, Rita Napier, Sue Ellmaker, Janet Sharistanian, Gina Morantz, George Ritzer, and Nancy Mueller. Our assistants, Sharon Gluck, Stella Vlastos, and Rose Schneider, have also provided invaluable help.

We are most grateful to our contributors not only for their intellectual contributions but also for their helpful partnership and good-natured patience with a lengthy process of editing and review. We are also indebted to Helen Mayer Hacker, Ronald Pavalko, and Sandra Schickele for their reviews of the manuscript; all shortcomings, however, are entirely our responsibility. Finally, we wish to acknowledge the staff of Mayfield Publishing Company, and our copyeditor, Zipporah Collins, for their helpful advice, professional expertise, and generous assistance.

We especially wish to thank our parents for encouraging us to embark on careers in sociology.

Ann H. Stromberg
Shirley Harkess

Introduction

In the United States two men meeting for the first time are likely to exchange names and then immediately ask each other, "What do you do?" This illustrates the central importance of a man's work in American society. His occupation determines, to a large extent, his friends, his leisure activities, the role he plays in his community, and the prestige and deference he is accorded. Because of the significance of his occupational achievement to others, it is also crucial in determining how a man feels about himself.

If two strangers meet and one is a woman, the scenario is likely to be somewhat different. She may well be asked, "What does your husband do?" This shift in questions reflects the fact that a different set of assumptions applies to women, their work, and its role in their lives. Women are usually assumed to be attached to a man whose occupational status determines their own. If a woman is in the labor force, her occupation is assumed to be inferior in status to her husband's and work is assumed to be of secondary importance to her. Her labor as a housewife is difficult to classify in the terms used for occupations pursued in the labor force and is ignored. Until recently, hardly anyone considered the impact on women's self-esteem of these assumptions, which devalue women's work and ascribe status to wives on the basis of their husbands' achievements rather than their own.

In the past, many social scientists have shared these assumptions about men and women, work, and marriage, and their research has reflected cultural stereotypes. Economists, for example, have used models of labor force participation that assume women, not men, have household responsibilities. As a result, these researchers have been unable to compare men and women workers on an equal basis (Bell).* Sometimes biases are introduced because economists must rely on existing data bases, such as the United States census, whose definitions understate the occupational skills of women and underestimate their rates of unemployment. In the hands of the unsophisticated, census data may contribute to the notion that women are dependents and secondary wage earners whose labor is less significant than men's. Whatever the source of the biases, they often mask women's economic contributions to their families and society.

Like labor economists, occupational sociologists have tended to develop models and to select data that emphasize the work of men. In theorizing, they have equated the norm with male behavior; in their empirical investigations, they have concentrated on male-dominated occupations and male workers, often treating employed women as de-

*References in parentheses are to chapters in this volume.

viants (Acker). Women have been asked, for example, why they are working. They are not asked why they are not working. This reflects the belief that occupational achievement inevitably comes second to homemaking for women (and investigators may not consider homemaking as work). Often sociologists have also accepted the conventional wisdom about women's behavior patterns in the labor force, contributing to the perpetuation of a series of myths: that women work only for income that is nonessential to the family; that they have higher absenteeism and withdrawal rates, which make them less dependable than men and more costly to employers in terms of training investment; that women do not want responsibility on the job and shy away from promotions; and that they, unlike men, do not mind boring, repetitious work.

Recently, economists and sociologists have recognized the need to reexamine the employment of women. Two developments have roused this interest. First, women's participation in the labor force has grown to such an extent that their experiences and contributions to the economy can no longer be viewed as unimportant. In the last decade women have accounted for three-fifths of the increase in the civilian labor force, and they now constitute approximately two-fifths of all employed persons. Women workers no longer differ from the general female population—they are young, middle-aged, and elderly; white and minority women; working and middle class; mothers of young and older children; and childless women. The majority of them say they entered the labor force for the same reason men do—economic necessity. Women's participation in the labor force, in short, cannot be viewed as a deviant or insignificant activity.

The second reason for increased attention to the work roles of women is that social scientists have recognized and begun to make explicit the biased models implicit in much past research. They have initiated empirical investigations on women workers, and they have started to develop the theories and methods that are needed for a better understanding of women's work and its personal and social significance.

This collection of readings reflects these new developments. It offers empirical data and analyses, critiques of previous theories and models, alternative theoretical bases, and some projections about the future. The status of women in the labor force today is described generally (Blau) and in specific occupational categories (chapters in section three). One fact that emerges from the readings on women's work status is that, while the female labor force has changed dramatically in composition and volume in recent decades, some characteristics of women's participation remain amazingly resistant to change: their concentration in sex-typed jobs, their disproportionate share of low-ranking positions, and their relatively low earnings compared to men of similar training and experience. A number of social forces, most notably the women's liberation movement and recent federal legislation, have produced some pressure for change in these respects. However, relatively few resources are dedicated to enforcement of the laws that combat deep-seated attitudes and institutionalized patterns of differential treatment of women and men. It may be a long time before women gain an equal place in the labor market (Eastwood).

A second theme that emerges in the collection is that women workers share some common experiences, but they are also a diverse group. Too often researchers have concentrated on workers who are most like themselves (professionals) to the neglect of other sectors of the female labor force. Several of the articles here help to fill gaps in our knowledge about employed minority group women (Almquist and Wehrle-Einhorn, Baker, Katzman) and women in little-studied occupations, including female-dominated professions (such as librarianship and social work), clerical occupations, blue-collar and service occupations, private household service, and homemaking (Grimm, Olesen and Katsuranis, Baker, Katzman, and Vanek, respectively). Women in the male-dominated professions, however, are not ignored (Patterson and Engelberg).

Several readings note the biased nature of much traditional economic (Bell) and sociological (Acker) research on employed women. The authors attempt, however, to move beyond critiques of earlier work to lay the foundation for a more accurate and profound understanding of women and their work. To explain the particular characteristics of women's labor force participation, the contributors focus on theories of sex-role socialization, the family roles ascribed to women, employer discrimination, and the structure of the marketplace (Stevenson; chapters in section two). These same factors help to explain women's status in particular occupational groups (chapters in section three).

In considering why women's work takes the forms that it does, many of the authors stress the influence of social policies; and to improve employment opportunities for women, they recommend specific changes in the policies of schools and vocational training institutions, government agencies, and private companies (Safilios-Rothschild; also Rosenthal, Ireson, Moore and Sawhill, Baker, Katzman, and others).

These overarching themes appear and reappear throughout the four sections of the volume. The first section presents an overview of the status of women in the labor force. It gives a brief history of women's employment in the United States and a comprehensive assessment of the current situation. It also reviews the laws aimed at eliminating discrimination in the marketplace. The chapters in this section provide essential background for the subsequent sections.

The contributions in section two critique old and offer new sociological perspectives on women and work. The authors explore a variety of factors that shape women's work patterns and often discourage their high occupational achievement.

Section three presents analyses of women's statuses, experiences, and problems in a variety of white-collar and blue-collar occupations. While the authors present a rich diversity in their approaches, they pursue some common themes in examining the sex-typing of occupations and specialties, the educational and recruitment processes by which aspirants enter an occupation, the availability of channels for upward mobility, and the informal side of the work world. These original contributions begin the task of balancing the preoccupation of earlier research with men's occupational experiences.

The concluding article, in section four, speculates about women's work roles in the future and advocates significant changes in social policies regarding work and the family. These recommendations are aimed at improving the quality of work and family life for both men and women.

Taken together, the readings make it clear that the work experiences of women and men differ and that it is invalid to study men and then generalize to women by implication. The work women do at home and in the marketplace differs from that of men; the combination of unpaid and paid work in their lives is special; the significance attributed to their labor is different. We now need to expand

our understanding of women's work—its characteristics and determinants, and its consequences for
other important social relationships and institutions. The articles in this collection constitute an
important step in achieving that understanding.

Contributors

Ann H. Stromberg is Assistant Professor of Sociology at Pitzer College in Claremont, California, where she is also active in the Women's Studies program. She did her undergraduate work at Pomona College, where she was elected to Phi Beta Kappa, and her graduate studies at Columbia University and Cornell University. Previously she directed research projects for the Pan American Development Foundation, Washington, D.C., and for the Institute of Social Research and Development, University of New Mexico. Her current interests are in sex roles, population studies, sociology of health and medicine, and Latin American studies. Her earlier publications include *Philanthropic Foundations in Latin America* (1968) and several articles on health services in the United States and Latin America. She is particularly interested in the innovative teaching of undergraduates and is currently developing a course on women, health, and medicine.

Shirley Harkess is Associate Professor of Sociology at the University of Kansas in Lawrence, where she teaches urban sociology, population, sex roles, and women's employment. In 1976 she became Coordinator of Women's Studies. She received her B.A. in sociology from the College of William and Mary, where she was a member of Phi Beta Kappa, and her M.A. and Ph.D. in the same field from Cornell University. Her areas of interest include sex roles, Latin American studies, and social demography. Research conducted in Colombia, South America, provided the basis for her articles "The Pursuit of an Ideal: Migration, Social Class, and Women's Roles in Bogota, Colombia" (in *Female and Male in Latin America: Essays*, edited by Ann Pescatello, 1973) and (with Patricia Pinzon de Lewin) "Women, the Vote, and the Party in the Politics of the Colombian National Front" (*Journal of Interamerican Studies and World Affairs*, 1975). Forthcoming is an article on "Family and Sex Roles in Urban Society" (in *The Handbook of Urban Life*, edited by David Street, 1978).

Joan Acker is Associate Professor of Sociology at the University of Oregon. She is also Director of the Center for the Sociological Study of Women and a member of the Women's Studies Council of the university. She has written on theoretical issues concerning sex inequality in the study of stratification (*American Journal of Sociology*, 1973) and in the study of organizational structure (*Administrative Science Quarterly*, 1974). She is currently working on a study of the process of transition from housewife to worker among middle-aged women.

Elizabeth M. Almquist is Associate Professor of Sociology at North Texas State University. She is author of *Sex Roles, Tradition and Change* (1977) and coauthor (with Janet Chafetz, Barbara Chance, and Judy Corder-Bolz) of *Men, Women and Society*, a nonsexist introductory sociology text. She and Shirley S. Angrist published *Careers and Contingencies: How College Women Juggle with Gender* (1975), which traces the development of women's career aspirations during their four years of college. They are currently investigating the career implementations and feminist activities of the same women during the ten years following college and graduation.

Sally Hillsman Baker is a Project Director in the Research Department of the Vera Institute of Justice in New York City. She holds a Ph.D. in sociology from Columbia University and has taught at Queens College of the City University of New York and Columbia University. She has published articles on the educational and labor market experiences of working-class women and on work behavior and its psychological correlates. She is past Chair of the Poverty and Human Resources Division of the Society for the Study of Social Problems and is currently directing a study of pretrial diversion in the New York City criminal courts.

Carolyn Shaw Bell holds the Katharine Coman chair in economics at Welles-
ley College. She serves on the Executive Committee of the American Economic Association, the Board of Governors of the Amos Tuck School of
Business Administration at Dartmouth College, the Board of Trustees of the
Joint Council on Economic Education, and several editorial boards. She
chairs the Federal Advisory Council on Unemployment Insurance and is a
member of the Board of Advisers to the Center for Women Policy Studies as
well as the Public Interest Economics Center. She served on Jimmy Carter's
Economics Task Force during his campaign for president. Her research on
applied microeconomics and the appropriate unit for analysis has led to
extensive publications dealing with employment and income, in *Challenge,
Social Science Quarterly, The Public Interest, Social Research, Social Policy,* and
other journals.

Francine D. Blau is Assistant Professor of Economics and Labor and Industrial
Relations at the University of Illinois at Urbana-Champaign, where her
teaching includes courses on women in the economy. She was a founding
member of the American Economic Association Committee on the Status of
Women in the Economics Profession. She is coauthor (with Adele Simmons
and others) of the background paper for *Exploitation from 9 to 5: Report of the
Twentieth Century Fund Task Force on Women and Employment.* Her published arti-
cles include "'Women's Place in the Labor Market" (*American Economic Review,*
May 1972); "Women in the Labor Force: An Overview" (in *Women: A Feminist
Perspective,* edited by Jo Freeman, 1975): "Sex Segregation of Workers by
Enterprise in Clerical Occupations" (in *Labor Market Segmentation,* edited by
Richard Edwards and others, 1975); and (with Carol Jusenius) "Economists'
Approaches to Sex Segregation in the Labor Market: An Appraisal" (*Signs,*
spring 1976).

Mary Eastwood is an attorney in the U.S. Department of Justice, Washington,
D.C. She was formerly a technical secretary for the Civil and Political Rights
Committee of the President's Commission on the Status of Women, and has
served as technical legal assistant to the Citizens' Advisory Council on the
Status of Women. She is the author of several articles on legal theory and
women's rights, and a founding member of the National Organization for
Women, Federally Employed Women, and Human Rights for Women, Inc.
She is a member of the board of directors of Human Rights for Women and
a member of the National Council of the National Women's Party.

Laurie Engelberg is an advanced graduate student and teaching associate at the University of California, Los Angeles. She has authored a number of papers addressing the role of women in contemporary American society. Her primary interest is women's health care, and she has served as a consultant to the Department of Health, Education, and Welfare in an evaluation of the use of female paramedics in obstetrical and gynecological settings.

James W. Grimm is Associate Professor of Sociology at Western Kentucky University. He has published several articles on aspects of the female-dominated professions, such as the attitudes of nurses and social workers toward abortion (*American Journal of Public Health*, May 1974) and the attitudes of social work students toward the poor (*Social Work*, January 1973). His article "Sex Roles and Internal Labor Market Structures: The 'Female' Semi-Professions," appeared in *Social Problems*, June 1974. His major research interests now focus on the relationship between work activity and other social roles. He is currently doing research on the effects of embourgoisement and proletarianization in the middle class and, with Carol L. Kronus, is preparing a textbook on occupations and work.

Carol Ireson is Assistant Professor of Sociology and Women's Studies at Pomona College and has also taught in the Women's Studies Program at Cornell University. She is currently studying the effects of sex-role socialization on the achievement of adolescent girls.

Frances Katsuranis is a Ph.D. candidate in sociology at the University of California, San Francisco. She currently holds an appointment as a NIAAA research fellow with the Social Research Group in Berkeley. Her dissertation is a study of the non-degreed alcohol counselor, with special attention to the issue of professionalization.

David M. Katzman is Associate Professor of History at the University of Kansas and is currently engaged in research on the black working class and the nature of work in industrializing America. His most recent book is on domestic service, *Seven Days A Week: Women and Domestic Service in Industrializing America* (1977). He has also written *Before the Ghetto: Black Detroit in the Nineteenth Century* (1973), and is coauthor of *Three Generations of Americans* (1976).

Larry H. Long is Chief of the Population Analysis Staff, a research unit within the Census Bureau's Population Division. His studies of income and receipt of welfare among interregional migrants have appeared in the *American Sociological Review* (February 1974) and the *American Journal of Sociology* (May 1975). His study with Celia Boertlein titled *The Geographical Mobility of Americans: An International Comparison* will be published by the Census Bureau. He and his colleagues are currently developing data to measure the costs and benefits of geographical mobility for various population subgroups.

Kristin A. Moore is a social psychologist at the Urban Institute, a policy-oriented research organization in Washington, D.C. As part of a project on the social and economic status of women, she has recently completed a research report for the Department of Health, Education, and Welfare on out-of-wedlock childbearing and has begun work on a two-year study of the consequences of early childbearing. Her doctoral dissertation explored fear of success among a noncollege population.

Monica B. Morris is a member of the sociology faculty of Pomona College. Her recent book, *An Excursion into Creative Sociology* (1976) attempts to "demystify" ethnomethodology and other theoretical approaches of the "new wave." She has published several articles on sociological theory (*American Sociologist,* August 1975) and the press (*Sociolinguistics Newsletter,* February 1976; *Journalism Quarterly,* spring 1973, *Sociology and Social Research,* July 1973). Her current interests are in media and in aging. She is executive producer of a proposed television series, "Celebrate the Years!" and is presently preparing a book of the same title.

Virginia L. Olesen is Professor of Sociology at the University of California, San Francisco. With Elvi Whittaker she is the author of *The Silent Dialogue: The Social Psychology of Professional Socialization* (1968) and numerous articles on professional socialization, methodology of field work, and women's issues. She is currently working on a study of temporary service employees.

Michelle Patterson is Assistant Professor of Sociology at the University of California, Santa Barbara. She has written and lectured extensively on women in higher education and the professions. Among her publications are "Sex and Specialization in Academe and the Professions" (in *Academic*

Women on the Move, edited by Alice S. Rossi, 1973), "Some Limitations on Traditional Research on the Benefits of Higher Education: The Case of Women" (in *Does College Matter? Some Evidence on the Impact of Higher Education,* edited by Lewis C. Solmon and Paul J. Taubman, 1973), and "Alice in Wonderland: A Study of Women Faculty in Graduate Departments of Sociology" (in *American Sociologist,* August 1971). She is currently studying the attempt of women to break into the world of high finance by forming financial institutions such as banks.

Evelyn R. Rosenthal is Assistant Professor of Sociology at State University of New York at Binghamton, where she helped organize the Women's Studies Program. She is the faculty representative to the program's Executive Committee and co-chair for 1976–77 of the SUNY Caucus for Women's Rights. She teaches statistics, research methods, and social psychology and has published articles on education (*Educational Forum,* May 1976), comparative methodology (*Cornell Journal of Social Relations,* spring 1972) and women doctorate recipients (*AAUW Journal,* spring 1967). At present, she is completing the analysis of a six-year panel study of the school experience and educational attainment of over 2,000 men and women from the high school class of 1970.

Constantina Safilios-Rothschild is Professor of Sociology and Director of the Family Research Center at Wayne State University. She has conducted cross-cultural research on the options of men and women and taught sociology of women at the University of Zurich, Switzerland, and the Free University of Brussels, Belgium. She is the author of *Toward a Sociology of Women* (1972) and *Women and Social Policy* (1974) as well as a number of articles on sex roles, family power, the dual links between family and work, women's work commitment, and women and development.

Isabel V. Sawhill is Senior Research Associate and Director of a Program of Research on Women at the Urban Institute in Washington, D.C. She has written extensively on the economics of sex discrimination and coauthored (with Heather L. Ross) a book entitled *Time of Transition: The Growth of Families Headed by Women* (1975).

Mary Huff Stevenson is Assistant Professor of Economics at the University of Massachusetts at Boston. Her published articles include "Women's Wages and Job Segregation" (*Politics and Society,* 1973) and "Relative Wages and Sex Segregation by Occupation" in *Sex, Discrimination and the Division of Labor* (edited by Cynthia Lloyd, 1975). She is a coauthor (with Barry Bluestone and W. Murphy) of *Low Wages and the Working Poor* (1973).

Joann Vanek is Assistant Professor of Sociology at Queens College of the City University of New York. Her work has focused on historical time budget data and includes the article "Time Spent in Housework" (*Scientific American,* November 1974).

Juanita L. Wehrle-Einhorn earned her M.A. at the University of Maryland and originated and taught a course in sociology of women at Washburn University. She is currently a doctoral student in sociology at the University of Kansas, where she is an assistant to the Dean of Men.

WOMEN WORKING
Theories and Facts in Perspective

ONE

WOMEN, WORK, AND THE LABOR FORCE

EDITORS' INTRODUCTION

If work is defined as goal-directed expenditure of energy,[1] it is apparent that almost everyone works—students, volunteers in community organizations, and housewives, as well as participants in the labor force. The work people do is of great personal and social significance. For young people, involvement in work-oriented relationships is an important part of socialization and preparation for adulthood. For people of all ages work establishes patterns of social interaction, drawing workers to common places where they meet, talk, and make friends. Moreover work imposes a schedule and pattern on our lives, providing individuals and society with a predictable structure.[2]

Work also plays an important role in helping individuals establish their identity and self-esteem. It contributes to people's self-esteem in two ways. First, people derive a sense of mastery over themselves and their environment through the awareness of their efficacy and competence in producing or accomplishing something. Secondly, by producing something valued by others, they gain a sense that they are needed.[3] People who value their work

3

highly *and* find that others agree with their estimate
are likely to have high self-esteem.

A more specific definition of work than the one
we gave at the outset is often used—participation
in the labor force. Paid employment by definition
fulfills the social and personal functions discussed
above. In addition, it serves two other key purposes.
Economically, it provides the goods and services
used by a society and gives individuals the financial
means to satisfy their own needs. Socially, labor
force participation confers status on individuals
and groups, most directly on men. A man's occupation, whether it falls high or low on the occupational scale, generally determines not only his
own but also his family's social class, neighborhood, friends, leisure time activities, and role in
the community.

Unpaid work may also be economically productive work. This is often not recognized by important
others, however, and it is not considered in the
computation of gross national product and other
economic statistics. One reason is that we have not
established feasible ways of measuring the contributions of unpaid workers. Socially, unpaid work,
like paid work, may confer status on a person. A
student who does extremely well in some task will
be recognized by others for his or her excellent
work, for example, and a housewife who heads a
prestigious and powerful community organization
will be accorded respect. Almost always, however,
status gained from unpaid work is secondary to
status conferred by paid work in the labor force.

Clearly, work is a phenomenon of great significance for individuals and for society. Like most
important social activities, it is pursued and experienced in different ways by different groups of
people. The purpose of this volume is to describe
and analyze the work women do, a matter too long

neglected by social scientists.

Men and women differ in their experiences with both paid and unpaid work. In comparison to men, for example, women do a disproportionate share of unpaid—and usually less valued—work. The characteristics of women's work in the marketplace are also distinctive, as the chapters in this section reveal.

One of the most striking features of women's labor force participation is its dramatic change in size and composition in the last several decades. During the first forty years of this century the labor force participation rate of women rose only slowly (from 20 to 29 percent), and the women seeking employment tended to be either single, middle-class, white-collar workers who retired from paid employment upon marriage, or poor, single or married women who worked in factories and in domestic service.[4] The heavy demand for labor created by World War II initiated a rapid growth in women's labor force participation. Then, continued prosperity and the expansion of white-collar and service jobs that were sex-typed for women sustained the demand for female workers in the postwar period. As the size of the female labor force grew, its composition also changed. Growing numbers of women of all ages, marital statuses, and maternal statuses sought paid employment.

While rapid change has marked women's labor force participation rates, continuity with the past is characteristic of women's occupational distribution. Despite some modest changes, women are still concentrated, as before, in a very narrow range of occupations compared to men. In 1973 more than two-fifths of all women in the labor force were found in ten occupations (secretarial work, retail trade sales, bookkeeping, private household work, elementary school teaching, waitressing, typing, cashiering, sewing and stitching, and registered nursing), whereas the ten largest occupations for men employed less than one-fifth of all male workers. Three-fourths of all employed women worked in fifty-seven occupations; only half of employed men worked in that number of occupations.

Another characteristic of employed women is their partial attachment to the labor force. In 1975, for example, only 43 percent worked full-time, year-round. While most women are satisfied with part-time jobs, a significant number of part-time women workers (1.1 million in April 1974) said they would prefer full-time employment and were working only part-time for economic reasons beyond their control. Women also participate in the labor force less continuously than men. Longitudinal studies reveal that the life cycle pattern of work of many married women displays several distinct stages. Between school and childbearing, there is a period of several years' continuous work. After the birth of the first child there is often a period of nonparticipation, which may last between five and ten years. This is generally followed by a period of intermittent participation starting when the youngest child reaches school age. Finally there may be a period of permanent labor force affiliation.

Another factor distinguishing women's labor force experience is that they receive low earnings. In 1973 full-time year-round women workers had a median income that was only 57 percent of the median for men ($6,488 compared to $11,468). Time series data show that the gap has widened in recent years, although women's educational and occupational achievements have been increasing along with those of men.[5] Data on full-time year-round workers in selected occupational groups reveal that this deterioration of women's relative income position has occurred in almost all occupational groups.[6]

The discussion in section one of these and other characteristics of women's labor force participation is initiated by three economists, Carolyn Shaw Bell, Francine D. Blau, and Mary H. Stevenson, since economics raises many of the issues and provides many of the data used by students in all fields who are interested in the study of work. The authors introduce basic definitions and data used in studies of labor force participation, review the historical and current status of employed women, and present several theoretical models used by economists to interpret women's relatively low wages. To complete this picture of women's labor force participation in the United States, a team of sociologists, Elizabeth M. Almquist and Juanita Wehrle-Einhorn, discuss differing patterns of labor force participation among minority group women, and an attorney, Mary Eastwood, examines the legal rights of women in the labor force. The materials presented in these chapters are a springboard to the chapters in subsequent sections of the volume. The growth in female labor force participation, women's concentration in sex-typed jobs, their part-time and intermittent patterns of employment, and their low pay, for example, are themes that reappear in sections two and three.

Carolyn Shaw Bell begins the discussion by defining several key terms, such as labor force participation and unemployment, and by describing the basic labor force data that economists have developed and that all students of the labor force use. Bell also highlights some of the shortcomings of these definitions and data for describing women's economic contributions and problems. The terms, data, and modes of analysis that Bell defines and critiques undergird the explorations undertaken in the chapters that follow.

Francine Blau's contribution is a keynote of this

collection. In it the author describes the historical development of women's labor force participation in the United States, presents a thorough, up-to-date overview of the current status of women in the labor force, and speculates about the future. Her myth-debunking discussions of the characteristics of employed women, their earnings, their unemployment, and their concentration in sex-segregated occupational categories provide the background on which subsequent articles elaborate.

Elizabeth Almquist and Juanita Wehrle-Einhorn expand upon Blau's overview with a detailed comparison of the different experiences of black, Spanish-origin, American-Indian, and Asian-American women in the labor force. The authors argue that most of these women are "doubly disadvantaged." Their class and ethnic group affiliations submit them to the same historical and social discrimination experienced by their male counterparts and are crucial in determining their relative status in the labor force. Their sex compounds the problems and may be even more important than ethnicity in determining their low wages and concentration in a narrow range of low-prestige jobs. While exposing the problems faced by minority women, Almquist and Wehrle-Einhorn alert us to the limitations of available data and underscore the need for more research on this important topic.

Mary Stevenson also explores an issue raised by Blau: women's low earnings relative to men's. Stevenson reviews a number of theoretical approaches that economists use to explain wage differences—the theory of individual human capital, several theories of employer discrimination, and the crowding hypothesis, which focuses on women's limited access to many occupations. The author elucidates the assumptions and implications of each theory, and she explains why she considers the crowding hypothesis to be the most plausible.

In the concluding article of the section, attorney Mary Eastwood discusses the federal laws and executive orders that protect women from sex discrimination in the marketplace by prohibiting differential treatment of women and men. As she notes, these laws represent a monumental change in approach from earlier legislation, which "protected" women by requiring employers to give them special treatment. In practice such protective legislation often restricted women's employment and preserved certain jobs as male enclaves. The problems faced by women in the labor force are still far from solved, however. The new legislation is inadequately enforced, and several concerns of employed women, such as maternity benefits and occupational health standards, are at issue in pending court and legislative battles.

NOTES

1   The notion of expenditure of energy is taken from V. Vroom, *Work and Motivation* (New York: John Wiley and Sons, 1964), p. 42. He gives a much fuller discussion of the characteristics of work.

2   *Work in America,* Report of a Special Task Force to the Secretary of Health, Education, and Welfare (Cambridge, Mass.: MIT Press, 1973), pp. 3–10.

3   Ibid., pp. 4–5.

4   These statistics and those in the subsequent paragraphs are from U.S. Department of Labor, Women's Bureau, *1975 Handbook on Women Workers,* Bulletin No. 297 (Washington, D.C.: Government Printing Office, 1975).

5   David L. Featherman and Robert M. Hauser, "Sexual Inequalities and Socioeconomic Achievement in the U.S., 1962–1973," *American Sociological Review* 41 (1976): 462–83.

6   *1975 Handbook on Women Workers,* pp. 131–32.

Women and Work:
An Economic Appraisal

Carolyn Shaw Bell

This book is a collection of articles in the social sciences. Its subject matter, women and their work, has never been categorically assigned to one discipline in the way that the chronology of kings belongs to history and the analysis of elections to political science. But the discipline of economics has a special relation to the other social sciences dealing with this subject, for the empirical data about work have been compiled largely in the course of economic inquiries. Hence this initial chapter: most of the authors of subsequent chapters use material derived, at least partly, from economists' interests and concerns.

Like other social scientists, economists have identified and collected data, analyzed the information, and presented research results within limitations imposed by a commonly accepted mode of thinking—a set of assumptions about men and women, work and marriage, dependence and security. This way of thinking has led economists to pose certain questions and to overlook others. Unlike other social scientists, economists have helped to develop and publish the bulk of the data used throughout this volume. The economist's way of thinking, therefore, deserves to be understood by anyone who uses such data.

This chapter attempts to describe the limitations of the existing data.

It assumes that before using data to test hypotheses, the researcher must identify the assumptions and understand the methodology embodied in the data. It presents the economist's point of view as the motivating force behind the existing data. Whether such a point of view is either necessary or sufficient for an adequate analysis lies outside the scope of this introductory chapter, but later writers will have much to say on both these points.

DEFINITIONS OF WORK AND THE LABOR FORCE

Basic to any economic model are the two fundamental economic processes: production and consumption. These both represent human activity—our mental and physical energies can be devoted to working (making physical products or performing services) or to using and enjoying the commodities that we and others produce. To apply such a model to any specific situation, such as the United States in the mid-seventies, we must rely, of course, on actual data. And most available data are shaped by the particular sources from which they originate.

We live in a market economy, so most economic data result from market activity. Employers record dollars of wages, numbers of employees, hours of work, quantities of output and similar facts for their own purposes, and these are readily available to data collectors.

The work that is done outside the market is not recorded in the same way, because it is not in anyone's interest to keep those records. Thus, the work of a canvasser for a local charity is not measured, while that of an Avon lady or Fuller Brush man is. The services of the teenager carrying a tray to an invalid parent go unrecorded, while those of a hospital attendant are recorded. The tutoring efforts of a skilled teacher donating time to a volunteer program will not automatically be noted, but the payroll of the local school is subjected to a careful accounting. Occupational data, therefore, refer only to people in the market. Although work is not synonymous with labor market activity or with paid employment, recorded and available economic data about work consist largely of facts about labor markets and the events that take place there.

A common accusation by the uninformed, including feminists, is that such data reflect a sexist attitude on the part of economists, and that economics denigrates women by failing to record or measure their work. But it was not economists who invented the market system, nor is it economists who determine what records are useful to employers, tax collectors, brokers, agents, and other economic entities to keep. Indeed, economists recognize the limitations of their data more than most critics realize.

It is worth documenting economists' concern with the fact that, for example, Gross National Product excludes the value of women's work at home and in the community (as it does the value of men's work there). Simon Kuznets, the economist chiefly responsible for the development of national income accounting (GNP and other measures) in the United States, wrote as early as 1941, "The exclusion of the products of the family economy, characteristic of virtually all national income estimates, seriously limits their validity as measures of all scarce and disposable goods produced by the nation."[1] Thirty years later, contributors to a volume celebrating the golden anniversary of the national income accounts repeated this concern. The following is typical of their comments:

> As presently constituted, the national income accounts do not pretend
> to be indicators of . . . all economic activity. Instead, they are . . .
> defined as recording those activities which either pass through markets
> or at least permit of market price imputation. The important economic
> activities which occur within households, . . . the considerable volume
> of criminal activity, . . . what students do in schools and universities
> are not defined as . . . economic activity.[2]

Why does this state of affairs persist? First, because abundant economic data have been obtained from existing records, making special surveys or investigations unnecessary. (As one result, however, economists tend to focus on problems revealed by these data or on questions that can be explored by means of such data.) If information on nonmarket activity were required, special records would have to be kept, probably by the individuals concerned. But hours and conditions of work reported by, for example, volunteers for a local hospital could not be relied on for accuracy the way a hospital's reports of hours of work by its paid employees can.

More importantly, the market provides a process of valuation that can be used to record wages, sales, inventories, and other components of production and consumption. Values for each of these items can be found in the market transactions of hiring, buying and selling, renting, storing, and so on. Economists call these values prices; wages are the price of labor and interest is the price of capital. Prices measure values differently for the buyer and for the seller. For example, a given wage paid to an employee means the employer values the worker's output at that amount or more. The same wage accepted by an employee means the worker values his or her own time at that sum or less.

The market's process of valuation and the prices and wages that result obviously do not exist where market transactions do not take place. Values for work performed outside the market (i.e., unpaid work) must be calculated, and the problems surrounding such value assignments have not generated much enthusiasm among economists. Many willing noneconomists, however, have calculated various sums purporting to represent the value of unpaid output.

Economists recognize that there may be insurmountable problems in imputing wages to unpaid work—to the value of singing in the church choir or campaigning for a political candidate or taking care of a preschool child. To use union wages for professional singers as a proxy for the value of choir

> 🙶 Women at work, their accomplishments, and even their productive potential are measured and analyzed by standards and terminology developed for the labor force, even where (as in the case of women's work at home) these are inappropriate. 🙷

singers, to calculate the output of a campaign worker in terms of commercial costs for advertising or marketing, to equate the value of child care to the salary paid a day-care center teacher flies in the face of economic reality. In the first place, if all the unpaid workers offered their services in the market, wages in these fields would be affected, and market values would be different. In addition, many unpaid workers perform services for themselves because they are not willing to pay current market prices for someone else to do the work. This means that they value their own time at a lower price than the prevailing market price for that work. For both these reasons,

therefore, it is inappropriate to use market wages, unadjusted, to value unpaid work.

There are other problems in imputing values to unpaid work. Arthur
Okun comments on the proposal that GNP accounts impute values for the
services of housewives:

> I find it a compelling argument that a housewife is not a maid—and
> that this difference is of a higher order of magnitude than the difference
> between the title to a house and a lease. The activity of a housewife
> is not that of a maid, and valuation of the housewife's hourly services in
> terms of the wage rate of maids, or any multiple thereof, would not
> translate her activity meaningfully into dollars and cents.
>
> I have never been disturbed by the well-known paradox that, when
> the bachelor marries his cook, the national product goes down. The
> GNP is measuring the output of market-oriented activity, and market-
> oriented activity is reduced by the cook's marriage. Whatever she does
> as the mistress of the household is a different type of activity, oriented
> toward different objectives than receiving her pay at the end of the
> week.[3]

Work is not synonymous with paid employment, nor are workers equivalent to those employed or seeking employment. Nevertheless, it is only for
the latter—people either seeking employment or holding paid jobs—that reliable data exist. This group of people, otherwise known as the labor force,
is referred to frequently in the following chapters. Women at work, their ac-
complishments, and even their productive potential are measured and analyzed by standards and terminology developed for the labor force, even
where (as in the case of women's work at home) these are inappropriate. It
is essential, therefore, to explore the meaning of the term *labor force* in some
detail.

WOMEN WORKERS AND THE LABOR FORCE

The measure of "work" or "productive work" was restricted to paid employment before the development of the national income data discussed a-
bove. As early as 1820, the Bureau of the Census reported data on "gainful
workers." The purpose of this decennial enumeration was to list the *occupations* of the population; whether or not an individual was currently employed was subsidiary to the occupation the person had, either currently or
at some previous time, for this census. The term "gainful worker" referred

to any person over ten years old "who followed an occupation in which he earned money or its equivalent, or in which he assisted in the production of marketable goods." To the extent that home production (chores and child care) did not result in marketable goods, or that wives, grandmothers, maiden aunts, and other women at home did not "earn money or its equivalent," this census definition excluded women workers from its count. This conclusion is confirmed by noting that in 1870, for instance, when gainful workers totaled 13 million, those employed in domestic service numbered only 920,000. Since there were over 15 million women over the age of ten in that year, clearly the occupation of "domestic service" did not include all the women who worked.

In 1940 the concept of *labor force* was adopted as the official measure of quantifiable workers in the economy. Refinements have been made in the sampling methods used, the type of questions asked, and the timing of the employment or job search experience referred to in measuring the labor force. At present, the definition is:

> Employed persons are (1) those who worked for pay any time during the week which includes the 12th day of the month or who worked unpaid for 15 hours or more in a family-operated enterprise* and (2) those who were temporarily absent from their regular jobs because of illness, vacation, industrial dispute, or similar reasons. A person working at more than one job is counted only in the job at which he or she worked the greatest number of hours.
>
> Unemployed persons are those who did not work during the survey week, but were available for work except for temporary illness and had looked for jobs within the preceding four weeks. Persons who were available for work but did not work because they were on layoff or waiting to start new jobs within the next 30 days are also counted among the unemployed. The unemployment rate represents the number unemployed as a percent of the civilian labor force.
>
> The civilian labor force consists of all employed or unemployed persons in the civilian noninstitutional population; the total labor force includes military personnel.[4]

The analysis of people *not* in the labor force requires some attention. Six categories exist:

---

* The Bureau of the Census uses the phrase "family farm or family business" instead of this term.

Persons not in the labor force are those not classified as employed or unemployed; this group includes persons retired, those engaged in their own housework, those not working while attending school, those unable to work because of long-term illness, those discouraged from seeking work because of personal or job market factors and those who are voluntarily idle. The noninstitutional population comprises all persons 16 years of age and older who are not inmates of penal or mental institutions, sanitariums, or homes for the aged, infirm, or needy.[5]

Although people give their own statements about their present activities in surveys to measure the labor force, they are fitted into one of the six classifications. "Retired" obviously implies previous employment; it is significant that 45 percent of the men not in the labor force are retired, compared to 3 percent of the women. By contrast 80 percent of the women not in the labor force are engaged in home responsibilities, compared to only 2 percent of the men.[6] For the women involved, household chores or duties at home clearly represent a particular occupation—a kind of work—from which these women, unlike men in paid employment, do not retire. That this particular occupation is not classified as "work" affects many kinds of employment analyses.

Our understanding of other occupations is colored by the widespread use of labor force data. To quote Census Bureau figures for the number of "laboratory technicians" or "architects" or "family counselors" or any other occupation reveals little about the number of people in the country qualified to perform technical work in a laboratory, to be architects, or to provide family counseling. Occupational data are not collected from an enumeration of the population. Only those who are either employed or actively seeking employment are questioned.

It follows that nothing like a national inventory exists of the human abilities, experience, and training that are available in the economy. The number of physicians who are qualified, licensed, and experienced exceeds by some unknown but significant figure the number of people classified as physicians according to the data on occupations. The same is true for many other types of employment. Because the number of women temporarily absent from the labor force exceeds the number of men, it is women's skills and abilities that are more frequently omitted from the occupational data. Analysts need to emphasize the warning that statistics on occupations refer primarily to job holders or job seekers, not to people in general.

Participation rates are calculated and analyzed from labor force data. The participation rate for any group consists of the number of those employed or seeking employment as a percentage of the total number of people in the group. Thus, to say that labor force participation rates are higher for women between the ages of eighteen and twenty-five than for women between fifty-five and sixty-four merely means that a larger proportion of the first age group than of the second is in the labor force. Population groups can be defined in terms of age, education, location, or any other useful characteristic, to compare differences in labor market activity from group to group or from one time period to another for the same group.

Labor force participation rates have universally been calculated separately for men and for women, and this implies much about the female role in the economy. The human activity of work consists of individual effort; and the amount and quality of that effort may represent psychological, physical, or mental differences among individuals. Differentials in employment, occupation, or productivity may well relate to certain variables, such as age and education, that directly affect human effort. Sex, per se, does not, but it does reflect cultural or legal constraints on the performance of work by men and women. If these constraints are investigated, the way in which they produce differentials in employment, occupation, or productivity should be clearly distinguished from the impact of other variables, such as age or physical condition.

A particularly frustrating problem in analyzing women's participation in the labor force is recognition of the limitations imposed by the cultural model used. For example, the monumental work by Bowen and Finegan, *The Economics of Labor Force Participation,* reports on the "individual characteristics" that influence presence in the labor market.[7] For men, these consist of marital status, color, schooling and job experience, health, other income, and age. For married women, health and age are omitted, while children, housing, employment of husband, and occupation of husband are added. Implicit in this structure for analysis, therefore, is the assumption that sex, per se, does affect work and participation in the labor force.

Most of the "individual characteristics" for men represent situational variables over which the worker has little control: age, color, and health, for example. The amount of schooling and of nonlabor income received often reflect decisions taken by other people, usually the individual's parents. There is very little a person can do to change these characteristics.

What about the "individual characteristics" for women? Color, schooling, and other income represent variables over which a person has little or no control, regardless of sex. But are the other factors in the Bowen and Finegan analysis also situational (as opposed to volitional) variables? The employment status and occupation of a married woman's husband are probably not under her control; is the same true of her children and her housing? Why are these variables included for women and not for men? The analyst will reply (and probably with some impatience) that these variables have proved significant in explaining employment patterns among married women, although correlation does not imply causation. Nonetheless, the analytical structure itself does imply, by these choices of variables, that women (and not men) have "home responsibilities" for child care and housework.

When the basic framework within which data are collected or the ways in which data are analyzed have been set up differently for men and for women, there is no way to escape the limitations that result: direct comparisons cannot be made.

SPECIAL DEFINITIONS FOR WOMEN

If a woman is defined primarily by one model, that is, in terms of her family role as wife, mother, or homemaker, the family is also defined primarily by one model, and this affects the basic data on people's economic status and work effort. Two notable problem areas exist: that of the "head of household" and that of the "secondary worker."

The Census Bureau uses the term *household*[8] (rather than family) in its data to recognize that some people live together who lack familial relation: two college roommates sharing an apartment after graduation, two or more couples buying a vacation home together, and so on. Moreover, some households contain more than one family: for example, the adult married son who lives with his wife and children in his parents' home, or the single mother who lives with her married brother and his wife. Families who share a dwelling unit, therefore, are identified as primary families and subfamilies, according to their relationship to the "head of the household or his wife."

Sound reasons exist for the notion of "head of household." If small groups of people (call them tribes or families or cells) are to be analyzed in terms of age, or education, or mobility, or other sociological indicators, then data for only one person must be used to classify the group (although different members may have different characteristics). This does not preclude picking up such data for all *individuals* (*persons* in the census lexicon) in other analyses, of course.

The precise definition of household head reads:

> One person in each household is designated as the "head," that is, the person who is regarded as the head by the members of the household. However, if a married woman living with her husband was reported as the head, her husband was considered the head for the purpose of simplifying the tabulations.[9]

There is nothing *inherently* sexist in this rule, any more than designating the oldest female present as household head would be inherently feminist.

> **There is no economic reason to evaluate an individual's labor or the income from it according to the individual's position in the family.**

Statisticians use conventions and make arbitrary distinctions for the sake of producing data that can be usefully analyzed. But other people have read into this particular convention the implication that the head is also the economic mainstay for, or the primary social influence on, the other members of the household. Such interpretations add little to our understanding of how people live and are clearly contradictory to reality in many households.

Determining or evaluating income seems to raise especially knotty problems. Most families, and some households, operate on the basis of shared income: individual members pool their earnings or property income to pay for the family's style of living. A good part of this living represents collective consumption, the shared use of homes, equipment, gardens, and services such as recreation and insurance. Data on *family* income have become more and more affected by the labor market earnings of women; in other words, distribution of income by families has changed over time, because women have dramatically increased their labor force participation rates. Education, employment, and the like, however, are measured by head of the household data, although the household is simultaneously classified by income that is partially earned by the wife or other household members.

Use of the term *secondary earner* can be particularly troubling. If it means anything, it indicates that family income consists primarily of the earnings of one person, and that the labor income of another family member is significantly less. It is an imprecise concept, because no data exist to identify all secondary earners in this fashion, and because earnings that are significantly less mathematically are not necessarily significantly less economically. The value of the marginal dollar of income can be determined only by the family involved, not by any outside observer or recorder of income. Most economic thinking suggests that this marginal income is worth more at lower income levels than at higher levels, but even this does not necessarily hold true for all families.

The term *secondary earners* sometimes suggests that the employment, working conditions, opportunities for promotion or training, and many other influences on the earning ability of these workers are less significant than those of primary earners. But there is no *economic* reason to evaluate an individual's labor or the income from it according to the individual's position in the family.

When the unjustified assumptions that secondary earners are women and that women are secondary earners are added to all these ambiguities, some remarkable errors of judgment can occur. Although few analysts equate the terms secondary earner and woman worker in unqualified statements, such an equation lurks beneath much of the analysis of recent trends in unemployment.

DEFINING WOMEN AS DEPENDENTS

Because the terms *head of household* and *primary earner* generally refer to men, only awkward terminology exists for other types of families. To some extent this leads analysts to avoid discussing them. *Female-headed families* is the best example—this jarring term follows inevitably from the Census Bureau's definition. An authoritative study of such families points out that

> the Census-imposed definition of husband-wife families as male-headed
> is a convention that offers little gain in simplicity for what it costs in
> observing household differences of possible interest. It is a convention

which assumes the social and economic dependency of wives without inquiring into the facts and as such is not only demeaning to many women but is also likely to become an increasingly obsolete description of reality over time.[10]

The dependent status of women, however, is more than a misguided assumption based on an outdated cultural model. Under both federal and state legislation women are assigned dependent status as wives or widows of wage earners. This general rationale exists, for example, in Social Security legislation, some types of government regulations on pensions, and certain state programs of unemployment insurance. Other legislation assigns a dependent status—dependent on a government agency—to women as mothers or caretakers of children. This occurs in Aid to Families with Dependent Children and, to some extent, in Social Security payments to widows with children.

Both state and federal inheritance tax laws contain provisions that make the wife or widow a dependent, and many court rulings do this in divisions of property in divorce or separation proceedings. In much of the legal language about married couples, the term "spouse" has not yet replaced "wife" or "widow." (Probably this change cannot occur until the characteristics of dependence have been thought through.) Finally, the income tax laws of the federal government and many states have provisions for married couples that clearly originated in the presumption that wives were economically dependent on husbands.

Most of these programs generate data, and some agencies, notably the Social Security Administration and the Treasury Department, turn out excellent research and analyses. But much of their basic data deal with women as dependents, not as individuals. Under the Social Security system, women have been treated differently from men in many ways—for example, eligibility for early retirement and proof of dependent status. Gradually some of the inconsistencies are being eliminated; for example, children of a deceased mother can now receive Social Security benefits based on her contributions, and a widower can claim survivor's benefits without proving his "dependence" when his wife was alive (see Mary Eastwood's chapter below). But these changes mean that the basic data of the system—figures for the number of beneficiaries and average benefit paid—will also change, leaving no way of comparing them accurately to data for earlier years.

CROSS-SECTIONAL VERSUS LONGITUDINAL DATA

Most of the data problems discussed concern cross-sectional or intertemporal analyses, and perhaps the failings of the data may stimulate more projects to generate longitudinal data. The basic shortcoming of cross-sectional analysis is that it gives inadequate results for building a dynamic model, although researchers are often tempted to make predictions based on it nevertheless.

Thus, if labor force participation rates by age are plotted, the curve may look like that in figure 1. It is easy to predict, from such a graph, that employment for women will peak during their late teen years, and that as women marry and have children they will leave the labor force until their late thirties, when their children require less maternal attention and, perhaps, more income. But the data say nothing whatsoever about the life pattern of any particular woman or group of women. Rather they reflect the patterns of about 18 million women, *of different ages,* in the year 1950. The danger in making such predictions can be seen from the curve of figure 2, again referring to all the women in the labor force, of different ages, but for the year 1974. The eighteen-year-old girl of figure 1 would be forty-two in 1974; the probability of her being employed was not correctly indicated by the height of the curve for forty-two-year-old women in 1950. (Of course, the same defect arises when a researcher uses cross-sectional analysis to build a dynamic model for men, but the changes that have occurred in the number of working women are much greater in size and significance than those for men.)

Despite these shortcomings, many analysts rely on cross-sectional data, because nothing else exists. Collecting data on an individual or a group through the course of their lives or even for ten to twenty years is a very expensive process. Significantly, one of the most valuable sources of longitudinal data was created not to provide statisticians with raw material but to provide the Social Security Administration with annual information about the earnings and eligibility of millions of individuals. "Lifetime" records for individuals therefore do exist, although the information they contain is extremely sparse.

Two other notable sources of longitudinal data should be mentioned. The Survey Research Center at the University of Michigan has conducted a number of surveys with a callback or follow-up on the same respondents. Most, however, span only a short period. The Center for Human Resource

Research at Ohio State University deals specifically with labor market experience and has collected data over a five-year period.

The most critical need for longitudinal data over a much longer time span—say, a lifetime or the period between leaving school and retiring from employment—is in human capital theory. This fairly new field of economics looks at the resources devoted to education, specialized training, certain types of health care, and other programs of human development as investments. Spending on a college education is like buying a long-term bond: it requires a large outlay of current funds in the expectation of future returns. The bond-buyer will receive interest income in the years to come; the college graduate will earn a higher income, in the years to come, than he

> **❝ It is likely that the lack of data on home production by women causes gross underestimates of their economic contribution, not only to current consumption and the comforts of home, but also to current investment and the future productivity of others. ❞**

or she would without a college degree. The same frame of reference can be used to evaluate spending on health programs: the prospective return in production and income from eradicating the common cold probably exceeds that from finding a cure for cancer. The economic theory involved has not been fully developed, but some interesting empirical tests of hypotheses have been conducted.

Most of the data on lifetime earnings or income, however, refer only to men. Data for lifetime earnings in specific occupations frequently refer only to white males. Such data cannot, on the face of it, be used to calculate prospective returns for investing in young women or in blacks of either sex. And if changes in employment practices take place, the data may not even be relevant to the future income of the young white men currently investing in their graduate or professional education.

A major return on investment in human resources consists of production outside the market, which of course is excluded from data on lifetime earnings. For instance, it has been known for several generations that the education of parents strongly correlates with the educational level of children, and recent research seems to indicate that much education, especially for the young child, takes place at home. This suggests that one valuable return from the capital represented by education consists of the educated parent's ability to develop educated, or educable, children. It also suggests that the hours spent in child care by educated mothers may represent a highly valuable kind of capital formation (this time in the child) that is excluded from calculations based on formal education.

Longitudinal studies, following a woman through all her investment years and calculating the returns from this investment in terms of her production both in and out of the labor market, would reveal totally different data from those presently available. The problem is not that the data do not exist, but that imperfect and incomplete cross-sectional analyses are substituted for valid longitudinal findings.

Finally, human capital theory does not come to grips with questions of ownership. Since we do not live in a slave economy, the earnings from human labor belong to the individual worker. But when an individual is enabled to earn higher labor income because he or she has higher human capital, derived from an investment in education, then the question arises, who paid for the investment? And does that person then have rights of ownership in the return? The individual who finances his or her own education clearly owns all the returns on that investment, but the same is not necessarily true for the individual whose education has been paid for by parents, society, or a spouse.

That millions of women seek employment in order to finance someone else's higher education is well documented. The gains from that investment flow to the children or husbands who are educated. In order for society to evaluate alternative investment choices properly, therefore, we need to understand not only the total costs and benefits of each but how the costs and benefits are distributed among particular individuals. It is likely that the lack of data on home production by women causes gross underestimates of their economic contribution, not only to current consumption and the comforts of home, but also to current investment and the future productivity of others.

Today's human capital theorists could regard all their work as an amplification of Alfred Marshall's observation almost a century ago: "The most valuable of all capital is that invested in human beings, and of that capital the most precious part is the result of the care and influence of the mother." Contemporary feminists, however, would perhaps prefer not to recall this quotation, since it continues, "so long as she retains her tender and unselfish instincts, and has not been hardened by the strain and stress of unfeminine work."[11]

CONCLUSION

Although we have touched on some of the implications of longitudinal data, most of the discussion in this chapter has dealt with cross-sectional analysis and static data. In some ways, the two approaches—cross-sectional and dynamic analysis—symbolize the two views of woman—as an individual and as a member of the feminine sex or gender. Ever since Simone de Beauvoir's *The Second Sex* was published, analysts have recognized that investigating the situation of women frequently means comparing it to that of men. This is cross-sectional analysis, using data classified by sex. We need additional data for such analyses, and some researchers are exerting pressure on the Bureau of Labor Statistics to require more, if not all, of the data it collects to be tabulated separately for men and women.

But the growth and development of an individual person, whether male or female, encompasses movement into and out of particular cells of a statistical table and particular sets of records. Such movement represents the influences of social and economic variables that can be quantified or at least identified; it also represents the individual choices of a human being, in the context of that human being's life history to date, perceptions of current reality, and expectations for the future.

During a time of social change, these individual choices change more readily. The process of choosing may also change, as tradition or law gives way to new assertions of the individual's right to decide. Both of these changes have a profound effect on institutions, laws, and economic activities, which ordinarily change more slowly than individuals responding to or struggling against a particular social environment. In a period of rapid social change, then, predictions should perhaps come rather low on the agenda of things to do.

If, in fact, the social, economic, and psychological climate surrounding women at their work alters in profound and irreversible ways, then much of

FIGURE 1   Labor Force Participation of Women, by Age Group, 1950

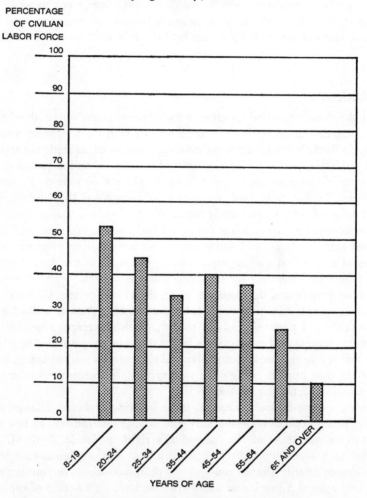

PERCENTAGE
OF CIVILIAN
LABOR FORCE

YEARS OF AGE

Source: U.S. Department of Labor, Bureau of Labor Statistics, *U.S. Working Women,* Bulletin no. 1880 (Washington, D.C.: Government Printing Office, 1976), chart 4.

the data we now use will become irrelevant. And this may be the most basic of shortcomings: that the facts we are recording will be of little use in seeking to understand the present and future and should be turned over to historians for interpretation of the past.

FIGURE 2   Labor Force Participation of Women,
by Age Group, 1974

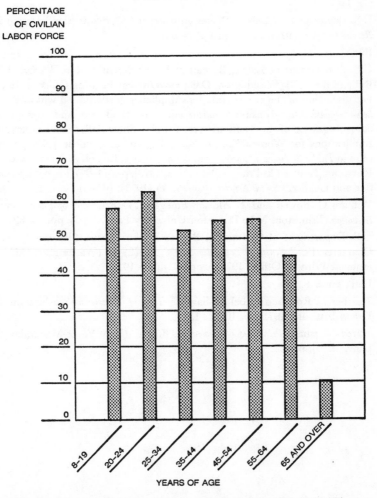

Source: U.S. Department of Labor, Bureau of Labor Statistics, *U.S. Working Women,* Bulletin no. 1880 (Washington, D.C.: Government Printing Office, 1976), chart 4.

NOTES

1 Simon Kuznets, *National Income and Its Composition, 1919–1938* (New York: National Bureau of Economic Research, 1941), p. 10.

2 Robert Lekachman, "The Income Accounts of Tomorrow," *Survey of Current Business* 51 (1971): 119.

3 Arthur Okun, "Social Welfare Has No Price Tag," *Survey of Current Business* 51 (1971): 34.

4 U.S. Department of Labor, "Notes on Current Labor Statistics," *Monthly Labor Review* (any month from August 1974 on).

5 Ibid.

6 U.S. Department of Labor, Bureau of Labor Statistics, *U.S. Working Women,* Bulletin no. 1880 (Washington, D.C.: Government Printing Office, 1976), p. 5. For discussion of the two occupations implicitly encompassed within the term *home responsibilities*—consumer maintenance and child care—and attempts to secure recognition of these activities, see Carolyn Shaw Bell, "Full Employment— Implications for Women," *Social Policy,* September/October 1972, pp. 12–19 (also in *Public Service Employment,* ed. Alan Gartner, Russell A. Nixon, and Frank Riessman [New York: Praeger Publishers, 1973], pp. 74–82); idem, "Economics, Sex and Gender," *Social Science Quarterly* 55 (1974): 615–31.

7 William G. Bowen and T. Aldrich Finegan, *The Economics of Labor Force Participation* (Princeton, N.J.: Princeton University Press, 1969), pp. 40, 89.

8 U.S. Department of Commerce, Bureau of the Census, "Persons by Family Characteristics," *Census of Population: 1970,* PC (2)–4B (Washington, D.C.: Government Printing Office, 1973), app. C, pp. 8–10.

9 Ibid., pp. 8–9.

10 Heather L. Ross and Isabel V. Sawhill, *Time of Transition* (Washington, D.C.: Urban Institute, 1975), p. 10, fn. 1.

11 Alfred Marshall, *Principles of Economics,* 8th ed. (New York: Macmillan Company, 1950), p. 564.

The Data on Women Workers, Past, Present, and Future

Francine D. Blau

Women have traditionally engaged in three types of economically productive work: producing goods and services for their family's own consumption; producing goods and services at home for sale or exchange on the market; and working for pay outside the home. The process of industrialization brought about a reallocation in the relative importance of these three types of activities, greatly increasing the absolute and relative numbers of women who sought and obtained paid employment. This chapter briefly traces the evolution of the working woman's role and summarizes the trends

Portions of the first two sections of this paper are from my article "Women in the Labor Force: An Overview," in *Women: A Feminist Perspective*, ed. Jo Freeman (Palo Alto, Calif.: Mayfield Publishing Company, 1975). The remainder of the paper is a revised and updated version of chapter 1 of *Exploitation from 9 to 5: Report of the Twentieth Century Fund Task Force on Women and Employment*, background paper by Adele Simmons, Ann Freedman, Margaret Dunkle, and Francine Blau (© 1975 by The Twentieth Century Fund, New York). I am grateful to the Twentieth Century Fund for granting permission for the publication of this material here, and to my coauthors for their valuable input into the original version. I would also like to thank Lawrence Kahn and Marianne Ferber for their helpful comments on an earlier draft of this paper. I am indebted to Theodore Miller and Kathryn Ross for their excellent research assistance in preparing the updated paper.

in women's involvement in work outside the home. It then reviews the current status of women in the labor market, describes the distribution of women among different industries and occupations, and shows how this distribution limits women's access to prestigious and highly paid jobs. The income differences between men and women are examined, and some of the popular myths that perpetuate discrimination against working women are explored. Finally, the future prospects for women in the labor market are investigated.

HISTORICAL PERSPECTIVE

In the preindustrial economy of the American colonial period, work was frequently allocated on the basis of sex, but there could be little question that the work of women was as essential to the survival of the community as that of men. Although women in England and the Continental countries were routinely employed as reapers, mowers, and haymakers, in the colonies agricultural work was mostly left to men, at least among the nonslave population.[1] This colonial departure from the customs of the mother country may have been due to the economic importance of the household industries carried on primarily by women and children, who produced most of the manufactured goods for the colonies. In addition to cleaning, cooking, and caring for their children, colonial women considered spinning, weaving, and making lace, soap, shoes, and candles part of their ordinary housekeeping duties, since the colonial economy at first provided no other sources for these goods and services.[2]

The pressures of a struggling frontier society, which was faced with a continual labor shortage and imbued with a puritanical abhorrence of idleness, opened up a wide range of business activities to women. They could be found working as tavern keepers, store managers, traders, speculators in commodities, printers, and publishers, as well as in the more traditional women's occupations of domestic servant, seamstress, and tailor.[3] But many of the colonial businesswomen were widows, frequently with small children, who carried on their husband's enterprises.[4] And in some cases opportunities for women to remain single and self-supporting were curtailed, perhaps because of women's economic value in the home. For example, although the early New England female family heads were given their portion of planting land, and in Salem even unmarried women at first also received a small allotment, "the custom of granting 'maid's lotts' . . . was soon discontinued in order to avoid 'all presedents and evil events of graunting lotts unto single maidens not disposed of.' "

Although conditions peculiar to the colonies may have contributed to the relatively high status of American women, the more general point has been made that, before the Industrial Revolution separated the home from the place of work, women were able to take a more active role in the economic life of the community.[6] The broad thrust of industrialization may indeed have diminished the participation of women in certain kinds of economically productive work. Particularly in America, however, women played a crucial role in the development of the first important manufacturing industry, the textile industry.

During the seventeenth century, when spinning and weaving were household industries done primarily by women and children, each household provided its own raw materials and produced cloth chiefly to meet its own needs. But it was not uncommon for women to market part of their output, selling directly to their own customers or to shopkeepers for credit against their accounts.[7] With the expansion of the industry in the latter half of the eighteenth century, it became more common for women to be employed by merchants to spin yarn in their own homes under a commission system. The merchants would either sell the yarn or commission other women to weave it into cloth. The first factories in the United States embodied no new technology. They were "merely rooms where several looms were gathered and where a place of business could be maintained." Women delivered yarn they had spun at home to these establishments and were paid for it there.[8]

The first textile factory to incorporate power machinery was established in Pawtucket, Rhode Island, in 1789 by Samuel Slater, a British immigrant. Slater's factory used a water-powered spinning frame. By 1800 fifteen mills had been established in New England for carding and spinning yarn. When the power loom was introduced in 1814, the whole process of cloth manufacture could be carried on in the new factories.[9] But although cloth was no longer made solely in the home, it was still made primarily by women and female children, who constituted the bulk of the new industrial work force.

The earliest factories did not open any new occupations to women. So long as they were only "spinning mills" there was merely a transferring of women's work from the home to the factory, and by the time that the establishment of the power loom had made weaving also a profitable factory operation, women had become so largely employed as weavers that they were only following this occupation, too, as it left the home. It may, in brief, be said that the result of the introduction of the factory system in the textile industries was that the work which women had been doing in the home could be done more efficiently outside of the home, but women were carrying on the same process in the making of yarn or cloth.[10]

Perhaps even more interesting than the pioneering role of women in industry is the reaction of illustrious contemporaries to the employment of women outside the home. Alexander Hamilton, for example, claimed that one of the great advantages of the establishment of manufacturing was "the employment of persons who would otherwise be idle (and in many cases a burthen on the community). . . . It is worthy of particular remark, that, in general, women and children are rendered more useful, and the latter more early useful, by the manufacturing establishments, than they would otherwise be."[11] The notion that a farmer's masculinity might be threatened by the entry of his wife and children into paid employment apparently did not trouble American men of the time. Hamilton noted, on the contrary, that men would benefit by having a new source of income in the family.[12] Others claimed that the new factories not only opened up a new source of income but also built character in their employees:

> The rise of manufactures was said to have "elevated the females belonging to the families of the cultivators of the soil from a state of penury and idleness to competence and industry". . . . In the same spirit of unreasoning exaggeration the women in villages remote from manufacturing centers were described as "doomed to idleness and its inseparable attendants, vice and guilt."[13]

Since the economy of the United States during this period was predominantly agricultural, with an extremely favorable land-to-labor ratio, women and children were virtually the only readily available sources of labor for the infant manufacturing industry. This seems to account for the approval with which women's entry into the wage-labor force was greeted. The existence of a factor of production, women, that was more productive in the new industrial pursuits than in the home, was cited as an argument for the passage of protective tariffs to encourage the development of the textile industry in a country that appeared to have a clear comparative advantage in agriculture. "To the 'Friends of Industry,' as the early protectionists loved to call themselves, it was . . . a useful argument to be able to say that of all the employees in our manufacturing establishments not one fourth were able-bodied men fit for farming."[14]

Later attitudes toward women working outside the home were not nearly so encouraging. Without undertaking a careful investigation of the causes for the change, it seems reasonable to suggest that the gradual diminution of the supply of unsettled land coupled with the waves of immigrants that provided a more abundant source of labor shifted public concern to the problem of providing sufficient employment for men. In any case, by the turn of the twentieth century sentiment against the "intrusion" of women into the industrial work force was strong enough to compel Edith Abbott to answer this charge specifically in her classic study, *Women in Industry*. Her words add a valuable perspective to contemporary discussions:

> ❝ In 1890 the two major groups of married women for whom work outside the home was fairly common were black women, most of whom lived in the South, and immigrant women in the textile-manufacturing towns of New England. ❞

Women have been from the beginning of our history an important factor in American industry. In the early days of the factory system they were an indispensable factor. Any theory, therefore, that women are a new element in our industrial life, or that they are doing "men's work," or that they have "driven out the men," is a theory unsupported by the facts.[15]

A careful investigation of the facts also leads us to further qualify the statement that the separation of the home from the place of work during the Industrial Revolution tended to reduce the participation of American women, particularly married women, in many kinds of economically productive work. For one thing, though it is estimated that in 1890 only 5 percent of married women had jobs outside the home,[16] this pattern did not prevail among all groups in the female population. For another, various types of work done in the home continued to be important in the economy throughout the nineteenth century.

The two major groups of married women for whom work outside the home was fairly common were black women, the majority of whom still lived in the South, and immigrant women in the textile-manufacturing towns of New England. In 1890 one-quarter of black wives and two-thirds of the large number of black widows were gainfully employed. Most of these women worked either as field hands or as domestic servants, work that black women had done under slavery.[17] Undoubtedly, the tendency of black wives to engage in market activity can be explained in large part by the low incomes of black men.

The women in the New England textile mills were carrying on a long tradition of participation by women in this industry. In two Massachusetts towns, Fall River and Lowell, for example, nearly one-fifth of all married women worked outside the home in 1890. Most were first- or second-generation immigrants of French Canadian or Irish ancestry. The low wages of men working in the textile mills frequently made it necessary for other family members, including children, to work in the mills too. Thus, Robert Smuts has suggested that married women went to work for family reasons as well as financial ones: "Since many of the older children worked in the mills, their mothers were not needed at home to care for them. Indeed, a mother whose children worked could look after them better if she went to work in the same mill."[18]

Married women from other sectors of the population were also forced to seek market work when they suffered misfortunes for which there was little social protection in the nineteenth and early twentieth centuries. Some indication of the kinds of problems these women faced can be gained from the results of a study conducted by the United States Bureau of Labor Statistics in 1908:

Among one group of 140 wives and widows who were employed in the glass industry, 94 were widows, or had been deserted, or were married to men who were permanently disabled. Thirteen were married to drunkards or loafers who would not work. The husbands of ten were temporarily unable to work because of sickness or injury. Seventeen were married to unskilled laborers who received minimum wages for uncertain employment. Only six were married to regularly employed workers above the grade of unskilled labor.[19]

As noted earlier, some women contributed to the incomes of their families by earning money for work performed in their own homes. The types of employment and working conditions of this group varied widely. Some women took in boarders or did laundry or sewing. Others, in New York, Chicago, and other major cities, eked out a meager existence doing work for the garment industry at home. Bohemian and German women in New York's upper East Side tenements provided a cheap source of labor for the cigar industry.[20]

Another element of work at home, the production of goods and services for the family's own use, remained extremely important throughout the nineteenth century, even in urban areas. Women frequently kept livestock and poultry and raised fruits and vegetables in small home gardens. Even foods bought at the market usually required processing at home. Preserving, pickling, canning, and jelly making, as well as baking the family bread, were normal household duties. The family's clothing, curtains, and linens were often sewn or knit in the home. And, of course, the housekeeping tasks of cleaning, washing, and cooking were accomplished without the benefit of modern appliances.[21]

In sum, women have consistently played a major role in the American economy. While their husbands tilled the fields, colonial women were engaged in household manufacturing. When a factory system was established in the textile industry, women and girls comprised the bulk of the new industrial work force. The broad sweep of industrialization drew men into the paid labor force at a faster pace than women. Nonetheless, married women contributed to the economic welfare of their families by producing goods and services for their families' own consumption and by earning money for work performed in their homes. Moreover, financial need drove a minority of married women, particularly those from the black and immigrant communities, to seek employment outside their homes.

A PROFILE OF THE FEMALE LABOR FORCE

While industrialization meant that many of the goods and services women traditionally produced in the home were increasingly provided by the market economy, it also brought ever-increasing numbers of women into the paid labor force. In this section, we review the trends in female labor force participation and then consider the factors that influence women to seek market work. Since fairly reliable data on the female labor force did not become available until 1890, we confine our discussion of participation trends to the period 1890–1974.

The data in table 1 indicate a relatively slow rate of increase in the proportion of women of working age who were in the labor force in the pre-1940 period. (There is some question whether there was any increase at all in female labor force participation during the 1890–1930 period. The 1910 census, in which enumerators were given special instructions *not* to overlook women workers, especially unpaid family workers, yielded a participation rate of 25 percent. Robert W. Smuts has argued that women workers were undercounted in the 1900, the 1920, and perhaps the 1930 censuses, but that, over the period, gradual improvements in technique, broader defini-

TABLE 1   Women in the Civilian Labor Force, 1890–1974

Year	Number (Thousands)	Percentage of all workers	Percentage of female population
1890	3,704	17.0	18.2
1900	4,999	18.1	20.0
1920	8,229	20.4	22.7
1930	10,396	21.9	23.6
1940	13,783	25.4	28.9
1945	19,290	36.1	38.1
1947	16,664	27.9	30.8
1950	18,389	29.6	33.9
1955	20,548	31.6	35.7
1960	23,240	33.4	37.7
1965	26,200	35.2	39.2
1970	31,520	38.1	43.3
1974	35,825	39.4	45.6

Note: Pre-1940 figures include women fourteen years of age and over; other years include women sixteen and over.

Sources: U.S. Department of Labor, Women's Bureau, *1969 Handbook on Women Workers,* Bulletin no. 294 (Washington, D.C.: Government Printing Office, 1969), p. 10; U.S. Department of Labor, Manpower Administration, *Manpower Report of the President, April 1975* (Washington, D.C.: Government Printing Office, 1975), p. 203.

tions of labor force status, and a redistribution of the female work force from unpaid farm work to paid employment resulted in an apparent rather than a true increase in the female participation rate.)[22]

Between 1940 and 1974, however, dramatic changes in women's labor force participation occurred. In 1940 less than 29 percent of the female population sixteen years of age and over was in the labor force. By 1974 the figure had risen to almost 46 percent, and 53 percent of all women between the ages of sixteen and sixty-four were working or seeking work.[23] Women workers increased from one-quarter to nearly two-fifths of the civilian labor force.

When we take into account the World War II experience, these changes look less impressive. Between 1940 and 1945 the female labor force expanded by 5.5 million, and 38 percent of all women sixteen and over were working. But the 1947 figures indicate that considerable ground was lost in the immediate postwar period. In fact, it was not until 1953 that the absolute number of women workers surpassed its wartime peak. Participation rates did not regain their 1945 levels until 1961.[24]

The long-term growth in the female labor force since 1940 was accomplished primarily by the entry of new groups of women into the labor market. Before 1940 the typical female worker was young and single. The peak participation rate by age group occurred among women twenty to twenty-four years of age. Over the next ten years, this pattern began to change as older married women entered or reentered the labor force in increasing numbers. The new trend continued, and by 1960 the contours of the "age profile" of the female labor force had undergone a major shift (figure 1). The percentage of women over thirty-four years of age who were in the labor force rose dramatically, with the largest increase in the forty-five to fifty-four age group. During the last fifteen years, more and more women have entered the labor force, with the most rapid increases in participation occurring among women in the twenty to thirty-four group, many of whom are mothers of preschool children. For example, the labor force participation rate of married women with children under six years old rose from 18.6 percent in 1960 to 36.6 percent in 1975.[25]

As a result of these postwar changes, the profile of the female labor force now corresponds more closely to the profile of the total female population: in terms of their racial composition, age, educational attainment, marital and family status, and other characteristics, women in the labor market now closely resemble the total female population. For example, in 1974, the median age of working women was thirty-six, only five years younger than the median for the entire female population—forty-one. Similarly, 50 percent of ever-married working women and 47 percent of all ever-married women had children under eighteen, while 19 percent of ever-married women workers and 22 percent of all ever-married women had children under six.[26] Thus, it is rapidly becoming more difficult to consider working women an unrepresentative or atypical group.

For obvious economic reasons, single, widowed, divorced, and separated women are more likely to work than married women. However, because married women are by far the largest group in the adult female population, the postwar increases in their labor market activity have meant that the majority of working women are now married. Married women living with their husbands comprised 30 percent of the female labor force in 1940 and 58 percent in 1975.[27]

One major factor in determining whether or not a married woman participates in the labor force is the presence of children, particularly young children. In March 1975, 36.6 percent of wives with preschool children were in the labor force, compared with 52.3 percent with children between the ages of six and seventeen only.[28] Since married women between the ages of twenty-five and thirty-four are the most likely to have young children, their labor force participation rate is still relatively low. However, as noted earlier, it is rising rapidly. The difficulty of obtaining and paying for adequate child care may be a serious deterrent to the entry of these women into the labor force. According to a recent study, mothers of small children are more likely to work if a relative is available to look after their children.[29]

Education is another major factor in determining whether a married woman will seek employment. The more education a woman has, the more likely it is that she will work outside the home. In March 1974, 32 percent of wives with less than four years of high school, 46 percent of wives who had graduated from high school, and 59 percent of wives with four or more years of college were in the labor force.[30]

Among both male and female workers, educational attainment generally affects employment opportunities and pay scales. Although the educated woman often meets with discrimination that keeps her from better-paid, more prestigious jobs, her opportunities are still greater than those of a less educated woman. Thus, the more education a woman has, the higher the "opportunity cost" to her of remaining out of the paid labor force (that is, she forgoes higher earnings by not seeking paid work). The attraction of market work is therefore greater for the more educated women. It may also be more feasible for such women to participate in the labor force, since the better a woman's educational credentials, the greater her chances of finding a job that pays enough for her to buy goods and services to ease the "double burden" of home chores and paid work. The correlation between educational attainment and employment may also reflect a process of self-selection: women who earn diplomas may be more strongly motivated, ambitious, and career-oriented than those who do not.

Financial need, as measured by a husband's income, may also affect a wife's decision to enter the labor force. Married women most frequently give economic reasons for their decision to seek work.[31] Whether husband and wife perceive the husband's income as adequate depends, among other things, on the size of the family, the standard of living to which they aspire, and their age: the same level of income may meet the needs of one family but not another. In addition, the response of a married woman to insufficient family income may depend on the kind of employment opportunities available to her and whether her earnings will cover the cost of services such as child care.

In recent years, the observed inverse relationship between husband's income and wife's labor force participation has become less consistent. For example, in 1951, participation rates of married women were highest among those whose husbands earned less than $3,000 (in 1973 dollars). By 1960, wives whose husbands' earnings were in the $5,000-to-$6,999 category (in 1973 dollars) were most likely to be in the labor force. And, by 1973, the highest participation rates were found among wives with husbands earning between $7,000 and $9,999.[32] This suggests that increased opportunities for educated married women to get jobs and to earn higher pay may be eroding the simple inverse relationship between husband's income and wife's labor force participation.

Proportionately more black women than white participate in the labor force, although the differential has been declining in recent years. In 1948, 31 percent of all white women and 46 percent of all nonwhite women sixteen years of age and over were working. By 1974, 45 percent of white women and 49 percent of nonwhite women were in the labor force.[33] A primary factor in the racial differential is the greater financial need of black women to earn money. A higher proportion of black women are widowed, divorced, or separated from their husbands. These women must rely heavily on their own earnings to support them and their families. Furthermore, the lower average income of black men increases the importance of their wives' contributions to family income.[34]

The labor force participation rates of women, particularly of married women and teenagers, are very sensitive to the general level of economic activity. The impact of economic conditions on female labor force participation can take two forms. In times of economic downturn, if the male family head becomes unemployed, the wife or other members of the household may enter the labor force to supplement the family income. These "additional workers" often leave the labor force once the major breadwinner is reemployed on a regular basis. In similar economic conditions, if a working woman loses her job and cannot find a new one after prolonged search, she may become a "discouraged worker" and leave the labor force. Other women, especially wives and teenagers, who are not yet working but were planning to look for jobs may postpone their entry into the labor market until economic conditions improve.

Studies show that the second group of discouraged workers predominates, so that the female labor force either declines or grows more slowly during periods of high unemployment.[35] Unemployment statistics then tend to underestimate the extent of female unemployment, particularly during periods of low economic activity. Thus, the gap between women's and men's unemployment rates tends to decline during recessions as women leave, or become discouraged from entering, the labor force and tends to widen when the economy is buoyant as women are drawn into the labor force by increased employment opportunities.

Regardless of the stage in the business cycle, however, the incidence of unemployment among women is considerably higher than among men, of the same race (although it is higher for nonwhites than for whites regardless of sex). For example, in 1974, the unemployment rates were 6.1 percent for white women and 10.7 percent for nonwhite women, compared to 4.3 percent for white men and 9.1 percent for nonwhite men.[36] Unemployment often creates serious economic hardship for women workers and their families. In March 1974, 54 percent of unemployed women workers were single, divorced, widowed, or separated from their husbands.[37] Even among wives, unemployment often undermines family welfare; for example, in March 1974, approximately one-half of married women workers had husbands whose 1973 earnings were less than $10,000.[38]

JOB OPPORTUNITIES AND LIMITATIONS

Once a woman decides to work, she finds only a limited number of jobs available. Despite the rapid growth of the female labor force in recent years, women are still primarily concentrated in certain industries and occupations. In March 1974, 76 percent of employed women worked in the service sector, broadly defined to include wholesale and retail trade, finance, insurance, real estate, and public administration, as well as professional, personal, entertainment, business, and repair services. An additional 21 percent worked in the manufacturing sector, including transportation and public utilities.[39] This concentration of women in service sector employment has increased somewhat since 1940, when 71 percent of employed women worked in services and 25 percent in manufacturing.[40]

> **Despite the rapid growth of the female labor force in recent years, women are still primarily concentrated in certain industries and occupations.**

Within the service sector, women tend to be concentrated in specific industries that have traditionally employed them. For example, in January 1973, women made up 46 percent of the employees in retail trade, but only 23 percent in wholesale trade; more than 80 percent of the workers in hospitals; and 61 percent of the employees in elementary and secondary schools, but only 42 percent in colleges and universities.[41]

In manufacturing also, certain industries are "women's industries." In January 1973, when women comprised 38 percent of all manufacturing workers, they were 46 percent of the work force in textile mill products, 81 percent in apparel and related products, 41 percent in electrical equipment and supplies, 60 percent in leather, and 42 percent in tobacco industries, but less than 10 percent in petroleum refining, primary metal, and lumber industries.[42]

Thus some industries rely more heavily on women workers and employ them more readily than others. But the representation of women workers in an industry gives an incomplete picture of the opportunities open to them. Within a given industry women may fill a broad or narrow range of jobs and have full or limited opportunities for career advancement. An industry in the service sector may have a high proportion of women in its work force simply because it employs large numbers in clerical jobs, not in professional, technical, and managerial positions. Similarly, manufacturing firms, may welcome women into their operative and clerical categories, but exclude them from their skilled craft and supervisory jobs. Thus, the occupational distribution of women workers reflects the differences in employment opportunities between male and female workers more accurately than does the industrial distribution (table 2).

Proportions of female and male workers by major occupation reveal striking differences between the sexes. In 1974, 57 percent of female white-collar workers (more than one-third of all employed women) worked in clerical jobs. Yet 69 percent of male white-collar workers (28 percent of the male work force) were in either professional and technical or managerial jobs.

Since 1960 women have been entering the skilled trades at a faster rate than men. There were nearly twice as many women in these trades in 1970 as in 1960.[43] Yet men continue to hold a disproportionate share of the highest-status, highest-paying blue-collar jobs. Only 10 percent of women blue-collar workers (fewer than 2 percent of employed women) were craftsmen or foremen in 1974. Yet 45 percent of the men in this group (21 percent of the male labor force) were categorized as craftsmen and foremen. Data collected by the Equal Employment Opportunity Commission indicate that even in industries where women represent a large proportion of operatives, they may be excluded from craft jobs. For example, in 1971, women comprised 66 percent of the operatives employed in the electronics industry in Boston, but were only 7 percent of the craftsmen. Similarly, in the instruments industry of that city, 44 percent of the operatives, but only 8 percent of the craftsmen, were women.[44]

While there has been considerable improvement in the occupational status of nonwhite women workers in recent years, their employment distribution remains skewed toward the lower rungs of the occupational ladder. In 1974, 37 percent of nonwhite working women were employed in service jobs, compared to 21 percent of all women workers. And 11 percent of nonwhite women workers were in the lowest-paying occupation, private household worker; they comprised nearly two-fifths of all women in this occupation. Only 42 percent of nonwhite women held white-collar jobs, and 60 percent of these white-collar workers were clerical workers.

Viewing the distribution of female employment by detailed occupations further highlights two aspects of the employment problems of women. First, women are heavily concentrated in an extremely small number of occupations. One indication of the limited job opportunities open to women is that half of all working women were employed in just twenty-one of the two

TABLE 2   Occupational Distribution by Sex and Race, 1974

Major occupation group	Percentage of employed labor force			
	Males	Females		
			Total	Nonwhite
White-collar workers	40.3		61.6	41.8
Professional and technical		14.0	14.9	11.7
Managers, officials, and proprietors		13.9	4.9	2.4
Clerical		6.4	34.9	24.9
Sales		6.0	6.8	2.7
Blue-collar workers	46.8		15.5	19.8
Craftsmen and foremen		20.9	1.5	1.4
Operatives		18.3	13.0	17.2
Nonfarm laborers		7.7	1.1	1.2
Service workers	8.0		21.4	37.3
Private household		0.1	3.6	11.3
Other		8.0	17.8	26.1
Farm workers	4.9		1.4	1.1
Farmers and farm managers		2.9	0.3	*
Farm laborers and foremen		1.9	1.2	1.0

*Less than 0.05 percent.

Sources: U.S. Department of Labor, Manpower Administration, *Manpower Report of the President, April 1975* (Washington, D.C.: Government Printing Office, 1975), p. 226; U.S. Department of Labor, *Employment and Earnings,* January 1975, p. 149.

hundred fifty occupations listed by the Bureau of the Census in 1969. Male workers were more widely distributed throughout the occupational structure, with half in sixty-five occupations. One-quarter of all employed women worked in only five jobs: secretary-stenographer, household worker, bookkeeper, elementary school teacher, and waitress.[45]

Secondly, most women work in predominantly female jobs. Women's share of total employment increased from 18 percent in 1900 to 33 percent in 1960, but the proportion of women in predominantly female occupations, occupations in which 70 percent or more of the workers were women, declined only slightly from 55 percent to 52 percent. Such a small change can hardly be interpreted as a trend toward reduced segregation.[46]

Another way of approaching the issue of the concentration of women in sex-segregated occupational categories is to construct an "index of segregation" based on the percentage of women in the labor force who would have to change jobs in order for the occupational distribution of women workers to match that of men. This index of segregation has remained almost the same since 1900: it was 66.9 in 1900 and 65.8 in 1970, suggesting that sex segregation has been virtually unaffected by the vast social and economic changes of the present century.[47] It is interesting to note that by this measure sex segregation in employment is even more severe than segregation by race.[48]

Thus, it appears that the growing numbers of working women have been absorbed into the labor force not through an across-the-board expansion of employment opportunites, but rather through an expansion of traditionally female jobs (particularly in the clerical and service categories), through the emergence of new occupations that were rapidly defined as female, and perhaps occasionally through shifts in the sex composition of some occupations from male to female. Indeed, a detailed analysis of employment data from the 1950 and 1970 censuses reveals that over this twenty-year period there was a larger net inflow of men into predominantly female occupational categories than of women into predominantly male occupations. For the most part this was the result of an increase in the participation of men in such female-dominated professions as elementary school teaching, librarianship, nursing, and social work.[49]

A number of variations on the theme of sex segregation are worth noting. The sex composition of occupations is subject to regional variation. For example, in the Midwest, cornhuskers are traditionally women, while trimmers are almost always men. In the Far West, cornhuskers are men and trimmers are women.[50] In addition to complete reversals of sex labels, the concentration of women in a job category may also vary geographically. For example, in 1960, 64 percent of spinners in textile mills were female in the Northeast, while 83 percent were female in the South.[51]

Since women are not evenly distributed among industries, an occupation that is predominantly female in one industry may be predominantly male in another. For example, in 1960 the census reported that 44 percent of all assemblers were women. This included assemblers in electrical machinery equipment and supplies, of whom 67 percent were women, as well as assemblers in motor vehicles and motor vehicle equipment, of whom only 16 percent were women.

Additional examples of regional and industrial differences may be drawn from data collected by the Equal Employment Opportunity Commission. For example, the occupation of salesworker exhibited a great deal of variation. In 1971, women comprised 25 percent of insurance sales personnel in Boston, but less than 5 percent in New York City. Moreover, the representation of women in an industry is frequently not a very good predictor of their access to higher-level jobs. In the Detroit electronics industry, 21 percent of all workers and 46 percent of sales workers were women; in Boston, although 38 percent of electronics workers were women, they held only 16 percent of sales positions.[52] It is doubtful that such large differences can be explained in terms of differences among the cities in industry composition or in the availability of qualified women.

The sex typing of a job may even vary from one business establishment to another. One firm may hire only men as elevator operators, while another may hire only women; many restaurants employ either waiters or waitresses, but not both. A recent study of employment patterns of male and female office workers in three large northeastern cities revealed a strong and consistent pattern of sex segregation by establishment among workers employed in the same occupational categories.[53]

United States census data tend to underestimate the extent of sex segregation in the labor market, because the tabulations are reported across regions, industries, and firms. Thus, predominantly male and predominantly female classifications may be combined to yield apparently integrated occupational categories. The variations in the sex composition of occupations also reveal the extremely arbitrary way in which many jobs are sex-typed. Efforts to justify the exclusion of one sex from a job on the basis of differences in training or ability are undermined by the evidence that a "man's job" in one locale, industry, or company may be classified as a "woman's job" in another.

INCOME DIFFERENCES BETWEEN MEN AND WOMEN

The pay differentials between men and women parallel and reflect the occupational differences, as well as income disparities within occupational categories. Statistics for full-time, year-round employees show that in 1973 the median annual income of women was $6,450, compared to $11,310 for men. Thus, women earned only 57 percent of the male median.[54] The sex differential in earnings is manifest among both whites and nonwhites. In 1973, the median income of white men was $11,800; of nonwhite men $7,953 (67.4 percent of the white male median); of white women, $6,598 (55.9 percent); and of nonwhite women, $5,595 (47.4 percent).[55] Earnings distributions also reveal major sex differences. For example, in 1973, 17 percent of year-round, full-time working women earned less than $4,000, compared to 5 percent of working men; only 16 percent of the women earned $10,000 or more, but 60 percent of the men were in that bracket.[56]

The gap between women's and men's incomes increased between 1956 and 1969 and, after a brief respite, has continued to widen in recent years. A large difference in earnings between male and female workers is found even when adjustments are made for sex differences in hours of work and educational attainment.[57]

Earnings differentials by sex still persist when we control for major occupation group. In 1974 the ratio of the median earnings of full-time, year-round women workers to those of full-time year-round men workers was 66 percent for professional and technical workers; 59 percent for managers, officials, and proprietors; 60 percent for clerical workers; 41 percent for sales workers; 54 percent for craftsmen and foremen; 58 percent for operatives; and 60 percent for service workers.[58] These pay differences are in large part due to sex segregation in employment, which means that even within broad occupational groups, men and women tend to be concentrated in different detailed occupational categories or to work in different industries.

The data on earnings suggest that the "separate but equal" doctrine has the same effect on the sexes in employment as it did on the races in education. The artificial division of occupations into men's and women's jobs results in substantially higher earnings for men than for women. This is because the demand for women workers tends to be restricted to a small number of occupational categories that are segregated by sex. At the same time, the supply of women available for work is highly responsive to small changes in the wage rate and to employment opportunities in general. Employers can often attract more women into poorly paid jobs simply by increasing the flexibility of work schedules. Thus, in most predominantly female jobs there exists a reserve pool of qualified women outside the labor market who would be willing to enter if the price or job or hours were right. The abundance of supply relative to demand, or what has been termed the "overcrowding" of female occupations, results in lower earnings for women's jobs.[59] This is not to say that men and women do not receive different pay for the same work even within the same establishment; they sometimes do.

> ❝ The gap between women's and men's incomes increased between 1956 and 1969 and, after a brief respite, has continued to widen in recent years. ❞

However, since most men and women do not work together in the same occupational classifications, such instances of "unequal pay for equal work" account for a relatively small proportion of the aggregate earnings difference. When this does occur, the problem may be complicated by the use of different job titles to disguise existing inequalities. And because the jobs open to women are so limited, they have few weapons against such wage discrimination except litigation.

One of the most popular explanations for the difference between men's and women's incomes is that women are merely secondary earners or, as one economist put it, "assistant breadwinners."[60] Even apart from the principle of equal pay for equal work, this is not a valid reason for paying women less. Of the women in the labor force in March 1973, 23 percent were single, 19 percent were widowed, divorced, or separated from their husbands, and 19 percent had husbands earning below $7,000.[61] Thus, a substantial proportion of the female labor force does not have other or adequate means of support. The economic plight of families headed by women is particularly serious. In March 1975, 7.2 million American families, one out of every eight families in the population, were headed by women.[62] Female-headed families constitute a large and growing proportion of the poverty population. In 1972, one-half of the families headed by women lived in poverty, while less than one-tenth of the families headed by men had incomes below the poverty threshold.[63] The majority of poor families with children are now headed by women.[64]

The financial contribution of the "assistant breadwinner," the working wife of a working husband, frequently is very important to the economic welfare of the family and may mean the difference between poverty and a decent standard of living. More than half (52 percent) of married women had work experience (worked at some time) during 1973, and they contributed a median 26 percent to the incomes of their families. Nearly one-quarter of this group contributed 40 percent or more of family income. Among white families, median family income was $15,042 if the wife worked during 1973, compared to $11,709 if she did not. Among nonwhites the corresponding figures were $12,360 and $7,247.[65]

Another frequently heard explanation of the difference between women's and men's incomes is that men are better trained. Occupations in which women predominate are often dismissed as unskilled or unimportant, even for men. Although it is extremely difficult to compare skill levels across occupations, educational attainment does provide a crude index. A recent study compared the levels of educational attainment and earnings of men and women workers within a number of predominantly female job categories in which both men and women workers had higher than the median educational level for the total male experienced civilian labor force (11.1 years). According to the study, the median income of the male workers was slightly above the median for the male labor force in six of the eleven cases; it was less in five cases; and in none was it commensurate with their educational attainment. In no case did the median earnings of female workers approach either those of the total male experienced civilian work force or those of their own male counterparts in the occupation. To put it another way, men were somewhat underpaid and women were severely underpaid, relative to their educational attainment, in these predominantly female occupations.[66]

A growing body of research into the question of male-female pay differences supports the view that discrimination accounts for a significant share of the differential. After controlling for education, experience, and other factors that might tend to cause productivity differences between men and women, the proportion of the sex differential attributable to pure discrimination has been estimated at between 29 and 43 percent of male earnings.[67]

TURNOVER

Somewhat different issues are raised by the argument that women workers are less likely than men to stay on the job, and therefore employers are justified in discriminating against them. Before considering the empirical evidence on this question, one point deserves special emphasis. Even if it were true that women were *on the average* more likely to quit their jobs than men, this would not justify treating *individual* women as if they all conformed to the average. Unless each female applicant is considered on the basis of her own job history and work aspirations, employers are discriminating against women as a group.

Are women workers less likely than men to stay on the job? Unfortunately, no evidence exists to answer this question definitely. According to the Bureau of Labor Statistics, in 1968 the average voluntary turnover rate for male factory workers was 2.2 per hundred compared to a somewhat higher 2.6 rate for female factory workers.[68] Further, in January 1973, men averaged 4.6 years of continuous employment at one job, while women averaged only 2.8 years.[69] However, overall averages can be misleading. A number of factors influence turnover rates for both sexes. What appear to be sex differences may actually be results of the differential impact of these factors on men and women.

Age is an important determinant of voluntary labor turnover. Younger workers of both sexes change jobs more often than older workers. They are often able to experiment with occupations to a greater extent than older workers, because generally they have fewer financial responsibilities, and, since they have little seniority to lose, they risk less by changing jobs. Their turnover also imposes less of a burden on the employer, because on the average they have not received as much training as older workers. Conversely, the longer a worker stays in a job, the more likely he or she is to remain. Length of service increases a worker's stake in the job in terms of nontransferable fringe benefits and seniority rights. Jobs that require substantial on-the-job training tend to have lower turnover rates in part because the job skills acquired may not be transferable. Good prospects for promotion and high salary levels also diminish a worker's incentive to change jobs.

A United States Civil Service Commission study of the voluntary turn-over rates of full-time employees in the federal government confirmed that, on average, women had a higher turnover rate than men.[70] However, the study also revealed that many more women were in the low-grade jobs that have the highest turnover rates for both sexes. Such things as age, grade level, type of job, and length of service were found to be more predictive of job success and retention than the single factor of sex. For example, women over thirty years of age had substantially lower turnover rates and were better employment risks than men between the ages of nineteen and twenty-four. The authors of the study conclude: "Much better predictions about the probability of loss can be made when age, grade level, etc., are taken into consideration than simply to assume that (1) probability of loss is the same for all women, and (2) probability of loss will be much greater for a woman than it would be for a man."[71]

The public's view of the sex differential in turnover rates evolved during the period when the typical woman worker was young, single, and apt to leave the work force permanently when she married. Today, the typical woman worker is thirty-six years old, married, and a mother. Women with children under six are the least represented but fastest growing group in the labor force. These factors have greatly increased the job stability of women workers and suggest that dramatically different work patterns are now developing.

However, women are frequently denied the incentives given to male workers to remain on the job. Employer practices that restrict women to low-paying, dead-end jobs and deny them access to training programs en-courage turnover. The lack of guaranteed maternity leave forces many younger women to leave their jobs permanently when they become preg-nant. Thus, a "vicious circle" may exist whereby employer views of women as unstable workers are constantly reaffirmed without giving women an opportunity to respond to a different structure of incentives.

FUTURE LEVELS OF PARTICIPATION

Even those who recognize the disadvantages women now face in the labor market are often fearful of the impact of remedies on the structure of the present labor force. A major concern is how an increase in the number of working women will affect unemployment rates. How many more women can we expect to enter the labor force? What kinds of jobs will they seek?

By analyzing trends in participation rates, this section will offer some tentative answers to these two questions.

FIGURE 1   Female Participation in the Labor Force,
by Age, 1940–74

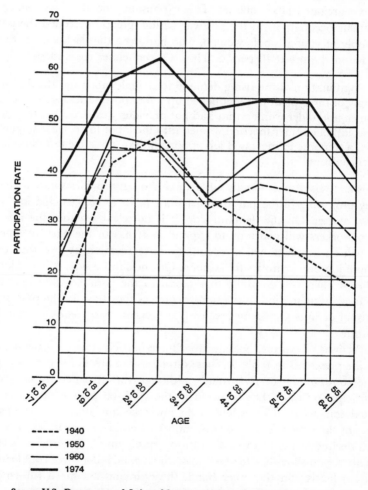

Sources: U.S. Department of Labor, Manpower Administration, *Manpower Report of the President, April 1975* (Washington, D.C.: Government Printing Office, 1975), pp. 206–9; U.S. Department of Labor, Women's Bureau, *1969 Handbook on Women Workers,* Bulletin no. 294 (Washington, D.C.: Government Printing Office, 1969), p. 18.

A study by Valerie Kincade Oppenheimer identified the increase in the *sex-specific* demand for women workers as the crucial factor in explaining the growth over time of the female labor force between 1940 and 1960.[72] The increasing importance of service industries and white-collar occupations has provided more job opportunities for women within the framework of a rigidly sex-segregated labor market. This expansion, and the development of new female occupations in the postwar period, greatly exceeded the potential supply of young, single women, who had been the backbone of the labor force in the pre-1940 period. Thus, Oppenheimer concluded,

> the combination of the rising demand for female labor and the declining supply of the typical worker opened up job opportunities for married women and older women that had not previously existed . . . the great influx of older married women into the labor force, was, in good part, a response to increased job opportunities— not a creator of such opportunities.[73]

This analysis of past female labor force growth provides some indication of why projecting future patterns of female labor force participation is not an easy matter. On the demand side, it is not clear whether the need for women workers will continue to expand as it has in the past, or whether there will be a breakdown of occupational segregation by sex, thus creating more job opportunities for women. On the supply side, it is not known whether women will continue to respond to the variables that determine labor force participation to the same degree as they have in the past. In the absence of definite knowledge, we can, at best, use past trends as a guide to the future.

Projections of expected female labor force participation over the next ten years are presented in table 3. These estimates are based, for the most part, on the continuation of past trends, although the extremely rapid growth in participation rates that occurred in the 1965–69 period have been discounted somewhat. The estimates do not take into account the possible impact of the women's movements, improved child-care facilities, or a continued decline in the birth rate on future employment patterns. It is therefore entirely possible that the growth of the female labor force could surpass predicted levels. On the other hand, the estimates assume a full-employment economy in the coming years. The entrance of women into the labor force in the past has been highly responsive to changes in the aggregate level of economic activity. If this pattern continues, future periods of relatively high unemployment can be expected to slow the growth rate of the female labor force.

With these factors in mind, we may proceed to examine the prospects for future growth in the female labor force. We can expect 43 million women to be working or seeking work in 1985. The projections indicate the possibility that 47 percent of all women will be in the labor force (54 percent of women between sixteen and sixty-four), and that these women will account

> **Projections indicate that by 1985 women will account for nearly 40 percent of the total labor force.**

for nearly 40 percent of the total labor force. If the labor force participation rates of men continue to decline, due to school attendance and retirement, beyond the level projected by the Bureau of Labor Statistics, the female proportion of the work force will be still higher.

FUTURE REQUIREMENTS AND PROBLEMS

Because this chapter was written during a period of less than full employment, the question arises whether the economy can generate enough jobs to absorb the anticipated increase in the number of women seeking work. The ability of the economy to provide employment for a larger female work force depends on two factors. First is the aggregate level of economic activity. To a great extent, this is within the control of our policymakers. Thus, it is extremely important that full employment be made a national goal of the highest priority and that the government take the necessary measures to assure a full-employment economy in the coming years.

Secondly, since women are heavily concentrated in a limited number of occupational categories, the ability of women to find employment depends not only on the aggregate number of jobs available, but on the *structure* of demand as well. The Bureau of Labor Statistics projections for 1980 indicate that the structure of demand will continue to favor the employment of women, even if the present uneven distribution of women among occupations persists. Above average rates of increase in employment are anticipated in the professional and technical, clerical, and service categories that employed 71 percent of women workers in 1974.[74] The rate of increase projected for these occupations, under conditions of full employment, exceeds the 2.4 percent annual rise in the female labor force estimated from the projections in table 3.

The aggregate statistics do, however, conceal certain problem areas. For example, elementary and secondary school teaching positions, which employed 36 percent of all professional women in 1969, are not expected to grow as rapidly as in the past. The Bureau of Labor Statistics projections indicate that the number of people seeking to enter the noncollege teaching profession could be as much as 75 percent above projected requirements.[75] Such shifts in demand are not unusual in a dynamic and changing economy. Under conditions of full employment, the decline in the need for teachers would be offset by expanding employment opportunities in other areas. However, given the sex segregation of the labor market and the long period of training required for most professional jobs, this shift in demand could pose serious problems for college-educated women. Present projections indicate that other traditionally female professions will not expand suffi-

TABLE 3   Projections of Total Female Work Force

Year	Women sixteen years and over in labor force		
	Number (Thousands)	Participation rate (Percentage)	Percentage of total labor force
Actual			
1960	23,272	37.8	32.3
1974	35,892	45.7	38.5
Projected			
1980	39,560	45.9	38.7
1985	43,018	47.1	39.5

Source: Computed from data and estimates in U.S. Department of Labor, Manpower Administration, *Manpower Report of the President, April 1975* (Washington, D.C.: Government Printing Office, 1975), pp. 203, 309.

ciently to compensate for the poor prospects in elementary and secondary education. Those professions in which demand is expected to expand rapidly—medicine, dentistry, architecture, science, and engineering—have not traditionally employed large numbers of women.[76] Unless efforts are made to encourage a substantial change in the type of training acquired by women at the college and graduate levels, college-trained women could well face serious underemployment.[77] In the absence of sufficient professional opportunities, women college graduates may begin to compete for jobs that have in the past been held by women with less education, adversely affecting that group of women workers as well.

While the trend toward growth of a service economy and white-collar employment does not in general indicate a worsening of the economic position of women, it does not necessarily imply an improvement. Lower earnings and higher unemployment rates will probably continue to plague the female work force as long as occupational segregation by sex persists. For this reason, the goal of equal employment opportunity is crucial to the economic welfare of women.

The evidence presented in the preceding sections shows that, until women have more occupational mobility, it is extremely unlikely that the pay differentials between female and male workers will be substantially reduced. Although it is not possible to predict exactly what the distribution of female employment would be if there were complete equality of opportunity in the labor market, it can reasonably be expected that women would be much more evenly distributed throughout the occupational structure.

The effort needed to change the occupational distribution of women workers substantially should not be underestimated. Not only are women heavily concentrated in a small number of occupations, but they also comprise nearly 40 percent of the civilian labor force. Nonetheless, a great deal can be accomplished by concentrating on *new* jobs created by the growth and replacement needs of the economy. This is illustrated by the data in figure 2. The 1980 projections show what the percentage of women in each occupation would be if, between 1969 and 1980, 40 percent of the new jobs in each category were allocated to women and 60 percent to men. The 40–60 ratio is, of course, purely illustrative, but the results do give some indication of the impact on the occupational distribution of women workers that a different distribution of job opportunities would have. Fairly large changes would apparently result. The female proportion of those employed as managers, officials, and proprietors would increase from 16 to 26 percent; the female proportion of craftsmen and foremen from 3 to 16 percent; the proportion of clerical employees would decline from 74 to 61 percent; and

FIGURE 2   Women as a Percentage of Total Employment
in Major Occupations, 1969, 1974, and 1980

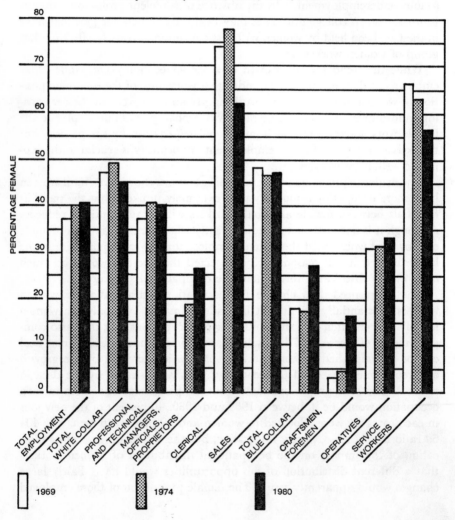

that of service workers would decline from 66 to 56 percent.

However, the actual figures for 1974, approximately midway through the eleven-year period, indicate that in most cases, progress fell far short of what was possible. By 1974, women comprised 19 percent of managers, officials, and proprietors, and fewer than 5 percent of craftsmen and foremen. Although the female proportion of service workers did decline by 3 percentage points between 1969 and 1974, women's share of clerical jobs increased by 4 percentage points. Thus, in 1974, the skewed occupational distribution of women workers continued to be a serious barrier to the economic equality of women.

An assessment of the future prospects of women in the labor market must also consider the impact of the level of unemployment on women's economic status. The adverse effect of periods of high unemployment on women cannot be overemphasized. First, since the unemployment rate of women is generally higher than that of men, women bear a disproportionate share of unemployment. Secondly, in times of high unemployment, many women become discouraged and drop out of the labor force; others postpone their entry until economic conditions improve. This kind of "hidden unemployment" is a particular problem for women. Finally, the level of unemployment will undoubtedly affect the social acceptance of programs designed to increase the opportunities for women in what are presently predominantly male jobs.

An unavoidable consequence of the effort to expand the employment opportunities open to women is that men will face a new source of competition. Thus, some men may find that they are unable to obtain employment in their preferred occupations. However, under conditions of full employment, they can find employment elsewhere. Buoyant demand conditions combined with a new occupational mobility for women workers will tend to reduce the former earnings differentials between jobs considered predominantly male and those traditionally considered female. Thus, men who are unable to enter the occupation of their choice may not suffer as great a loss as they would under different conditions. On the other hand, during a period of high unemployment, public support for a fundamental change in women's employment status may diminish. Moreover, since the jobs that are most likely to become available to women are the new jobs that become available in a growing, healthy economy, the maintenance of full employment is important if we are to move *rapidly* toward the goal of economic equality for women.

NOTES

1 Edith Abbott, *Women in Industry* (New York: D. Appleton and Company, 1910), pp. 11–12.

2 Eleanor Flexner, *Century of Struggle: The Women's Rights Movement in the United States* (New York: Atheneum Publishers, 1968), p. 9.

3 Abbott, *Women in Industry*, pp. 13–18. "It should be noted that the domestic servant in the seventeenth and eighteenth centuries was employed for a considerable part of her time in processes of manufacture and that, without going far wrong, one might classify this as an industrial occupation." Ibid., p. 16.

4 Flexner, *Century of Struggle*, p. 9.

5 Abbott, *Women in Industry*, pp. 11–12, quoting Herbert B. Adam, "Allotment of Land in Salem to Men, Women, and Maids," *Johns Hopkins University Studies*, 1st ser., vol. 9–10, pp. 34, 35.

6 Viola Klein and Alva Myrdal, *Women's Two Roles* (London: Routledge and Kegan Paul, 1956), p. 1.

7 Abbott, *Women in Industry*, pp. 18–19.

8 Ibid., p. 19; for quote, p. 37.

9 Elizabeth Faulkner Baker, *Technology and Women's Work* (New York: Columbia University Press, 1964), p. 5.

10 Abbott, *Women in Industry*, p. 14.

11 Alexander Hamilton, *Report on Manufactures*, vol. 1, cited in Baker, *Technology and Women's Work*, p. 6.

12 Hamilton, *Report on Manufactures*, cited in Abbott, *Women in Industry*, p. 50.

13 Abbott, *Women in Industry*, p. 57.

14 Ibid., p. 51. Abbott noted (p. 52) that "manufactures are lauded because of their 'subserviency to the public defense; their employment of women and children, machinery, cattle, fire, fuel, steam, water, and even wind—instead of our ploughmen and male laborers.'"

15 Ibid., p. 317.

16 Robert W. Smuts, *Women and Work in America* (New York: Columbia University Press, 1959), p. 23.

17 Ibid., pp. 10, 56.

18 Ibid., p. 57.

19 Ibid., p. 51.

20 Ibid., pp. 14–17.

21 Ibid., pp. 11–13.

22 Robert W. Smuts, "The Female Labor Force," *Journal of the American Statistical*

Association 55 (1960): 71–79. For a discussion of this issue, see Valerie Kincade Oppenheimer, *The Female Labor Force in the United States,* Population Monograph Series, no. 5 (Berkeley: University of California, Institute of International Studies, 1970), pp. 3–5.

23   U.S. Department of Labor, Manpower Administration, *Manpower Report of the President, April 1975* (Washington, D.C.: Government Printing Office, 1975), p. 223, table A–14.

24   U.S. Department of Labor, Manpower Administration, *Manpower Report of the President, March 1970,* (Washington, D.C.: Government Printing Office, 1970), p. 217.

25   U.S. Department of Labor, Manpower Administration, *Manpower Report of the President, April 1975* (Washington, D.C.: Government Printing Office, 1975), Howard Hayghe, "Marital and Family Characteristics of the Labor Force, March 1975," *Monthly Labor Review,* November 1975, p. 53.

26   Howard Hayghe, "Marital and Family Characteristics of the Labor Force, March 1974," Special Labor Force Report no. 173 (Washington, D.C.: U.S. Department of Labor, Bureau of Labor Statistics, 1975), pp. A–11, A–17.

27   U.S. Department of Labor, Women's Bureau, *1969 Handbook on Women Workers,* Bulletin no. 294 (Washington, D.C.: Government Printing Office, 1969), p. 24; Hayghe, "Marital and Family Characteristics, March 1975," p. 53.

28   Hayghe, "Marital and Family Characteristics, March 1975," p. 53.

29   Elizabeth Waldman, "Marital and Family Characteristics of the U.S. Labor Force," *Monthly Labor Review,* May 1970, p. 25.

30   Hayghe, "Marital and Family Characteristics, March 1974," p. A–23.

31   "Why Women Start and Stop Working: A Study in Mobility," *Monthly Labor Review,* September 1965, pp. 1077–82, cited in Vera C. Parella, "Women and the Labor Force," Special Labor Force Report no. 93, (Washington, D.C.: U.S. Department of Labor, Bureau of Labor Statistics, February 1968), p. 4.

32   *Manpower Report of the President, April 1975,* p. 59.

33   Ibid., pp. 208–9.

34   For a fuller discussion of racial differences in labor force participation rates, see T. Aldrich Finegan, "Participation of Married Women in the Labor Force," in *Sex, Discrimination and the Division of Labor,* ed. Cynthia B. Lloyd (New York: Columbia University Press, 1975).

35   Gertrude Bancroft McNally, "Patterns of Female Labor Force Activity," *Industrial Relations* 7 (1968): 209.

36   *Manpower Report of the President, April 1975,* p. 230.

37   Hayghe, "Marital and Family Characteristics, March 1974," p. A–10.

38   Ibid., p. A–21.

39   Ibid., pp. A–11, A–14. This definition of the service sector follows that used by Victor Fuchs in *The Service Economy* (New York: National Bureau of Economic Research, 1968).

40   *1969 Handbook on Women Workers,* p. 110.

41   Elizabeth Waldman and Beverly McEaddy, "Where Women Work," *Monthly Labor Review,* May 1974, p. 6.

42   Ibid.

43   Janet Neipert Hedges and Stephen Beims, "Sex Stereotyping in the Skilled Trades," *Monthly Labor Review,* May 1974, p. 16.

44   U.S. Equal Employment Opportunity Commission, *Employment Profiles of Minorities and Women in the SMSA's of 20 Large Cities, 1971,* Research Report no. 43 (Washington, D.C.: Government Printing Office, July 1974).

45   Janet Neipert Hedges, "Women Workers and Manpower Demands in the 1970's," *Monthly Labor Review,* June 1970, p. 19.

46   Valerie Kincade Oppenheimer, "The Sex-Labeling of Jobs," *Industrial Relations* 7 (1968): 220.

47   The source for the 1900 figure is Edward Gross, "Plus Ça Change . . . ? The Sexual Structure of Occupations Over Time," *Social Problems* 16 (1965): 202. The 1970 figure was computed from U.S. Department of Commerce, Bureau of the Census, "U.S. Summary," U.S. Census of the Population, Detailed Characteristics, Final Report PC(1)–D1, (Washington, D.C.: Government Printing Office, 1973), pp. 718–24.

48   Gross, "Plus Ça Change," p. 202.

49   Francine D. Blau, "Pay Differentials and Differences in the Disbribution of Employment of Male and Female Office Workers" (Ph.D. diss., Harvard University, 1975), p. 29.

50   National Manpower Council, *Woman Power* (New York: Columbia University Press, 1957), p. 91, cited in Oppenheimer, *The Female Labor Force,* p. 66.

51   Oppenheimer, "The Sex-Labeling of Jobs," p. 222.

52   U.S. Equal Employment Opportunity Commission, *Employment Profiles of Minorities and Women.*

53   Francine D. Blau, "Sex Segregation of Workers by Enterprise in Clerical Occupations," in *Labor Market Segmentation,* ed. Richard C. Edwards, Michael Reich, and David M. Gordon (Lexington, Mass.: Lexington Books, 1975). See also John B. Buckley, "Pay Differences between Men and Women in the Same Job," *Monthly Labor Review,* November 1971, pp. 36–39.

54 Thomas Bradshaw and John F. Stinson, "Trends in Weekly Earnings: An Analysis," *Monthly Labor Review*, August 1975, p. 26.

55 "Money Income in 1973 of Families and Persons in the U.S.," *Current Population Reports*, Series P-60, no. 97, January 1975.

56 Ibid.

57 *Manpower Report of the President, April 1975*, p. 62.

58 "Money Income in 1974 of Families and Persons in the U.S.," *Current Population Reports*, Series P-60, no. 101, January 1976.

59 Barbara R. Bergmann, "Occupational Segregation, Wages and Profits When Employers Discriminate by Race or Sex," *Eastern Economic Journal* 1 (1974): 103-10. See also Francine D. Blau, "Women's Place in the Labor Market," *American Economic Review* 62 (1972): 161-66.

60 Georgina M. Smith, *Help Wanted—Female: A Study of Demand and Supply in a Local Job Market for Women* (New Brunswick, N.J.: Rutgers—The State University, Institute of Management and Labor Relations, n.d.), p. 2.

61 "Why Women Work," mimeographed (Washington, D.C.: U.S. Department of Labor, Women's Bureau, May 1974), p. 2.

62 Hayghe, "Marital and Family Characteristics, March 1975," p. 55.

63 *Manpower Report of the President, April 1975*, p. 70.

64 Heather L. Ross and Isabel V. Sawhill, *Time of Transition: The Growth of Families Headed by Women* (Washington, D.C.: Urban Institute, 1975), p. 15.

65 Hayghe, "Marital and Family Characteristics, March 1974," pp. A-22, A-23, A-27.

66 Oppenheimer, *The Female Labor Force*, pp. 100-101.

67 See Isabel Sawhill, "The Economics of Discrimination Against Women: Some New Findings," *Journal of Human Resources* 8 (1973): 383-96, for a review of this research.

68 U.S. Department of Labor, Bureau of Labor Statistics, *Facts on Absenteeism and Labor Turnover among Women Workers* (Washington, D.C.: Government Printing Office, 1969), p. 2.

69 Howard Hayghe, "Tenure of Workers, January 1973," *Monthly Labor Review*, December 1973, p. 53. It is important to note that, since a higher proportion of women than men are relatively new entrants into the labor force, not all of the difference in job tenure is attributable to higher turnover rates.

70 U.S. Civil Service Commission, President's Commission on the Status of Women, *Report of the Committee on Federal Employment* (Washington, D.C.: Government Printing Office, 1963), app. F.

71 Ibid., p. 24.

72 See Oppenheimer, *The Female Labor Force*.

73 Ibid., p. 187.

74 U.S. Department of Labor, Bureau of Labor Statistics, "The U.S. Economy in 1980: A Preview of BLS Projections," *Monthly Labor Review*, April 1970, pp. 21–24.

75 Janet Neipert Hedges, "Women Workers and Manpower Demands in the 1970's," *Monthly Labor Review*, June 1970, p. 22.

76 Ibid.

77 Current trends in female enrollment in professional training appear to point in the right direction. See John B. Parrish, "Women in Professional Training an Update," *Monthly Labor Review*, November 1975, p. 49.

The Doubly Disadvantaged: Minority Women in the Labor Force

Elizabeth M. Almquist
and
Juanita L. Wehrle-Einhorn

Many minority women in American society suffer a double disadvantage as a result of their status as both women and minority group members. The effects of this dual status are reflected in minority women's patterns of labor force participation. In this chapter we examine these patterns—the extent of minority women's participation in the labor force, their occupational distribution, and their earnings. At appropriate points we compare minority women with other groups, such as white women or minority men, in order to place our data in context. We explore some possible reasons for each group's labor force experience, and in the concluding section we draw certain comparisons among minority women, including an assessment of the relative effects of gender and minority group status on occupational status and income.

By *minority women* we mean women of races other than white, and white women of Spanish descent. Such women compose more than 18 percent of the female population in the United States, and there are more than 5 million in the labor force.

With the rebirth of feminism in the 1960s, women have become increasingly aware of the effect their gender has on their occupational opportunities. The rationale that a man needs higher pay because he has a family to support has become far less persuasive than it once was, and women as a group are beginning to regard themselves as objects of collective discrimination.

Minority women who share this view find themselves members of two minorities. Accordingly, their feminism is tempered by their experience with ethnic discrimination, and minority feminists tend to form organizations independent of white feminists. Black women, for example, have formed two national organizations;[1] Mexican-American women have organized caucuses within the Chicano movement; and American Indian women are holding conferences[2] to evaluate their double minority status.

Minority women constitute 16 percent of all women in the United States labor force.[3] Although studies have been made of women in the labor force, the term *women employees* has generally meant white women; studies of black workers have focused almost exclusively on black men; and research concerning minority women other than black women is extremely scarce, because blacks constitute nearly 90 percent of the minority population in the United States.[4] This absence of references to minority women in analyses of the labor force seems puzzling at first glance, in view of the availability of data published by the Census Bureau and the Department of Labor. There are, however, three serious obstacles to the use of these data.

The first obstacle is confusion generated by the multiplicity of overlapping terms used by the Census Bureau to define minority groups. In general, minority group members are self-defined: the interviewee designates his or her own race; unless otherwise indicated, the data we have used are of this type. However, for certain purposes "objective" standards are used; for example, the Census Bureau tabulates and publishes data for persons whose surnames are designated by the Census Bureau itself as being of Spanish origin. Brief reflection reveals that the two groups, "persons of Spanish surname" and "persons of Spanish origin," are not identical, although the groups overlap. Similar overlapping is found between those groups and "persons of Spanish language," "persons of Spanish heritage," and "persons of Puerto Rican birth or parentage." This problem is compounded by the fact that the definitions of these terms as used in the census have varied over the last thirty years.[5]

The second major problem with census data is the inadequacy of published data for within-group comparisons. Although it is possible, for example, to compare the median income or educational level of Japanese-Americans and of American Indians, the published data are inadequate to study the relationship between level of income and education within either group.

Finally, the data in different census publications are sometimes inconsistent. In May 1974, for example, the Women's Bureau of the Department of Labor estimated that 93 percent of women of Spanish origin were white;[6] in 1975 the estimate was 98 percent.[7]

Despite these problems, government data do provide us sufficient information to analyze certain aspects of minority women's labor force experience. Since race is currently most prominent among the three components of ethnicity (race, religion, and nationality) that limit assimilation into American society, we will consider mainly women of racial minority groups. Since national origin is an important determinant of assimilation in certain areas of the United States, we will also consider women of Spanish origin, almost all of whom, as we noted, are classified as white by the Census Bureau.[8]

Women of Spanish origin are represented here by Mexican-American (Chicano), Puerto Rican, and Cuban-American women; Asian-American women are represented by Chinese-American, Japanese-American, and Filipino-American[9] women. We discuss each group separately, presenting data that reflect its labor force experience; where appropriate, comparisons are made with certain "reference" groups, such as white women, white men, or minority male counterparts. The data we discuss are shown in tables 1 and 2.

For the purpose of this discussion it is helpful to recall the differing circumstances surrounding the entry of the various minority groups into the United States. Native Americans were, as the name implies, indigenous to the territory that became the United States. They did not come to America by choice; the nation developed around them. Equally involuntary was the entry of blacks, who arrived as slaves in the eighteenth and nineteenth centuries and were confined for more than a century to that status. Many Mexican-Americans "entered" the United States involuntarily in the nineteenth century with the Mexican cession of the southwest territory and the annexation of Texas; others entered voluntarily in search of employment and shelter. Puerto Ricans came to the United States as American citizens seeking work, from a nearby United States commonwealth acquired in the war against Spain in 1899 and still torn between independence and association with the United States. Most Cuban-Americans arrived in the United States as refugees from the Castro government within the last twenty years.

TABLE 1 Rank-ordered Socioeconomic Characteristics of Minorities and Whites

	White	Black	Spanish origin			American Indian	Asian origin		
			Mexican origin	Puerto Rican	Cuban origin		Japanese origin	Chinese origin	Filipino origin
Population (thousands)	178,107 (1)	22,550 (2)	4,532 (3)	1,429 (4)	545 (7)	764 (5)	588 (6)	432 (8)	337 (9)
Labor force participation rate									
Of women sixteen and over (percentage)	40.6 (6)	47.5 (5)	36.4 (7)	31.6 (9)	51.0 (2)	35.3 (8)	49.4 (3)	49.2 (4)	55.2 (1)
Of wives (percentage)	44 (6)	48 (3.5)	29 (8)	28 (9)	49 (2)	36 (7)	51 (1)	48 (3.5)	46 (5)
Of men (percentage)	77.4 (4.5)	69.8 (8)	77.4 (4.5)	75.5 (6)	83.7 (1)	63.4 (9)	79.3 (2)	73.2 (7)	79.0 (3)
Median income									
Of women sixteen and over (dollars)	3,738 (1)	2,041 (7)	1,892 (8)	2,938 (4)	2,825 (5)	1,697 (9)	3,236 (3)	2,686 (6)	3,513 (2)
Of men sixteen and over (dollars)	7,875 (1)	4,158 (8)	4,735 (7)	5,105 (5)	5,532 (3)	3,509 (9)	7,574 (2)	5,223 (4)	5,019 (6)
Education, median years of school completed, all persons twenty-five and over	12.1 (4)	9.8 (6.5)	8.1 (9)	8.7 (8)	10.3 (5)	9.8 (6.5)	12.5 (1)	12.4 (2)	12.2 (3)

High school graduates, percentage of all persons twenty-five and over	54.7 (3)	57.8 (2)	68.8 (1)	33.3 (6)	43.9 (5)	23.4 (9)	24.2 (8)	31.4 (7)	54.5 (4)
Average family size	4.23 (3)	4.01 (6)	3.67 (8)	4.46 (2)	3.74 (7)	4.15 (4.5)	4.64 (1)	4.15 (4.5)	3.57 (9)
Percentage of husband-wife families with at least one child under six	42 (3)	33 (6)	37 (5)	40 (4)	30 (8)	45 (2)	46 (1)	32 (7)	27 (9)
Percentage of families with female head	9 (8)	7 (9)	10 (7)	18 (3)	12 (5)	24 (2)	13 (4)	27 (1)	11 (6)
Percentage of families with female head with at least one child under six	39 (2)	12 (9)	24 (6)	32 (3)	16 (8)	46 (1)	30 (4.5)	30 (4.5)	17 (7)

Sources: U.S. Department of Commerce, Bureau of the Census, *Subject Reports of the 1970 Census:* PC (2)–1B, Negro Population; PC (2)–1C, Persons of Spanish Origin; PC (2)–1D, Persons of Spanish Surname; PC (2)–1E, Puerto Ricans in the United States; PC (2)–1F, American Indians; and PC (2)–1G, Japanese, Chinese, and Filipinos in the United States (Washington, D.C.: Government Printing Office, 1973).

TABLE 2   Occupational Distribution and Income of Minority and White Women and [

	Median income			White		Bla
Job category	W	M	Women's as percentage of men's	W	M	W
*Professionals, technical workers	$6,675	$11,577	58	16	15	11
*Managers, administrators (except farm)	5,523	11,292	49	4	12	1
*Sales workers	2,279	8,321	27	6	7	3
*Clerical workers	4,646	7,965	58	37	8	21
Craft workers, foremen	4,276	8,833	48	2	22	1
Operatives	3,885	7,017	55	14	19	17
Nonfarm laborers	3,151	4,839	65	1	6	1
Farmers, farm managers	—	3,859	—	0	3	—
Farm laborers, foremen	1,166	2,238	52	0	1	1
Nonhousehold service workers	2,541	5,568	46	14	7	25
Private service workers	825	—	—	2	0	18

*White collar.

Sources: U.S. Department of Commerce, Bureau of the Census, Subject Reports of the 1970 Census: PC (2)-1B, Negro Population; PC (2)-1C, Persons of Spanish Origin; PC (2)-1D, Persons of

Asian-American men arrived after a voluntary journey of thousands of miles, planning to return home with their fortunes made. Asian-American women, on the other hand, arrived for the most part as wives of white men or betrothed to Asian-American men as "picture brides," a phenomenon not unlike the mail-order brides of the old west.

It is clear that each group has had its own version of the "American dream," and that the dreams have been quite different. Some groups have sought wealth or prestige; some have sought assimilation; and others have sought to be let alone. Recognizing that the values of these groups are not

	Percentage of labor force												
Spanish origin						American Indian		Asian origin					
xican igin	Puerto Rican		Cuban origin		American Indian		Japanese origin		Chinese origin		Filipino origin	
M	W	M	W	M	W	M	W	M	W	M	W	M
5	7	5	9	13	11	9	16	21	19	29	32	18
4	2	4	1	7	2	5	4	12	4	11	2	3
3	4	4	5	6	4	2	7	6	5	4	4	2
6	30	11	26	25	25	6	34	9	32	9	29	9
21	2	16	3	18	2	22	2	20	1	7	1	13
27	40	34	43	24	19	24	13	10	23	10	11	14
13	1	8	1	6	1	13	1	10	1	3	1	8
1	0	0	0	0	1	2	1	3	0	4	0	1
9	0	1	0	0	2	6	1	2	0	0	2	11
10	12	17	11	14	26	10	17	6	13	24	17	20
0	1	0	1	0	7	0	4	0	2	0	2	0

Spanish Surname; PC (2)-1E, Puerto Ricans in the United States; PC (2)-1F, American Indians; and PC (2)-1G, Japanese, Chinese, and Filipinos in the United States (Washington, D.C.: Government Printing Office, 1973).

necessarily the same as those espoused by white America, we may proceed to discuss the labor force experience of each group.

BLACK AMERICANS

Blacks are the most numerous racial minority in the United States. A relatively high proportion (47.5 percent) of black women are in the labor force, a higher proportion than for white women and all other minority women studied except Asian-Americans. Since 1900 the rate of black women's participation in the labor force has been higher than that of white women, but the rate of increase has not been as sharp for black women as it has for white women. As a result, only a slightly higher proportion of black women than white women were in the labor force in 1970.

The median income among employed black women is very low ($2,041), perhaps because of their occupational distribution. An exceptionally large proportion (43 percent) of employed black women are service workers, and a relatively small proportion (21 percent) are in clerical positions. Nearly one out of five black women in the labor force is a domestic servant, compared with only one out of fifty white women. Between 1960 and 1970, however, black women dramatically altered their labor force status. During that decade nearly one-fourth of employed black women changed occupations, shifting the occupational distribution of black women toward clerical occupations and female-dominated professions.[10] Still, black women have the smallest representation in clerical occupations of all the groups of women considered here.

The relatively high rate of labor force participation of black women and their occupational distribution reflect a number of historical and social factors. First, black men have a rather low rate of labor force participation (69.8 percent), exceedingly only that of American Indians among minority men. Black men tend to occupy relatively low-paying, nonsupervisory, blue-collar occupations. Therefore black women need to work to supply adequate family income.

Joyce Ladner has found that career pursuits are not regarded by black girls as unfeminine, primarily because an employed mother is normative.[11] Although black women would often prefer to marry men for support and protection, they cannot rely on marriage for security. The career aspirations of black girls may also be explained in part by the high educational aspirations black families have for their daughters.[12]

Cynthia Epstein has observed that black professional women experience less family–career conflict and feel more confident in their roles than do white women.[13] She further argues that the doubly negative status of "female" and "black" actually aids black professional women, because the two negatives either cancel each other out or form a unique status. Note, however, that Epstein's sample size was small and that the sample was admittedly distorted by including numerous highly career-oriented immigrants from the West Indies.

The key historical factor for black American women is their heritage of slavery and degradation. Black female slaves were taught only limited domestic skills; on the plantation, white women were hired to spin, sew, and make clothing.[14] Consequently the needle trades and early textile industry jobs were closed to blacks. Having demonstrated their manual dexterity in the textile factories, white women were permitted to operate a new machine, the typewriter, and established their preeminence in clerical and secretarial positions.[15] Black women continued as unskilled laborers, service workers, and farm laborers.

> 66 Between 1960 and 1970 nearly one-fourth of employed black women changed occupations, shifting the occupational distribution of black women toward clerical occupations and female-dominated professions. 99

The recent increase of black women in clerical and professional work represents a marked improvement of their status, if not their earnings. The professions entered by black women are generally the "female" professions: they become nurses, teachers, librarians, etc. Women are 61 percent of the black professionals, but they constitute only 16 percent of black doctors and dentists, 13 percent of black lawyers, and 5 percent of black engineers.[16] Black women have been moving to occupations with career ladders, but, as is true for whites, the high-paying, high-prestige professions remain "male" professions.

WOMEN OF SPANISH ORIGIN

Mexican-Americans

Of the 9 million persons of Spanish origin in the United States, nearly half are of Mexican origin; approximately 80 percent of these Mexican-Americans were born in the United States. It is estimated that nearly 90 percent of all Mexican-Americans reside in Arizona, California, Colorado, New Mexico, and Texas.[17]

A rather low proportion (36.4 percent) of Mexican-American women are in the labor force, exceeding only the proportions of Puerto Rican and American Indian women. The median income for employed Mexican-American women ($1,892) is also low, surpassing only that of American Indian women. Unlike black women, however, a relatively small proportion (5 percent) of employed Mexican-Americans are domestic service workers; nearly three-fourths of employed Mexican-American women are in clerical (26 percent), operative (26 percent), and nonhousehold service (21 percent) occupations. In addition, the proportion of Mexican-American women who are farm laborers (4 percent) is the highest among the groups studied. And 9 percent of Mexican-American men are also farm laborers. This pattern reflects the large proportion of migrant farm workers in the Southwest who are Mexican-American.

It appears that Mexican-Americans are torn between the need to assimilate into American society and the desire to preserve their Mexican heritage.[18] It has also been suggested that one aspect of the "machismo" attitude of Mexican-American men makes them embarrassed to have their wives employed outside the home.[19] Nearly half of the Mexican-American families have at least one preschool child, and the average family size (4.64 members) is the largest among the groups studied. The median educational level (8.1 years) of Mexican-Americans is the lowest among the groups studied, perhaps because bilingual educational facilities are lacking. These three characteristics—low level of education, large family size, and presence of small children in the home—together with a cultural norm against career pursuits, appear to explain the relatively low proportion (6 percent) of Mexican-American women in the professions.

In a recent study of Mexican-Americans, Rosemary Cooney rejected the arguments of previous researchers attributing the low rate of labor force participation of Mexican-American women either to high fertility rates or to a special cultural emphasis on motherhood and family obligations.[20] She found that, when she controlled for socioeconomic factors that generally influence participation rates, the difference in 1970 participation rates for Mexican-American and Anglo women virtually disappeared. Among childless women with some college education, for example, 87.8 percent of Mexican-Americans were in the labor force, compared with 85.3 percent of Anglos. Cooney's data must be interpreted cautiously, however, because a cultural emphasis on the family might *indirectly* influence labor force participation rates by directly affecting those factors for which Cooney controlled, such as educational level and presence of preschool children in the home.

Puerto Ricans in the United States

More than half (56 percent) of the 1.4 million Puerto Ricans in the United States were born in Puerto Rico. Puerto Ricans are heavily concentrated in east coast urban centers; an estimated 60 percent live in New York City.[21]

An unusually large proportion of employed Puerto Rican women (40 percent) are operatives. Among the female minorities considered, they have the strongest representation in that category except for Cuban-American women. Clerical work also draws a rather large proportion (30 percent) of employed Puerto Rican women. There is a correspondingly low proportion of Puerto Rican women (13 percent) in service occupations. Puerto Rican men also have the highest proportion (34 percent) of operatives among male minorities, and they rank lowest among the male groups in the proportion of professionals (5 percent).

Puerto Ricans' educational level is very low; they have the smallest proportion of high school graduates among the groups studied. A very large proportion of families (45 percent) have at least one preschool child, and a slightly larger proportion (46 percent) of female-headed families have at least one preschool child. In view of these data, it is not surprising that Puerto Rican women have the lowest labor force participation rate of all groups studied.

Another factor, however, makes Puerto Ricans in the United States an even more distinct group. As previously mentioned, more than half the Puerto Ricans in the United States were born in Puerto Rico and immigrated to the United States. Lourdes King has described the problem of transience encountered by Puerto Rican women: "The Puerto Rican woman in the United States fits the historical pattern of the immigrant woman who worked alongside her man, sharing the burden of work and responsibilities. Unlike any other woman who has preceded her, however, she is a member of a group in continuous flux, moving between the United States and Puerto Rico for varying lengths of time throughout her life."[22]

According to King, Puerto Rican women tend to return to Puerto Rico following traumatic events, for example, when marital dissolution takes place, loss of employment occurs, or the youngest child leaves home. It is not unusual for a Puerto Rican woman to be separated from her husband and children while she works on the mainland if they remain at home on the island, or she may pioneer with her husband on the mainland while a grandparent at home cares for the children. Thus, many Puerto Ricans in the United States experience a transience similar in certain respects to that of migrant Mexican-American farm workers, limiting the opportunities for educating their children and assimilating the family into American society. The Puerto Rican experience also appears to resemble that of American Indians, who leave the reservation to seek work in the cities and occasionally return home to resume ties of kinship and friendship.

Cuban-Americans

Cubans are the most recent large minority group to come to the United States. Large numbers of Cubans entered the country following Fidel Castro's victory in the Cuban revolution and implementation of socialist programs. The rate of immigration increased further in 1961–62 when tensions between the United States and Cuba heightened. Nearly three-fourths of the Cuban-Americans have entered the United States since 1959.[23]

An extraordinarily large number of employed Cuban-American women (43 percent) are operatives, and a rather small proportion (26 percent) are in clerical positions. Very few Cuban-American women are managers (1 percent) or private household workers (1 percent), and relatively few are nonhousehold service workers (11 percent). A high proportion of Cuban-American women are in the labor force (51 percent). This finding is not surprising in light of the fact that both the educational level for Cuban-Americans and the median income level of Cuban-American women are somewhat higher than average among the groups considered.

Compared with other minority men, a high proportion of Cuban-Americans are in clerical positions (11 percent), professional occupations (13 percent), and operative jobs (24 percent). They have the highest rate (87.3 percent) of labor force participation of all groups considered, including whites, although their median income ranks third, below the income of white males and Japanese-American males.

Many of the recent immigrants encounter a language barrier that results in their underemployment. This may explain why such large proportions of

Cuban-Americans are in semiskilled positions, although they were generally middle- or upper-class citizens of Cuba before the revolution.[24]

AMERICAN INDIANS

The Native American population is composed of several hundred separate groups, each having its own culture and pattern of contacts with whites. The various cultures, however, almost uniformly value mutual effort, sharing, and cooperation, in contrast to the typical American belief in competition and free enterprise as the engines of progress. "Rugged individualism" and the desire for acquisition are foreign concepts to many American Indian cultures.[25]

American Indians constitute the most economically depressed and least acculturated minority group in the United States. More than a quarter of the American Indians still live on reservations, where their average life expectancy is only 43.5 years.[26]

> 〰 Japanese-Americans have the highest educational level among the groups considered, including whites. 〰

The major occupations for American Indian women are in nonhousehold service work (26 percent), clerical positions (25 percent), and operative jobs (19 percent). Only 35.3 percent of American Indian women are in the labor force, the second lowest proportion among the groups studied; similarly, only 63.4 percent of American Indian men are in the labor force, lowest among the male groups considered. Median annual income for employed American Indians is also lowest among the groups considered: $1,697 for women and $3,509 for men.

The *Farmington Report,* which describes the employment situation in San Juan County, New Mexico, illustrates the conflicts and difficulties encountered by American Indians. The four private companies that dominate the area's economy pay royalties to the Navaho Nation for use of the land; in addition, the companies have contracted to hire Navaho workers (who represent two-thirds of the local labor force) on a preferential basis. However, union seniority rules determine promotions, and whites tend to have seniority; the Navaho have also had difficulty enforcing the preferential hiring provisions. As a result, Navaho employees are heavily concentrated in low-skilled blue-collar positions, and whites virtually monopolize the management positions.[27]

Although the cultures are varied among American Indian groups and subgroups, Laila Hamamsy's study of the Navaho provides insight into the relationship between family functions and the economic position of American Indian women.[28] Navaho society was historically organized on a matrilineal and matrilocal basis, with extended families the norm. Upon marriage the woman received a "bride price," and the couple lived with or near her family. Thus Navaho women had opportunities for visiting their families and sharing the care of small children.

Men did the heavy farm work and tended livestock; women herded the sheep and wove blankets from the wool. Since inheritances were not apportioned on the basis of sex, the economic contribution of women was comparable to that of men, and Navaho women had substantial influence in family decision-making.

Three major factors have reduced the Navaho woman's prestige: (1) federal government policies dictated that only male heirs would inherit land; (2) sheep raising declined in economic importance; and (3) American Indian men began to seek work beyond the reservation. Thus, men became the primary breadwinners, women's economic existence became precarious, and the extended family system evolved to a nuclear family norm.

As the locus of employment of American Indians has shifted from the reservation to urban centers, federal government policies have taken on added significance. The Bureau of Indian Affairs (BIA) provides aid to persons living on the reservation, but not to those living off the reservation. The availability of BIA assistance, together with the ties of kinship and friendship at the reservation, tend to engender a transience among American Indians similar to that experienced by Puerto Ricans. American Indians, especially women, have entered only tentatively into the mainstream of American economic life.

ASIAN-AMERICANS

Few women participated in the early migration of Chinese, Japanese, and Filipino people to the United States. Chinese men, who began arriving on the west coast with the California gold rush of 1848, were imported in large numbers in the 1870s to work in the lumber, construction, and railroad industries.[29] Large numbers of Japanese men immigrated to the United States beginning in 1900,[30] and Filipino men began to immigrate following World War I,[31] although they were ineligible for citizenship until after World War II.[32]

Japanese-Americans

Japanese-American women have an occupational distribution very similar to that of white women. Indeed, the only variation of more than one percentage point between the two groups occurs in clerical positions, which employ 37 percent of white women, compared with 34 percent of Japanese-American women. However, the median income of Japanese-American women ($3,236) is less than that of white women ($3,738). A larger proportion of Japanese-American women (49.4 percent) than of white women (40.6 percent) are in the labor force.

The proportion of Japanese-American men in the labor force (79.3 percent) is the second largest among the groups considered, including white men. Japanese-Americans have the highest educational level among the groups considered, including whites; the family size is nearest to the white family size; and the occupational distribution of Japanese-American men is similar to that of white men, except that Japanese-American men are more strongly represented in the professions (21 percent) and less strongly represented in operative jobs (10 percent).

The strong presence of Japanese-Americans in professional and management occupations probably results in part from their social and economic experience in the United States. Early Japanese immigrants encountered stiff resistance from whites. Trade unions in the early twentieth century excluded them from various industries, and white farm workers tried to prevent competition from Japanese-Americans. Laws were enacted to prevent Japanese-Americans from leasing land for agriculture. Perhaps because they were denied land for agricultural purposes and excluded from a variety of trades, an experience similar to that of the Jews in Europe, Japanese-Americans turned to education and entrepreneurship. Before World War II Japanese-Americans had the highest percentage of college graduates of any racial minority in the United States.[33]

During World War II Japanese-Americans were evacuated from the west coast and forced to move into relocation centers,[34] costing them an estimated $400 million in property.[35] Joseph Roucek argues that one beneficial result of this ordeal was that Japanese-Americans who had to find new employment in the growing American economy after the war entered industries that had previously been closed to them.[36]

Since World War II, Japanese-American women have substantially abandoned their traditional roles, often despite opposition from the Japanese-American community. The two main obstacles have been that assertiveness conflicts with the traditional Japanese values of passivity and submissiveness for women and that the public recognition often received by a competent woman conflicts with Asian women's traditional modesty.[37]

Chinese-Americans

The occupational distribution of Chinese-American women also closely parallels that of white American women. A larger proportion of Chinese-American women are in professional (19 percent) and operative (23 percent) occupations than the corresponding proportions of white women (16 and 14 percent, respectively); a larger proportion of white women (37 percent) than of Chinese-American women (32 percent) are employed in clerical positions.

Chinese-American men are very strongly represented in the professions (29 percent) and nonhousehold service occupations (24 percent). The Chinese-American level of education is second only to that of Japanese-Americans among the groups considered (including whites). The rate of participation in the labor force is very high for women (49.2 percent) and moderately high for men (73.2 percent). However, the median income of Chinese-American men is the fourth highest among the groups considered (including whites), while the median income of Chinese-American women ranks only sixth among the female groups. One reason such a large proportion of Chinese-American women are in the labor force despite a relatively low median income may be derived from the fact that a very small proportion (12 percent) of families with female heads have preschool children, indicating that most female heads of families are relatively free to seek employment outside the home.

Rose Hum Lee has observed that the refusal of whites to serve Chinese immigrants was a major factor causing the Chinese immigrants to establish service enterprises, such as restaurants, laundries, and rooming houses.[38] Additional factors were that restaurant and laundry work involved minimal personal competition with hostile white neighbors, and that the ineligibility of Chinese immigrants for American citizenship excluded them from many occupations.[39]

The major breakthrough for Chinese-Americans came with World War II, in which the United States and China were allies. As industry boomed and Japanese-Americans were removed to relocation camps, Chinese-American men were able to enter engineering and technical fields.[40] Simultaneously, changes in United States immigration laws enabled increasing numbers of Chinese women to enter the country.[41] The Chinese-American population changed from 74.1 percent male in 1940 to 53 percent male in 1970.[42] Thus the influx of Chinese women into the United States coincided with a period of economic boom for Chinese-Americans. This timing may be another factor contributing to the high labor force participation rate of Chinese-American women.

Filipino-Americans

The occupational distribution of Filipino-American women is generally similar to that of white women, except that nearly one-third (32 percent) of employed Filipino-Americans are in the professions, an extraordinarily large proportion A relatively small proportion (11 percent) of Filipino-American women are operatives. Filipino-American women also have the highest labor force participation rate (55.2 percent) of any group of women considered, including whites, and a median income second only to whites among groups of women.

Filipino-American men are poorly represented in management (3 percent), operative (14 percent), and craft (13 percent) positions. They do have the highest proportion (11 percent) in farm labor occupations and a high proportion (20 percent) in nonhousehold service positions, second only to Chinese-Americans among groups of men in these service positions.

Filipinos were the last group of "Asians"[43] to migrate in large numbers to the United States before 1970. Like other groups, Filipino immigrants generally hoped to earn their fortunes and return home. The immigrants were predominantly male—143 men per woman in the early twentieth century.[44] Because of this, and because the chief employment opportunities on the west coast were in agriculture when the Filipinos arrived, they tended to become migrant farm laborers.[45]

Before 1935, Filipinos were able to enter the United States as nationals without a quota because the Philippines had become an American colony as a result of the Spanish-American War. However, in 1934 Congress passed a law granting the Philippines gradual independence over the next ten years. Filipinos in the United States were then rendered ineligible for federal government relief measures during the depression.[46] Since World War II, the proportion of Filipino-American women has increased rapidly, and in 1970 men constituted only 55 percent of the Filipino-American population.

TENTATIVE CONCLUSIONS: THE DOUBLE DISADVANTAGE

In general the occupational distributions of minority women are more like the distribution of white women than those of their minority male counterparts. We have computed an index of dissimilarity comparing the occupational distribution of each group of minority women with that group's male counterpart and with white women. The index represents the percentage of minority women who would have to change occupations in order to achieve the same distribution as the reference group. The results of our computations are shown in table 3.

Using the first group listed in table 3 for purposes of illustration, we find an index of dissimilarity of 29.0 for the occupational distribution of black women compared with the distribution of white women, and 46.5 for black women compared with the distribution of black men. Thus 29 percent of employed black women would have to change occupations in order for black women to have the same occupational distribution as white women; 46.5 percent would have to change in order to have the same distribution as black men. Since fewer black women must change to have the same distribution as white women, it is clear that the occupational distribution of black women is more similar to that of white women than to that of black men. Accordingly, we conclude that gender is more important than minority status in determining occupational distribution for black women.

It is important to note that the differences between indexes of dissimilarity vary a great deal among the different groups of minority women. Thus, although it appears that gender is more important than ethnicity in determining the occupational distribution for each group of minority women, gender is much more important than race for Japanese-American and Chinese-American women, while gender and ethnicity appear to have nearly equal influence for Puerto Rican and Cuban-American women.

TABLE 3   Indexes of Occupational Dissimilarity:
Minority Women Compared to
White Women and Minority Men

| Minority group | Reference group | | Difference |
	White women	Minority men	
Black	29.0	46.5	17.5
Mexican-American	24.5	39.5	15.0
Puerto Rican	25.0	28.5	3.5
Cuban-American	28.5	34.5	6.0
American Indian	22.5	45.5	23.0
Japanese-American	5.5	43.5	38.0
Chinese-American	10.5	39.5	29.0
Filipino-American	18.0	37.0	19.0
Mean	20.4	39.3	18.9

Note: The index of dissimilarity indicates the percentage of employed women in the named minority group who must change occupations in order for the minority women to have the same occupational distribution as the reference group. A high index means a large percentage of minority women must change occupations; a low index indicates close similarity between the minority women and the reference group. The column headed *Difference* shows how much greater the index is when the minority group men are the reference group than when white women are the reference group. A larger difference means a relatively stronger influence of gender on occupational distribution.

Sources: U.S. Department of Commerce, Bureau of the Census, *Subject Reports of the 1970 Census:* PC (2)-1B, Negro Population; PC (2)-1C, Persons of Spanish Origin; PC (2)-1D, Persons of Spanish Surname; PC (2)-1E, Puerto Ricans in the United States; PC (2)-1F, American Indians and PC (2)-1G, Japanese, Chinese, and Filipinos in the United States (Washington, D.C.: Government Printing Office, 1973).

Having observed that gender appears to be more important than ethnicity in determining occupational distribution, let us now consider the data we discussed previously on income levels of minority women. First, we must note that *median income* is not equivalent to *median earnings;* rather, median income includes earnings plus income from all other sources, such as pensions, alimony, welfare, and insurance. We have treated income as if it were equivalent to earnings, however, because data concerning earnings are not readily available for the groups we have considered.

We must also note that *median income* represents the median income of all persons at least fourteen years old who received income. Median income figures include the earnings of those who work part-time or part-year. Since men are more likely than women to work full-time, year-round, median income figures are more representative of men's earnings than of women's earnings. The median earnings of full-time employed minority women are probably closer to the median earnings of full-time employed minority men than is suggested by a comparison of median incomes.

Our comparison of median incomes is also skewed somewhat as a result of different geographic distributions of the various minority groups. Earnings and other income are generally higher in urban than in rural areas, and higher on the east and west coasts than in the Southwest. Thus the median incomes of American Indians and Mexican-Americans are depressed somewhat by geography, and the median income of Puerto Ricans is inflated.

Recognizing these shortcomings in the data, we may examine apparent relationships between income and certain other group characteristics presented in table 1. First we note that for the minority group women considered, labor force participation rate has a moderately high positive correlation with median income (rho[47] = +0.596). This may mean either that low potential earnings discourage minority women from entering the labor force or that a low rate of participation in the labor force results in a low median income for minority women.

We have found that minority women's labor force participation rate shows a moderately high (rho = +0.583) positive correlation with the proportion of employed women who are in professional and management positions; a high positive correlation (rho = +0.730) with median educational level; a slight negative correlation (rho = −0.286) with the proportion of husband–wife families with at least one preschool child; and a high negative correlation (rho = −0.690) with the proportion of families headed by women. Women's median income has a moderately high positive correlation (rho = +0.554) with median educational level, but no correlation (rho = −0.024) with the proportion of families with female heads. Finally, we find a moderately high negative correlation (rho = −0.571) between median male income and the proportion of families with female heads.

The emerging pattern of correlations, based solely on the summary data available, suggests that labor force participation of minority women is influenced by those factors generally thought to influence labor force participation of white women. The correlations among participation, income, education, and the proportion of women in high-pay, high-status occupations suggest that increasing earning potential and possible job satisfaction will encourage minority women to enter the labor force.

It appears, however, that the presence of young children in the home is not quite as strong a deterrent to the employment of some minority women outside the home as it is for white women. This phenomenon may result from either (1) the fact that the minority male's income is less than that of the white male, and therefore supplementary income is needed more; or (2) the fact that kinship patterns (such as the traditional American Indian

> ❝ There is a growing body of evidence that wage discrimination is more extensive and costly when based on sex than when based on race. ❞

kinship system) provide sufficient child care so that the minority mother feels less uncomfortable than the white mother in seeking outside employment; or (3) the fact that traditional attitudes are consistent with the employment of women outside the home (for example, the fact that, among black women, employment has been a norm).

There is a growing body of evidence that wage discrimination is more extensive and costly when based on sex than when based on race. Larry Suter and Herman Miller[48] found that women[49] are unable to translate their educational and occupational achievements into earnings at the same rate as white men. Isabel Sawhill has concluded from a regression analysis of individual data that variations in education, occupation, etc., explain a large portion of the income disparity between blacks and whites, but do not explain a comparable portion of the disparity between men and women.[50]

The "double disadvantage," then, reflects two distinct types of disadvantages. Because of indirect disadvantages or discrimination (for instance, where the expenditure of funds per pupil in a school district varies inversely with the proportion of blacks per school), minority group members tend to be disadvantaged in terms of education and therefore type of occupation available. As a result of more direct disadvantages or discrimination, women who have achieved a given educational or occupational level are less able than men to reap the desired rewards in terms of earnings or status.

SUMMARY

As we have seen, minority women are not uniformly disadvantaged. Asian-American women are very close to white women in occupational status and earnings. Like their male counterparts they aim for the professions but tend not to enter management positions.

The Puerto Rican population is relatively new to the mainland and has not become assimilated, in part because of the relationship between Puerto Rico and the United States, which leads Puerto Ricans in the United States to maintain close ties with family members in Puerto Rico. As the proportion of Puerto Ricans born and raised on the mainland increases, the educational level of Puerto Ricans in the United States is expected to increase, enabling Puerto Ricans to achieve a more balanced occupational distribution.

The Cuban-American population is also new to the United States, but its members have generally arrived as refugees and have not maintained the same ties with Cuba that the Puerto Ricans have with Puerto Rico. Since the refugees were for the most part members of the Cuban middle and upper classes, Cuban-Americans may escape their disadvantages more rapidly than the other minorities we have considered.

Mexican-American women will probably enter the labor force in increasing numbers as industrialization of the Southwest requires more workers. Meanwhile, the extremely low educational level and the high proportion of families with preschool children will maintain the disadvantages suffered by these women.

Black women dramatically altered their labor force status from 1960 to 1970, and the trend is expected to continue. The shift of black women has been toward the white-collar clerical and female-dominated professional fields, and the changes have improved their status more than their income.

One unanswered question is whether black women in this decade or the next will begin to aim for management positions and the male-dominated professions.

American Indian women continue to confront the most difficult problems facing minority women. Although the reservation may not be a very attractive place, it does provide some basic services and a measure of security. The reservation offers the warmth of family ties and friendships, but the programs sponsored by the Bureau of Indian Affairs have not been very successful at either preserving American Indian values or reconciling those values with the demands of white society. The American Indian woman's problem is compounded by her decreasing power within the family and the rupture of her traditional kinship ties if she leaves the reservation.

In our analysis of labor force data we have found that minority women are indeed "doubly disadvantaged," although certain of our conclusions are very tentative because of the nature of the available data. While our discussion presumes that economic achievement is desirable, we do not seek to impugn, for example, the distaste of American Indians for competition, the desire of Mexican-Americans to preserve their culture and heritage, or the traditional values of Asian-Americans. Rather, we have sought to identify obstacles faced specifically by minority women who want, and are entitled to seek, full participation in American society.

NOTES

1 The black feminist organizations are Black Women Organized for Action and the National Black Feminist Organization.

2 *Wassaja, A National Newspaper of Indian America,* September, 1975, published by the American Indian Historical Society.

3 U.S. Department of Labor, Women's Bureau, *1975 Handbook on Women Workers* (Washington, D.C.: Government Printing Office, 1975) p. 48; U.S. Department of Commerce, Bureau of the Census, *A Statistical Portrait of Women in the United States* (Washington, D.C.: Government Printing Office, 1976), pp. 32, 62, 67, 77.

4 U.S. Department of Labor, Women's Bureau, *Facts on Women Workers of Minority Races* (Washington, D.C.: Government Printing Office, 1974), p. 1.

5 Jose Hernandez, Leo Estrada, and David Alvirez, "Census Data and the Problem of Conceptually Defining the Mexican American Population," *Social Science Quarterly* 69 (1973): 671.

6 *Facts on Women Workers of Minority Races.*

7 *1975 Handbook on Women Workers,* p. 48.

8   Ibid.

9   Filipinos have a Spanish heritage and have not considered themselves Orientals. See Salvatore J. La Gumina and Frank J. Cavaioli, *The Ethnic Dimension in American Society* (Boston: Holbrook Press, 1974), pp. 99–100. We have included Filipino-Americans among Asian-Americans because they are nonwhite and likely to be defined by white Americans as Asian-Americans.

10 Elizabeth M. Almquist, "Untangling the Effects of Race and Sex: The Disadvantaged Status of Black Women," *Social Science Quarterly* 56 (1975): 138.

11 Joyce A. Ladner, *Tomorrow's Tomorrow: The Black Woman* (Garden City, N.Y.: Doubleday and Company, 1971).

12 Dennis B. Kandel, "Race, Maternal Authority and Adolescent Aspirations," *American Journal of Sociology* 76 (1971): 999–1020.

13 Cynthia Epstein, "Positive Effects of the Multiple Negative: Explaining the Success of Black Professional Women," *American Journal of Sociology* 78 (1973): 912–35.

14 Julia Cherry Spruill, *Women's Life and Work in the Southern Colonies* (New York: W. W. Norton and Company, 1972).

15 Dale Hiestand, *Economic Growth and Employment Opportunities for Minorities* (New York: Columbia University Press, 1964).

16 Almquist, "Untangling the Effects of Race and Sex."

17 Leo Grebler, Joan Moore, and Ralph Guzman, *The Mexican-American People* (New York: Free Press, 1970).

18 Jack D. Forbes, "Mexican-Americans," in *Viewpoints: Red and Yellow, Black and Brown*, ed. Clifford L. Snyder (Minneapolis: Winston Press, 1972), pp. 41–46.

19 Consuelo Nieto, "Chicanos and the Women's Rights Movement," *Civil Rights Digest* 6 (1974): 36–42.

20 Rosemary Cooney, "Changing Labor Force Participation of Mexican-American Wives: A Comparison with Anglos and Blacks," *Social Science Quarterly* 56 (1975): 252–61.

21 Lourdes Miranda King, "Puertorriquenas in the United States: The Impact of Double Discrimination," *Civil Rights Digest* 6 (1974): 20–27.

22 Ibid., p. 22.

23 La Gumina and Cavaioli, *The Ethnic Dimension*, pp. 269–70.

24 Richard R. Fagen, Richard A. Brady, and Thomas J. O'Leary, *Cubans in Exile: Disaffection and the Revolution* (Stanford, Calif.: Stanford University Press, 1968), p. 16.

25 Joan Ablon, "Cultural Conflict in Urban Indians," *Mental Hygiene* 55 (1971): 199–205.

26   Robert Burnette, "The Long and Losing Fight of the American Indian," in *Viewpoints: Red and Yellow, Black and Brown,* ed. Snyder, pp. 23–31.

27   *The Farmington Report: A Conflict of Cultures,* Report of the New Mexico Advisory Commission to the United States Commission on Civil Rights (Washington, D.C.: Government Printing Office, 1975).

28   Laila Sheekry Hamamsy, "The Role of Women in a Changing Navaho Society," *American Anthropologist* 59 (1957): 101–11.

29   S. W. Kung, *Chinese in American Life* (Seattle: University of Washington Press, 1962), pp. 64–68.

30   La Gumina and Cavaioli, *The Ethnic Dimension,* p. 99.

31   Ibid.

32   Ibid., pp. 127–28.

33   Joseph S. Roucek, "Japanese Americans," in *One America,* ed. Francis Brown and Joseph S. Roucek (New York: Prentice-Hall, 1952), pp. 319–34.

34   Harry L. Kitano, *Japanese Americans: The Evolution of a Subculture,* 2d ed. (Englewood Cliffs, N.J.: Prentice-Hall, 1976).

35   Michi Weglyn, *Years of Infamy: The Untold Story of America's Concentration Camps* (New York: William Morrow and Company, 1976), p. 276.

36   Ibid.

37   Irene Fujitomi and Diane Wong, "The New Asian-American Women," in *Female Psychology: The Emerging Self,* ed. Sue Cox (Chicago: Science Research Associates, 1976), pp. 236–48.

38   Rose Hum Lee, "Chinese Americans," in *One America,* ed. Brown and Roucek, pp. 309–18.

39   Kung, *Chinese in American Life,* pp. 180–81.

40   Ibid.

41   Betty Jung, "Chinese Immigrants," *Civil Rights Digest* 6 (1974): 46–47.

42   Ibid.

43   See La Gumina and Cavaioli, *The Ethnic Dimension,* pp. 99–100.

44   John H. Burma, *Spanish-speaking Groups in the United States* (London: Cambridge University Press, 1954), pp. 138–55.

45   Ibid.

46   Ibid.

47   Rho, sometimes called *rank difference correlation,* is a simple estimate of the correlation of rank orders. The value of rho falls between $+1.0$ (perfect positive correlation) and -1.0 (perfect negative or inverse correlation). Where rho $= 0$, there is no correlation. For additional information concerning computation and

use of rho, see G. David Gorson, *Handbook of Political Science Methods* (Boston: Holbrook Press, 1971), pp. 182–84.

48   Larry E. Suter and Herman P. Miller, "Income Differences between Men and Career Women," *American Journal of Sociology* 73 (1973): 962–74.

49   The analysis treated all women as a group; some consideration was given to black women as a subgroup, but other minorities were not discussed separately.

50   Isabel V. Sawhill, "The Economics of Discrimination against Women: Some New Findings," *Journal of Human Resources* 8 (1973): 383–96. See also Ronald Oaxaca, "Sex Discrimination in Wages," in *Discrimination in Labor Markets,* ed. Orley Ashenfelter and Albert Rees (Princeton, N.J.: Princeton University Press, 1973).

Wage Differences between Men and Women: Economic Theories

Mary Huff Stevenson

Economists have been pondering the general question of wage differences between workers since before the time of Adam Smith. Recently, attention has been focused on the applicability of different economic theories to the specific question of wage differences between men and women. This chapter discusses several approaches to the issue, including explanations based on productivity differences and explanations based on labor market discrimination. It then concentrates on the implications of the "crowding hypothesis," and analysis that links wage differences to restrictions on women's access to the full range of occupations.

WAGE DIFFERENCES AND PRODUCTIVITY

One way in which economists have attempted to explain wage differences between men and women is through application of the human capital theory of wage determination.[1] This theory states that in a competitive economic system wage differences are a product of differences in human capital between workers. Human capital consists of the things workers could do to make themselves more productive, such as improving their education or skill level. Proponents of the human capital approach argue that human capital is analogous to physical capital—it is a stock that is subject to depreciation over time, and it can be increased through the process of investment. Like investment in physical capital, investment in human capital has a return associated with it—in the form of higher future earnings—and costs—both direct (books, tuition) and indirect (earnings forgone during the investment period). It is assumed that individuals compare the probable returns with the costs in order to decide how much time they should allocate to investment in human capital and at what stage in their lives. Individual choice plays a prime role, according to the theory. As Jacob Mincer states, "human capital models single out individual investment behavior as a basic factor in the heterogeneity of labor incomes."[2] Wage differences, then, become a function of variables over which individuals are presumed to have a large measure of control.

The human capital approach also implies that wage differences between workers are primarily a result of differences in their productivity. Because of its focus on worker attributes that affect productivity, and its attempt to explain wage differences as a function of variables such as a worker's age, education, training, migration, and labor force experience, the human capital theory is often referred to as a theory of the "supply" side of the labor market.

Economists have used this theory to analyze male–female wage differences by emphasizing the factors that tend to reduce women's stock of human capital. They argue that women typically leave the paid labor force in order to bear and raise children, and that during this time out of the labor force their stock of human capital deteriorates. Therefore, women's shorter and more intermittent labor force experience reflects their lower productivity, which in turn accounts for their lower wages. This pattern of women's labor force participation also reduces their wages indirectly because women will choose to invest less in their own human capital, reasoning that, since they will reap the rewards over a shorter time span, the cost of investing in human capital is too large compared to the probable return.

Since male–female wage differences are viewed by human capital proponents as reflecting differences in productivity, and since the decision to invest in human capital is assumed to be made as a free choice by individuals, this approach may be used to justify women's present economic position.[3]

Differences in human capital, however, seem to have only limited ability to account for wage differences between men and women. In a recent study of an urban labor market, Albert Rees and George Schultz examined a dozen occupations, only three of which had sufficient numbers of men and women for purposes of comparison, a fourth mixed occupation being created by combining two separate categories (janitor and janitress).[4] The subsample used to make sex comparisons included only 27 percent of the females, since the other 73 percent of the females were in exclusively female occupations.[5] Using regression analysis, Rees and Schultz found that, after controlling for differences in human capital due to age, seniority, education, and experience, women in these occupations could expect earnings 8 to 18

> 𝟲𝟲 **Male-female wage differences are viewed by human capital proponents as reflecting differences in productivity.** 𝟵𝟵

percent lower than men's: 11 percent lower for female accountants; 14 percent lower for female tabulating machine operators; 8 percent lower for female punch press operators; and 18 percent lower for janitresses.[6] In view of these substantial differences, which apparently cannot be explained by differences in human productivity, Rees and Schultz conclude that:

> Not all employer preferences among workers are related to quality in the sense of objective performance on the job. To no one's surprise, we find clear evidence of wage differentials in favor of males over females, whites over nonwhites, and other whites over those with Spanish surnames. Employers may view these preferences as indexes of quality, but there is no reason for the objective observer to do so.[7]

Another recent study, more comprehensive in scope and applying to a broader segment of the work force, shows even larger differentials. Larry Suter and Herman Miller find an unexplained wage gap of 38 percent even after male–female differences in education, occupational status, year-round full-time work, and lifetime work experience have been taken into account.[8]

This casts further doubt on the usefulness of the human capital approach in explaining wage differentials between men and women.[9]

WAGE DIFFERENCES AND DISCRIMINATION

Another approach to the question of wage differences between men and women concentrates on the role of discrimination. Although J. E. Cairnes, in 1874, discussed the notion of "noncompeting groups" resulting from social stratification in the labor force, systematic economic analysis of discrimination began with Gary Becker's *Economics of Discrimination*, published in 1957.[10] Most of the theoretical work on discrimination (including that of Lester Thurow and Barbara Bergmann, discussed below, as well as Becker's) was done in the context of black–white differences, but it has generally also applied to the question of male–female differences.

The "Conservative" Theory

Becker's theory defines discrimination as a preference or "taste," for which someone is willing to pay. For example, employers with a "taste for discrimination" would hire white workers, rather than hiring blacks who are equally productive, even if they had to pay the white workers a higher wage. Discrimination represents an inefficiency in the allocation of resources causing national output to be lower than it would be in a nondiscriminatory situation.

In Becker's model, white workers gain from employer discrimination: white workers still compete with each other for jobs, but they are protected from competition with black workers (much in the same way that import restrictions protect domestic products from foreign competition). Employers who discriminate hurt themselves (although not as much as they hurt black workers) because they are operating inefficiently. The Becker model implies that employers have strong motives to operate efficiently and therefore to desist from discriminating.

Becker assumes that most markets are characterized by some measure of real competition. In a competitive economy, the degree of discrimination will decline over time, since less discriminatory employers, being more efficient, will expand at the expense of more discriminatory employers. Becker's theory may be called "conservative," because it assumes that a laissez-faire market mechanism will, by itself, solve the problem of discrimination over the long run.

The "Liberal" Theory

In response to Becker's conservative theory, Lester Thurow developed a "liberal" theory of discrimination.[11] Thurow assumes that, under present conditions, the economy is not characterized by a substantial degree of competition, and there is no reason to expect that discrimination will fade away through the normal operation of a competitive market mechanism. Instead, Thurow believes that government intervention is necessary to combat persistent discrimination.

In contrast to Becker's view of a competitive society, Thurow sees whites acting as a monopoly in their dealings with blacks; therefore all whites, employers and workers, gain from discrimination, at the expense of all blacks.

Thurow also points out that the Becker view of discrimination is far too simple: white employers do not usually have a general aversion to hiring blacks. They are perfectly willing to hire them in menial roles, but not in supervisory roles. Therefore, it is not physical distance that employers try to maximize, but social distance. Thurow catalogs several different ways in which discrimination can occur: in labor markets by imposing lower wages, higher unemployment rates, and restricted choices of occupations on minorities; in markets for human capital by limiting their access to financing and credit (for example, for education or home mortgages); and in product markets by forcing minorities to buy at higher prices or sell at lower prices. Thurow believes that these varied forms of discrimination are mutually reinforcing and perpetuate discrimination from one generation to the next.

The theory of "statistical discrimination," recently developed by Edmund Phelps and others, is consistent with Thurow's assumption that white employers gain from discrimination and inconsistent with Becker's model.[12] This theory states that an employer may maximize expected profits by minimizing hiring costs. If it is expensive to collect detailed information on each individual job applicant, a rational employer may simply use categories such as race, sex, or age to distinguish among applicants. The employer simply assumes that average differences between groups apply in each individual case (e.g., each black worker is assumed to have the traits of the "average black worker"; each teenager is assumed to behave the way the "average teenager" does; each woman is assumed to have the intermittent work force pattern of the "average woman"). Although it may be rational, profit-maximizing behavior for an employer to use such stereotypes, it is nonetheless discriminatory. Discrimination is not likely to decrease over time, since those who do the discriminating benefit as a result.

The "Radical" Theory

The "radical" theory of discrimination, embodied in neo-Marxist labor market segmentation theory, posits that one way employers can preserve their own power vis-à-vis workers is by creating divisions among workers and discriminating against certain segments: for instance, those in secondary (low-wage, high-turnover, dead-end) jobs versus those in primary (high-wage, low-turnover, chance for promotion) jobs; blacks versus whites; and women versus men.[13] This theory traces the origin of the employer's need for labor market segmentation to the late nineteenth century, when small-scale competitive capitalism was rapidly being replaced by large-scale "monopoly capitalism."

The emergence of the large corporation meant that, in some industries, a few producers accounted for the bulk of the industry's output. As John Kenneth Galbraith has argued,[14] the advent of oligopoly (an industry controlled by a few producers) meant that large corporations, protected from the full force of competition, could turn their attention from short-run maximization of profits to planning strategies for long-run survival. These strategies involved establishing some measure of control over the markets in which the corporation operated: the product market in which it sold its goods and the factor market in which it hired the labor, machinery, and raw materials used to produce the goods.

Standard economic analyses have focused on the behavior of oligopolies in the product market. They have tried to explain why oligopolists tend to compete on the basis of advertising and product differentiation but not on the basis of price. This need to maintain price discipline without overt collusion (which would be prohibited by antitrust law) has led to practices such as price leadership, in which one firm announces its price changes and the others play follow-the-leader. By recognizing their mutual interests, oligopolists can maintain price discipline without conspiring and therefore without running afoul of the antitrust laws.

Labor market segmentation theory focuses on the behavior of oligopolies in the factor market, specifically the market in which the corporation hires its labor. In the late nineteenth century, growth in the size of firms and the advent of standardization tended to bring together large numbers of workers whose jobs were similar. This contributed to widespread labor militance, which was perceived by corporate owners and managers as a threat to their control. Labor market segmentation theorists argue that, although technological changes themselves would have led to greater similarity of jobs and hence organization of workers, employers imposed hierarchical job categories and fostered racial, ethnic, and sexual antagonisms, to deter the formation of strong, unified employee organizations.

Although some critics of this theory argue that it assumes there was a nefarious capitalist conspiracy, overt collusion between capitalists is not necessary for labor market segmentation to occur, as collusion is not necessary for oligopoly price discipline to be maintained. As David Gordon writes, "it has not always been necessary for capitalists to conspire in order to perceive their common interests and pursue them."[15]

In the radical view, labor market segmentation benefits employers, helping them to preserve their power over employees. It does so by (1) creating divisions among workers that prevent worker solidarity from developing; (2) limiting workers' own aspirations by creating relatively short job ladders that do not provide for continuous upward occupational mobility; and (3) using institutional sexism and racism to legitimize the authority of white male supervisors over minority subordinates.

Applying the Theories to Sex Discrimination

These three theories of discrimination differ from each other at a number of points. Applying the theories to discrimination against women workers, Becker's theory would imply that employers (male) lose from discrimination while male workers gain, and that over a period of time discrimination against women will fade away as less discriminatory employers expand. Thurow's theory implies that all males, whether workers or employers, gain from discrimination against women, and that such discrimination is not likely to fade away because it is so pervasive—not only in labor markets, but in human capital, credit, and product markets, with each type of discrimination reinforcing the others. Labor market segmentation theorists imply that all employers gain from discrimination against women, but that all workers, whether male or female, lose, since they are prevented by their separate experiences and beliefs from joining together to demand greater concessions from their employers. This disagreement on the nature and consequences of discrimination remains unresolved. The empirical evidence that would overwhelmingly confirm or deny the validity of each theory has not yet been provided, and where an individual stands depends on his or her political perspective.

WAGE DIFFERENCES AND CROWDING

The crowding hypothesis was first developed in post-World War I England. Millicent Fawcett suggested that women's low wages were a result of restricted access to occupations, and this observation was elaborated on by F. Y. Edgeworth.[16] Recently, the Edgeworth analysis was updated and expanded by Barbara Bergmann.[17]

Stated simply, the crowding hypothesis argues that women are allowed to enter relatively few occupations, while access to all others is restricted; women's wages are artificially low and men's wages artificially high, because so many women are available for so few opportunities. Bergmann attempts to merge the theoretical discussions of wage differences with those on occupational segregation in order to produce a unified theory. She presents a theoretical model in which there are only two occupations, in which all workers are equally productive and are paid according to their productivity, and in which marginal product[18] declines linearly as additional workers are hired. If entrance to one of the occupations is restricted, so that only members of a favored group are admitted, the supply of workers to that (prestige) occupation will be artificially reduced, while the supply of workers to the other (menial) occupation will be artificially expanded. As a result, marginal productivity and, therefore, wages will be higher in the prestige occupation than they would be if free access to occupations were allowed, while marginal productivity and wages will be lower than otherwise in the menial occupation. The size of the prestige occupation will be artificially small and the size of the menial occupation artificially large. Workers outside the favored group will be willing to accept employment in the prestige occupation at lower wages than can be obtained by those in the favored group. This occurs because the unfavored have a less attractive alternative, namely the wages they are paid in the menial occupation. Unlike Becker, who believes that the discriminatory employer sacrifices some profit in order to indulge his discriminatory "taste," Bergmann seems to agree with Thurow that, to the extent employers can act as a cartel to limit the opportunities of unfavored groups, they may transfer income from the unfavored group to themselves.

The distinction between productivity theories and discrimination theories becomes somewhat blurred in the crowding hypothesis, which sees discrimination, in the form of restricted access to occupations, as causing productivity differences that would otherwise not exist. Therefore, the crowding hypothesis shares with human capital theory the notion that wages are related to a worker's productivity, but it diverges from human capital theory in implying that productivity differences result from discrimination against women, rather than from their free choice.

The crowding hypothesis seems to imply that male workers gain from employers' restrictions of female occupations, and this would put it in conflict with labor market segmentation theory, which implies that all workers, male and female, are hurt by discrimination. The two theories may be reconciled, however, in my opinion. Crowding can be seen as one mechanism by which labor market segmentation is maintained. By perpetuating and encouraging distinctions between men's jobs and women's jobs (crowding), employers distort relative wages between men and women workers,

> ⁇ The crowding hypothesis argues that women's wages are artificially low and men's wages artificially high, because so many women are available for so few opportunities. ⁇

making men workers better off than women workers. However, this distortion in the relative wage may be seen as a device by which employers prevent men and women workers from unifying and demanding a higher wage for all workers (as the labor market segmentation theory implies). In other words, through the mechanism of crowding, employers segment their labor force by conceding a somewhat higher wage to men as compared to women, in order to prevent men and women from uniting to raise the absolute level of workers' wages compared to employers' incomes.[19]

A more detailed expositon of the crowding hypothesis is given in the appendix at the end of this chapter.

Implications of the Crowding Hypothesis

As mentioned above, the crowding hypothesis implies that women would be willing to accept employment in a "male" occupation at a somewhat lower wage than men (since their alternative is even lower wages in a "female" occupation). If employers could hire women in male occupations at a lower wage than men, why don't they do just that? How can sex segregation be maintained, if it is unprofitable for employers? The answer lies in explaining the model from the point of view of the individual firm.

In product markets that are not competitive (e.g., monopolies or oligopolies), whether the individual firm gains or loses from a sex-segregated market depends on the particular combination of workers that it hires.[20] Firms that hire many more workers in female occupations than male occupations can gain from sex segregation: the bargain rates they pay for their female workers outweigh the higher prices they pay for their male workers, compared to a sex-blind situation.

What about the employers who hire many more workers in male occupations than female occupations? In comparison to a sex-blind situation, the higher price they pay for their male workers may outweigh the savings they gain in the wages of female workers, so that the sex-segregated situation is unprofitable. What deters those employers from hiring women at cheaper rates for the male occupations? At this juncture it may be useful to refer again to Thurow's discussion of how discrimination against blacks is enforced. That discrimination takes a number of different forms—job discrimination, housing discrimination, schooling discrimination—and each type reinforces the others:

> If the various types are viewed separately, there seem to be powerful economic pressures leading to their elimination. Suburban homeowners could gain by selling to Negroes. White employers could increase profits by hiring Negroes. When the several types of discrimination are viewed together, however, the economic pressures are either not present or present in a much more attenuated form.[21]

This interdependence of various types of discrimination may explain the refusal of employers to hire women in male occupations even when it would add to their profits to do so. Sex-role stereotypes that pervade our culture may lead employers to believe that women would be such inefficient workers in male occupations that they would not be worth hiring, even at lower wages. This viewpoint may clearly be mistaken, but employers will never discover their mistake, since their beliefs prevent the very employment of women that would disprove those beliefs.[22]

Even if the employer does have an accurate assessment—even if he knows that female applicants would be as productive as males and could be hired more cheaply—he still may not sacrifice very much by refusing to hire them if few women are likely to apply because of other social forces. Sex-role socialization, learned at home, at school, through the media, as part of the everyday environment, may deter women from aspiring to work in male occupations, if they are told that such aspirations are inappropriate, unfeminine, and unattainable anyway. When few women apply for "male" occupations, there is little opportunity for employers to gain by hiring them at lower wages.

In some cases, employers may be deterred from hiring women in previously all-male situations if hiring them involves additional expenses (if new rest rooms or locker rooms must be built or old ones partitioned, for instance). Even employers who are willing to hire women in male occupations may not do so if they anticipate that the reaction of their male employees will make integration unprofitable. If male employees feel their manliness is enhanced by engaging in all-male activities (whether at a working-class tavern or the Harvard Club), then they may feel that working in an integrated occupation, with women as peers, is a demeaning and intolerable reduction of the social distance between the sexes. They may create inefficiencies in production because of personnel frictions and exert pressures on the employer to return to segregated occupations. If enough women are available, the employer might be tempted to shift from a high-priced male work force to a lower-priced female work force, but, in the absence of sufficient numbers of women, the occupation will tend to remain all male.

Finally, employers may not hire women in male occupations, even though it would be profitable, because the individuals who do the discriminating may not be the ones who lose as a result of it. As Harriet Zellner points out, those in charge of hiring may be free to exercise their preferences and prejudices regarding women, since their own salaries will be only minimally affected, even though it may be unprofitable for the firm.[23]

Crowding and Women's Labor Force Participation

If segregated labor markets yield restricted occupational choices and lower wages for women workers than would otherwise be available to them, sex segregation may cause the female labor force to be smaller than it otherwise would be, since incentives to enter the labor force are artificially reduced.[24] Alternatives to paid employment then become relatively more inviting.

The primary alternative for most women is probably unpaid work in the household; thus, as a result of crowding, the number of unpaid household workers is larger than it otherwise would be. Indirectly, employers may benefit from this. Without the alternative source of income that working wives could provide, married male workers may be less willing to risk a strike than they would be if their wives had easy access to well-paying jobs. When an employer hires a married male worker he also benefits in other ways from the free service of the housewife: he is not pressured into providing day-care facilities or allowing much time off for family emergencies, since the wife takes care of all the family maintenance problems that might otherwise reduce the male worker's productivity on the job. The husband's productivity may be increased if the wife performs valet and personal service tasks to keep him well-clothed and well-fed without depriving him of leisure time. It has also been argued that having a wife who can devote time and energy to social and entertainment duties is essential to men in some professions: "Professional men, ministers and ambassadors require home settings that need the services of wives, and they are judged in part on the performance of their wives."[25]

The volunteer work that many women do is another alternative to paid work in the labor force. The combination of sense of purpose and flexible scheduling is an attractive aspect of volunteer work and one that is difficult to find in paid employment. Institutions that use volunteer workers (such as schools, hospitals, and charitable agencies) benefit because they are able to provide a higher level of service than their budgets allow. In the absence of the volunteer work done by women, these institutions would have to forgo some services or find funds to pay for them. When volunteers do work for municipal institutions that paid workers would otherwise have to do, one result of crowding, which expands the pool of volunteers, is a somewhat lower tax rate: services that would be paid for by tax revenues are obtained free. This effect is probably more than offset, however, by another effect of crowding: women on welfare have fewer opportunities to earn their way off welfare, so they are induced to remain at home.

A third alternative to paid employment in the labor force, though one that is not as important as housework or volunteer work, is illegal economic activity, such as prostitution. Reformers of the progressive era around the turn of the twentieth century argued that the practice of paying women less than subsistence wages on the false notion that they were not self-supporting drove many women to prostitution:

Nearly all the investigators of women's labor gave some attention to the connection between low wages and prostitution. Miss Butler's comment was typical: "So long as custom or fact renders the payment of a full living wage nonessential, economic needs impel many a girl toward a personally degrading life."[26]

Although at any given time crowding and its artificially low wages may reduce women's labor force participation rates below what they otherwise would be, over the long run other factors may operate to produce a rising female labor force participation rate. The observation that women's labor force participation rates have been rising, but are still lower than men's, is consistent with the discussion of the preceding paragraphs; in other words, the effect of crowding is to keep participation rates below what they would be as a result of other economic forces.

But what happens as women's labor force participation rises over time? Assume that there is population growth but no change in men's labor force participation rates, and that, as the male working population grows, job opportunities for men grow at the same rate. If there is sex segregation, demand for workers in the women's sector (existing female occupations plus newly created female occupations) will have to grow as fast as new women enter the labor force in order to maintain the relative wage rate between men and women. Women can *increase* their relative wages under segregated conditions only if the demand for workers in their sector grows faster than the number of new women moving into the labor force. If, however, the increase in women entering the labor force outstrips the growth of demand for workers in women's occupations, and if men's occupations remain closed to women, the result will be a decline in women's relative wages. This situation typifies the actual experience of women workers in the United States over the past thirty years. Their increased labor force participation has been accompanied by a decline in their relative wages.[27]

This model does not assume that sex segregation will gradually be reduced until it disappears. On the contrary, it acknowledges that sex segregation benefits male workers in a relative sense, compared to female workers; that it may well benefit employers in an absolute sense, in terms of the total income accruing to employers versus the total income received by all workers, male and female; and that labor market segregation on the basis of sex will probably be maintained with the aid of other cultural forces even by employers who find it unprofitable.

CONCLUSION

This paper has discussed several economic approaches to wage differences between men and women, including those based on productivity differences and those based on discrimination. Conservative, liberal, and radical theories of discrimination were briefly discussed and compared. The crowding hypothesis was discussed as an eclectic theory that combines elements of the productivity and discrimination theories, by assuming that discrimination causes productivity differences that would otherwise not exist. Some implications of the crowding hypothesis were explored to see how well it explains the economic status of women and the continued existence of labor market discrimination.

APPENDIX: EXPOSITION OF THE CROWDING HYPOTHESIS

The model used in the following discussion is based on the work of F. Y. Edgeworth and Barbara Bergmann. For expository convenience, this analysis uses three occupations instead of two, but retains their other assumptions (see the discussion in the text of this chapter). Additionally, this analysis explicitly assumes that the supply of workers is fixed and that the proportion of women in the labor force is greater than the proportion of occupations open to them in a segregated market[28] (for example, that one-third of the occupations are open to women, but women constitute more than one-third of the labor force).

In a completely sex-blind labor market consisting of three occupations with the same marginal productivity curve for each (that is, the same demand for labor), the labor force would be distributed in equal numbers in the three occupations, and the sex composition of each occupation would be randomly determined. This model is shown in figure 1. If more than one-third of the labor force enters any one of the occupations, the wage (equal to the marginal productivity) of the last workers hired in that occupation would be lower than that of the last worker hired in the others, and workers would therefore be induced to move to the other occupations, where their wage (marginal productivity) would be higher. When a competitive equilibrium is reached, the marginal productivity of the last worker hired would be equal across the three occupations, and there would be no further wage incentive for any worker to move. Therefore, the outcome of a sex-blind labor market in three occupations of equal marginal productivity, would be equal wages for all workers, equal numbers of workers in each occupation, and a random distribution of women across the occupations.

If the labor market is not sex-blind, a different situation occurs (shown in figure 2). This model adds one assumption to those in figure 1: women are allowed to work in only one of the three occupations. For simplicity, Occupation III is designated as the women's occupation, while Occupations I and II are reserved for men. In this case, more than one-third of the labor force (all the women) will work in Occupation III, while less than two-thirds of the labor force (all the men) will be evenly divided between Occupations I and II, with less than one-third in each. Thus, Occupation III has a larger number of employees compared to the sex-blind situation, while Occupations I and II have smaller numbers. As a result, marginal productivity and wages are lower in Occupation III, compared to the sex-blind situation, and higher in Occupations I and II, even though all three occupations require equally qualified (productive) workers.

An additional result of crowding is that women would be willing to work in Occupations I and II for lower wages than men, since they have fewer

FIGURE 1   The Sex-blind Labor Market

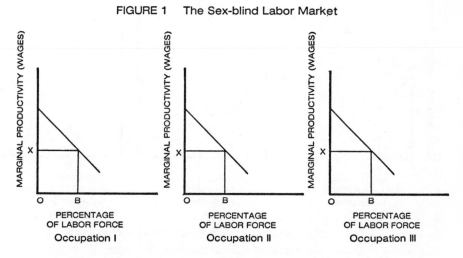

OB = 1/3 of the labor force in each occupation

OX = marginal product in each occupation

desirable alternatives (the wages ,they earn in Occupation III). Another result is that resources are misallocated. Occupation III has more workers
than it otherwise would have; the marginal product of labor is lower in
equilibrium than in Occupations I and II; and the gross national product
(GNP) is lower than it would be if barriers did not prevent labor from moving from the low productivity sector to the higher ones.

Let us now relax the assumption that all three occupations have the same
marginal productivity curve. Allowing for differences in the economic environment, some occupations may have higher marginal productivity curves.
For instance, assume that the marginal productivity curve of Occupation
I has shifted upward as a result of improved technology, while marginal
productivity in Occupations II and III remain the same. This situation is
illustrated in figure 3. If there is discrimination against women, formal and
informal methods will be used to keep them out of the occupation with
the higher productivity, so Occupation I will be closed to women. Let Oc-

FIGURE 2   The Sex-segregated Labor Market

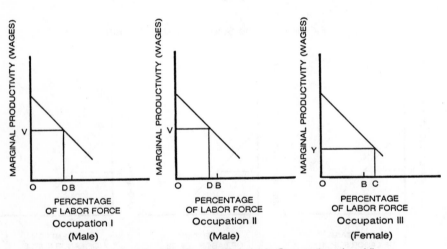

OD < 1/3 of the labor force (all male) in Occupations I and II

OC > 1/3 of the labor force (all female) in Occupation III

OV > OY (productivity and therefore wages are greater in
Occupations I and II than in Occupation III)

cupation III again be the only outlet for women's work. Compared to the previous model of sex segregation, the following results emerge: the size of Occupation III and its marginal productivity in equilibrium are unchanged; changes occur in Occupations I and II, however. Men previously employed in Occupation II are attracted to Occupation I by the higher marginal productivity and therefore higher wages; male workers leave Occupation II and enter Occupation I until the marginal productivities are equalized at some level higher than before; Occupation I now accounts for somewhat more than half of the male labor force, and Occupation II accounts for somewhat less; most importantly, the male–female wage difference has increased, both relatively and absolutely.

FIGURE 3   The Sex-segregated Market with Unequal
Occupational Marginal Productivities

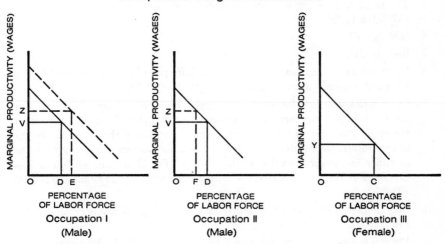

PERCENTAGE
OF LABOR FORCE
Occupation I
(Male)

PERCENTAGE
OF LABOR FORCE
Occupation II
(Male)

PERCENTAGE
OF LABOR FORCE
Occupation III
(Female)

OC > 1/3 of the labor force (all female) in Occupation III

OE > 1/2 of the male labor force in Occupation I

OF < 1/2 of the male labor force in Occupation II

OE + OF < 2/3 of the labor force (all male) in Occupations I and II

OZ > OV > OY

NOTES

1 For an exposition of human capital theory, see Gary Becker, *Human Capital: A Theoretical and Empirical Analysis, with Special References to Education* (New York: National Bureau of Economic Research, 1964).

2 Jacob Mincer, "The Distribution of Labor Incomes: A Survey, with Special Reference to the Human Capital Approach," *Journal of Economic Literature* 8 (1970): 6.

3 Although a recent study by Jacob Mincer and Solomon W. Polachek, "Family Investments in Human Capital: Earnings of Women," *Journal of Political Economy*, March/April 1974, pt. 2, pp. S76–S108, attributes up to 70 percent of the wage difference between men and women to differences in work experience, this study was based on miscoded data and is now in the process of being reassessed with corrected data.

4 Albert Rees and George P. Schultz, *Workers and Wages in an Urban Labor Market* (Chicago: University of Chicago Press, 1970).

5 The percentage of females was computed from ibid., p. 60, table 5.1, and p. 167, table 11.12.

6 Ibid., p. 167.

7 Ibid., p. 219.

8 Larry Suter and Herman Miller, "Income Differences between Men and Career Women," *American Journal of Sociology* 78 (1973): 962–74.

9 Other rationalizations for women's low relative wages include allegedly higher absenteeism and turnover rates. However, the actual male–female differences are small and seem to be more related to the status of the job than the sex of the worker. Economic studies have shown absenteeism and turnover to be of minor importance (see Isabel V. Sawhill, "The Economics of Discrimination Against Women: Some New Findings," *Journal of Human Resources* 8 (1973): 383–96.

10 Gary Becker, *The Economics of Discrimination* (Chicago: University of Chicago Press, 1957).

11 Lester Thurow, *Poverty and Discrimination* (Washington, D.C.: Brookings Institution, 1969).

12 Edmund Phelps, "The Statistical Theory of Racism and Sexism," *American Economic Review* 62 (1972): 659–61.

13 Michael Reich, David M. Gordon, and Richard C. Edwards, "A Theory of Labor Market Segmentation," *American Economic Review* 63 (1973): 359–65.

14 John Kenneth Galbraith, *The New Industrial State* (New York: Signet, New American Library, 1968).

15 David M. Gordon, *Theories of Poverty and Underemployment* (Lexington, Mass.: D. C. Heath and Company, 1972), p. 80.

16 Millicent Fawcett, "Equal Pay for Equal Work," *Economic Journal* 28 (1918): 1–6; F. Y. Edgeworth, "Equal Pay to Men and Women for Equal Work," *Economic Journal* 32 (1922): 431–57.

17 Barbara Bergmann, "Occupational Segregation, Wages, and Profits when Employers Discriminate by Race or Sex," mimeographed (College Park: University of Maryland, December 1970).

18 In economists' terms, a worker's addition to total output is referred to as her or his marginal product. Marginal product declines as additional workers are hired because, if the amount of machinery and raw materials remains constant, each additional worker hired will contribute less to total output than the one before. This is because, as additional workers are hired, each worker has a smaller share of the machinery and raw materials with which to work.

19 For some evidence on a related argument, see Michael Reich, "The Economics of Racism," in *Problems in Political Economy: An Urban Perspective,* ed. D. M. Gordon (Lexington, Mass.: D. C. Heath and Company, 1971).

20 For an interesting discussion of the employer's enhanced ability to discriminate in noncompetitive *factor* markets (that is, monopsony, in which there is only one buyer of labor, as in a "company town"), see Janice F. Madden, *The Economics of Sex Discrimination* (Lexington, Mass.: D. C. Heath and Company, 1973).

21 Thurow, *Poverty and Discrimination,* p. 127.

22 Harriet Zellner, "Discrimination against Women, Occupational Segregation, and the Relative Wage," *American Economic Review* 62 (1972): 157–60.

23 Ibid.

24 Several of the arguments presented in this and the following paragraphs were inspired by Daniel R. Fusfeld's *Basic Economics of the Urban Racial Crisis* (New York: Holt, Rinehart and Winston, 1973), chap. 5.

25 Caroline Bird, *Born Female* (New York: Pocket Books, 1969), p. 60.

26 Robert Bremner, *From the Depths* (New York: New York University Press, 1956), p. 239.

27 Other possibilities are also consistent with the observed decline in relative wages. For instance, if wages are correlated with labor force experience, and women entering the labor force have less experience than workers already employed, then a rise in the participation rate of women while men's participation rates remain constant might result in a widening of male–female differences in experience, and therefore a reduction in the relative wage.

28 For a similar treatment of the crowding hypothesis, see Fusfeld, *Basic Economics of the Urban Racial Crisis.*

Legal Protection against Sex Discrimination

Mary Eastwood

A dramatic change in the thrust of the laws that apply to the working woman began to develop in the 1960s. This change—from laws "protecting" women by requiring employers to give them special treatment to laws prohibiting different treatment of women to protect them from sex discrimination—came about through enactment of several federal statutes and executive orders, judicial decisions in cases brought by women workers to enforce these laws, and pressure by the women's movement on the government agencies responsible for implementing the federal nondiscrimination laws.

New federal requirements of nondiscrimination on the basis of sex had the effect of superseding or nullifying the impact of various state laws that required employers to treat women workers differently from men workers by limiting the amount of weight women could lift on the job, limiting the number of hours per day or week women could work, excluding women entirely from certain jobs, and prohibiting women in some occupations from working at night. The alleged purpose of these state laws was to protect the health of women; the effect was to encourage or even to require employers to discriminate against women workers and to limit their employment opportunities.

As a result of the federal nondiscrimination laws, employers must now treat men and women workers without distinction because of sex in terms of pay, job assignments, fringe benefits, and other conditions of employment.

The following is a summary of federal statutes and executive orders prohibiting discrimination against women in employment. (Many states now have similar nondiscrimination laws on these subjects.)

FEDERAL NONDISCRIMINATION LAWS

Equal Pay

The Equal Pay Act was enacted in 1963 as an amendment to the minimum wage provisions of the Fair Labor Standards Act of 1938. It prohibits employers from discriminating on the basis of sex in paying wages for "equal work on jobs the performance of which requires equal skill, effort, and responsibility, and which are performed under similar working conditions."[1] Different pay rates are allowed if they are based on a nondiscriminatory seniority system, a merit system, or a system that measures earnings by quantity or quality of production.

The Equal Pay Act did not prohibit discrimination in any form other than wage rates. That is, it did not require nondiscrimination in hiring, promotions, and work assignments. It was designed to help only those women who were doing work substantially equal to that done by men but who were paid less for it. Despite this narrow applicability, the United States Department of Labor, which administers the Fair Labor Standards Act, reported that from 1965 to May 1976, more than $130 million were found due to women under the act.[2] Nondiscrimination is costing employers, but the amounts due measure the extent to which working women were cheated in the past.

Equal Employment Opportunity

The equal employment opportunity provisions (Title VII) of the Civil Rights Act of 1964, as amended, prohibit discrimination in all aspects of employment, including hiring, firing, promotions, training, fringe benefits, seniority, and retirement, on the basis of race, color, religion, sex, or national origin.[3] The act also prohibits the segregation or classification of employees in any way that would tend to deprive an individual of employment opportunities because of race, color, religion, sex, or national origin. It prohibits discrimination by employment agencies and labor organizations as well as by employers. The act is administered by the federal Equal Employment Opportunity Commission, and litigation alleging discrimination by state and local government agencies is handled by the Department of Justice.

Title VII for the first time gave women a legal basis for insisting that they be allowed to compete with men for jobs and promotions, as well as that they be paid the same as men once they got those jobs or promotions.

Employment Under Government Contracts

Executive Order No. 11246 of September 24, 1965,[4] prohibited discrimination in employment under federal contracts and subcontracts on the basis of race, color, religion, and national origin, but not sex. The order was later amended by Executive Order No. 11375 of October 13, 1967, to add a prohibition against sex discrimination. The order as amended requires that each federal contract contain a nondiscrimination clause in which the contractor agrees not to discriminate in any aspect of employment. The order is enforced by the Office of Federal Contract Compliance Programs of the Department of Labor. The government has the power to enforce the non-discrimination clause by canceling, terminating, suspending, or delaying the contract if the contractor discriminates.

Labor Department regulations require employers of fifty or more employees that contract with the government for $50,000 or more worth of business to develop affirmative action compliance programs.[5] If an analysis of the contractor's employment statistics shows it underutilizes women or minority group members compared to their proportions in the available work force, the contractor must set up an affirmative action program with goals and timetables for increasing its employment of women and minorities. The contractor is committed to making "every good faith effort" to achieve the goals, but the regulations prohibit setting "rigid and inflexible quotas."[6]

Federal Government Employment

Executive Order No. 11478 of August 9, 1969, prohibits discrimination on the part of the federal government itself as an employer. It also applies to employment by the District of Columbia government. The order is administered by the United States Civil Service Commission and the various employing agencies. Civil Service Commission regulations provide a procedure for handling complaints of discrimination.[7] Federal employees and applicants for employment file complaints directly with the agency alleged to have done the discriminating, and that agency itself decides whether it has discriminated. This "self-enforcement" procedure does not encourage compliance with the requirements of nondiscrimination, because government agencies naturally do not like to admit that they have discriminated. The 1972 amendments to Title VII of the Civil Rights Act of 1964[8] allow government employee complainants, as well as employees in the private sector, to file suit in federal district court if they are not satisfied with the disposition of their cases by the agency or the Civil Service Commission.

Discrimination in Federally Funded Educational Programs

Title IX of the Education Amendments of 1972[9] prohibits discrimination on the basis of sex under educational programs or activities receiving federal financial assistance, with certain exemptions. The prohibition covers discrimination in employment of teachers and other school personnel as well as in admissions, financial aid, and access to educational programs and activities.

Age Discrimination

The Age Discrimination in Employment Act of 1967[10] prohibits government employers, private employers, employment agencies, and unions from discriminating against persons between the ages of forty and sixty-five because of their age. It is administered generally by the Department of Labor and with respect to federal employees by the Civil Service Commission. Older working women are frequently discriminated against in favor of younger men or, particularly in female-dominated occupations such as secretarial work, younger women (see Evelyn Rosenthal's chapter below). For women in traditionally female occupations, protection against age discrimination is especially necessary, because they frequently cannot establish a case of sex discrimination.

HISTORY OF WOMEN'S LABOR LEGISLATION

Before the enactment of the various nondiscrimination laws, most states had some restrictions on the employment of women, in the guise of "protecting" them. Women were excluded from working in certain occupations (such as bartending or mining) in some states; most states restricted the hours per day or week that employers could permit women to work; some prohibited night work by women in certain occupations; others limited the amount of weight women were allowed to lift on the job; and others required special facilities for women employees such as seats or restrooms.[11]

This body of special laws for women workers developed in part as a result of a Supreme Court decision in 1905, *Lochner* v. *New York.*[12] The Court held that a state law limiting hours of work for both men and women violated the due process clause of the Fourteenth Amendment to the United States Constitution[13] by restricting the right to liberty of contract for employment. The Court at that time found it not permissible for a state to protect workers (of both sexes) from excessive hours of labor.

Three years later, in *Muller* v. *Oregon,*[14] the Supreme Court upheld an Oregon statute that limited the hours *women* could work, on the theory that the state has a legitimate interest in protecting women's motherhood functions; special treatment of women workers is necessary, the Court decided, to compensate for their weaker physical structure and special maternal burdens. It reasoned:

> That woman's physical structure and the performance of maternal functions place her at a disadvantage in the struggle for subsistence is obvious. This is especially true when the burdens of motherhood are upon her. Even when they are not, by abundant testimony of the medical fraternity, continuance for a long time on her feet at work, repeating this from day to day, tends to injurious effects upon the body, and as healthy mothers are essential to vigorous offspring, the physical well-being of woman becomes an object of public interest and care in order to preserve the strength and vigor of the race. . . . The two sexes differ in structure of body, in the functions to be performed by each, in the amount of physical strength, in the capacity for long-continued labor, particularly when done standing, the influence of vigorous health upon the future well-being of the race, the self-reliance which enables one to assert full rights, and in the capacity to maintain the struggle for subsistence. This difference justifies a difference in legislation and upholds that which is designed to compensate for some of the burdens which rest upon her.[15]

In 1917, restrictions on working hours for both sexes were upheld by the Supreme Court in *Bunting* v. *Oregon.*[16] Although the Court did not expressly overrule *Lochner, Bunting* had the effect of invalidating that decision. Nevertheless, many state laws regulating terms and conditions of employment continued to apply to women workers only, and special restrictions on hours[17] and night work[18] and special requirements for minimum wages[19] for women were upheld by the Supreme Court.

Early feminists, such as suffrage leader Alice Paul, recognized that laws placing special restrictions on labor by women hampered women's job opportunities and encouraged further discrimination against working women. Getting rid of the so-called "protective" laws was one of the main objectives Dr. Paul and her followers had in drafting the Equal Rights Amendment first introduced in Congress in 1923. Special restrictions on working women

> 🙙 Before the enactment of the various nondiscrimination laws, most states had some restrictions on the employment of women, in the guise of "protecting" them. 🙚

continued, however, until these laws clashed with and were superseded by the equal employment opportunity provisions of Title VII of the Civil Rights Act of 1964.

ENFORCING EQUAL EMPLOYMENT OPPORTUNITY

The prohibition against sex discrimination was not included in Title VII of the civil rights bill originally introduced in Congress but rather was added on the House floor. The National Woman's Party, the only organization devoted exclusively to women's rights at the time, lobbied strenuously for including sex discrimination in the bill. Although he was opposed to civil rights legislation in general, Representative Howard Smith introduced the sex amendment on the House floor, at least in part on the basis of the NWP request.[20] Persuasive arguments by the women in Congress for inclusion of a sex discrimination provision in Title VII ultimately secured passage of the amendment.

Both proponents and opponents of the sex amendment expressed the view that the nondiscrimination requirement might strike down state laws regulating the employment of women.[21] However, some officials of the Equal

Employment Opportunity Commission—the agency charged with enforcing Title VII—simply declined to take the prohibition against sex discrimination seriously. A few even stated publicly that they thought the sex provision was a fluke or a joke and should not be enforced on the same basis as prohibitions against other forms of discrimination. Not only did the EEOC initially resist carrying out its duty of enforcing the sex provision, but it even encouraged such discrimination against women by publishing guidelines that expressly allowed employers to place ads in classified columns that were labeled by sex (help wanted—men; help wanted—women).[22] While the initial EEOC regulations on job opportunity advertising in 1966 provided that help wanted ads "may not indicate a preference based on sex unless a bona fide occupational qualification makes it lawful," the regulations let employers "place advertisements for jobs open to both sexes in columns classified by publishers under "Male" or "Female" headings to indicate that some occupations are considered more attractive to persons of one sex than the other."[23]

After pressure from the women's movement, these guidelines were replaced by ones prohibiting discrimination in job advertising.[24] It was the EEOC's reluctance to enforce the law that triggered formation of a new feminist organization, the National Organization for Women (NOW) in 1966.

One of the first key sex-discrimination cases filed under Title VII was that of Velma Mengelkoch, an electric assembler for North American Rockwell Corporation in Anaheim, California. She and other women employees of the corporation challenged the validity of a California law restricting hours of work for women to eight per day and forty-eight per week. Mengelkoch claimed that women were denied promotions and opportunities to earn premium pay for overtime by the California statute. The EEOC advised her that the conflict between Title VII and the state hours laws would have to be resolved in the courts.

She also challenged the constitutionality of the statute under the Fourteenth Amendment: she argued both that the employer discriminated, in violation of Title VII, and that the state discriminated by enforcing a law requiring unequal treatment of women workers.

The case had several complex jurisdictional issues and was appealed both to the United States Court of Appeals for the Ninth Circuit and the United States Supreme Court. It was ultimately settled by a consent decree in which the State of California and North American Rockwell were enjoined from discriminating against women by enforcing or relying on the state hours law for women.

The Ninth Circuit Court of Appeals distinguished *Mengelkoch* from *Muller* v. *Oregon,* the 1908 case that justified special protective legislation for women (quoted above). The 1971 court said in part:

> In our case, the constitutional attack against a state statute is mounted, not by an employer, but by an employee. The employee, Velma Mengelkoch, unlike the employer in *Muller,* does not question the state's police power to legislate in the field of hours of labor. Unlike *Muller,* she invokes the Equal Protection Clause, and she does so not to preserve the right of employers to employ women for long hours, but to overcome what she regards as a system which discriminates in favor of male employees and against female employees. In *Muller,* the statute was upheld in part because it was thought to be a necessary way of safeguarding women's competitive position. Here the statute is attacked on the ground that it gives male employees an unfair economic advantage over females.[25]

The Court of Appeals also noted that the Supreme Court in *Muller,* countering the *Lochner* ruling, which limited the state's authority to regulate hours of work, was led "to emphasize differences in the station which men and women occupied in the society of that day,"[26] but that those differences were no longer applicable.

Other cases also challenged state maximum hours laws and weight lifting limits for women workers, under Title VII. In *Rosenfeld* v. *Southern Pacific Company,*[27] Leah Rosenfeld alleged she had been denied a position as a railroad agent-telegrapher by Southern Pacific Company, in part because to hire a woman for that job would require the company to violate California laws limiting the weight to be lifted and hours to be worked by women workers. The United States Court of Appeals for the Ninth Circuit held that the state's labor laws for women "run contrary to the general objectives of Title VII . . . and are therefore, by virtue of the Supremacy Clause,[28] supplanted by Title VII," and that "state labor laws inconsistent with the general objectives of the Act must be disregarded."[29]

In *Weeks* v. *Southern Bell Tel. & Tel. Co.,* another case involving a thirty-pound weight lifting limit for women workers, Lorena Weeks was denied a job as a switchman for Southern Bell because of the Georgia regulation that imposed the weight limit. The Court of Appeals for the Fifth Circuit, ruling in favor of Weeks, rejected Southern Bell's claim that it was concerned about "protecting" women from certain hazards of the switchman's work:

> Title VII rejects just this type of romantic paternalism as unduly Victorian and instead vests individual women with the power to decide whether or not to take on unromantic tasks. Men have always had the right to determine whether the incremental increase in remuneration for strenuous, dangerous, obnoxious, boring or unromantic tasks is worth the candle. The promise of Title VII is that women are now to be on an equal footing.[31]

In the first sex discrimination class action[32] decided under Title VII, *Bowe* v. *Colgate Palmolive Co.,*[33] Georgianna (Sue) Sellers and other women at the Colgate-Palmolive plant at Clarksville, Indiana, sued the company for excluding women from jobs that required lifting more than thirty-five pounds. The limit was imposed by Colgate, with the cooperation of the union, in order to reserve the better-paying jobs (which were in fact easier) for men. Jobs that were reserved for men under the policy *began* at the highest wage rates paid for jobs open to women. The federal district court approved the policy of placing a special weight lifting limitation on women for their "protection," but the Court of Appeals for the Seventh Circuit said that the lower court's ruling was "based on a misconception of the requirements of Title VII's anti-discrimination provisions."[34] The appeals court ordered Colgate to give all its women workers the opportunity to bid on and fill any job at the plant they were entitled to by their seniority rights and to pay them back wages at the highest rate they could have earned had they not been the victims of discrimination. More than $400,000 in back pay was paid to women at the Indiana plant as a result of this case.

Limits on women lifting weight on the job were defended by employers as "bona fide occupational qualifications" justifying the exclusion of women from better-paying jobs. Title VII allows discrimination or the exclusion of a class from certain jobs where sex (being male or being female) is a bona fide occupational qualification reasonably necessary to the normal operation of the business.[35] The *Weeks* and *Bowe* cases effectively prevented the phrase *bona fide occupational qualification* from being used by employers as a loophole to escape the discrimination prohibitions of Title VII.

As a result of these and similar cases, special state limitations on women's hours of work and weight lifting on the job were nullified or superseded by

Title VII. Thus Title VII accomplished one of the major purposes of the proposed Equal Rights Amendment to the United States Constitution, now pending ratification by the states, which would provide: "Equality of rights under the law shall not be denied or abridged by the United States or by any State on account of sex." Although ratification of the ERA is important for other reasons, it would not further change the law on women's employment rights.

MOTHERHOOD AND EMPLOYMENT

Other cases concerning working women relate to the treatment of women's functions as childbearers and mothers. Ida Phillips, who had been turned down for a job as an assembly trainee at Martin Marietta Corporation in Florida, secured the first Supreme Court decision under Title VII. She was told by a company official that the corporation did not consider female applicants with pre-school-age children. The United States Court of Appeals for the Fifth Circuit held that, although discrimination solely on the basis of sex was a violation of Title VII, discrimination on the basis of "sex plus" another factor, such as having pre-school-age children, was not. The Supreme Court, however, reversed the decision, in 1971, holding that Title VII prohibits an employer from having one hiring policy for women and another for men.[36]

School board practices requiring pregnant schoolteachers to take leave without pay after their fifth (in Cleveland, Ohio) and fourth (in Chesterfield County, Virginia) months of pregnancy were challenged by teachers in those states. The Supreme Court ruled those mandatory terminations of employment unconstitutional under the Fourteenth Amendment, stating:

> This Court has long recognized that freedom of personal choice in matters of marriage and family life is one of the liberties protected by the Due Process Clause of the Fourteenth Amendment. . . . [N]either the necessity for continuity of instruction nor the state interest in keeping physically unfit teachers out of the classroom can justify the sweeping mandatory leave regulations that the Cleveland and Chesterfield County School Boards have adopted. While the regulations no doubt represent a good-faith attempt to achieve a laudable goal, they cannot pass muster under the Due Process of the Fourteenth Amendment, because they employ irrebuttable presumptions that unduly penalize a female teacher for deciding to bear a child.[37]

The Court's decision did not rest on the issue of discrimination on the basis of sex in that the termination policy could apply only to female and not to male teachers. Rather the court relied on the fact that the rule did not give a pregnant teacher any opportunity to show that she was able and willing to keep teaching past the fourth or fifth month. This deprived her of her job without due process of law.

In *Geduldig* v. *Aiello*,[38] the Court upheld the constitutionality of the California disability insurance system, which provided benefits to private employees temporarily disabled from work but denied benefits to women unable to work because of normal pregnancy and childbirth. Benefits were allowed under the California system if the pregnancy involved medical complications. The Court held that California was not required to include all risks of disability in its insurance system and that its exclusion of normal pregnancy and childbirth did not violate the Fourteenth Amendment equal protection clause. The Court discussed the sex-discrimination issue—the fact that only women can incur the risk of normal pregnancy—in a footnote:

> The California insurance program does not exclude anyone from benefit eligibility because of gender but merely removes one physical condition—pregnancy—from the list of compensable disabilities. While it is true that only women can become pregnant, it does not follow that every legislative classification concerning pregnancy is a sex-based classification . . . . Normal pregnancy is an objectively identifiable physical condition with unique characteristics. Absent a showing that distinctions involving pregnancy are mere pretexts designed to effect an invidious discrimination against one sex or the other, lawmakers are constitutionally free to include or exclude pregnancy from the coverage of legislation such as this on any reasonable basis, just as with respect to any other physical condition. . . . The program divides potential recipients into two groups—pregnant women and nonpregnant persons. While the first group is exclusively female, the second includes members of both sexes. The fiscal and actuarial benefits of the program thus accrue to members of both sexes.[39]

The issue in *Geduldig* was the constitutionality of excluding maternity benefits from state disability coverage. In *General Electric Company* v. *Gilbert*, decided December 7, 1976,[40] the Supreme Court held that an employer's disability insurance plan that excludes pregnancy-related disabilities from coverage does not violate the Title VII prohibition against sex discrimination. Sex discrimination means difference in treatment between men and women; difference in treatment based on pregnancy—a temporary function of only some women—does not itself constitute sex discrimination. However, the Court in *General Electric*, as in *Geduldig*, said that, if the exclusion of pregnancy benefits were shown to be a "mere pretext designed to effect an invidious discrimination" against women, it would be unlawful. Female employees of General Electric were already getting greater dollar benefits from the insurance system than male employees, so no adverse impact on women as a class resulted from the exclusion of pregnancy benefits.

> **In Geduldig v. Aiello, the Court upheld the constitutionality of the California disability insurance system, which denied benefits to women unable to work because of normal pregnancy and childbirth.**

The question of whether employer disability insurance plans should cover pregnancy-related disabilities is thus one of policy. The increased costs to the employer of such benefits might encourage employers required to provide the benefits to discriminate in hiring of women of childbearing age. The fact that such discrimination is unlawful would be of small comfort to the female applicant who must file a lawsuit to prove her case. Moreover, women often stay home from work for a far longer period than they are actually disabled from work, in order to care for their children themselves and to save child-care costs. Doctors are generally agreeable to approving such extended leave on "disability" grounds, particularly where maternity benefits are available from the employer, even though it is in fact "child care" leave. Where the employees directly or indirectly share in the cost of such benefits, there is little justification for assessing nonparent workers for child-care costs. Finally, there is no present need to encourage population growth.

The role of mothers as family wage earners was involved in a case questioning the constitutionality of the "mother's insurance benefit" provision of the Social Security Act.[41] When a working father covered by Social Security died, the statute provided benefits for both the surviving widow and her minor children. But when a covered working mother died, the act provided benefits for the minor children only, not the widower. Paula Weisenfeld died in childbirth, and her husband, Stephen, was left with the sole care of their infant son. Although he obtained Social Security survivors' benefits for his son, he was denied benefits for himself as a widower. The statute authorized payments only to widows, allowing women to choose not to work but rather to stay home to care for their children. The Supreme Court held the denial of benefits to Stephen Weisenfeld violated his right to equal protection of the laws secured by the Constitution. The Court stated:

> Obviously, the notion that men are more likely than women to be the primary supporters of their spouses and children is not entirely without empirical support. . . . But such a gender-based generalization cannot suffice to justify the denigration of the efforts of women who do work and whose earnings contribute significantly to their families' support.[42]

The Court went on to say that the Constitution forbids sex distinctions that give lesser benefits to the families of female workers who pay Social Security taxes than to the families of male workers.

The Court discussed the rights of children and fathers as well as the rights of working mothers, noting:

> Given the purpose of enabling the surviving parent to remain at home to care for a child, the gender-based distinction of sec. 402(g) is entirely irrational. The classification discriminates among surviving children solely on the basis of the sex of the surviving parent. . . . The fact that a man is working while there is a wife at home does not mean that he would, or should be required to, continue to work if his wife dies. It is no less important for a child to be cared for by its sole surviving parent when the parent is male rather than female. And a father, no less than a mother, has a constitutionally protected right to the "companionship, care, custody, and management" of "the children he has sired and raised. . . ."[43]

Thus, the 1975 Supreme Court cites equal rights and responsibilities of fathers in childrearing to strike down a legal distinction based on sex. This forms a sharp contrast to the 1908 Court's reliance on women's special and different functions as mothers as the basis for upholding a restriction on their hours of work in *Muller* v. *Oregon.*

The justification for laws discriminating against women in the past has been to "protect" women's childbearing and maternal functions, and all women, regardless of their life-style or age, were essentially regarded by the law as reproductive machines rather than individuals. The recent cases show the Supreme Court taking a more enlightened view of women's rights under the Constitution, and it no longer allows differential treatment of men and women in the laws relating to work.

NOTES

1   29 United States Code §206(d).

2   U.S. Department of Labor, "Equal Pay Findings," mimeographed sheet, July 16, 1976.

3   42 United States Code §§2000e et seq.

4   An executive order is a formal document issued by the president and has the force of law. Executive orders are compiled in Title 3 of the *Code of Federal Regulations.*

5   41 Code of Federal Regulations pt. 60–2.

6   41 Code of Federal Regulations §§60–2.10, 60–2.12(e).

7   5 Code of Federal Regulations pt. 713.

8   86 Statutes at Large 103 (1972).

9   20 United States Code §§1681 et seq.

10   29 United States Code §§621 et seq.

11   See U.S. Department of Labor, Women's Bureau, *1965 Handbook on Women Workers,* Bulletin no. 290 (Washington, D.C.: Government Printing Office, 1966), pp. 233–46.

12   198 U.S. 45 (1905).

13   The Fourteenth Amendment provides, in part: "No State shall make or enforce any law which shall abridge the privileges or immunities of citizens of the United States; nor shall any State deprive any person of life, liberty, or property, without due process of law; nor deny to any person within its jurisdiction the equal protection of the laws."

14   208 U.S. 418 (1908).

15   208 U.S. at 421–23.

16 243 U.S. 426 (1917).

17 See Miller v. Wilson, 236 U.S. 373 (1915); Bosley v. McLaughlin, 236 U.S. 385 (1915); Riley v. Massachusetts, 232 U.S. 671 (1914).

18 Radice v. New York, 264 U.S. 292 (1924).

19 West Coast Hotel Co. v. Parrish, 300 U.S. 397 (1937).

20 The history of the sex discrimination provision in Title VII is best described in Berger, "Equal Pay, Equal Employment Opportunity and Equal Enforcement of the Law for Women," Symposium on Women and the Law, *Valparaiso University Law Review* 5 (1971): 326.

21 See 110 Cong. Rec. 2577–78, 2580, 2732 (1964).

22 31 Federal Register 6414 (1966).

23 Ibid.

24 See 29 Code of Federal Regulations §1604.5.

25 Mengelkoch v. Industrial Welfare Commission, 442 F.2d 1119, 1123 (9th Cir. 1971).

26 442 F.2d at 1123.

27 444 F.2d 1219 (9th Cir. 1971).

28 The "supremacy clause" of the Constitution (article VI, clause 2) provides: "This Constitution, and the laws of the United States which shall be made in pursuance thereof; and all Treaties made, or which shall be made, under the Authority of the United States, shall be the supreme Law of the Land; and the Judges in every State shall be bound thereby, any Thing in the Constitution or Laws of any State to the Contrary notwithstanding."

29 444 F.2d 1225–26.

30 408 F.2d 228 (5th Cir. 1969).

31 408 F.2d at 236.

32 A class action is a case filed by one or more individuals in behalf of other persons similarly situated, e.g., in behalf of all other female employees of an employer.

33 416 F.2d 711 (7th Cir. 1969); 489 F.2d 896 (7th Cir. 1973) (second appeal).

34 416 F.2d at 715.

35 42 United States Code §§2000e-2(e).

36 Phillips v. Martin Marietta Corp., 400 U.S. 542 (1971).

37 Cleveland Bd. of Educ. v. LaFleur, 414 U.S. 632, 639–40, 647–48 (1974).

38 417 U.S. 484 (1974).

39 417 U.S. at 496–97.

40   45 U.S. Law Week 4031 (Dec. 7, 1976).
41   42 United States Code §402(g).
42   Weinberger v. Weisenfeld, 420 U.S. 636, 645 (1975).
43   420 U.S. at 651–52.

TWO

SOCIOLOGICAL PERSPECTIVES ON WOMEN WORKING

EDITORS'
INTRODUCTION

Carolyn Shaw Bell, in section one of this volume, provided examples of biases in economic concepts and data that limit our understanding of women's occupational skills and contributions to the economy. Such biases are also present in sociological studies of work. In some cases sociologists have ignored women's work or passed it over lightly. Empirical investigations have tended to concentrate on male-dominated occupations to the neglect of women's most common occupations, and studies of mixed male and female worker groups have often treated all alike on the assumption that gender does not make a difference in occupational and organizational behavior.[1]

Sociologists who *have* directed their attention to women workers, and have found that women's patterns of labor force participation differ from those of men, have sometimes worn blinders of other sorts. As members of the society they study, they have tended to rely on cultural myths and stereotypes in their explanations of differences between male and female workers. For example, in one frequently cited study of labor in four industries, the author states that women in the blue-collar jobs discussed are "more content than men with work that is of little challenge."[2] The major reason that "they are not dissatisfied" with their positions in the "least skilled, the most repetitive, and the least free" jobs, he asserts, is that "work does not have the central importance and meaning in their lives that it does for men since their most important roles are those of wives and mothers."[3]

In a similar vein, the authors of a well-known study of female-dominated professions, such as nursing and social work, observed that the work settings of these professions are more bureaucratic than those of the male-dominated professions and concluded that women require and accept the control inherent in bureaucratic structures. As they explain:

> A woman's primary attachment is to the family role; women are therefore less intrinsically committed to work than men and less likely to maintain a high level of specialized knowledge. Because their work motives are more utilitarian and less intrinsically task-oriented than those of men, they may require more control. . . .[5]

These investigations illustrate some of the problems found in a number of older sociological studies of women's work. First, it is noteworthy that, while the authors recognized women's disadvantaged position in the occupations they studied and while they identified discrimination and exploitation as contributing factors, their explanations emphasized women's low aspirations and submissive personalities which result from their sex-role socialization, or women's greater commitment to the family than to work, or both. Certainly socialization and women's family roles cannot be discounted in explaining women's occupational and organizational behavior. Too many studies, however, have introduced them as post hoc explanations for differences found in men's and women's behavior, and they have given too little attention to exploring other possible explanations. Studies that have sought further evidence have found possible answers arising from the work situations of women, characteristics of the jobs they have, and power differentials on the job that parallel the hierarchy of the sexes in the outside world.[6] Such situational explanations deserve far more attention than they have received in the literature, while explanations focusing on socialization and family structure need to be examined more critically.

Still another problem in the sociological study of work arises from sex biases built into basic concepts or their operationalization. Take, for example, the concepts of occupational status and occupational mobility. As Joan Acker explains in the first chapter in this section, the most widely used measure of occupational status was derived from a process that intentionally excluded women. This is not the only way in which women are ignored, however. Most stratification studies based on measures of occupational status ignore women's achievement by using the family as the unit of analysis and assigning even the most industrious employed woman the status of her husband. (For a more charitable interpretation of this problem, see Carolyn Shaw Bell's chapter in section one.) Likewise, most studies of both intra- and intergenerational occupational mobility have focused on men, although Acker discusses some recent exceptions.

These biases illustrate the sexist cast that has characterized much of the sociological study of work in the past. Exploring them in depth in her critique of the sociology of work, Acker first identifies some sources of male bias in the field and then shows how these biases have influenced not only basic concepts but also the statement of research problems and the research process itself.

Monica Morris then presents a veiled critique of these same biases in a more light-hearted chapter originally prepared as a classroom lecture. She explores the applicability of several sociological paradigms to women's role in the labor force, beginning with functionalism, which has been widely used to explain women's generally subordinate status. After showing how it may be applied to the more specific question of women's inferior labor force status, she demonstrates that exchange theory and conflict theory offer equally plausible explanations.

Together these two chapters begin the process of unmasking bias and hidden assumptions. This is only the first step toward improving our understanding of work and its place in women's lives. The next step is to lay the foundations of an adequate explanation of women's status in society and the labor force. This challenge has inspired a growing body of recent literature, including the remaining articles in this section. Although it is difficult to date precisely the beginning of the burgeoning sociological interest in women's employment in the contemporary period, Valerie Kincade Oppenheimer's 1970 study of women's labor force participation[7] is certainly a benchmark, along with Cynthia Fuchs Epstein's 1971 book on women professionals.[8] These investigations delineated what are now well-known features of women's labor force participation, and they inspired discussion of the underlying causes. Among the features brought to light were those discussed in section one: the rapid changes in the size and composition of the female labor force and women's second-class status in the world of work—their partial attachment to the labor force, their concentration in relatively few and sex-typed occupations, and their low earnings compared to those of men.

Sociologists have offered a variety of explanations of women's inferior status in the labor force. As we noted earlier, many analysts have stressed the importance of socialization, the process whereby a person's attitudes and behavior are shaped by the expectations of significant others. According to this approach, girls are encouraged to develop "feminine" personality traits and to pursue activities that prepare them to acquire "appropriate" statuses, primarily those of wife and mother. Certain characteristics of women's labor force behavior, such as their concentration in low-paying sex-typed jobs, may then be viewed as the result of their socialization, a channeling that prepared them to choose positions considered compatible with "feminine" personality traits and women's responsibilities as wives and mothers.

There is no doubt that socialization helps to explain the labor force behavior of women, particularly young women. However, analyses that offer this explanation uncritically or that focus too narrowly on socialization ignore women's individual experiences, particularly as adults, and disregard the situational factors that may greatly influence their employment experiences. For this reason a number of sociologists have stressed the effects of women's current circumstances more than their past socialization, in seeking to explain their status in the labor force. The family and the structure of the workplace are two situational factors that have been singled out for attention.

Epstein and others have emphasized the limitations imposed on married women's occupational achievement by household maintenance and child-care duties, tasks considered primarily women's work. If women are employed, their "double duty" may limit the location, hours, and types of jobs they can accept. Further, they may find their careers completely interrupted by geographical moves related to their husbands' jobs or by difficulties in finding adequate child care.

Family structure, like socialization, is a crucial factor in explaining women's inferior position in the labor force, but it, too, has sometimes been relied on too heavily. It is important to recognize that limited opportunities confront aspiring workers. Rosabeth Moss Kanter and Joan Acker are among those who have recently urged sociologists to give more attention to the nature of hierarchy and organizations as they seek to understand women's labor force status. These analysts argue that complex organizations have opportunity and power structures that routinely disadvantage some kinds of people, such as women.[9] They suggest that the creation of a class of disadvantaged people generates certain attitudinal and behavioral consequences, such as apathy and low aspirations, that may be used to "blame the victim." In this view, the primary causal factor is the nature of the hierarchical power structure that keeps women from rising.

The last four selections in this section illustrate these various explanations of women's status in the labor force. It is informative to examine not only how these approaches differ but also how they complement each other in helping to explain women's experiences in the world of work.

Carol Ireson discusses the socialization of girls and young women for occupational achievement. She examines girls' academic achievement and occupational aspirations as preludes to their occupational achievement as adults. Ireson identifies critical points in the young women's lives when their academic achievements and occupational aspirations decline, and she discusses the agents—parents, schools, peers (especially boyfriends), and the media—that influence young women's decisions. Ireson's chapter not only brings together many studies of the antecedents of women's achievement but also outlines directions for future research on this topic.

Kristin Moore and Isabel Sawhill consider a later stage in the life cycle: they analyze the present —and future—situation of women by exploring the relationship between family structure and women's labor force participation. The authors assess the impact of changing patterns of female labor force participation on marriage, divorce, parenthood, and child rearing. They also discuss the other side of the coin—ways in which family structure affects women's labor force participation. Their chapter reveals the complex relationship between these mutually influential phenomena; women's labor force participation and family structure and process. Moore and Sawhill conclude by considering public policies affecting women's familial roles and occupational pursuits.

Like Moore and Sawhill, Larry Long looks at the relationship between a wife's labor force participation and her family, but he pinpoints an aspect of family life that has rarely been studied: geographic mobility. Tracing first the effect of a wife's employment on her husband's movement, he finds that it promotes intracounty mobility (presumably because her income allows the family to afford a better house) and slightly discourages long-distance migration, but only after the age period when the husband's career is likely to be well established. The effects in the other direction are much more striking: women's careers are often interrupted by their husbands' migrations. Long concludes that such interruptions in a wife's employment are likely to lower her earnings. He thus makes a case for including family movement as a significant factor in the study of income differences between women and men.

Evelyn Rosenthal discusses the influence of both the family and the job market on the occupational experience of middle-aged women. Motivating her analysis is the apparent contradiction between older women's choices of sex-atypical occupations and their endorsement of sex-stereotyped family roles. Rosenthal resolves this contradiction by suggesting that mature women entering the labor force choose occupations that, regardless of their sex labels, enable the women to fulfill their traditional responsibilities as wives and mothers. In reaching this conclusion, Rosenthal evaluates the opportunities offered to and constraints imposed on older women by employers, by social policies, and by their families. Her chapter emphasizes the ways employers manipulate features of a job to attract older women when other workers are unavailable or more demanding.

These chapters, with their varying emphases on socialization, family structure, and the structure of the workplace, illustrate directions that theories about women's employment may take. Together, they suggest that the relative influence of each factor may vary with differing stages in a woman's life cycle. Along with the discussions by Acker and Morris, the chapters in this section contribute to the reexamination of old and the development of new sociological perspectives on women's place in the labor force.

NOTES

1   Ann Oakley, *The Sociology of Housework* (New York: Pantheon Books, 1974), pp. 1-28; Rosabeth Moss Kanter, "Women and the Structure of Organizations: Explorations in Theory and Behavior," in *Another Voice: Feminist Perspectives on Social Life and Social Science,* ed. Marcia Millman and Rosabeth Moss Kanter (Garden City, N.Y.: Anchor Books, Doubleday and Company, 1975), pp. 34-74; Joan Acker and Donald R. Van Houten, "Differential Recruitment and Control: The Sex Structuring of Organizations," *Administrative Science Quarterly* 19 (1974): 152-63; see also Joan Acker's chapter below in this volume.

2   Robert Blauner, *Alienation and Freedom* (Chicago: University of Chicago Press, 1964), p. 121.

3   Ibid., p. 81.

4   Richard L. Simpson and Ida Harper Simpson, "Women and Bureaucracy in the Semi-Professions," in *The Semi-Professions and Their Organization,* ed. Amitai Etzioni (New York: Free Press, 1969), pp. 196-265.

5   Ibid., p. 199.

6   See especially Rosabeth Moss Kanter, "Women and Hierarchies" (paper presented at the annual meeting of the American Sociological Association, San Francisco, August 1975); idem, "Women and the Structure of Organizations"; Acker's chapter below.

7   Valerie Kincade Oppenheimer, *The Female Labor Force in the United States,* Population Monograph Series, no. 5 (Berkeley: University of California, Institute of International Studies, 1970).

8   Cynthia Fuchs Epstein, *Woman's Place* (Berkeley: University of California Press, 1970).

9   Kanter, "Women and Hierarchies"; idem, "Women and the Structure of Organizations"; Acker's chapter below.

Issues in the Sociological Study of Women's Work

Joan Acker

INTRODUCTION

There are problems in any sociological study of women, because sociology has been, on the whole, the study of male society.[1] This is as true of the study of work as of any other area of sociology. Theoretical analyses of social processes and societal structure are supposedly sex-neutral; on close examination, they usually refer only to the world of men. Females are often absent from empirical work that is supposedly about "people" or "workers." When women are not simply missing, they are peripheral, dealt with in a footnote. If their inferior status is noticed, it is explained as necessary for stability, for the functioning of the economic system, or to provide for adequate socialization. Perhaps the greatest difficulty is that many sociological concepts simply do not fit well with the facts when those facts begin to include information about the female half of humanity.[2] Consequently, in any study of women, it is wise to start with an assessment of the effects of male bias on the concepts and methods conventionally used to deal with the subject matter. It is not sufficient to begin simply applying the available ideas to the topic of women; instead we must alter the angle of our vision and raise questions about many things that were previously taken for granted. This I propose to do here. I will not discuss in any detail the expanding number of articles, reports, and books (including this one) that are already correcting the male bias.[3] Although this new literature is rapidly producing a new area of specialization, elsewhere male bias is still alive and well, and we still need to understand it. Toward that end, I will discuss (1) the sources of male bias in the structure of our society, in the discipline of sociology, and in the structure of our thought; (2) how that bias affects the problems examined, the concepts used, and the methods followed in the study of women's work; and (3) resolutions—not only how we can eliminate sexism from our efforts to understand the world of work, but also what kinds of questions we need to ask in order to help change this world in which women are still the second sex.

SOURCES OF MALE BIAS

The Male Origins of the Discipline

A male bias was built into sociology from the time it began to emerge as a separate intellectual discipline during the nineteenth century.[4] Sociology developed as part of a series of massive societal changes, which included the growth "of the most thoroughgoing system of sex-role differentiation ever seen in American history."[5] Recent feminist historians have provided new understandings of the importance of this process of sex-role differentiation and how it was rooted in the separation of the home and the world of public affairs produced by the rise of capitalist industrial production.[6] The world of public affairs was a male domain, and it was there that the critical events transforming the society seemed to take place. Confined to the home, which had a diminishing part to play in the production of income and wealth, and completely excluded from positions of power, women were easily defined as irrelevant to the important questions about society. It is not surprising that, as the new sciences of society were defined, the questions raised and the concepts used reflected the reality of the public domain, and thus reflected a male reality. In addition, almost all sociologists were male; the patterns of dominance in the economic and political arenas also held in the world of ideas. In looking at the society, these sociologists inevitably looked through male eyes. Those were the eyes of the dominant group in society, and few members of dominant groups question the arrangements that solidify and justify their preeminence. Consequently, sociology developed as a male enterprise, defined by males, and overwhelmingly concerned with questions about the aspects of society that were almost entirely populated by males. Even though sociology has had an inherent male bias, the sociological visibility of women has varied. Some periods in the history of the discipline have produced more studies of women and work than others. Much research on women in working-class jobs was published between 1900 and the World War I period.[7] After 1925, there was a definite decline in such research, and almost nothing further was published until the early 1970s. This rise and fall coincides with the periods of high activity of the suffrage movement, the decline of the movement after the vote was obtained, the long period of quiescence in the forties and fifties, and the reemergence of the women's movement in the late sixties and early seventies. We might conclude that the effects of the male bias are reduced when women question through their own actions the assumptions of that bias. It should be noted, however, that most of the writers and researchers who have made contributions during both the early and the present periods have been women. We have little evidence that male bias has been eroded among men; they are simply moved to give a little space and a small measure of legitimacy to women studying women during periods when male definitions and dominance are openly challenged.

The Assumptions of Male Social Science

Male bias has another, and closely related, source in a set of assumptions that reflect and reinforce the male dominant structure. These assumptions are unstated, but they lead to conceptualizations that perpetuate the bias in empirical research.

The basic assumption is: male = general.[8] What is typical, usual, or to be expected of human beings is equated with the male. This equation can be seen clearly in sociological studies of "workers," which are almost always studies of male workers. It is reflected in studies of sex stereotyping, in which the stereotype of *human being* is very similar to the stereotype of *male*.[9] It can be intuitively grasped when we recognize the difficulty we have in using the term *woman* to refer to all human beings. The term *woman* does not evoke images of men.[10]

The corollary to the first assumption is: female = the particular, the "other," the residual. If the male is taken as the general, it follows that the female, to the extent that she is defined as socially and/or psychologically different from the male, is something other than the general human being.

Two additional and related assumptions follow: the female, the residual category, by implication has her fate determined by the characteristic that defines the category—her sex. Female is, thus, at root, a biological category. The male, on the other hand, as the general category, is not explained in terms of his sex, but rather in terms of his relationship to the means of production, his position in the occupational hierarchy, or the historical-political factors of a particular time and place.

Certain problems of conceptualization follow from these assumptions. First, the equation of the general and the male becomes obscured. We think and talk about society in general, and in the process we assume that females and males live in the same sociocultural world, within the same systems of meaning.[11]

Then, too, analytic categories that are developed with these implicit assumptions are consistent with male experience and the structuring of male lives. Measures of equality are measures of approximation to male norms or male standards. Females are those who deviate from the general.

The residual category, female, tends to be relatively invisible and is considered relatively uninteresting. Females are defined as a subgroup, analytically equated with youth, blacks, the aged.

We end up *without* a theory that systematically conceptualizes society as containing both sexes as equally significant participants. The structure of our male-dominant thought creates other problems in the study of women, stemming from the conservative nature of the social and behavioral sciences. These sciences are based on the idea that there are regularities in human behavior and that it is possible to discover the "laws" of these regularities; knowledge of the laws is supposed to enable us to explain and to predict behavior.[12] What exists is studied and then generalized as a description of behavior in general. As Shanley and Schuck point out, "the belief that forms of government are based upon the discernible laws of human behavior which are analogous to physical laws gave existing social and political arrangements an aura of inevitability."[13] A social science that can only describe and extrapolate from the present and the past inevitably ties women—and men, too—to what they have been historically. The potential, the emergent, the possible is not easily predictable from "data." Since most of us who are studying women have a commitment to change and liberation, a theoretical approach that mires us in the past has obvious limitations.

The effort of social scientists to develop predictive theories based on what presently exists is related to the discipline's overwhelming emphasis on models that can be dealt with in quantitative terms, in "hard data." Jessie

Bernard points out that this represents a "machismo element in research," and that quantitative research is considered the most prestigious and "most scientific."[14] This approach is concerned with control, mastery, and prediction, with the construction and manipulation of variables. The living, moving actuality of human experience is carved up into discrete pieces, which are assigned numbers and manipulated in more and more abstract ways. There is no question about the effectiveness of this approach for answering certain kinds of questions—for example, what are the social characteristics of women in the labor force; what variables explain the wage gap between women and men. But, this approach has been a spectacular failure at anticipating social change. We are continually and repeatedly surprised, caught off guard, by new developments in our society—for example, no sociologists predicted the reemergence of the women's movement. Perhaps social science has been so poor at predicting because the theories appropriate to its methods fail to grasp the nature of human existence. This issue goes beyond the scope of the present subject—the sociology of women's work. However, we must recognize that the study of women in relation to the sex structuring of society is a subject that forces us back into a consideration of the most basic questions about the nature of the social sciences and the nature of human reality.

THE EFFECTS OF MALE BIAS ON THE STUDY OF WOMEN'S WORK

In the following section, I discuss specific ways in which male bias operates in the study of women and work, by defining concepts in terms of the male reality, by consigning women to the residual category, by defining the central questions so that women are eliminated, or by failing to notice the operation of sex-differentiating processes.

Bias in the Definition of the Subject

The concept of *labor force* has established the boundaries of what is to be studied in the sociology of work. As Carolyn Shaw Bell noted above in this volume, the labor force includes those working for pay and those actively seeking work; it excludes those doing unpaid work such as housework or volunteer jobs. These activities are, by implication, defined as nonwork. Thus, the analytic category *labor force* is much more consistent with the work experience of men than with the work experience of women; when we discuss work as labor force participation, we are much more likely to encompass the significant elements of male lives than the significant elements of female lives.

Analytic categories are only ways of dividing up the empirical world so that we can talk about it. Why have we divided it up in such a way that what has been predominantly the work of men is considered the proper object of study, while what has been predominantly the work of women is considered a subject of little interest? This way of sectioning reality reflects the hidden assumption that the male is the norm, the general. But there are other factors involved. One is that sociologists tend to study what is problematical for the groups in the society that have power and control; much

> ❝ When we discuss work as labor force participation, we are much more likely to encompass the significant elements of male lives than the significant elements of female lives. ❞

of the research on work and the organization of work has been on issues of interest to employers—issues such as efficiency, job satisfaction, and commitment to work. It matters little to employers whether the wives of their workers are doing efficient jobs of homemaking, unless the activities of the wives are seen as affecting the husband's work significantly—as those of the wives of corporate executives are.[15]

An additional reason for the choice of this analytic category as the proper definition of work is, undoubtedly, that, as industrial capitalism developed, paid work became increasingly essential for survival. More and more of what any family needed had to be purchased for money. It made some sense, then, to define work as those activities that brought in money. A final factor has to do with the availability of data, as Bell noted above. It is easier to count and to place a value on work that is done for wages and recorded by employers. Although economists have long recognized that this definition excludes many valuable activities, they have only very recently begun attempts to place a monetary value on housework and to calculate a hypothetical gross national product that includes activities not previously assessed in terms of money.[16] Sociologists are only beginning to cope with the reconceptualization required to include housework within the definitions of occupation and work. Some of these efforts are discussed later in this chapter.

One effect of the traditional definition of work has been to obscure the fact that almost all women work, as do almost all men, and that their work is essential to the socioeconomic structure and to their own survival. The description of women's lifetime careers and how they take action to ensure their economic survival in a competitive, individualistic society has never been a major focus of sociological study.[17] The blinders that have kept us from seeing that this is an interesting—as well as a vital—question include not only the definition of work but also the comfortable assumption that women exist within the confines of the family, enjoying the economic support of men, and that this existence is not problematic. Elsewhere, I have pointed out that this assumption is only partially supported by the facts.[18] The recent rise in the proportion of mother-headed households suggests that this traditional view of women's lives is becoming less and less consistent with reality.[19]

Because the actual labor force participation of women was seen as relatively unimportant compared to that of men, it has received cursory attention until recently. We are now beginning to learn something about the factors associated with the female–male wage gap[20] and something about the sex segregation of occupations,[21] but aside from these topics our knowledge—particularly about women who are not professionals—is sparse. Sociologists and historians are only beginning to search out and bring together information about women's economic activities that will give us a clearer picture of the work lives of women in different classes and during different historical periods. When this picture is fully drawn, we will see—I am sure—that we cannot talk about women as simply a biological category, that their life and work situations have been as varied as those of men, determined by socioeconomic forces as much as by their sex. In this effort we will have to look seriously at the "nonoccupations" of women, such as being a prostitute[22] or a maiden aunt.[23] We will have to assess more carefully the differences in class, country, and time. This may lead us to question certain generalizations about women's labor force participation and the female–male division of labor in industrial society. We may find, for example, that males in general have never been the ideal-typical breadwinners and that women in general have never been the ideal-typical unpaid workers confined to the private sphere. Hilary Land suggests that this may be so in an article noting that the typical lifetime working pattern of the working-class nineteenth-century Englishwoman may have been quite similar to the pattern we identify as new in the United States today.[24] In other words, women generally worked for pay, with a temporary interruption for childbearing.

A redefinition of labor force might facilitate a better understanding of the work lives of women. How would labor force be defined if the female experience were taken as the norm, the general? All people who work, whether for pay or not, would be included. The work lives of all individuals would be described in terms of transition or movement from paid to unpaid activities, the proportion of time they spend in the two types of work, and how they combine the two. We now have some data on this process for women, although it tends to focus primarily on movement in and out of paid work, with little attention given to the unpaid part of the process.[25] We might, further, ask how different combinations of paid and unpaid work affect a person's consciousness and attribution of legitimacy to the existing socioeconomic system. We might speculate that those who are denied the experience of both realms would have narrower views of human capacity and narrower ranges of behavior than those who participate in both. We might ask about the social and personal costs to men of the denial of the alternatives open to women. Combinations of paid and unpaid work might be calculated and indexes of the sex distribution of paid and unpaid work might become important indicators of change and societal strain, just as measures of unemployment now are. To develop perspectives that will allow us to ask new and more revealing questions, it may be necessary to reverse our thinking and define the female as the norm in this way.

It would be possible to extend the definition of labor force to include more of the female population, however, without turning our thinking upside down completely. Some moves to extend the definition have recently been taken by the Bureau of Labor Statistics. It is now gathering data on adults who are outside the labor force and the reasons for their nonparticipation. Of course, the majority of adults outside the labor force are women. A category called *discouraged worker*, the worker who wants a job but has given up trying to find one, has been established, and suggestions are being made that these persons be counted as part of the labor force for purposes of calculating rates of unemployment and subemployment.[26]

This is only a small move in the direction of redefinition; it does not, of course, deal with the issue of unpaid work and how to conceptualize an occupational system that contains both paid and unpaid positions.

Bias in the Definition of Key Questions

Some of the most central sociological questions—those dealing with societal stability and change, order and chaos—have been about work, how it is organized, and its unequal distribution. These dimensions of social structure and social stratification have been defined in terms of male work. Consequently, females have been ignored, in both Marxist and non-Marxist traditions, in efforts to deal with certain basic issues about society. The resulting problems in understanding women's work can best be illustrated by a discussion of two key concepts, one from the non-Marxist study of social stratification—"occupational status"; the other from Marxist theory—"the working class."

Occupational status is an important concept in the study of work because it provides us with one way of talking about equality and inequality and because it links questions about work with larger questions about the structure of society. One way of thinking about the structure of society is in terms of social stratification—society, let us say, is a system of interrelated but unequal positions and the most important system-defining positions are those that involve work. Occupational status is an indicator of where any particular kind of work falls in the hierarchy. An important process in the society—social mobility—is the movement of individuals and groups from one occupational status to another. Basic changes in the society may be reflected or signaled by the disappearance of clusters of occupations at a similar status or by the expansion of groups of occupations at a similar status. For example, unskilled manual occupations with a low status have been disappearing in the United States, an important fact related to such disparate developments as the increase in the welfare recipient rolls in the central cities and the high proportion of young people who go on to higher education. In these senses, questions about occupational status are at the heart of important questions about society—but in most formulations it is male status that is at the heart, not female status.

Females are obviously absent from studies of social mobility, which are most often studies of occupational status mobility.[27] Studies of the occupational structure and of occupational mobility have usually used male samples, probably because of the underlying assumption that it is the occupational positions of males that determine the contours of the larger society. Thus, most generalizations, based on studies of occupational status, about the extent of opportunity and the openness of our society are really only generalizations about male society. But the difficulties go much deeper than that, right into the construction of the concept itself and its transformation into a variable that can be measured.

Occupational status is defined as the prestige of the occupation or the social standing of people in the occupation. The most widely used measure of occupational status, the Duncan scores of socioeconomic status,[28] was devised by using prestige scores developed in the National Opinion Research Center study of 1947.[29] The NORC researchers deliberately chose to study occupations held primarily by men to eliminate the confounding effect of sex. The Duncan scores were derived using weights based on the income and education of males in forty-five occupations that had NORC prestige scores.[30] Females and their work attributes were intentionally excluded in the development of the measure. An additional and major defect of commonly used measures of occupational status, including the Duncan scores, is that they do not include the largest female occupation—that of housewife. Thus, the measures of occupational status that have been widely used in American sociology are male biased and of questionable utility in the study of women.

Researchers have recognized that both the studies and the measures of occupational status ignore the existence of women, and some have made an effort to alter the situation. For example, Bose has developed occupational scores that intentionally include the effect of sex on status.[31] Other studies published in the last four years have been concerned with questions of sex inequality in occupational status and occupational mobility.[32] They raise a number of new questions and, I think, indicate that some of the old questions were trivial. I will briefly summarize where these recent studies seem to have taken us.

What we now know about occupational status differences between females and males can be summed up as follows: (1) female-typed jobs have a lower prestige than male-typed jobs;[33] (2) that difference is not very great;[34] (3) "the average status of all working men is only slightly above the average status of working women because of the distribution of people in jobs";[35] (4) the occupation *housewife* has an unexpectedly high status, higher than 70 percent of the other female-dominated occupations;[36] (5) the occupation househusband has an extremely low level of prestige;[37] (6) it is not clear whether or not there is more intergenerational occupational mobility among men than among women,[38] but it is clear that within any generation women do not rise to even the first levels of supervision and management at the rate that men do; (7) the relationship between income and occupational prestige is different for women and men.[39]

The last finding seems to me to be the most important. For women, prestige and income are not as closely intertwined as' they are for men. A woman's prestige may rise although her income remains low and close to the average for all women.[40] It is not that income is irrelevant to women, but rather that they cannot expect significant income increases from greater work effort, although they can expect some gains in the respect and approval they receive as workers. This is true of women in labor force jobs. If we also include women in the occupation of housewife the disparity between status and income is even more glaring. The housewife position has fairly high status rewards but no direct income rewards at all.

These studies of female occupational status suggest some different ways of looking at the lifetime careers of women. Over a lifetime, women are presented with fewer choices than men, but they have the possibility of being housewives, an occupation that is not generally available to men. Most women cannot reasonably expect what a majority of men can expect—that competence and hard work will bring them an adequate income. Moreover, most cannot expect jobs that give them autonomy or power. They may be given respect for the work they do, but the low monetary rewards carry the opposite connotation in a society that measures almost all value in dollars. Is it possible, then, that women live in a different social reality from that of men, a reality that they experience and interpret differently? Do competence, hard work, and status have the meanings for women that they have for men?

The recent studies of occupational status differences also raise some questions about the concept of occupational prestige and its measurement. Prestige is an ambiguous concept, operationally defined by rating occupations on a scale from 1 to 9. It is not completely clear what respondents mean when they make such a rating. Are they rating on the basis of what they think or on the basis of what they think others believe? The high status of housewife found in Bose's study is particularly puzzling, since we know from other studies using different methods that housewives themselves often do not give high status to their work.[41] In addition, differences in prestige do not adequately reflect differences in other aspects of work that may matter more to women workers, such as income inequities, the subtleties of power relationships on the job, the lack of significant decision-making positions, and the unequal distribution of autonomy and responsibility between the sexes. Finally, the focus on status mobility obscures important questions such as the lack of mobility between female and male work domains (noted in detail by Francine Blau above). In sum, occupational status may not be the most appropriate measure to use in studies of social stratification or social mobility.

Working class is a central concept for Marxist theorists concerned with questions about the revolutionary transformation of capitalist society. It has also been marred by a male bias. Working class has a specific meaning in Marxist thought. It refers to those people who sell their labor for wages, having no ownership of the means of production or of the product itself.

> **❝ Is it possible that women live in a different social reality from that of men, a reality that they experience and interpret differently? Do competence, hard work, and status have the meanings for women that they have for men? ❞**

The workers are inherently in conflict with the bourgeoisie, the class that owns the means of production and the product and that pays workers for their labor power while appropriating part of the value the workers create. Thus, class membership is defined by the part a person plays in the process of commodity production; it can be seen immediately that housewives are in an anomalous position in this conceptualization. Since they do not produce products for sale or work for wages, do they have any class position at all? Are they simply appendages of men—is their class position determined by the position of the men to whom they are attached by kinship? Clearly, Marx thought that working-class women would be drawn into industrial production in the same way that men were, and that eventually each woman as well as each man would be a member of the working class by virtue of her own participation in industrial production.[42] This did not happen; later Marxists adopted the solution of non-Marxists to the problem of the class identity of the unpaid female worker—she was to take the identity of her husband. Women were seen, then, as full participants in the society only when they were wage workers; as unpaid workers they were seen as members of the working class only indirectly, through their husbands.

This essential male bias in Marxist thought produced a theory that could not adequately explain the continuing subordination of women in the family or their inequality in the occupational structure. The only explanation offered for the economic subordination of women was that they constituted a reserve labor force that could be hired either to replace men (thus forcing down wage rates) or to meet excess demand for labor (and could easily be fired when no longer needed). Thus, women were—even more than men—at the mercy of employers and forced to accept low wages and poor working conditions. This explanation for their low wages and their exclusion was seen to be inadequate as more and more women entered the labor force. They went, in vast numbers, into sex-segregated, female-typed jobs where pay was low partly because of a reserve of women workers anxious for a job at almost any wage.[43] However, women did not replace male workers. Indeed, another reason for their low pay was that they were barred from replacing male workers.[44] The argument had to be more complex; what was needed was an explanation of why women were not used as a reserve army of labor for male jobs except during times of war.[45]

The male bias in Marxist theory also obscured the possibility that the interests of women, both as housewives and as workers, might frequently be in conflict with the interests of men; grounds for division within the working class were given insufficient attention.[46] This weakened the analysis of one of the central issues of Marxist theory—how and under what conditions workers become a class-conscious political force. Instead of seeing women as workers with particular interests related to their position in the system of production, Marxist theory pushed women to the side as unimportant, involved in precapitalist production, a regrettably conservative group afflicted with a lack of class consciousness.

Contemporary neo-Marxists have attempted to correct this male bias. Their efforts seem to be going in two directions. One group analyzes the special relationship of women to the means of production in an attempt to show that women as housewives are part of the working class and a part that is exploited in a particular way.[47] A second group converges with a number of non-Marxists studying the sex segregation of occupations.[48] These theorists analyze the structure of labor markets within the capitalist economy and how women and men are distributed differently in the economy as a whole and in specific firms or organizations. The basic idea is that women and men operate within different labor markets, with no bridges between them; the private secretary is not in the pipeline for promotion to department chief. The concepts of occupational segregation, dual labor markets, and internal labor markets allow us to understand the limits and restrictions on the work available to women. They also suggest explanations of wage inequities and blocked opportunities that do not blame the victim, do not hold women responsible for their particular place in the work world because of their passivity and dependence.

The reconceptualization of the Marxist working class and the place of women within it is incomplete; it still splits the lives of women between the world of wage work and housework. As wage workers women are almost identical to men in this reconceptualization, but as nonwage workers they are different. The theory has not yet been able to capture the unified reality of female lives.

Studies of Organizations and Work Behavior

Up to this point, the discussion of male bias has focused on concepts—labor force, occupational status, working class—that relate the work of individuals to the structure of the society; in other words, they are structural concepts. In fact we have seen that work has been the basis for conceptualizing the whole structure of society, and that these central concepts in the study of work had a bias that excluded women by definition or failed to encompass aspects of existence that occur primarily in female lives. The concepts were based on the assumption that the general is the male.

I now turn to studies of organizational and work behavior that provide additional examples of the problems and pitfalls of male bias. The dominant paradigms of organizational structure and processes were heavily influenced by their origins in male sociology, as Kanter points out in a recent article.[49] She notes that the classical, rational models of the organization saw organizations as rational, goal-seeking systems, hierarchically arranged for efficient goal achievement. The interest of investigators was therefore centered on those positions and persons who set the goals and carried out the main goal-oriented activities. They paid little attention to those whose functions were mainly supportive. Since support personnel were primarily women, women received little attention in studies conducted within this tradition.

Studies of female work behavior provide good examples of the assumption that women are a residual category. A typical argument runs as follows: differences between women and men are found; the deviance of the female from the male is interpreted as the result of female socialization or greater female commitment to family than to work. Neither of these explanations is supported by data from the study; they are post hoc explanations indicating that the researchers did not anticipate finding females or sex differences and therefore did not gather data relevant to explaining the differences. Explanations are seldom based on factors in the work situation of women, in the characteristics of the work that women perform, or in the sex power differentials at work, which parallel the hierarchy of the sexes in the outside world. Although some changes have occurred in recent sociological studies, the typical pattern is so widespread in the existing literature that a review of a few outstanding examples should be instructive.

A number of studies attribute the work attitudes and behaviors of women to attachment to home and family rather than to the work situation itself even though the authors provide no information on home and family ties. For example, a study of factory workers in West Germany[50] looked at the relationship between certain worker variables and the structure of the work situation. Of the seven chemical factories studied, six had a work force that was 100 percent male, while one had a work force that was 92 percent female. The researchers found a number of differences in attitudes between the workers in the female factory and the workers in the other factories, including some indications that female workers were more alienated than male workers. They also found many more of the objective conditions of alienation in the organization of the female factory—particularly, far less control over the work process itself. In addition, almost all of the women workers earned less than the lowest paid men. The authors did not analyze these findings or speculate about why the women workers were not even more alienated than they were, given their work conditions. Rather, the authors dismissed the attitudinal differences between the females and the males with two sentences about how married women have different values from other workers.[51]

Not only are women as a category assumed to be primarily attached to home and family, but they are also assumed to be less aggressive and more submissive to authority than men. These alleged personality characteristics are used to explain differences in work experience as well as differences in the structure of work organizations. For example, Amitai Etzioni, in discussing the differences between professional organizations and what he calls semiprofessional organizations, notes, "Part of the problem is due to the fact that the typical professional is a male, where the typical semi-professional is a female. Despite the effects of emancipation, women, on the average, are more amenable to administrative controls than men. It seems that, on the average, women are also less conscious of organizational status and more submissive in this context than men."[52]

Whether or not women *are* psychologically more submissive than men is still, in my opinion, an unresolved question. There is no question, however, that more women than men work in situations in which they are under the direct and continuous control of others—the others very often being men.[53] Reactions to this situation that are labeled submissiveness may merely be attempts to live with the inevitable. In examining the work behavior of women, we need to consciously assess the structural conditions, limitations, and demands of the work situation, rather than simply interpret behavior as a consequence of some female personality deficit.

Some of these conditions became clear in a reexamination I did with Donald Van Houten of the famous Hawthorne studies.[54] Our second look suggested that women workers may be subjected to special processes of selective recruitment and control that, in at least some situations, makes their work behavior look different from that of men. The Hawthorne studies,[55] which began in the 1920s, were the first extensive study of human relations in the workplace and had a great impact on subsequent writing and research. This research project was the first to demonstrate that increased autonomy and benign supervision in the work setting led to the development of group solidarity among workers. In one of the Hawthorne experiments, group cohesion seemed to foster a cooperative spirit toward management, along with increased output. In another experiment, group solidarity seemed to result in defiance of management directives and restriction of output. What was ignored in the many later interpretations of this research was that the group that increased output, the Relay Assembly Test Room, was all female, while the group that restricted output, the Bank Wiring Room, was all male. Van Houten and I looked at accounts of the original research in order to decide if these differences constituted evidence that the women workers were more submissive than the men workers.

We found in these research reports evidence of subtle and overt coercion in the treatment of the women workers. The women in the Relay Assembly Test Room were repeatedly confronted by powerful males—supervisors, researchers, and even the plant superintendent. Although these contacts were intended to be supportive, the power differential itself could have been subtly demanding of conformity to the expectations of the powerful. There were instances of open coercion as well as paternalistic rewards and manipulations. For example, the workers were asked for suggestions about the research and told that their opinions were important, but the power to make decisions was always retained by the male researchers and supervisors. "In summary," we argued, "it appears that the cumulative effect of coercion, paternalistic treatment, and special rewards resulted in a rise in productivity."[56] The rise cannot be attributed to female submissiveness; it *can* be attributed to the ways in which the women were treated by male superiors and to the position of the women in the sex hierarchy. The treatment of the men in the Bank Wiring Room was very different. In the absence of coercion and of special rewards, and to provide mutual protection, these men developed ways of controlling and limiting their production as a group.

Women may, indeed, be controlled by rewards and punishments that are somewhat different from those meted out to men and that are related to the norms of sex stratification in the work place. For example, many women secretaries and clerical workers may be rewarded with approval from their male supervisors for being attractive and may be punished with disapproval for being "unfeminine" and assertive. Of course, the punishment may be much more severe than mere disapproval. The power strategies available to women workers may be different from those available to male workers. For example, open and assertive power plays may be much more available to men than to women. Because such behavior is more expected from men, the sanctions for exhibiting it may not be as great for men. Similarly, this approach may explain the scattered evidence that women are disproportionately recruited into jobs demanding passivity—subordinate jobs in the office hierarchy or highly routine jobs in which machines largely control the work. Perhaps women are preferred for these jobs because of implicit understandings that women do not complain and that, if they do, there are other women available to take their places. I am arguing, of course, that it may be the structure of the work situation that produces the behavior, not the personality orientations of women workers.

Many of the problems I have been discussing here reflect the assumption that women workers operate in the same cultural-structural environment as men. The question, Why aren't women more assertive, more ambitious, more career-oriented? is essentially a question about why women aren't more like men, and it assumes that they work in the same world as men. We could assume, as suggested above, that women live and work in a different cultural-structural environment from that of men. In this environment they are viewed as outsiders in a place where they are not expected to be.[57] They are also seen as people who are by definition either too passive or too aggressive, people who have a proper place in supportive but not in leadership roles. If we made those assumptions, we might ask why women are not even more different from men and wonder where women find the tremendous capacity to persevere in a work world in which they are tolerated but rarely welcomed. It must take a high level of economic need as well as ambition, assertiveness, and career orientation to survive in such an environment. Differences between women and men could be seen as responses to different environments. For example, Kanter reports that the only fairly consistent differences between women and men shown in empirical studies of single-sex work groups occur in orientation toward interpersonal relationships and level of aspirations.[58] These can be interpreted, as she points out, as realisitic adaptations by women workers to reality.

The assumption that the core of feminine identity is the self as wife and mother affects not only the interpretation of findings but also the choice of questions to ask. For example, researchers rarely ask whether or not work, achievement, and competence are important to women as a source of meaning and satisfaction in life. Sociologists have considered this issue, primarily in the case of professional women,[59] but have not given it the extensive attention they have devoted to the meaning of work to male identity. Recent studies showing that married nonworking women have more mental health problems than either working married women or single women[60] suggest that paid employment may have much more significance for women than is implied by descriptions of women workers as less committed to and less involved in work than male workers.[61]

Bias in the Research Process

The conceptual problems I have discussed so far have a primary effect on what sociologists have seen as problems worthy of study, how they have conceptualized those problems, and how they have interpreted data. There is a further problem: the effect of sex can enter into the research activity

itself, clouding the vision of the observer and structuring the responses of
the observed. Researchers often see what they expect to see. If their expectations are that they will see passive and compliant behavior on the part of
women, that is what they are likely to see. If researchers are not aware that
sex might make a difference, they may miss some important aspects of a
situation simply because they are not looking for them. For example, in a
well-known study, Michel Crozier analyzed the patterns of work relationships in two French bureaucracies.[62] He paid little attention to the fact that
most of the workers in both were women, while most of the supervisors and
union leaders were men. In one bureaucracy, Crozier found conflict and
antagonism that he attributed to centralization and impersonality. Some of
the conflicts could just as well have resulted from antagonism between the
sexes, between women workers and their male supervisors who, in the es-
timation of the women, did not understand females.[63]

The sex hierarchy may also have an effect on the people who are being
studied, particularly if the researchers are male and the subjects are female.
It has been demonstrated that people often behave as they are expected
to behave, responding most to the expectations of those with power or authority.[64] Researchers often have some measure of authority, especially if
they are doing research in work settings under the sponsorship of management. Males generally have more power in this society than do females. The
combination of male researcher and female subject may, therefore, produce
findings quite different from those of a female researcher and female subject. The Hawthorne researchers, discussed above, were completely unaware
that their identity as male authority figures might have effects on the findings of their study. Even where no overt coercion or deception is used to get
research subjects or carry out the research, the fact that the investigator is a
male may be subtly coercive or manipulative, just as the presence of one or
two males in a discussion group of women may undermine the freedom of
the women to discuss the topics in which they are most interested. The general problem of response bias may also be escalated when male researchers
attempt to study females. We can at least speculate that women may be
more likely to give conventional responses to men than to women.

RESOLUTIONS

The first step in the process of correcting a bias is to make it visible, to
uncover its social sources and its hidden assumptions. When I talk about

correcting bias, I of course do not mean completely eliminating bias, in the sense of removing subjectivity and value commitment; I mean developing an alternative view of the world, with different values consciously articulated, allowing investigators to ask new questions, directed toward different goals.

Sociology has at least three possible political functions or consequences: (1) control—to maintain the status quo; (2) unmasking—to reveal how the status quo is maintained; and (3) liberation—to help change the status quo for the better. In my discussion of male bias in the study of women's work I have tried to demonstrate the processes through which much of the sociology of work has helped to maintain the status quo of sex stratification. I have also attempted to demonstrate that male bias is formed in all the major theoretical perspectives in sociology. I hope this analysis has had an unmasking effect. Much of the sociological study of women and work that

> **The first step in the process of correcting a bias is to make it visible, to uncover its social sources and its hidden assumptions.**

is being carried out today also has an unmasking function. This research is revealing the processes that consign women to sex-segregated jobs,[65] exposing the working conditions of poor women in the most menial jobs,[66] examining the mechanisms that truncate opportunity for women,[67] laying bare the reasons women earn less than men.[68] This unmasking effort is extremely important, for we know so little about the worlds of women—their subjective worlds and their social and material environments. Of course, we each know our own world, but we are only beginning to combine that knowledge into some composite understanding.

The new knowledge we are producing, which unmasks previously ignored realities, also makes a contribution to liberation, because we must know what stands in the way in order to anticipate necessary changes. For example, equality between the sexes in all aspects of paid employment is, I believe, an essential component of liberation.[69] Therefore, a sociology of women's work that is informed by a feminist dedication will emphasize questions that help us understand how women are kept unequal within the occupational structure; how organizational processes channel women into sex-segregated positions and keep them there; how sex segregation and the female–male wage gap are maintained; who profits and how, from sex inequality. Any future society I can imagine will be one in which many—perhaps most—people will work within large organizations. Unless we know how the conditions of women's work are controlled and shaped in male-run organizations, work inequalities may persist under even a radically changed economic and political system. Ultimately, to solve the riddle of female inequality, we are going to have to open that black box in the heads of men—their beliefs, their attitudes, even their sense of self—that, at least partially, leads them to exclude women from male preserves.

Equality is not liberation. Women could be equal to men, at least hypothetically, without either women or men achieving liberation. Women could be equally employed along with men in dreary and deadening work, for little pay, and without much choice. Liberation, on the other hand, involves some vision of human beings doing work that is personally and intrinsically satisfying as well as socially useful within a society that offers the individual wide choices. Our images of a liberated society are hazy; we need to give them more shape and focus. At the very least, a liberated life for women must imply a liberated life for men. Again, we see the need for a theory that encompasses all society: not just a theory of male society—or an alternative theory of female society—but a theory free of sex bias.

A sociology of liberation must give us ideas about how to get to the future as well as ideas of what it might look like. For this endeavor, I think we need to take seriously the very sociological insight of the contemporary women's movement: the personal is political and the political is personal. This is not a new idea. But, to understand how we can contribute to change, we need to find a better way of exposing and comprehending the nexus between the individual life, its meaningful interpretation, and the larger structural events that define the boundaries of the possible. This, of course, is what C. Wright Mills defined as the sociological enterprise;[70] our attempts to understand the situation of women simply make it more imperative that we see the enterprise in that way.

We also need a better understanding of what structures will allow liberation and how those might emerge out of present conflict and contradiction. In that regard, many serious feminists now consider themselves to be socialists, because they cannot imagine equality, let alone liberation, emerging within the capitalist economic system—a system in which the primary objective is profit making rather than equality and improvement of the conditions of life for all. They contend that as long as the unequal situation of women does not interfere with production and profits, little will be done to effect real changes. Under our present system, only when the productive machine has an unusual need for women will the barriers come down and serious innovative attempts be made to integrate women into the work force.

How a transition to socialism might come about and how women, along with men, might participate in that transition then become central questions in thinking about women's work and how it might be changed. Academic studies of women at work and treatises clarifying conceptual biases that denigrate women workers will not make much difference in the outcome, in whether or not we achieve a fundamental reordering of our economic and personal lives. Such intellectual enterprises may, however, make a small difference to some people—and big differences sometimes erupt ultimately from the accumulation of small differences.

NOTES

1 There is a growing body of feminist criticism of the male bias in sociology. See, for example, Joan Acker, "Women and Social Stratification: A Case of Intellectual Sexism," *American Journal of Sociology* 78 (1973): 936–45; Pauline B. Bart, "Sexism in Social Science: From the Gilded Cage to the Iron Cage, or, the Perils of Pauline," *Journal of Marriage and the Family* 33 (1971): 734–45; Jessie Bernard, "My Four Revolutions: An Autobiographical History of the ASA," *American Journal of Sociology* 78 (1973): 773–91; Cynthia Fuchs Epstein, "A Different Angle of Vision: Notes on the Selective Eye of Sociology," *Social Science Quarterly* 55 (1974): 645–56; Judith Long Laws, "A Feminist Review of the Marital Adjustment Literature: The Rape of the Locke," *Journal of Marriage and the Family* 33 (1971): 485–516; Marcia Millman and Rosabeth Moss Kanter, eds., *Another Voice* (Garden City, N.Y.: Anchor Press, Books, Doubleday and Company, 1975); Ann Oakley, *The Sociology of Housework* (New York: Pantheon Books, 1974); Dorothy E. Smith, "Women's Perspective as a Radical Critique of Sociology," *Sociological Inquiry* 44 (1974): 7–13.

2 Acker, "Women and Social Stratification," p. 938.

3 For reviews of the literature and discussions of needed research on women and

work, see Arlene Daniels, "Feminist Perspectives in Sociological Research," Rosabeth Moss Kanter, "Women and the Structure of Organizations: Explorations in Theory and Behavior," and Pamela Roby, "Sociology and Women in Working-Class Jobs," all in *Another Voice*, ed. Millman and Kanter. See also Martha Blaxall and Barbara B. Reagan, eds., *Women and the Workplace*, issue of *Signs* 1, no. 3, pt. 2 (1976).

4   I take the position that value-free social science is impossible. As human beings, we live within the subject matter we study as scientists; we are our own subject matter. As participants in society, we take sides, we have our own interests to look out for, we have personal standards and values. Our values help to define what we are. The ideas and words that we use reflect commonly held assumptions about how things are; values pervade our very process of thought. As thinkers, we must use the words and concepts available to us. Although sometimes we can and must develop new ones, new concepts reflect our changing experiences. We cannot step outside of our own heads and observe our subject matter from a distance. We can attempt to identify our own positions in the social world, to recognize our own values and biases, to make our assumptions conscious, to check and recheck our observations. This, I think, is as close as we can get to objectivity.

5   John Demos, "The American Family in Past Time," *American Scholar* 43 (1974): 442–46.

6   Ann D. Gordon, Mari Jo Buhle, and Nancy E. Schrom, "Women in American Society," *Radical America* 5 (1972): 4–66; Alice Kessler-Harris, "Stratifying by Sex: Understanding the History of Working Women," in *Labor Market Segmentation*, ed. Richard C. Edwards, David M. Gordon, and Michael Reich (Lexington, Ky.: Lexington Books, 1976); Heidi Hartmann, "Capitalism, Patriarchy and Job Segregation by Sex," *Signs* 1 (1976): 137–69; Elise Boulding, "Family Constraints on Women's Work Roles," *Signs* 1 (1976): 95–117.

7   Roby, "Sociology and Women in Working-Class Jobs," p. 203.

8   Nicole-Claude Mathieu, "Notes for a Sociological Definition of Sex Categories," *International Journal of Sociology* 5 (1976): 14–38; Joan Acker, "Introduction—Women and Work," *International Journal of Sociology* 5 (1976): 3–13.

9   Inge K. Broverman, Donald M. Broverman, Frank E. Clarkson, Paul S. Rosenkrantz, and Susan R. Vogel, "Sex-Role Stereotypes and Clinical Judgments of Mental Health," *Journal of Consulting and Clinical Psychology* 34 (1970): 1–7.

10   It may be that we cannot talk about the social existence of human beings in general. I frequently meet people who object on humanitarian grounds to this insistence on the theoretical importance of the sex dichotomy. "We are all human beings," they say. "There are more similarities than differences between the sexes. We must not see ourselves in opposition if we are to build a better

society." These noble sentiments help to hide the equation of the general and the male, the fact that the lives of females are different from the lives of males, and the fact that this differentiation pervades all aspects of our culture.

11 Smith, "Women's Perspective."

12 Mary L. Shanley and Victoria Schuck, "In Search of Political Women," *Social Science Quarterly* 55 (1974): 632–44.

13 Ibid., p. 641. See also Thelma McCormack, "Toward a Nonsexist Perspective on Social and Political Change," in *Another Voice*, ed. Millman and Kanter.

14 Bernard, "My Four Revolutions," p. 784.

15 Robert Seidenberg, *Corporate Wives—Corporate Casualties?* (Garden City, N.Y.: Anchor Press, Doubleday and Company, 1975).

16 One example of these efforts is work done at Cornell. See Kathryn E. Walker and William H. Gauger, *The Dollar Value of Household Work*, Information Bulletin no. 60 (Ithaca, N.Y.: Cornell University, New York State College of Human Ecology, n.d.).

17 The studies of women's careers that have been done deal almost exclusively with professional women; class bias, as well as sex bias, is a problem. See, for example, Cynthia Fuchs Epstein, *Woman's Place* (Berkeley: University of California Press, 1970); Ruth B. Kundsin, ed., *Women and Success: The Anatomy of Achievement* (New York: William Morrow and Company, 1974); Athena Theodore, ed., *The Professional Woman* (Cambridge, Mass.: Schenkman Publishing Company, 1971). However, see also Judith Mayo, *Work and Welfare* (Chicago: University of Chicago, Community and Family Study Center, 1975).

18 Acker, "Women and Social Stratification."

19 Isabel Sawhill, "Discrimination and Poverty among Women Who Head Families," *Signs* 1 (1976): 201–12.

20 For example, see Larry E. Suter and Herman P. Miller, "Income Differences between Men and Career Women," in *Changing Women in Changing Society*, ed. Joan Huber (Chicago: University of Chicago Press, 1973); Donald J. Treiman and Kermit Terrell, "Sex and the Process of Status Attainment: A Comparison of Working Women and Men," *American Sociological Review* 40 (1975): 174–200.

21 Valerie K. Oppenheimer, *The Female Labor Force in the United States: Demographic and Economic Factors Governing Its Growth and Changing Composition*, Population Monograph Series, no. 5 (Berkeley: University of California, Institute of International Studies, 1970); E. Waldman and B. J. McEaddy, "Where Women Work: An Analysis by Industry and Occupation," *Monthly Labor Review*, May 1974, pp. 3–13.

22 Marion Goldman, "Prostitution and Virtue in Nevada," *Society (Transaction)*, November/December 1972, pp. 32–38.

23   Olive Banks and J. A. Banks, *Feminism and Family Planning in Victorian England* (New York: Schocken Books, 1964).

24   Hilary Land, "The Myth of the Male Breadwinner," *New Society,* October 9, 1975, pp. 71–73.

25   Beth Niemi, "The Female-Male Differential in Unemployment Rates," *Industrial and Labor Relations Review* 27 (1974): 331–50; Sookon Kim, Roger D. Roderick, and John R. Shea, *Dual Careers: A Longitudinal Study of Labor Market Experience of Women* (Columbus, Ohio: Ohio State University, Center for Human Resource Research, 1972); James A. Sweet, *Women in the Labor Force* (New York: Seminar Press, Academic Press, 1973).

26   Christopher G. Gellner, "Enlarging the Concept of a Labor Reserve," *Monthly Labor Review,* April 1975, pp. 20–28.

27   Peter M. Blau and Otis Dudley Duncan, *The American Occupational Structure* (New York: John Wiley and Sons, 1967).

28   Otis Dudley Duncan, "A Socioeconomic Index for All Occupations," in *Occupations and Social Status,* ed. Albert J. Reiss, Jr., et al. (New York: Free Press, 1961).

29   Paul K. Hatt, "Occupation and Social Stratification," *American Journal of Sociology* 55 (1950): 533–43.

30   Duncan, "A Socioeconomic Index"; Christine E. Bose, *Jobs and Gender: Sex and Occupational Prestige* (Baltimore: Johns Hopkins University, Center for Metropolitan Planning and Research, 1973).

31   Bose, *Jobs and Gender.*

32   Peter Y. DeJong, Milton J. Brawer, and Stanley S. Robin, "Patterns of Female Intergenerational Occupational Mobility: A Comparison with Male Patterns of Intergenerational Occupational Mobility," *American Sociological Review* 36 (1971): 1033–42; Elizabeth M. Havens and Judy Corder Tully, "Female Intergenerational Occupational Mobility: Comparison of Patterns?" *American Sociological Review* 37 (1972): 774–77; Natalie Rogoff Ramsoy, "Patterns of Female Intergenerational Occupational Mobility: A Comment," *American Sociological Review* 38 (1973): 806–7; Andrea Tyree and Judith Treas, "The Occupational and Marital Mobility of Women," *American Sociological Review* 39 (1974): 293–302.

33   Bose, *Jobs and Gender,* p. 2.

34   Tyree and Treas, "Occupational and Marital Mobility," p. 294; Treiman and Terrell, "Sex and the Process of Status Attainment"; Bose, *Jobs and Gender.*

35   Bose, *Jobs and Gender,* p. 2.

36   Ibid., p. 146.

37   Ibid.

38　The results of the mobility studies are equivocal. DeJong et al. found no significant differences in the intergenerational mobility of women and men. Tyree and Treas, using different methods to reanalyze the same data, found considerably greater differences.

39　Bose, *Jobs and Gender;* Suter and Miller, "Income Differences"; Treiman and Terrell, "Sex and the Process of Status Attainment."

40　Bose, *Jobs and Gender,* p. 32.

41　Oakley, *Sociology of Housework.*

42　Karl Marx, *Capital* (New York: Modern Library, Random House, 1906), p. 536.

43　Barbara Deckard and Howard Sherman, "Monopoly Power and Sex Discrimination," *Politics and Society* 4 (1974): 475-82.

44　Hartmann, "Capitalism, Patriarchy and Job Segregation."

45　William H. Chafe, *The American Woman* (London: Oxford University Press, 1972).

46　Hartmann, "Capitalism, Patriarchy and Job Segregation"; Linda Gordon, "Are the Interests of Men and Women Identical?" *Signs* 1 (1976): 1011-18.

47　Wally Seccombe, "Housewife and Her Labour under Capitalism," *New Left Review* 83 (1974): 3-24; Margaret Coulson, Branka Magas, and Hilary Wainwright, "The Housewife and Her Labour under Capitalism—a Critique," *New Left Review* 89 (1975): 59-72; Jean Gardiner, "Women's Domestic Labour," *New Left Review* 89 (1975): 47-58.

48　Oppenheimer, *The Female Labor Force;* Barbara Deckard and Howard Sherman, "Monopoly Power and Sex Discrimination," *Politics and Society* (1974): 475-82; Barbara Ehrenreich, "The Health Care Industry: A Theory of Industrial Medicine," *Social Policy,* November–December 1975, pp. 4-11.

49　Kanter, "Women and the Structure of Organizations."

50　Friedrich Furstenburg, "Structural Changes in the Working Class: A Situational Study of Workers in the Western German Chemical Industry," in *Social Stratification,* ed. John A. Jackson (London: Cambridge University Press, 1968).

51　Ibid., p. 159.

52　Amitai Etzioni, *The Semi-Professions and Their Organizations* (New York: Free Press, 1969), p. xv.

53　M. Patricia Marchak, "The Canadian Labour Farce: Jobs for Women," in *Women in Canada,* ed. Marylee Stephenson (Toronto: New Press, 1973).

54　Joan Acker and Donald Van Houten, "Differential Recruitment and Control: The Sex Structuring of Organizations," *Administrative Science Quarterly* 19 (1974): 152-63.

55   F. J. Roethlisberger and William J. Dickson, *Management and the Worker* (Cambridge, Mass.: Harvard University Press, 1939); T. North Whitehead, *The Industrial Worker* (London: Oxford University Press, 1938), vol. 1.

56   Acker and Van Houten, "Differential Recruitment," p. 156.

57   McCormack, "Toward a Nonsexist Perspective."

58   Kanter, "Women and the Structure of Organizations."

59   E.g., Lynda Lytle Holmstrom, *The Two-Career Family* (Cambridge, Mass.: Schenkman Publishing Company, 1972); Alice S. Rossi and Ann Calderwood, eds., *Academic Women on the Move* (New York: Russell Sage Foundation, 1973).

60   Walter Gove, "The Relationship Between Sex Roles, Mental Illness, and Marital Status," *Social Forces* 51 (1972): 34–44; Lenore Radloff, "Sex Differences in Depression," *Sex Roles: A Journal of Research* 1 (1975): 249–66. These are only two examples of an emerging body of literature that is already showing conflicting and contradictory findings.

61   Constantina Safilios-Rothschild, "The Influence of the Wife's Degree of Work Commitment upon Some Aspects of Family Organization and Dynamics," *Journal of Marriage and the Family* 32 (1970): 681–91.

62   Michel Crozier, *The Bureaucratic Phenomenon* (Chicago: University of Chicago Press, 1964).

63   Acker and Van Houten, "Differential Recruitment."

64   Robert Rosenthal and Lenore Jacobson, *Pygmalion in the Classroom* (New York: Holt, Rinehart and Winston, 1968).

65   For example, see Gail Warshofsky Lapidus, "Occupational Segregation and Public Policy: A Comparative Analysis of American and Soviet Patterns," *Signs* 1 (1976): 119–36.

66   Rosalyn Baxandall, Linda Gordon, and Susan Reverby, *America's Working Women: A Documentary History—1600 to the Present* (New York: Random House, 1976); Nancy Seifer, *Nobody Speaks for Me!* (New York: Simon and Schuster, 1976).

67   For example, see Frank H. Cassell, Steven M. Director, and Samuel I. Doctors, "Discrimination within Internal Labor Markets," *Industrial Relations* 14 (1975): 337–44; James W. Grimm and Robert N. Stern, "Sex Roles and Internal Labor Market Structures: The Female Semi-Professions," *Social Problems* 21 (1974): 690–705; Edward Sternberg, "Upward Mobility in the Internal Labor Market," *Industrial Relations* 14 (1975): 259–65.

68   For a summary and critique of the many studies on this problem, see Francine D. Blau and Carol L. Jusenius, "Economists' Approaches to Sex Segregation in the Labor Market: An Appraisal," *Signs* 1 (1976): 181–200.

69 For one set of recommendations for achieving this goal, see *Exploitation From 9 to 5: Report of the Twentieth Century Fund Task Force on Women and Employment,* background paper by Adele Simmons, Ann Freedman, Margaret Dunkle and Francine Blau (New York: Lexington Books, 1975).

70 C. Wright Mills, *The Sociological Imagination* (New York: Oxford University Press, 1967).

Inequalities in the Labor Force: Three Sociological Explanations

Monica B. Morris

The facts pertaining to the present position of women in the labor force are well documented and widely known. It is not the purpose of this chapter to restate the statistics on inequalities in pay and opportunities in the world of work. (These are detailed in Francine Blau's chapter, above.) Suffice it to say here that women earn less than men for performing the same tasks; the salary gap has widened rather than narrowed over the years; and many fields remain virtually closed to women.

How can these facts be explained? Following the suggestion put forward in a recent paper by Slawski[1] I will attempt to apply a number of sociological theories to one concrete situation so that the relative value of each theory may be appraised.

Sociology offers several theoretical approaches for such an exercise, each approach based on somewhat different assumptions about the nature of humankind and about what constitutes reality. Some deal in grand theoretical terms with whole social systems, and others are used to discover the meaning conveyed by the flutter of an eyelid. The three theoretical approaches I

"Inequities in the Labor Force: Three Sociological Explanations," *International Journal of Contemporary Sociology* 12 (July–October, 1975). Reprinted by permission of the publisher and the author.

will apply here to the position of women in the work force are functionalism, exchange theory, and conflict theory. This chapter cannot study all aspects of these theories exhaustively or compare them in more than superficial ways. Its purpose is merely to demonstrate the usefulness of abstract theories in examining a concrete sociological question. Space limits preclude the inclusion of other theories that might also have been used to address the problem, including symbolic interactionism, ethnomethodology, and labeling theory.

As Slawski reminds us, theory is another word for *explanation.* If theories are at all useful they should also have some *predictive* power, and they should be testable. Predictive power does not mean that theories should enable us to foresee the future. Rather, given a theory, it should be possible to make some "if-then" statements and to test them in some way. We should, for instance. be able to say something like, "*if* the assumptions of our theory are sound, *then,* under such and such circumstances, we should expect that the following has a given probability of occurring." The greatest value of a theory, however, lies in its explanatory power.

FUNCTIONALISM

Functionalism has been the prevailing sociological model for describing society for three or four decades. Its greatest influence has been felt since World War II. When many of the sociologists teaching in colleges and universities today did their graduate work, functionalism was the theory they unquestioningly accepted. A large number of introductory textbooks in sociology have an underlying framework of functionalism.

Briefly and simply put, this theory applies the biological or organic analogy of *system* to society. In an organic system, such as the human body, there are a number of subsystems, each of which contributes to the equilibrium, homeostasis, or maintenance of the body. The digestive system, the respiratory system, the urinary system, among others, are interdependent, each contributing to and with the others to maintain the system as a whole. If one of the organs is sick or fails, the rest of the organs suffer, and, at worst, the entire body dies.

Subsystems are "healthy" as long as they contribute to the maintenance of the system as a whole. If they do not, they are seen as "pathological"; the system will try to expel or destroy the "sickness" before it destroys the system.

In the functionalist approach, the system to be maintained is the society.

Functionalist theory comes to us from anthropology, by way of Alfred Radcliffe-Brown and Bronislaw Malinowski, and the sociologists Emile Durkheim and Talcott Parsons. In anthropology it was used to explain, for instance, the existence and persistence of the family. The family is ubiquitous. It has existed in some form or another universally. Sociologists have devoted their energies to explaining a number of such persistent features in society in terms of their contribution to the maintenance of society. Social phenomena exist because they are "functional for" society or for certain segments of society.

We might assume from this that such features as crime and corruption in their various forms are seen as "pathological" or dysfunctional. Functionalist theory does not necessarily find this to be the case, however. Robert K. Merton, in his now classic essay on the corrupt political machine of the turn of the century[2] advises readers to put their moral indignation to one side, because such allegedly deplorable organizations contribute to the maintenance of society in many ways. The boss system, for instance, provided a means for otherwise unemployable immigrant groups to climb the ladder of prosperity—the Irish in particular used those means. It also enabled illegal goods and services, such as prostitution and gambling, to be made available to those who desired them.

When I first read Merton's piece as a college senior, I found it delightfully humorous, thinking it was written as a joke, tongue-in-cheek. It was not. Durkheim had used a similar argument about crime. A certain amount of crime in a society is necessary, he contended. It is functional for the maintenance of society; it helps to reinforce the boundaries of right and wrong. The punishment of some for their crimes serves as a reminder to the others that they may go so far but no farther. It allows us to see what evil looks like.[3]

How might functional theory be used to explain the position of women in the labor force? Some of the suggestions presented here will quickly be recognized as part of what Galbraith has termed "the conventional wisdom."

1. If girls and women are not encouraged to enter rewarding careers, they will be easily persuaded to leave the labor force, marry, and raise families. The family, it is constantly reiterated, is the backbone of society. The family serves to maintain the society in a number of ways, including caring for the young and helpless, socializing children into the ways of society, pro-

viding legitimate sexual outlets, serving as a haven of peace, comfort, and relaxation for those who must do the world's work. It is, then, functional for society to have women relatively uncommitted to careers. A large and imposing body of literature stresses the function of the family in maintaining society.[4]

2. Society is served better if women are not financially independent. This point follows from the one above. The family needs women to lead it; high-paying occupations, which might attract women away from their natural function of running the home, are not functional. Women are, *by nature*, equipped to bear children and nurse them. They are better equipped than men to deal with small children and household matters. There has never been a society without families, therefore society will not be able to survive without them. (Logicians among the readers may wish to argue with this.)

3. Women are less stable than men, more emotional. When their work or social relationships become difficult, they are likely to cry, scream, faint, or become inefficient. It is clearly less functional for society to place women rather than men in positions of responsibility. This argument is current in many forms. One example is: Women should not be commercial airline pilots because before and during menstruation—and perhaps after it—they are unable to remain cool, calm, and collected. By *nature* they are unsuited for work of major importance. If the rejoinder is made that some women (for instance, Golda Meir and Indira Gandhi) have obviously been able to handle the most important tasks of the nation, this is countered by noting that during their terms of office both these women were past childbearing and menstruation; in any case, these women are exceptional in that they "have the minds of men."

4. The positive functions that may be found for sexual inequality are countless, but as a final example an unusual but functional argument by George Gilder[5] must be mentioned. In *Sexual Suicide* Gilder maintains that if the present inequalities between the sexes are changed very much, the result will be the destruction of society as we know it and the development of a species of uncivilized males. In fact, he says, men are essentially unnecessary. Their only real function is sexual intercourse. Besides this, their role is trivial and easily dispensable. If we reduce their part in procreation by introducing large-scale artificial insemination, they are virtually useless. It is women who conceive, bear, and suckle the young. Childbirth can proceed, and usually does, without the father's help. It is the male, Gilder maintains, who is inherently inferior, whose role is societally contrived, and who must

be made equal by the culture. Woman's role is indispensable. The institution of marriage gives men a role and creates order where none would otherwise exist. Marriage has a civilizing effect on men. The argument, in brief, is that if women take over the tasks that society has found for men to do, men will lose their responsibilities—those culturally contrived responsibilities—feel themselves to be useless, and become sexual hedonists and parasites. "At this point," writes Gilder, "any serious government campaign for equal pay for equal work would be destructive."

While he agrees that the feminists are right when they say that: (a) men get paid more than women, (b) women are persistently discouraged from competing with men, (c) the minority of women who are sufficiently motivated can perform almost every job in society as well as men, (d) job assignments by sex are arbitrary and illogical, (e) most women do work because they have to, and (f) the lack of child-care facilities does prevent women from achieving real financial equality of opportunity, Gilder insists that if we change the present situation, where men have a position of economic superiority over women, men, in their search for ways to affirm their masculinity, will revert to brutality, perversion, and crime. The present situation of inequality is functional for the maintenance of civilized society and, we are warned, must not be undermined.

EXCHANGE THEORY

The names most closely connected with exchange theories are George Homans, Peter Blau, and John Thibaut and Harold Kelly.[6] Exchange theory has a number of variants. The one I will use here is a simple, economics-based theory that can be stated in terms of an equation: profit equals reward minus cost.

In attempting to explain the position of women in the work force, we must remember that, by and large, women have *not* risen up by the millions to protest their unequal place—and there are over 30 million women in the labor force. If any gains have been made in equalizing salaries in some fields, they have come through the efforts of a small number of dedicated persons, both male and female, mainly in professional and business organizations. It is notoriously difficult to organize women into labor unions and studies have found that women, after waging their long struggle for suffrage, generally voted in the same way as their men and frequently vote more conservatively.[7]

The women of the suffrage movement were seen by most other women of the time as nuts and loons. Even today, many women as well as men are likely to dismiss active feminists as lesbians, as women who cannot get a man, or as somehow unhappy and insecure people. For example, a recent review of an anti-women's-liberation book by a woman reviewer closes:

To the writer of this book—as to the writer of the present review— the vociferous Women's Libber, far from being free or adult or the "equal" of an adult of either sex, is a frightened creature wanting to retreat back into the irresponsibility of little girlhood, self-absorbed, happiest with other little girls, believing that menstruation is dirty and that men are baddies out to get her with machiavellian schemes—in a word, that very same inadequate being which she claims, in the circular argument of the Movement, that "male domination" has made her. The dependent, self-indulgent habit of blaming others for her own disabilities seems to be the last of the old-style feminine privileges which your dedicated modern feminist will abandon.[8]

Keeping in mind this perspective of some women on feminists, let's examine how exchange theory can explain the situation of women in the labor force. First we'll look at working-class women—those who are least likely to be among women's rights and women's liberation groups. For them, the work world may not appear pleasant. They watch their men leave home early in the day and return late, after having struggled through the rush-hour traffic both going to and coming from their place of work. After spending eight hours at the workbench, the men return home exhausted, often dirty, and unable to do much more than slump down in front of the television set.[9] For working-class women the world of work offers the same unattractive prospects and, if their men earn enough to allow them to stay at home, they consider themselves fortunate indeed.[10] The world of work does not offer working-class women opportunities for "self-fulfillment and personal satisfaction" and the "cost" of staying home to care for the family is a small one compared to the "reward."

Many middle-class women, whose career opportunities might be more attractive than those open to working-class women, appear to find that being women gives them very real rewards that might be reduced if their position in the work world were to equal that of men. Over and over again, middle-class women in my study samples and classes have demonstrated that rewards are found in the *security* that a man can offer them. When asked what they like most about being women, subjects frequently answer that they *like* the fact that they need not work unless they choose to—that they can lean on a man financially.[11] There are clearly some costs for this security—particularly loss of independence—but few women appear to prize independence very highly. Housework *is* seen as drudgery by many but, exchange theory would suggest, the rewards of not being committed to a career are still greater than the cost. If women were expected to be breadwinners equally with men—to compete with men for the same jobs on an equal basis— they might have to give up the choice they now have, to work or not, as they will. Men do not presently have that choice. Their rewards must stem from other sources. Exchange theory would predict that as long as women perceive the costs as lower than the rewards, the situation will remain largely unchanged. If they see the costs as too high, however, perhaps because of "raised consciousness," they will exert pressure for change.

An example supporting the version of exchange theory presented above is the unexpected outcome of Bell Telephone Company's policy, forced into effect by the government's Equal Employment Opportunity Commission, to open previously sex-typed jobs to both sexes. "Male" jobs were largely outdoor jobs with higher pay scales than "female," indoor jobs. Figures for the second quarter of 1973 showed that the number of women who accepted formerly male jobs was less than half that of men who accepted formerly female jobs. When questioned, some of the female employees said they feared that outside jobs would take greater strength than they possessed or subject them to more discomfort than they wanted to endure; others seemed to feel that such jobs were incompatible with their femininity.[12] In exchange theory terms, the costs of lower pay and dead-end prospects were still outweighed by the rewards of comfort and cleanliness and the opportunity to remain "feminine," as traditionally defined.

CONFLICT THEORY

Conflict theory differs from functionalism in that it posits *constant conflict,* rather than equilibrium, as the natural state of society. It is a theory that concerns itself with *power*—on all levels: between persons, between whole classes of persons, between nation states. Power may be of various kinds: economic, political, and physical, among others.

In simplest terms, society is divided into opposing groups: those who have power and those who have less power or no power. Power, according to Max Weber, may be defined as the ability of a person or a group of persons to work its will, even against the resistance of others.[13] Among the many varieties of power are *force,* or coercion of various kinds, and *authority,* or legitimated power. Legitimation grants power to certain persons by virtue of their position or status. Among the many theorists who have described the world in these terms are Weber, Sigmund Freud, Georg Simmel, and Karl Marx.

Conflict theory has several variations, so that the position of women in the work force can be explained by this theoretical view from a number of starting points. Randall Collins offers an explanation of women's inferior position in the labor force using sex drives and physical force as the basis to explain both the history of sexual stratification and its persistence.[14] He bases his argument on the work of Freud and Weber. Freud's major discoveries were the biologically universal drives of sexuality and aggression— and the repression of these drives through idealized moralism. From Weber, Collins takes the insight that people struggle for as much dominance as their resources permit; changes in resources lead to changes in the structure of domination; ideals are used as weapons both to unify status groups and to justify power interests.

Society, Collins says, is stratified by sex—a form of stratification different from the economic, political, or status-group stratification systems. In this stratification system women are subordinates. For example, even if women reach supervisory status, rarely do they supervise men. Their subordinate position at work may be viewed as a continuation of their subordinate position at home.

What is the basis for their subordinate position at home? The strong sexual and aggressive drives of human beings coupled with the fact that men are physically stronger than women have made men the sexual aggressors and women the sexual prizes. Strength is the crucial factor; men can force themselves on women, says Collins, and this coercion is influential in shaping women's role.

The present situation, Collins suggests, stems from the institution of sexual property. Men *own* women. Although we are not likely to think of male-female relations in these terms, the pattern of sexual ownership is supported by church and state: marriage is usually not legal until sexually consummated, sexual assault within a marriage is not legally a rape, and a major ground for divorce is sexual infidelity. Collins traces four types of social structures and describes the dominant sexual ideology and sex roles in each. These depend on the relative power of each sex. The tasks that women perform in the division of labor vary with the level of technology of the society.

In *low-technology tribal societies,* all members must work to survive. Premarital sexual permissiveness is found, because, with little economic surplus, women are not used as property in a marital bargaining system. With economic surplus and the change to the *fortified households* of preindustrial societies, the head of the household, or the estate, treats all subordinates as servants. Women are highly exploited sexually and as laborers. They become important as exchange property for the substantial dowries or brideprices they bring and are closely guarded so as to retain their market value. The ideals of premarital virginity and female chastity are an aspect of male property rights, enforceable only by men. Women are sexual objects for the men who own them.

As the state, rather than household heads, claims a monopoly on the legitimate use of violence, smaller *private households* replace the fortified household. While men remain heads of households and control the property, the relationship between men and women changes; women are seen not only as sexual objects and domestic laborers but also as companions. The ideology of romantic love prevails.

This ideology demands the chastity of women but, within marriages built on the notion of romantic love, women can make demands that husbands, too, be chaste and faithful and that women be cared for, cherished, and respected. Romantic love is a key weapon giving women a measure of power to rise from their subordinate position. Collins says, however, that the romantic ideal has one weakness as strategy for improving the status of women. It demands that women be relatively inaccessible as sexual objects; it is a strategy of remaining "hard to get." Women are offered devotion and care in return for giving men sexual access. This strategy, Collins says, serves to maintain the barrier between men and women. The idealization of women as people to be protected from conflict—in politics, economics, and aggressive sexuality—reinforces men's control of the economic world. Women, especially middle- and upper-middle-class women, have idealized themselves out of the competitive world. While they do exact deference from men, they are trapped in a narrow, female role.

As long as men controlled all economic resources, women's primary strategy was to emphasize the feminine ideal. In the Western world now, however, with an *advanced market economy,* women are free to go to school and to go to work. They are gaining some economic power, but, because their position in the occupational world is not equal to men's, female attractiveness still tends to be traded for economic prospects. This varies by social class. In general, the higher the income of the wife relative to that of her husband, the greater her power within the family. However, says Collins, force is still available as a male resource—even in the modern middle class. As a general principle, he suggests, the more male violence is allowed to be used in a sexual market, the more puritanical the female ideology is, that is, the more women themselves will condemn females who are readily available sexually. This, in turn, reinforces the existing inequality of the sexes. Women can use sexual attractiveness as a bargaining resource only to the extent that sexual favors are not simply given away. With further equalization of the economic positions of the sexes, sexual ideologies will shift in women's favor but, as long as men monopolize higher occupational positions, the emphasis on the trading of female attractiveness in return for economic gains remains. This is strongly reminiscent of the exchange theory explanation above.

Collins, then, uses sexual drives and aggressions as the basis for explaining the history of sexual stratification—a form of stratification that rests on sexual attractiveness itself. The two groups in basic conflict, in his view, are men and women.[15]

Another conflict theory approach, however, might come to a different conclusion. Karen Beck Skold[16] offers the suggestion that Marx's theory of the role of ideas in history should explain the origins and persistence of any type of idea. She couples it with Marx's belief that the basic conflict in society is between economic classes—not between men and women—to formulate another explanation. Skold suggests that the ideology of women as people to be cherished, protected, and supported is a distortion of real social relations. It conceals the fact of women's oppression—an oppression that she sees as benefiting the owners of the means of production (the rulers) in a number of ways, just as the ideology of the inferiority of blacks and other ethnic and religious groups benefited those owners. For example, when men and women are seen as having different roles to play, an attempt by women to change their position will be resented by men. The energy men use to defend their petty privileges against women draws their attention away from the fact of their mutual oppression by the ruling class. In similar ways, the division between blacks and whites, and among black groups themselves, diverts their attention and energy from what really oppresses them. The use of women as scapegoats, then, encourages men to vent their hostilities on women, a so-called inferior group, instead of directing their resentment against those who really control their lives. The system thus has a safety valve that increases its stability.

Further, women provide a huge pool of unpaid labor. Part of the ideal of the good, middle-class woman is that she engages in volunteer work—work that contributes untold millions of dollars to the coffers of the ruling class. The ideology of men as breadwinners encourages women to work for less pay uncomplainingly, benefiting no one but the employer.

Collins's explanation, from this Marxist point of view, would probably be seen as a "ruling class" explanation, which sets men against women instead of have-nots against haves.

DISCUSSION

It soon becomes obvious that the examples of functional analysis presented above are ways of *justifying* what is, rather than explaining it. This kind of reasoning, however, filters through from policymakers to the general public and becomes established as conventional wisdom—"facts" that "everybody knows," and that women subscribe to as wholeheartedly as men do. As John Maynard Keynes wrote:

> the ideas of economists and political philosophers, both when they are right and when they are wrong, are more powerful than is commonly understood. Indeed, the world is ruled by little else. Practical men, who believe themselves to be quite exempt from any intellectual influences, are usually the slaves of some defunct economist. Madmen in authority who hear voices in the air, are distilling their frenzy from some academic scribbler of a few years back.[17]

Further support for the notion that theories themselves may have an effect on what they purport to explain is offered by a recent letter to the editor of the *Los Angeles Times* about research and study to be conducted in India by American scholars:

> Ambassador Daniel P. Moynihan's statement that programs of Indian studies at American universities have benefitted India is erroneous. The idea that "an objective search for the truth" has universal relevance is a scholarly rationalization. . . . Research reflects the ethnocentric concerns of the researcher.
>
> Just as Margaret Mead gained notoriety by upsetting Western assumptions about sex roles and adolescence with her South Sea

research, American researchers today study caste because a caste-like organization appears to exist in the United States, and the role of Indian women sheds light on the feminist movement. . . . In their "functional" explanations of why and how caste and the traditional role of women persist, Western scholars present a conservative, idealized picture. Such research is not relevant to the goals of enlightened social reformers in India who seek to eliminate caste and enhance the role of women. Not only have Indian studies reflected Western biases, but the studies themselves helped to perpetuate features in Indian society which might have disappeared otherwise. It is possible that the caste system might have disintegrated with industrialization, but Western scholars' concentration on caste created a new social reality; Indians themselves quote Western "scholarly works" as scientific truth to support their caste and racial claims.[18]

Functionalism is of little use in prediction. It refers to the existence of a situation or item of social behavior in terms of its "function for" the maintenance or equilibrium of society. Since any behavior that does not contribute to the maintenance of society will be attacked or destroyed by the society, if an element exists and persists, it *must*, by definition, be functional. This is a tautological tangle from which there is no escape.

Exchange theory offers an apparently plausible explanation of why women tolerate their inferior position in the labor force. The explanation is limited in terms of its level of abstraction, because it deals with a concrete issue as viewed by the persons directly concerned. It leaves much still to be explained, such as the manner in which women are socialized to accept the feminine role, and how pressures are exerted on women, and men, to conform to societal expectations of their behavior. Within its limits, though, it appears to offer some predictions about the changes in profit that might be expected, given certain changes in women's awareness of rewards and costs.[19] Using exchange theory, it appears possible to explain either equilibrium or change, depending on the weights entered into each side of the equation.

Possibly explanations using exchange theory can be subsumed under the broader and more abstract conflict theory approach. Conflict theory, for instance, might account for a power structure that is able to persuade or coerce the relatively powerless into thinking styles that benefit the powerful. Marx maintained that the owners of the means of production also own the means of intellectual production, so that their ideas become the ideas of the ruled. It is possible, however, with "consciousness of kind," "class consciousness," or "raised consciousness" for the oppressed to realize their oppression and, with that realization, form a movement toward change.

CONCLUSION

Three kinds of theories have been used in an attempt to explain the position of women in the world of work. Some of the explanations presented will seem plausible to the reader, some will not. Some are readily testable, others not so readily. Plausible or not plausible, testable or not testable, the theories of scientific thought become amalgamated with political thought— an amalgamation that, Karl Mannheim has said, has both negative and positive effects. Scientific ideas become so diffused that even the average citizen looks for theoretical justifications of what exists. As Mannheim reminds us, theories can be used by the dominant to maintain their dominance or by the oppressed to gain release from their oppression. Both oppressed and oppressors can also *misuse* theory, citing only the aspects that serve them and casting a blind eye over those that would shake their beliefs or temper their desire to change things.[20]

NOTES

1 Carl Slawski, "Evaluating Theories Comparatively," *Zeitschrift für Sociologie* 3 (1974): 397–408.

2 Robert K. Merton, *Social Theory and Social Structure* (New York: Free Press, 1967).

3 Emile Durkheim, *The Division of Labor in Society* (New York: Free Press, 1964).

4 See, for instance, Rose Laub Coser, ed., *The Family: Its Structures and Functions,* 2d ed. (New York: St. Martin's Press, 1974); Talcott Parsons, "The Incest Taboo in Relation to Social Structure and the Socialization of the Child," *British Journal of Sociology* 5 (1954): 101–17; William F. Ogburn and Clark Tibbitts, "The Family and Its Functions," in *Recent Social Trends,* ed. President's Research Committee on Social Trends (New York: McGraw-Hill Book Company, 1934); and D. F. Aberle, A. K. Cohen, A. K. Davis, H. J. Levy, Jr., and F. X. Sutton, "The Functional Prerequisites of a Society," *Ethics* 60 (1950): 100–111. A useful, functionalist approach to the topic of this paper is given by Rose Laub Coser and Gerald Rokoff, "Women in the Occupational World: Social Disruption and Conflict," *Social Problems* 18 (1971): 535–52.

5 George Gilder, *Sexual Suicide* (New York: Bantam Books, 1975).

6   George Homans, *Social Behavior: Its Elementary Forms* (New York: Harcourt, Brace and World, 1961); Peter M. Blau, *Exchange and Power in Social Life* (New York: John Wiley and Sons, 1964); and John W. Thibaut and Harold H. Kelly, *The Social Psychology of Groups* (New York: John Wiley and Sons, 1967).

7   See, for instance, Corinna Adam, "Why Women Aren't Socialists," *New Statesman,* July 9, 1971.

8   Gillian Tindall, "Msconceptions," *New Statesman,* September 28, 1973.

9   Kenneth Lassen, *The Workers* (New York: Bantam Books, 1971).

10 See Lillian Rubin, "Liberation: Is the Definition Class-bound?" (paper presented at the annual meeting of the Pacific Sociological Association, Portland, Oregon, April 1972).

11 Monica B. Morris, "I Enjoy Being a Girl: The Persistence of Stereotypic Views of Sex Roles" (paper presented at the annual meeting of the American Sociological Association, Montreal, Canada, August 1974).

12 "Employment: Crossed Wires at Bell," *Time Magazine,* October 22, 1973, p. 79.

13 Max Weber, *The Theory of Social and Economic Organization* (New York: Free Press, 1947), p. 152.

14 Randall Collins, "A Conflict Theory of Sexual Stratification," *Social Problems* 17 (1971): 3–21.

15 For another version of the view of men as the oppressors of women, see Shulamith Firestone, *The Dialectics of Sex* (New York: Bantam Books, 1970).

16 Karen Beck Skold, "Woman's Place and Woman's Nature: The Theories of Knowledge of Marx and Durkheim" (paper presented at the annual meeting of the Pacific Sociological Association, Scottsdale, Arizona, May 1973).

17 John Maynard Keynes, *The General Theory of Employment, Interest and Money* (London: Macmillan and Company, 1936).

18 E. T. Jacob-Pandian, "Research in India," letter to the *Los Angeles Times,* October 10, 1973.

19 See Catherine Arnott and Vern L. Bengtson, " 'Only a Homemaker': Distributive Justice and Role Choice among Married Women," *Sociology and Social Research* 54 (1970): 495–507, for a discussion of the feelings of status deprivation that housewives may experience once they become conscious of status as a valued reward.

20 Karl Mannheim, *Ideology and Utopia* (New York: Harcourt, Brace and World, 1936), p. 37.

Girls' Socialization for Work

Carol Ireson

Conflict between traditional notions of femininity and occupational or intellectual achievement is experienced by many girls and women.[1] Achievement is highly valued and rewarded in American society, yet it is often viewed as unfeminine. This culturally induced conflict, buttressed by various social institutions, may partially account for women's limited success in the world of paid employment.

As pointed out in other chapters, women's potential for occupational achievement is underdeveloped, underutilized, and underrated in American society today. Occupational achievement is the major area of adult achievement, but about half the women in the United States are not pursuing paid occupations. Despite their talents, training, and individual identities these nonemployed women are almost all working at the same job: that of full-time homemaker. About two-thirds of all job categories are virtually closed to the women who are employed for pay, so nearly 80 percent of women employees are found in dead-end clerical, factory, service, or sales jobs, while only 40 percent of employed men end up in such jobs.[2]

The conflict between femininity and achievement affects girls long before they enter the work force. Both the academic achievement and the occupational aspirations of many girls seem to be adversely affected by socialization for femininity. In fact, some girls never confront this conflict; due to their early experiences, they espouse feminine goals (attractiveness, domesticity, helping others) early in their lives. Other girls achieve intellectually and maintain high occupational aspirations throughout childhood, but in adolescence they encounter increased demands for nonachieving, unambitious, feminine behavior. Some girls continue to achieve and aspire throughout adolescence but then change to more feminine behavior at marriage or during college. Some women never resolve this conflict by choosing one alternative. They attempt to achieve occupationally and also fulfill feminine goals of attractiveness, wifehood, and motherhood.[3]

In childhood and adolescence girls, unlike boys, seem to experience social

> **Both the academic achievement and the occupational aspirations of many girls seem to be adversely affected by socialization for femininity.**

pressure to be feminine rather than to achieve or to prepare for careers. This social pressure emanates from many sources, including family, school, and peers. Characteristics of the girls themselves may also affect their achievement behavior and occupational aspirations. This chapter describes girls' achievement patterns in detail and discusses the people and institutions that influence these patterns. First I describe how and when girls lower their academic achievement and limit their occupational aspirations. Next I discuss the various factors that support and encourage these patterns of decline and limitation. Finally I pinpoint new directions in the socialization of girls for achievement and future employment and new research that needs to be done in this area. Before beginning the discussion, however, I want to define a few basic concepts.

CONCEPTS AND DEFINITIONS

The basic thesis of this chapter is that socialization, particularly socialization into a female sex role, negatively affects girls' achievement patterns and occupational aspirations. Four basic terms, then, require definition: socialization, sex role, achievement, and occupational aspirations.

The interactional process by which a person's behavior and personality characteristics are modified according to the expectations of others is known as *socialization*.[4] Whenever a person acquires a new social position, for example, becoming a "teenage girl," the person is socialized into the role associated with that position. Socialization is a cumulative process; present socialization pressures depend, in part, on the individual's responses to previous socialization pressures.

Important socializing agents (the people and institutions that influence a person's behavior and characteristics) vary somewhat depending on the age of the person being socialized. In childhood, important socialization agents initially include family members, especially parents, and later include teachers, friends, and communication media. In adolescence all these agents are still important, but the influence of peers seems to increase. Boyfriends especially may be important socialization agents for many teenage girls.

A *sex role* is a set of behavior patterns and personality characteristics that is expected of a person solely on the basis of gender. The sex-role-related behavior and characteristics assigned to females in our society fall into two main groups: (1) incompetence (for example, dependence, submissiveness, passivity, and low self-confidence); and (2) warmth and emotional expressiveness (for example, talkativeness, gentleness, tactfulness, awareness of others' feelings, and the ability to express tender feelings).[5] As part of the adequate performance of sex roles, girls and women are generally expected to manifest these attributes of traditional femininity, espouse traditional sex-role values (such as "a woman's place is in the home"), and seek feminine goals (such as attractiveness, domesticity, and helping others).

Achievement is commonly defined as competent performance in a situation where standards of excellence apply. However, only certain kinds of achievement are relevant to a discussion of socialization for future occupational participation. In this chapter, then, achievement refers to intellectual and academic achievement. A girl's achievement may directly affect the kinds of jobs she can obtain as an adult. Achievement is not incompatible with the sex-role definitions of young girls, but it is often expressly excluded from the sex-role definitions of adolescent girls and adult women.

The occupations a person desires to enter indicate that individual's *occupational aspirations*. Research on the occupations that people expect to enter indicates that their *aspirations* may be quite different from their *expectations.* For girls, both aspirations and expectations may be influenced by sex-role socialization. In general, the process by which girls and boys come to know what kind of occupational role they will enact is called *occupational development.*[6]

Neglect and mythic thinking about girls and women characterize much of the theoretical work on occupational development. Most theorists of occupational development think of this as a decision-making process controlled by the individual. However, a girl's choices are constrained to a narrow range of occupations, and it is almost inevitable that she will be a housewife, no matter what else she may do (see Joan Acker's chapter, p. 134). Some theories ignore girls almost entirely; others claim to be applicable to females although their models are based on male occupational patterns. Even the best theory among these, while it could be extended to include girls and women, has serious shortcomings.[7]

Socialization is a complicated process. An outcome or product of socialization at one point may later influence other socialization outcomes. The learning and subsequent effects of traditional sex-role values illustrate this complex relationship between socialization outcomes and inputs. Two traditional sex-role values are: (1) the woman's place is in the home, and (2) the man is responsible for the economic support of the family. Girls may learn these sex-role values from parents who espouse traditional roles, from media that portray men and women in traditional roles, and from other sources. Once learned, the traditional values are likely to restrain girls' achievement behavior and limit their occupational aspirations in adolescence. Thus, sex-role values can be both an outcome of sex-role socialization and an input into this process.

Ridicule or rejection is the price a person pays for violating dearly held social expectations. These are powerful sanctions; they are powerful enough to induce girls to be somewhat "feminine," even though the male role is more highly valued in our society than the female role is.[8]

The socialization of girls for work roles in adulthood is complex. It is a cumulative process involving a wide variety of socialization agents, in which earlier socialization outcomes influence the course of later socialization. Figure 1 illustrates some of this complexity. At any given time, parents, peers, school, and other influences on a girl's socialization affect her characteristics, which in turn affect her academic and intellectual achievement and occupation-related behavior. The specific socialization agents and individual characteristics that influence achievement and occupation-related behavior are listed within the circles.

FIGURE 1   Socialization Influences that May Affect a Girl's
Achievement and Aspirations

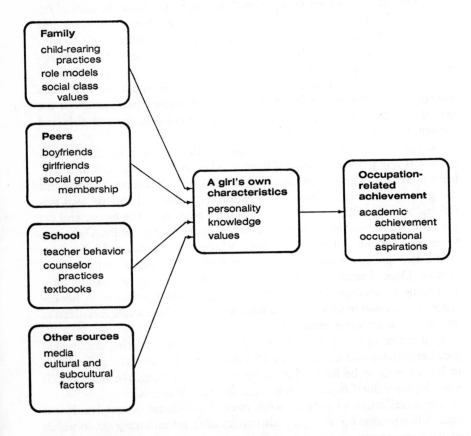

GIRLS' PATTERNS OF ACHIEVEMENT
AND OCCUPATIONAL DEVELOPMENT

Young girls are often excellent students with high aspirations for themselves, but in the course of growing up this excellence is often lost and the high aspirations often forgotten. How can I explain this tragic loss? I will begin by describing its occurrence.

The academic achievement of preadolescent girls is higher than that of boys: girls perform better in school[9] and are more likely than boys to work to their full ability in school.[10] Research done during the 1950s showed that early in adolescence a sizable minority of girls began to decline in school achievement and that this drop in grades continued throughout junior high and high school.[11] More recent research suggests that this adolescent decline may still occur.[12] If a girl's desire to achieve in school is still intact in late adolescence, it may be thwarted in college.[13]

A pattern of limitation is also evident in girls' occupational development. Young girls indicate much less varied occupational aspirations than young boys, and both boys and girls consider fewer kinds of jobs open to women. In adolescence and in college those females who still aspire to professional jobs often lower their aspiration in preparation for their actual work participation.

When asked, "What do you want to be when you grow up?" many young boys say they want to be adventurers: astronauts, famous athletes, scientists, or cowboys. Most girls are not so adventurous: they want to be teachers, secretaries, and stewardesses.[14] Even as preschoolers, girls choose fewer occupations than boys do[15] and are more likely than boys to project themselves into a parent role.[16] Tyler shows that the activity likes and dislikes of ten-year-old girls and boys are based on whether the activities are "appropriate" or "inappropriate" for their sex, rather than the "goodness" or "badness" of that activity. This rejection of inappropriate activity seems to occur very early, affecting their vocational choices in nursery school. Earlier research found that, even in first grade, girls did not develop skills (or aspirations) to match their interests.[17] Instead, their aspirations and skill development seemed to be guided by the feminine value of helping others.[18] Thus, in middle childhood and perhaps earlier, girls' activities and skills are often limited by being female: "inappropriate" unfeminine activities are rejected, and the feminine value of nurturance determines the selection of "appropriate" activities and skills.

The resulting narrow range of female job choices continues throughout childhood and adolescence, although fifth-grade girls are more likely than fifth-grade boys to say that a particular job is open to both sexes.[19] Thus Iglitzin finds that some girls want to be artists and veterinarians. Of the 7,000 ninth-grade girls first studied by Astin in 1960, 16 percent planned to have careers in the natural sciences or the professions (excluding teaching); except for nursing, these are male-dominated fields.[20] When these same girls were studied four years later, only 5 percent of them planned to have natural science or professional careers.

Girls' occupational aspirations often decline, then, at the same stage of the life cycle when substantial numbers of girls also decline in I.Q.[21] and in academic achievement.[22] This pattern of declining occupational aspirations also occurs during college as many women give up plans to become high-level professionals and plan instead to become housewives or middle-level professionals such as teachers.[23]

Thus, during their adolescent and college years, girls' academic achievement is likely to decline, and the relatively narrow range of occupations chosen by young girls becomes even further constricted. It seems likely that many achieving girls or girls who make sex-atypical career choices in childhood are forced by social pressure from family, school, or peers or by their own awareness of appropriate sex-role behavior either in adolescence or during college to give up their "unfeminine" achievement behavior and "unrealistic" career plans. This decline may occur in adolescence and college because during these years girls begin to look like adult women and are expected to act accordingly. Behavior, such as achievement-related behavior, that is incompatible with the adult sex roles of wife and mother may then be discouraged by socialization agents.

Spurred by the women's movement and other social forces, however, women's roles are rapidly changing, or so it is commonly believed.[24] Do females' occupational plans reflect any changes? Various studies give conflicting answers. In a national sample survey, high school juniors of 1970 were asked about their career plans, and their responses were compared with those of juniors from some of the same high schools in 1960. The girls of 1970 expressed much more interest in male-dominated job categories such as biological scientist, lawyer, and economist, and fewer planned to enter female-dominated occupational roles such as nurse, office worker, beautician, and housewife.[25] The other study compared college seniors in 1972 with those of 1961. There was little change in the career plans of either sex. Most women expected to become teachers, social workers, counselors, and nurses. The one major difference between the earlier and more recent classes in this study was the greater emphasis both sexes put on the importance of family and human relations—hardly a turn away from traditional values for the women.[26]

INFLUENCES ON GIRLS' ACHIEVEMENT AND OCCUPATIONAL DEVELOPMENT

Information about and social pressure affecting girls' achievement and occupational development emanate from several principal sources: family, school, peer group, and communication media. The characteristics of the girls themselves may also be an important influence.

Family Influences

Families, especially parents, can greatly influence girls' achievement behavior and girls' perceptions of and plans for employment. Influence may come from several specific familial sources: socioeconomic status, race, parents' child-rearing practices, the presence or absence of a brother, parental values communicated to daughters, and the presence or absence of an achievement-oriented mother.

Social class is positively related to academic achievement and occupational choice: the higher a girl's social-class origins, the higher her school achievement[27] and the higher the level of occupation she chooses.[28] Realistically, a working-class girl has a narrower range of occupations to choose from than a middle-class girl does. Her choices are also limited by the occupational aspirations of her parents and friends, by the values she expects her future husband to espouse, by lack of money for further education, and by lack of professional role models. As a result, more working-class girls than middle-class girls want to be office workers, and fewer want to be teachers or professionals.[29] Most working-class girls see obstacles to the achievement of even their modest aspirations: only one-fourth expect to enter the occupation of their choice, while most of the rest expect to be housewives.

Black children and adolescents generally have lower occupational aspirations than white children. In fact, black children seem to be less able to see themselves working at a job than white children. When asked what they wanted to be when they grew up, black preschool children were more likely than white children to say "a man" or "a woman" or an answer meaning an older child. White children were more likely to respond with a particular occupation.[30] Black adolescents were also less likely than white adolescents to see themselves as future workers in an occupation.[31] These differences by race in occupational development are undoubtedly influenced by black children's perceptions of the occupational effects of racism: that there are only limited opportunities to enter jobs and that these jobs are likely to be undesirable or low paying. Unlike many black children and adolescents, most black college women do see themselves as future workers in the labor force. A study of career orientations of white and black college women found that a large number of black women expected to have more career involvement than they wanted, while almost half the white women expected to have less career involvement than they wanted.[32]

Child-rearing practices may also influence girls' achievement patterns and occupational orientation. "Smother love" (maternal protectiveness and control) seems to be negatively related to the development of an achievement orientation in girls[33] and to work orientation in college women.[34] Maccoby notes that "nonhelpful" mothers may actually elicit achievement in daughters.[35] Hoffman speculates that the seeds of a later achievement decline are planted early in childhood when a girl's achievement behavior is linked to the satisfaction of social needs. As a result of more restrictive child-rearing practices, girls are more likely than boys to lack confidence in their ability to cope with their environment alone and are more likely to fear abandonment by those they depend on for help.[36] Thus, Hoffman says, girls are likely to achieve as long as the people they depend on approve of their achievement. When approval is no longer bestowed, these girls will stop achieving rather than risk alienating the people on whom they depend. However, other researchers do not find that girls are more sensitive than boys to social approval.[37] The rewarding of achievement behavior in young children has a positive effect on the achievement behavior of both sexes.[38] A decline in girls' achievement may simply be linked to a decline in social approval, from parents and others, for achievement.

The presence or absence of brothers may affect the career orientation of a girl. A smaller proportion of career-oriented college women than home-oriented women had older brothers in one study.[39] The number of brothers a girl has may also affect her parents' willingness and ability to finance her college education.[40] However, brothers do not always have a negative effect on career development: girls who have brothers are more likely to be tomboys, and tomboys are more likely to be achievement-oriented.[41]

Parental values and encouragement seem to be influential for both educational and occupational plans. A mother's encouragement of college attendance positively affects her child's educational plans, and her influence seems to have a greater effect if the child is a girl. This influence persists throughout the high school years.[42] Encouragement to attend college is also related to high occupational aspirations among teenage girls.[43] Parental values stressing competitiveness and the equality of women are also related to strong career orientations among white college women.[44] Parents' valuation of the domestic role for women adversely affects girls' occupational choices. Perrone shows this in a longitudinal study of teenagers and their parents from seventh through twelfth grades.[45] When the daughters reach the ninth and tenth grades, many parents begin to value the development of homemaking qualities and a domestic orientation in their daughters. By the late high school years, these parental values are reflected in their daughters' newly adopted occupational values: helping others and working with people. By the time these girls are seniors, their occupational aspirations are lower than boys' aspirations for the first time.

> **Parental values stressing competitiveness and the equality of women are related to strong career orientations among white college women.**

Fathers and mothers can have differing effects on their daughters. College women who aspire to careers in male-dominated fields are somewhat more likely than other women to perceive similarities between themselves and their fathers, but they do not feel particularly close to their fathers, and they do not select their fathers as role models. Instead, there is some evidence that these women are more likely than other women to have college-educated working mothers as role models.[46] A greater proportion of college women who are career-oriented than those who are home-oriented have working mothers.[47] The mother's occupational level, her interest in work, and her attitude toward the future employment of her daughter make her a more or less viable role model for her daughter.[48] For women, having a role model who successfully integrates work and family life seems to facilitate career orientation (as Kristin Moore and Isabel Sawhill point out in the next chapter of this book).

School Influences
Schools influence girls' achievement behavior and occupational develop-

ment both directly (by differentially reinforcing female and male achievement and by channeling girls toward female occupations) and indirectly (by encouraging traditionally feminine behavior and values). School structures and processes, interactions with teachers and counselors, and textbooks affect girls' achievement patterns and occupational plans.

"Open" schools, stressing a less structured curriculum and classroom than traditional schools, foster less stereotyped sex-role conceptions among elementary school children of both sexes, while traditional schools foster more stereotyped role conceptions.[49] It is not clear, however, which aspects of the two kinds of educational methods are responsible for the differing role conceptions.

Vocational education trains girls for low-paying jobs and, to compound the problem, provides a large pool of women for a narrow range of occupations (see Sally Baker's chapter below). Girls are usually trained in home economics, business education, and health, while boys receive training in agribusiness, technical fields, and skilled industrial trades. Vocational education graduates in business education (mainly girls) earn much less than technical education and industry trade graduates (mainly boys).[50]

High school mathematics is a "critical filter" in the job market, according to Sells.[51] Statistics from the University of California at Berkeley show that, of the freshman class, 57 percent of the men and only 8 percent of the women had taken four years of high school math. That amount of math is required for entry into the basic college math course at Berkeley, and that basic math course in turn is required for all majors except humanities, social sciences, education, and social welfare—the traditionally female fields. Thus high school girls who drop out of the four-year math sequence in high school effectively close off their career options in male-dominated fields. Adolescents in general think that boys are better at mathematics than girls are.[52] This is reflected in high school girls' lower concept of their ability in mathematics[53] and may influence girls' decisions to drop math.

High school training is different for boys and girls in some other ways. While girls are more likely than boys to discontinue math, they are more likely to be trained for unpaid domestic pursuits or low-paying office jobs. These training differences affect the college fields girls are able to enter and the jobs they eventually hold.

Teachers sometimes reward girls and boys for different kinds of behavior. Preschool girls in one study were more likely to gain the teacher's attention if they stayed near the teacher, while boys received attention whether they were nearby or across the room.[54] Overall, however, preschool girls and boys received the same amounts of praise or reward from their teachers.[55] Teachers of fifth and sixth graders have been found to rate socially oriented achievement more highly than task-oriented achievement among girls but not among boys.[56] In addition, teachers usually pay less attention to girls than to boys, and their attention to girls is likely to reinforce cultural notions of girls' incompetence: girls are more likely to be reprimanded by teachers for lack of skill and knowledge, while boys are reprimanded for violations of rules.[57] These studies suggest that girls are rewarded as preschoolers for staying near the teacher, rewarded in elementary school for achievement behavior manifested in a social way, and reprimanded in ways that tend to emphasize their academic incompetence when it occurs. Boys, on the other hand, are not as likely to be rewarded for teacher dependence and socially oriented achievement, and teachers' reprimands do not emphasize boys' academic failures.

As recently as the late 1960s counselors were being told by colleagues to give adolescent boys (but not girls) more opportunities to explore and plan for their future.[58] Counselors' perceptions of the "maleness" of certain occupations influence their advice to girls making career decisions.[59] Male counselors have more restrictive views of appropriate careers for women, so they may be somewhat more likely to steer girls toward traditionally female occupations.[60] A study of female counselors-in-training notes that a high proportion did not think men held rigid, stereotyped notions of appropriate female behavior. With this notion of male acceptance, perhaps these future counselors will find a wide range of career choices acceptable for the women they advise.[61]

One study showed that children's books strongly sex-type the activities and characteristics of females and males.[62] Career roles are similarly stereotyped. Sixteen different series of books commonly used in grades one through ten were reviewed for their portrayal of males and females in careers. Females enacted only 14 percent of the career roles portrayed. Males enacted five times as many career roles as females.[63]

Peer Influences

The influence of friends on girls' achievement patterns and occupational aspirations seems to be greater in adolescence than in childhood. Among adolescents, brilliance or academic success is devalued, especially if manifested in girls.[64] In Coleman's 1961 study of the adolescent subculture, intelligence was especially devalued in middle-class girls: popular, good-looking girls were much more likely than smart girls to be wanted as friends, to be respected as role models, and to gain admittance to the "leading crowd." In the lives of some teenage girls, achievement becomes unfeminine; many respond by getting lower grades or by hiding their high grades.

Boyfriends may be particularly influential in female achievement or occupational development, since girls and women often think the price for unconventional female achievement will be lowered marriage chances. There is some empirical support for this notion. In one study, for example, subjects judged women with feminine sex-role preferences to be more attractive and more desirable as work partners than women with masculine sex-role preferences;[65] and achievement-oriented women may be perceived as having masculine sex-role preferences. Thus, male support and encouragement of females with career goals may be important in the attainment of those goals, especially for females planning to enter male-dominated occupations. Explicit support of career plans rather than mere lack of disapproval may be necessary for high school girls, since they tend to attribute sex-role values to boys that are more traditional than the ones boys actually have.[66]

Black college women who are career-oriented are more likely than their home-oriented peers to report that the men in their lives prefer to have a working wife.[67] College women who aspire to male-dominated occupations have men friends who are more supportive of their career plans than the men friends of women planning feminine careers.[68] It is not clear that supportive male friends are responsible for their sex-atypical career orientation; however, college women determined to have a nontraditional career are more concerned with male support than other women are[69] and may seek out men who provide it.

The influence of girlfriends has been important in the past because females interpret to each other what boys and men expect of them. In the future, however, informal groups of nontraditional girls or women may be important sources of support and encouragement for individual women.

Media Influences

The communication media, particularly television, may also affect girls' occupational development. Children's television programs and advertisements portray sex roles in rigid stereotyped ways.[70] Children who frequently watch television reflect this rigid sex stereotyping in their own sex-role development and career choices. Elementary school children who watch more than twenty-five hours of television per week are significantly more traditional in their sex-role development than children who watch fewer than ten hours a week,[71] and heavy television watchers among preschoolers are more likely to show interest in sex-typed careers for themselves than moderate television watchers.[72]

Influence of Females' Own Characteristics

A girl's sex-role values seem to influence her academic achievement. Sex-role values, combined with knowledge and personality characteristics, seem to distinguish girls and women planning a career from those who do not have career plans. They also differentiate females who choose male-dominated occupations from those who choose female-dominated occupations.

"A woman's place is in the home," some women still believe. However, adolescent girls and young women who are achievement-oriented do not espouse traditional female sex-role values.[73] Teenage girls who agree that "a woman should not work if she has children," but should "care for the house and children while her husband works," are less likely to do well in school than are girls who disagree with these statements.[74] This relationship is strongest for older adolescents.

Another way girls may cope with the conflict between achievement and femininity is to define femininity in a general way. This enables girls who value femininity to remain feminine while continuing to achieve in areas typically labeled masculine. For example, if a girl thinks math is a feminine area of study, she is likely to want to do well in math. This will have a positive effect on her mathematical performance.[75]

High school girls holding traditional sex-role values about a "woman's place" do not plan as realistically for future employment as less traditional girls[76] and plan to discontinue their education earlier than less traditional girls.[77] College women espousing those traditional values are less career-oriented than nontraditional women.[78] Among college women, a desire for an early marriage and several children is related to home orientation and selection of a feminine career.[79]

Knowledge may also affect occupational interest. Knowledge of sex discrimination may have a negative effect, while knowledge of the job options available may have a positive effect. Adolescent girls' educational plans are negatively affected by their awareness of sex discrimination;[80] their occupational plans might also be negatively affected. Work experience, which increases information about occupations, is positively related to career orientation: college women with work experience in various jobs are more likely to select male-dominated occupations than those with little work experience.[81]

Personality characteristics may also be related to achievement and career orientation. For example, adolescent girls with high self-esteem have more realistic occupational plans than girls with low self-esteem,[82] while motivation to avoid success, also called "fear of success," may depress the achievement and aspirations of girls and women.[83] Fear of success has been used recently to explain the differential achievement of women and men. There are several criticisms of the concept, but its problems and potential deserve further discussion.

Horner, in attempting to account for the inconsistencies in studies of female achievement motivation,[84] proposed that fear of success inhibits female achievement motivation under competitive conditions. She saw fear of success as a result of the internalization of societal sex-role stereotypes that depict competition and achievement as unfeminine. Women who have internalized the dominant stereotypes then expect negative consequences from success in competitive, achievement-related situations. This expectation inhibits their achievement and their levels of aspiration.[85] In her original work Horner found that college women were much more likely to fear success (67 percent) than college men (8 percent). College women high in fear of success were also likely to perform better in noncompetitive than in competitive situations. Horner's later work shows that fear of success in females seems to increase from early adolescence (47 percent) to college (64 percent) and the work world (for example, secretaries: 88 percent). She suggests that fear of success in women may be responsible for women's relative lack of occupational success.

Horner's work stimulated much other research on fear of success. The additional studies and critiques of Horner's work have pointed out several shortcomings in the concept of "fear of success." Several studies were unable to replicate Horner's original findings that women have more fear of success than men[86] and that the performance of women who are motivated to avoid success is adversely affected by competitive conditions.[87] Other research suggests that the motive might be better labeled "fear of sex-atypical behavior." Horner's original work used stories written about success in a male-dominated field: medicine. Success in a female-dominated field (elementary education) elicited much less fear of success from female subjects.[88] One later study found that women with high fear of success perform better on female sex-typed tasks, while women with low fear of success perform better on male sex-typed tasks.[89] Other critics suggest that fear of success measures may not be tapping a motive at all but rather a cultural stereotype. Men also manifest fear of success when responding to female success in a "masculine" field. This indicates hostility toward females who do not fit traditional female stereotypes, rather than high fear of success.[90] Sex-role stereotypes reflect cultural norms; as a culture changes, these stereotypes may also change, affecting related personality characteristics such as fear of success. For example, a comparative study found higher fear of success manifested by Australian women than by American women. Australian sex-role changes have lagged behind American changes. Recently, women's fear of success in Australia has also declined.[91] In short, the personality characteristic called fear of success may have a negative effect on achievement and occupational participation, but this effect will not be certain until shortcomings in the concept are corrected and until the sociocultural context in which fear of success occurs is clarified.

NEW DIRECTIONS

Counteracting Traditional Occupational Socialization

Young girls, as we have seen, quickly learn about the narrow range of occupations open to women. The occupational aspirations of adolescent and college females are further constrained by various influences and tend to decline throughout the high school and college years. Parents, aspects of the school, peers, the media, and a female's own characteristics are all important influences in this process. Amazingly, some women who graduate from high school and college are still strongly career-oriented. What enables these women to emerge relatively unscathed?

Research already mentioned suggests certain childhood and family conditions that may affect girls' perceptions of the female role as well as directly influence their career orientation. Girls who are not subjected to "smother love" and are even given positive encouragement to undertake independent exploration may learn how to control their environment and develop self-confidence in their abilities. A mother who works to fulfill her own achievement needs may be a positive role model for her daughter, and other achieving role models might also be used by girls.[92] By late adolescence, girls who have not been overprotected and rewarded for dependence or "ladylike" behavior, who have been encouraged to develop their skills both in and out of school, and who have had achieving role models to imitate are more likely than other girls to be career-oriented.

These career-oriented women are likely to have a broader definition of "a woman's place" than more traditional women. They are likely to seek out men who agree with their ideas and who will support their career goals. Career-oriented girls and women, like most females, want to be "feminine," but their definitions of feminine may not be contradicted by careers in such occupations as law, medicine, computer programming, and cross-country truck driving.

Knowledge of the circumstances that tend to minimize the effect of traditional sex-role socialization on girls leads to knowledge of changes in family, school, and other areas that might weaken the effect of such socialization on most females. Some family changes that might facilitate girls' career development include child-rearing practices encouraging independence, exploration, and competence in girls and father involvement in a daughter's skill development. School changes might encompass increasing the number of achieving woman role models in all areas of school life, especially in administration and athletics, and actively recruiting female students into traditionally male courses (such as "shop" and physics) and vice versa. Fortunately, most schools are required by Title IX of the Education Amendments of 1972 to discontinue formal channeling by sex (see Mary Eastwood's chapter above). These changes may have a liberalizing effect on the sex-role definitions of future generations of children but will do little to help today's adolescents and adults who are unhappy with the characteristics they have developed in the course of their own sex-role socialization. Perhaps "de-stereotyping" programs could be developed for this group.[93] Since traditionally socialized women may lack competence outside the domestic sphere, such a program might attempt to develop female competence in other areas. The increase in competence that could result from any of these changes would be partly expressed in careers: more talented women would be free to develop their career interests, and would do so in a wide range of areas.

It is clear that changes in the female role toward greater career orientation can have only limited success unless changes also occur in the male role. Boys are much more stringently socialized into their sex role[94] and receive more rewards than girls do when they enact their sex role "properly." Thus, they are less likely to be aware of the costs of being the strong, competitive breadwinner. Ultimately, if women become more career-oriented without men becoming more family-oriented, more and more women will carry a "double burden" of both family and career responsibilities (see the chapter by Kristin Moore and Isabel Sawhill next).

The women's movement seems to have had some effect on the direction in which sex roles are changing, and it is likely to continue its influence. It is impossible, however, to disentangle the effects of the women's movement from other social influences on changing sex roles. In any case, the women's movement seems to be affecting female attitudes toward employment.

> ❝ It is clear that changes in the female role toward greater career orientation can have only limited success unless changes also occur in the male role. ❞

First, vociferous women's groups have highlighted the incongruence between women's traditional expectations of and training for an adulthood limited to domestic roles and their actuality of an adulthood of both domestic and work-related responsibilities. Secondly, women's organizations have lobbied for laws to require equal pay and equal employment opportunities for women. Thirdly, women's groups in many colleges and universities and in a few high schools function as support groups for career-oriented women. Fourthly, the growth of women's studies as a discipline now enables many women to learn about the forces that keep women in their "proper" place. This knowledge, properly applied, may help women cope more effectively with both overt discrimination and more subtle put-downs encountered in the work place.

Research Needed

Chronic neglect characterizes some areas of research, while other areas have only recently received attention. Research on the development of work orientation among females is not plentiful, and the research that exists is almost entirely concerned with white, middle-class females. Black, Chicana,

Oriental, and working-class white females have been consistently ignored. Since this chapter is a review of existing studies, it too has this shortcoming. The development of work orientation among all groups, especially those that are not white and middle class, must be studied in greater detail.

The increasing interest of boys and men in family values, as they begin to question "success" values, suggests that the father's role may be expanding.[95] More research is needed about the father's influence on a daughter's sex-role and career development.

Recent questioning of traditional sex roles suggests the need for more information about possible changes in sex roles that would affect female career development. Valuable information might include: family situations and forms of school organization that facilitate strong work orientation among females; the characteristics and background of males who are not intimidated by work-oriented females; and the process by which women become work-oriented in adulthood, after years of strongly traditional sex-role socialization.

Theory development relevant to female as well as male career development is sorely needed. If new research has inadequate theoretical bases, it will have only limited usefulness.

Finally, the temporal order of the various influences in the female career development process needs to be better understood. Times in the life cycle when various influences are most critical could be pinpointed, and possible causal links could be established. This, of course, calls for longitudinal research.

NOTES

1 Cynthia Epstein, *Woman's Place* (Berkeley: University of California Press, 1971). My thinking about female occupational socialization has been stimulated by the ideas of Judith Long Laws. Some of her views on this topic are contained in an article entitled "Work Aspirations of Women: False Leads and New Starts," *Signs* 1, no. 3, pt. 2 (1976): 33–50.

2 Sandra Bem and Daryl Bem, "Training the Woman to Know Her Place: The Power of a Non-conscious Ideology," in *Roles Women Play: Readings toward Women's Liberation,* ed. Michelle Garskof (Belmont, Calif.: Wadsworth Publishing Company, 1971), pp. 84–96.

3 The result of not resolving this conflict in favor of femininity is often labeled "role strain." However, the rewards of accumulating roles other than domestic roles should not be overlooked. Sieber suggests that people who enact many

roles are more highly regarded and allowed more flexibility in their performance of these roles than people who enact fewer roles. Sam Sieber, "Toward a Theory of Role Accumulation," *American Sociological Review* 39 (1974): 657–78.

4   Paul Secord and Carl Backman, *Social Psychology* (New York: McGraw-Hill Book Company, 1964).

5   Inge Broverman et al., "Sex-Role Stereotypes: A Current Appraisal," *Journal of Social Issues* 28 (1972): 59–78.

6   Samuel Osipow, *Theories of Career Development* (New York: Appleton-Century-Crofts, 1968).

7   Donald Super, *The Psychology of Careers* (New York: Harper and Row, Publishers, 1957); Barbara Putnam and James Hansen, "Relationship of Self-Concept and Feminine Role Concept to Vocational Maturity in Young Women," *Journal of Counseling Psychology* 19 (1972): 436–40; Ronald Pavalko, *Sociology of Occupations and Professions* (Itasca, Ill.: F. E. Peacock Publishers, 1971).

8   A. Rudy, "Sex Role Perceptions in Early Adolescence," *Adolescence* 3 (1968–69): 453–70; Ann Beuf, "Doctor, Lawyer, Household Drudge," *Journal of Communication* 24 (1974): 142–45.

9   W. Emmett, "Secondary Modern and Grammar School Performance Predicted by Tests Given in Primary Schools," *British Journal of Educational Psychology* 24 (1954): 91–98.

10 David Lavin, *Prediction of Academic Performance* (New York: John Wiley and Sons, 1965). For a detailed review of sex differences that might influence achievement, see Eleanor Maccoby and Carol Jacklin, *The Psychology of Sex Differences* (Stanford, Calif.: Stanford University Press, 1974).

11 Merville Shaw and John McCuen, "The Onset of Academic Underachievement in Bright Children," *Journal of Educational Psychology* 51 (1960): 103–8.

12 Patricia Campbell, "Feminine Intellectual Decline During Adolescence" (Ph.D. diss., Syracuse University, 1973); Eleanor Maccoby, *The Development of Sex Differences* (Stanford, Calif.: Stanford University Press, 1966).

13 Reported in Matina Horner, "Toward an Understanding of Achievement-related Conflicts in Women," *Journal of Social Issues* 28 (1972): 157–75.

14 Leona Tyler, "The Antecedents of Two Varieties of Vocational Interests," *Genetic Psychology Monographs* 70 (1964): 177–227; Beuf, "Doctor, Lawyer, Household Drudge."

15 E. Kirchner and S. Vondracek, "What Do You Want to Be When You Grow Up? Vocational Choice in Children Aged 3–6" (paper presented to the meeting of the Society for Research in Child Development, Philadelphia, March 1973) (ERIC document ED 076 244); Robert O'Hara, "Roots of Careers," *Elementary School Journal* 62 (1962): 177–80.

16 Kirchner and Vondracek, "What Do You Want to Be."

17 Leona Tyler, "Relationship of Interests to Abilities and Reputation among First Grade Children," *Educational and Psychological Measurement* 11 (1951): 255-64.

18 Tyler, "The Antecedents"; O'Hara, "Roots of Careers."

19 L. Iglitzin, "What Fifth Graders Think about Sex Roles," *Education Digest* 38 (1973): 39-41.

20 Helen Astin, "Stability and Change in the Career Plans of Ninth Grade Girls," *Personnel and Guidance Journal* 46 (1968): 961-66.

21 Campbell, "Feminine Intellectual Decline."

22 Shaw and McCuen, "The Onset of Academic Underachievement."

23 Geraldine Homall, Suzanne Juhasz, and Joseph Juhasz, "Differences in Self-Perception and Vocational Aspirations of College Women," *California Journal of Educational Research* 26 (1975): 6-10; D. Klemmack and J. Edwards, "Women's Acquisition of Stereotyped Occupational Aspirations," *Sociology and Social Research* 57 (1973): 510-25.

24 "Women of the Year: Great Changes, New Chances, Tough Choice," *Time,* January 5, 1976, pp. 6-16.

25 John Flanagan, "The First Fifteen Years of Project TALENT: Implications for Career Guidance," *Vocational Guidance Quarterly,* September 1973, pp. 8-12.

26 D. Gottlieb, "Work and Families: Great Expectations for College Seniors," *Journal of Higher Education* 45 (1974): 535-44.

27 Upper-class students, however, are an exception to this general finding. Lavin, *Prediction of Academic Performance.*

28 Steve Picou and E. Curry, "Structural, Interpersonal and Behavioral Correlates of Female Adolescents' Occupational Choices," *Adolescence* 8 (1973): 421-32; Astin, "Stability and Change."

29 Ethelyn Davis, "Careers as Concerns of Blue-Collar Girls," in *Blue-Collar World: Studies of the American Worker,* ed. Arthur Shostak and William Gomberg (New York: Prentice-Hall, 1964), pp. 154-64.

30 Kirchner and Vondracek, "What Do You Want to Be."

31 E. Ansell and J. Hansen, "Patterns of Vocational Development in Urban Youth," *Journal of Counseling Psychology* 18 (1971): 505-8.

32 Turner, "Socialization and Career Orientation"; Turner and McCaffrey, "Socialization and Career Orientation."

33 Lois Hoffman, "Early Childhood Experiences and Women's Achievement Motives," *Journal of Social Issues* 28 (1972): 129-56.

34 Sara Kriger, "*n Ach* and Perceived Parental Child-rearing Attitudes of Career Women and Homemakers," *Journal of Vocational Behavior* 2 (1972): 419-32.

35 Eleanor Maccoby, "Sex Differences in Intellectual Functioning," in *Development of Sex Differences*, ed. Eleanor Maccoby (Stanford, Calif.: Stanford University Press, 1966), pp. 25-55.

36 For a discussion of mastery and achievement, see Bernard C. Rosen and Roy D'Andrade, "The Psychosocial Origins of Achievement Motivation," *Sociometry* 22 (1959): 185-218.

37 Maccoby and Jacklin, *Psychology of Sex Differences.*

38 Vaughn Crandall, Anne Preston, and Alice Rabson, "Maternal Reactions and the Development of Independence and Achievement Behavior in Young Children," *Child Development* 31 (1960): 243-53.

39 A. Stewart and D. Winter, "Self-Definition and Social Definition in Women," *Journal of Personality* 42 (1974): 238-59.

40 Suggested by George Psathas in "Toward a Theory of Occupational Choice for Women," *Sociology and Social Research* 52 (1968): 253-68.

41 Jerome Kagan and Howard Moss, *Birth to Maturity* (New York: John Wiley and Sons, 1962); Elizabeth Douvan and Joseph Adelson, *The Adolescent Experience* (New York: John Wiley and Sons, 1966).

42 Denise Kandel and Gerald Lesser, "Parental and Peer Influence on Educational Plans of Adolescents," *American Sociological Review* 34 (1969): 213-23.

43 Picou and Curry, "Structural, Interpersonal, and Behavioral Correlates."

44 B. Turner, "Socialization and Career Orientation among Black and White College Women" (paper presented at the meeting of the American Psychological Association, Honolulu, 1972) (ERIC document ED 074 412).

45 Philip Perrone, "A Longitudinal Study of Occupational Values in Adolescents," *Vocational Guidance Quarterly* 22 (1973): 116-23.

46 Sandra Tangri, "Determinants of Occupational Role Innovation Among College Women," *Journal of Social Issues* 28 (1972): 177-99.

47 Elizabeth Almquist and Shirley Angrist, "Role Model Influences of College Women's Career Aspirations," *Merrill-Palmer Quarterly* 17 (1971): 263-79; Stewart and Winter, "Self-Definition."

48 Alberta Siegel and Elizabeth Curtis, "Familial Correlates of Orientation toward Future Employment among College Women," *Journal of Educational Psychology* 54 (1963): 33-37.

49 Patricia Minuchin et al., *The Psychological Impact of School Experience: A Comparative Study of Nine-Year-Old Children in Contrasting Schools* (New York: Basic Books, 1969).

50 J. Trecker, "Room at the Bottom—Girls' Access to Vocational Training," *Social Education* 38 (1974): 533-37, 607-8.

51   Lucy Sells, "High School Mathematics as the Critical Filter in the Job Market" (unpublished paper, University of California, Berkeley, March 1973).

52   John Ernest, *Mathematics and Sex* (Santa Barbara, Calif.: Mathematics Dept., University of California, 1976).

53   Wilbur Brookover, S. Thomas, and Ann Paterson, "Self-Concept of Ability and School Achievement," *Sociology of Education* 37 (1963): 271–78.

54   L. Serbin, K. D. O'Leary, R. Kent, and I. Tonick, "A Comparison of Teacher Response to the Preacademic and Problem Behavior of Boys and Girls," *Child Development* 44 (1973): 796–804.

55   Claire Etaugh, Gene Collins, and Arlene Gerson, "Reinforcement of Sex-typed Behaviors of Two-Year-Old Children in a Nursery School Setting," *Developmental Psychology* 11 (1975): 255.

56   Pauline Sears, *The Effect of Classroom Conditions on the Strength of Achievement Motive and Work Output of Elementary School Children*, Cooperative Research Project no. 873 (Washington, D.C.: U.S. Office of Education, 1963). Socially oriented achievement in this study was measured by the number of social remarks, interactions, and social actions that related to the school work being done.

57   L. Zach and M. Price, "The Teacher's Part in Sex Role Reinforcement," Yeshiva University (ERIC document ED 070 513).

58   Hubert Clements and M. Oelke, "Factors Related to Reported Problems of Adolescence," *Personnel and Guidance Journal* 45 (1967): 697–702.

59   Nancy Schlossberg and John Pietrofesa, "Perspectives on Counseling Bias: Implications for Counselor Education," *Counseling Psychologist* 4 (1973): 44–54.

60   Nancy Friedersdorf, "A Comparative Study of Counselor Attitudes toward the Further Educational and Vocational Plans of High School Girls," *Dissertation Abstracts International* 30 (1970): 4220–21.

61   Peggy Hawley, "Perceptions of Male Models of Femininity Related to Career Choice," *Journal of Counseling Psychology* 19 (1972): 308–13.

62   Lenore Weitzman et al., "Sex Role Socialization in Picture Books for Preschool Children," *American Journal of Sociology* 77 (1972): 1125–50.

63   Gwyneth E. Britton, "Sex Stereotyping and Career Roles," *Journal of Reading* 17 (1973): 140–48.

64   James Coleman, *The Adolescent Society* (New York: Free Press, 1961); A. Tannenbaum, *Adolescent Attitudes toward Academic Brilliance* (New York: Columbia University, Teacher's College, Bureau of Publications, 1962).

65   D. Shaffer and C. Wegley, "Success Orientation and Sex-Role Congruence as Determinants of the Attractiveness of Competent Women," *Journal of Personality* 42 (1974): 586–600.

66   J. P. McKee and A. C. Sherriffs, "Men's and Women's Beliefs, Ideals, and Self-Concepts," *American Journal of Sociology* 64 (1959): 356–63. Positive encouragement from family, school, and other sources is also important; see Jo Freeman, "How to Discriminate against Women without Really Trying," in *Women: A Feminist Perspective*, ed. Jo Freeman (Palo Alto, Calif.: Mayfield Publishing Company, 1974), pp. 194–208.

67   B. Turner and J. McCaffrey, "Socialization and Career Orientation among Black and White College Women," *Journal of Vocational Behavior* 5 (1974): 307–19.

68   Tangri, "Determinants of Occupational Role Innovation."

69   Hawley, "Perspectives of Male Models."

70   Sara Sternglanz and Lisa Serbin, "Sex Role Stereotyping in Children's Television Programs," *Developmental Psychology* 10 (1974): 710–15.

71   Terry Frueh and Paul McGhee, "Traditional Sex Role Development and the Amount of Time spent Watching Television," *Developmental Psychology* 11 (1975): 109.

72   Beuf, "Doctor, Lawyer, Household Drudge."

73   Kagan and Moss, *Birth to Maturity.*

74   Carol Ireson, "Effects of Sex Role Socialization on the Academic Achievement, Educational Expectations, and Interpersonal Competence of Adolescent Girls" (Ph.D. diss., Cornell University, 1975).

75   Aletha Stein, "The Effects of Sex-Role Standards for Achievement and Sex-Role Preference on Three Determinants of Achievement Motivation," *Developmental Psychology* 4 (1971): 219–31.

76   Putnam and Hansen, "Relationship of Self-Concept and Feminine Role Concept."

77   Ireson, "Effects of Sex Role Socialization."

78   F. Karmen, "Women: Personal and Environmental Factors in Career Choice" (paper presented to the meeting of the American Educational Research Association, New Orleans, 1973) (ERIC document ED 074 400); Turner, "Socialization and Career Orientation."

79   Klemmack and Edwards, "Women's Acquisition."

80   Ireson, "Effects of Sex Role Socialization."

81   Tangri, "Determinants of Occupational Role Innovation."

82   Putnam and Hansen, "Relationship of Self-Concept and Feminine Role Concept."

83   Matina Horner, "Sex Differences in Achievement Motivation and Performance in Competitive and Noncompetitive Situations" (Ph.D. diss., University of Michigan, 1968).

84 David McClelland et al., *The Achievement Motive* (New York: Appleton-Century-Crofts, 1953).

85 Horner, "Toward an Understanding."

86 Lois Hoffman, "Fear of Success in Males and Females: 1965 and 1971," *Journal of Consulting and Clinical Psychology* 42 (1974): 353–58; Adeline Levine and Janice Crumrine, "Women and the Fear of Success: a Problem in Replication," *American Journal of Sociology* 80 (1975): 964–74.

87 David Tresemer, "Fear of Success: Popular, But Unproven," *Psychology Today*, March 1974, pp. 82–85.

88 Carolyn Breedlove and Victor Cicirelli, "Women's Fear of Success in Relation to Personal Characteristics and Type of Occupation," *Journal of Psychology* 86 (1974): 181–90.

89 S. Karabenick and J. Marshall, "Performance of Females as a Function of Fear of Success, Fear of Failure, Type of Opponent and Performance-Contingent Feedback," *Journal of Personality* 42 (1974): 220–37.

90 Lynn Manahan, Deanna Kuhn, and Phillip Shaver, "Intrapsychic versus Cultural Explanations of the 'Fear of Success' Motive," *Journal of Personality and Social Psychology* 29 (1974): 60–64.

91 N. T. Feather and A. C. Raphelson, "Fear of Success in Australian and American Student Groups: Motive or Sex-Role Stereotype?" *Journal of Personality* 42 (1974): 190–201.

92 Tangri, "Determinants of Occupational Role Innovation."

93 Eileen Nickerson et al., *Intervention Strategies for Changing Sex Role Stereotypes* (Dubuque: Kendall/Hunt Publishing Company, 1975).

94 Maccoby and Jacklin, *Psychology of Sex Differences;* Ruth Hartley, "Sex-Role Pressures in the Socialization of the Male Child," *Psychological Reports* 5 (1959): 457–68.

95 Mirra Komarovsky, *Dilemmas of Masculinity* (New York: W. W. Norton and Company, 1976); Hoffman, "Fear of Success."

Implications of Women's Employment for Home and Family Life

Kristin A. Moore
and
Isabel V. Sawhill

Over the last few decades, an unprecedented rise in the employment rate of married women has significantly altered the economic role of women while the emergence of a new feminist movement in the early 1960s has influenced many people's perceptions of women's place in our society. Given women's traditional commitment to home and children—a commitment that now appears to be weakening as new options become available—it would be surprising if these changes had no impact on the American family. There is, in fact, evidence of widespread dislocation in that venerable institution. Demographers have faithfully recorded some of the essential changes. They have found that young women now marry at a later age, a dramatic upsurge has occurred in divorce rates, and birth rates have declined sharply, although the proportion of births occurring outside of marriage has risen (see table 1). While these changes cannot be definitively linked to changes in the social or economic position of women, there is some evidence that the two sets of trends are related, and the shifts of family structure that have

This is a slightly revised version of Kristin A. Moore & Isabel V. Sawhill, 'Implications of Women's Employment for Home and Family Life,' from *Women In the American Economy* by The American Assembly © 1976, Columbia University, New York, New York. Reprinted by permission of Prentice-Hall, Inc., Englewood Cliffs, New Jersey.

occurred to date may well be only minor harbingers of much more fundamental shifts to come.

The increased employment of women means that they have less time to devote to home and family and that they have more economic resources with which to choose a wider variety of life-styles—some of them less family-oriented—than in the past. These possibilities raise quesitons about the welfare of children, the size of families, the stability of marriages, the quality of relationships between men and women, the division of labor within the household, and the distribution of family income. What changes have already occurred in each of these areas, if any, and what kinds of new policy issues are raised by the prospect of further change? Can society adjust to, even plan for, these changes, or will we simply muddle through, as we have so often in the past?

THE FUTURE OF MARRIAGE

Economic and Social Bases of Marriage

In the past, women have had fewer opportunities to earn a living on an equal basis with men, and as a result marriage has been essential to their economic welfare. Economists—who view the married household as a small unit of production that allocates the time of its various members among different tasks according to each individual's talents—argue that, as long as women are at least as efficient as men in producing household goods and services but have lower market earnings, an efficient allocation of resources requires that women specialize in home production and men in market production. Through marriage each can gain the benefits of this specialization. Thus, the traditional division of labor between husbands and wives is in part economically determined, although social expectations clearly play a major role as well. The consequence of this particular division of labor is that wives are dependent on their husbands for the necessities of life that can only be bought in the market. Although much has been made of the implicit value of a housewife's services, the important fact is that, in our market-oriented society, homemaking services command a high return in the form of other goods, services, and prestige only within the context of the family (see Joann Vanek's chapter later in this book).

Even in our present, partially liberated culture, the most important decision a young woman faces is likely to be the choice of whom to marry.

Unlike her male counterpart, she must bear in mind that her social and economic standing may depend much more on the outcome of this decision than on her own education, family background, or occupational prospects. To be sure, these other factors help determine whom she associates with and eventually marries, but it is the marriage itself that secures her position in the social system. For this reason, a father traditionally worries about a young man's potential ability to support his daughter, a mother teaches her daughters to use female wiles to entice the "right" young man into marriage, and an adolescent girl may give more thought to marriage than to her own education or career.

In the past, women have had very little choice in these matters. Those who did not marry were viewed with pity and often had great difficulty earning a living. Few achieved high incomes or status in their own right. Those who married took on the usual domestic responsibilities of wife and mother happily in response to both social custom and a lack of good economic alternatives. This very specialization, of course, leads to still greater dependence, because over the life cycle a wife's productivity within the home increases relative to her productivity in the market, while her husband's productivity in the market increases relative to his productivity in the home. By the time a woman who has devoted herself to home and family reaches middle-age, she typically has few marketable skills that would enable her to support herself outside of marriage. Thus, she is more dependent than ever on a marital tie. Women's dependence on marriage is further reinforced by a shortage of alternative partners if the marriage is terminated. The ratio of unmarried women to unmarried men increases dramatically with age, partly because of higher mortality rates and partly because men tend to remarry women considerably younger than their first wives. As a result, female prospects for remarriage decline precipitously as women grow older.

Marrying and remaining married, then, are economic as well as social necessities for women deprived of an independent means of support. Men, too, tend to be bound to their marriages by a sense of social responsibility to their wives and children and by the knowledge that the costs of supporting more than one family may be prohibitively high.

One result of this state of affairs is the prevalence of what William Goode has called "empty shell" marriages—marriages in which there is little love or real caring but a reasonably high degree of stability because social and economic constraints inhibit formal dissolution of the marriage relationship.[1]

If this is a reasonable description of the traditional marriages that have characterized Western nations (with some modifications) since the Industrial Revolution, the next question is how marriages of the future will look (assuming marriage survives). How will they differ from those of the past?

If women move into the labor force in increasing numbers and gain a more favored position in the occupational structure, this will tend to undermine the traditional division of labor within the household and the interdependence this specialization implies. Marriages based on economic considerations alone will give way. The utilitarian basis of marriage will be eroded, and love, companionship, and perhaps children, will become the only reasons for maintaining a particular relationship. These marriages are likely to be less stable than marriages of the past, although those that do endure will probably provide greater satisfaction to the participants than economically motivated and socially constrained alliances.

At the present time, the institution of marriage lies somewhere between the totally egalitarian marriages that could emerge in the future and the highly traditional marriages of the past. Although almost half of American married women are working, their jobs are often viewed as secondary to their family responsibilities and their income as supplementary rather than essential. Partly for this reason, but also because of the strength of ingrained attitudes, men have continued to maintain their authority as household heads, to consider their work as primary, and to share little in the unpaid work of the household. Although most American marriages are based on a democratic commitment to shared decision-making, in fact they tend to be partnerships in which the wife is clearly the junior partner and there are "separate but equal" spheres of influence.

Effects of Women's Employment on Marriage and Divorce

Our discussion above suggests that the future of marriage is linked to changes in the economic and social status of women. There are already indications that when a young married woman has a high income she is less likely to marry (or more likely to postpone marriage) and that when a wife works and contributes to the family income a divorce is more likely to occur. A number of studies have now documented the inverse relationship between, on the one hand, women's high education, high earnings, or strong commitment to the labor force and, on the other, low rates of marriage or high rates of divorce (see figure 1).[2] Some of the data on this question make it impossible to conclude which is cause and which is effect—for example, one possible interpretation is that women who are not very marriageable or who choose not to marry have to work and therefore have a greater need to stay in school and to earn a good income. Another possible interpretation is that men find high-achieving women threatening or less desirable as mates. Some new research on this question, involving a representative national sample of families whose marital behavior was monitored over a period of years, shows that, other things being equal, the likelihood of divorce is greater where wives have had access to an independent source of income while married.[3] One plausible interpretation of this finding is that, among marriages that are tension-ridden or unsatisfactory for some reason, the costs of divorce are lowest for those in which the wives are capable of self-support. Another possibility is that failure to conform to societal norms

> ❝ A number of studies have documented the inverse relationship between, on the one hand, women's high education, high earnings, or strong commitment to the labor force and, on the other, low rates of marriage or high rates of divorce. ❞

about appropriate sex-role behavior is itself tension-producing for one or both spouses. We suspect that both interpretations are true. If we are right, the recent upsurge in divorce rates reflects both greater economic independence among women and the marital strains engendered by changing attitudes about the position of women. Once society has adjusted to more egalitarian norms, the divorce rate might decline somewhat, but if the economic achievements of women continue to undermine the utilitarian character of traditional marriages, a permanently higher rate of divorce is a likely outcome. Furthermore, as divorce becomes more common, it is by definition less deviant and is considered more acceptable; this change in attitudes further erodes the constraints that currently inhibit marital dissolution. Thus, while individual marriages may dissolve for countless reasons that have nothing to do with the changing status of women, it is this more fundamental change in sex roles that creates the environment in which these changing behavior patterns emerge.

At the same time, other forces are at work that may increase rather than reduce the stability of the family. Younger single women now have the economic resources to establish their own independent households before marriage to a much greater extent than they did in the past. Thus many do not need to marry in order to escape their parental homes. For this and other reasons, large numbers of them are delaying marriage: the average age at first marriage has moved up gradually since 1962. If this trend continues, or at least is not reversed, it may mean greater marital stability in the future, since marriage at an early age is highly correlated with later divorce or separation. Thus, as the economic imperatives for women decline, and as more permissive attitudes about premarital sex gain acceptance, it is quite possible that young people will choose a mate more slowly and wisely and that the resulting marriages will rest on more solid foundations.

Relationships between Husbands and Wives

A second consequence of women's greater commitment to work and increased access to economic resources is likely to be a shift in the relationships between men and women within marriage.

A number of studies have found that wives who are employed exercise a greater degree of power in their marriages. Marital power is higher among women employed full-time than those working for pay part-time or not at all, and it is greatest among women with the most prestigious occupations, women who are most committed to their work, and those whose salaries exceed their husbands'. Working women have more say especially in financial decisions. This tendency for employment to enhance women's power is strongest among lower- and working-class couples.[4]

The resource theory of Robert Blood and Donald Wolfe provides an explanation for these findings:

> The sources of power in so intimate a relationship as marriage must be sought in the comparative resources which the husband and wife bring to the marriage, rather than in brute force. A resource may be defined as anything that one partner may make available to the other, helping the latter satisfy his needs or attain his goals. . . . The partner who may provide or withhold resources is in a strategic position. . . .

Hence, power accrues spontaneously to the partner who has the greater resources at his disposal.[5]

Thinking along these lines, it does not seem surprising that employed women appear to have more power than nonemployed women: they contribute to family income, and their experiences on the job may provide them with valuable new knowledge and contacts. Of course, factors other than income can act as resources as well—for example, physical attractiveness, skill in cooking or entertaining, and a prestigious family background. Working women may lose power, too, if they have to seek help from their husbands to accomplish household tasks that the husbands consider part of the wives' role and that paid workers would not do or do as well (such as caring for sick relatives or running errands).

The existing literature on marital power has been criticized on the ground that concepts such as "resources" and "power," are difficult to measure and quantify objectively.[6] The basic theory outlined here, however, suggests that, as women move into the labor force and contribute a larger fraction of total family income, they will acquire new rights as wives and improve their bargaining position within marriage. The wife who once had to ask her husband's permission to buy a new dress will have a new freedom to decide the matter herself, in addition to the higher prestige that generally accrues to income-earning adults.

The Division of Household Work

Closely related to the issue of marital power is the question of how the employment of women affects both the division of tasks between husband and wife and the total amount of work done in the household. In general, husbands of working wives engage in slightly more child care and housework than do husbands of women who are not earning income, although it does not appear that the rapid movement of women into the labor force has been matched by a very significant increase in husbands' willingness to help around the house. Data based on household interviews with married couples in Detroit suggest that little change occurred in the distribution of household tasks between 1955 and 1971.[7] Of the tasks considered, three functions were preponderantly the wife's responsibility—doing the dishes, making breakfast, and straightening up the living room. Decisions about the house, the car, life insurance, and the husband's job, as well as responsibility for household repairs, tended to fall into the husband's realm; responsibility for grocery shopping, taking care of money and bills, and decisions about the food budget and the wife's employment were either joint concerns or fell within the wife's domain. Although some changes did occur in the allocation of tasks—for example, a greater proportion of husbands always got their own breakfasts in 1971—the more notable finding was a lack of the kind of change that we might have expected to accompany the movement of women from the home into the labor market. Indeed, in 1971, a *greater* proportion of women than in 1955 always did the grocery shopping and the evening dishes, and a smaller proportion made decisions about life insurance, what house or apartment to take, and whether they themselves should go to work or quit work. Perhaps it takes some time for an adjustment to be worked out, but it does not seem, at least in the short run, that women have traded one kind of work for another. Instead they seem to have taken on a new set of activities without forgoing their traditional responsibilities. Whether this is because men are still the primary breadwinners in most families (that is, they still have substantially higher earnings than their wives), or whether it simply reflects deeply ingrained male attitudes that are resistant to change, is difficult to say.

One sort of accommodation that working women have made is a reduction in the number of hours spent doing household tasks. Joann Vanek has reported that, despite new convenience appliances, nonemployed urban women spent an average of fifty-five hours per week in the 1960s doing household tasks that nonemployed rural women spent fifty-two hours on in 1924. Employed women, on the other hand, spent only half as many hours on housework. This difference holds true after accounting for the fact that full-time housewives have more children, younger children, less household help, a different social class, and a different marital status than employed women.[8] The latter may have lower housekeeping standards, purchase more goods and services in the market (restaurant meals, commercial laundering, etc.), or simply do their work more efficiently. As we have seen, working women get very little extra help from their husbands, so they must be compensating in other ways.

Adjustments for Men

Deciding who does the housework is only one area in which the increased employment of married women is likely to affect the lives of men, yet relatively little research has been done on these effects. The traditional male role has been as provider and protector. As women demand more male participation in activities traditionally defined as feminine, and as they begin to share and sometimes usurp men's traditional roles, some response on the part of men is inevitable.

Mirra Komarovsky[9] and more recently Matina Horner[10] have both written on the threat that female competence poses for males. Being married to a woman with a busy schedule, an income of her own, outside friendships and commitments to non-family-members may produce feelings of insecurity and perhaps bewilderment in a husband. The result may be strain or even resentment.

Although this kind of competition is uncommon at present, since so few women approach their husbands' earning abilities, it is likely to be more common as women pursue careers in earnest, without frequent interruptions,

> **66 Will men increasingly turn down overtime, refuse travel, and reject transfers because of the work commitments of their wives and the needs of their children? 99**

and as employers come to honor the slogan "equal pay for equal work." Even now the impact of women's employment is being felt. For example, Kristin Moore reports that white women who make as much or nearly as much money as their husbands are more likely to tell fear of success stories, emphasizing the difficulties and costs attendant on high achievement for a woman.[11] And Larry Long reports, in the next chapter, that men with working wives are slightly less likely to be involved in long-distance mobility. While the reason for this association is not presently clear, it seems likely that women with job attachments, experience, and seniority are more resistant to moves that may advance their husbands' careers at the expense of their own opportunities. The inability to locate suitable employment for both spouses may create strain.

Traditionally, the woman's job commitment has been viewed as secondary to her domestic responsibilities. A child's illness or a family crisis interrupts the mother's day rather than the father's, a tendency that Joseph

Pleck refers to as "the differential permeability of the boundaries between work and family roles for each sex."[12] Serious, steady commitment to a job by a woman will require that her husband share the dislocations and interruptions caused by family needs. A woman's home life has tended to intrude on her work life; a man's work life had tended to intrude on his family life. As the wife's employment comes to require the husband's contribution at home, it may become impossible for him to leave on frequent business trips, work overtime shifts, and bring work home in the evening. The man with a working wife may find himself at a competitive disadvantage compared to a man who can work sixty to seventy hours a week because his wife takes complete charge of the home front.

On the other hand, the man with a working wife may not need to work overtime himself and may find that his wife's income gives him the security to refuse demands from an employer that intrude on his home life. Vital statistics show that, at the present time in the United States, the life expectancy of males is sixty-seven years, whereas for females it is nearly seventy-five. In addition, life expectancy is increasing faster for females than for males. One factor in the relative disadvantage of men is probably the strain of employment. Many men may welcome both the opportunity to share the burden of family support with their wives and the chance to spend more time with their children.

The implications of these changes for male employment and life-styles are unclear. Will men increasingly turn down overtime, refuse travel, and reject transfers because of the work commitments of their wives and the needs of their children? If men are able to share the burden of family support and develop the ability to express their feelings and emotions more openly, will male mortality rates fall? The implications of the rising rate of female employment on the lives of males have yet to be seen and remain largely unexplored. But the reaction of men to greater participation by women in the world outside the home will be an important determinant of how rapidly and how smoothly changes occur and ultimately how society judges this evolution.

To summarize, married couples face new opportunities and new pressures as women's involvement in the world of work increases. These changes are likely to have a destabilizing impact on marriage, to improve the bargaining power and rights of wives, and to unsettle the lives of husbands. As women take on new responsibilities outside the home, they devote less time to housework and child care. To date, there is no evidence that most men have moved toward meaningful sharing of these tasks. A critical issue, then, is what will become of children in a society where almost everyone is committed to activities outside the home.

THE FUTURE OF PARENTHOOD

Child-Care Arrangements of Working Mothers

Although the total number of children under age eighteen in the United States has been declining because the birth rate is falling, the number of children with working mothers has been increasing rapidly.[13] In 1973, 44 percent of mothers were employed, compared to 34 percent in 1964 and 22 percent in 1950. Mothers of school-age children are even more likely to work—53 percent worked in 1973—although one-third of mothers with preschool children were employed as well. In fact, the number of preschool children with working mothers has increased by over one-third in the last decade.

The arrangements working mothers make for the care of their children vary widely. Although the proportion of children in day-care centers doubled between 1965 and 1970, these centers still provide care for only 10 percent of preschool children of working mothers. The remaining 90 percent are cared for informally—some in their own homes by a father, a sibling, another relative, or a paid worker, and some in the homes of family day-care workers.

Most family day-care workers who take in children are themselves mothers, and they take care of only a few children at a time. They choose this work so that they can stay home with their families while earning some money; sometimes their motivation is to provide company for themselves and their children as well. Parent satisfaction with these informal arrangements has been found to be high, although only 1 or 2 percent of these homes are estimated to be licensed, and the quality of care undoubtedly varies widely.

Since an estimated 6 million children under age six required some sort of child care in 1972, and only about 1 million were cared for in day-care centers or licensed homes, there is pressure for the federal government to provide day-care services on a greatly expanded basis. At least three different groups support an expanded government role in this area. One consists of women who believe that their opportunities or their ability to cope with the dual responsibilities of home and job are limited by the lack of day-care facilities. Another group is concerned about the early environment of children and has argued that quality child care can enhance child development and provide greater equality of opportunity for children from poor families. A third group feels that day-care programs will enable poor women who head families to work and thus reduce welfare costs. Opposition to federal involvement in day-care programs focuses on the cost, concern for the quality of mass child-care services, preference for home-centered family day care, and concern that the availability of low-cost child care might encourage people to have more children and thus aggravate population pressure.

Since quality day care is labor intensive and expensive, especially if it emphasizes child development rather than custodial care, much debate has raged about who should pay and how much. Parents are currently allowed a tax deduction for child-care expenses, and most proposals for an expanded government role include a sliding fee schedule that provides free or very low cost services to poor women.

Consequences for Children

Much of the controversy over whether women should work or not centers around the question of whether children are adversely affected if mothers delegate child care to other persons while they are away at work.

One reason for the expectation that maternal employment harms children lies in early research on young children separated from their mothers for long periods or placed in institutions. The severe deprivation of attention and stimulation that these children suffer tends to produce intellectual retardation and social apathy or unresponsiveness. These effects have been extrapolated to suggest that the children of working women will not develop adequately. However, the separation of mother and child for routine, brief, nontraumatic periods does not seem to be harmful if adequate substitute care is provided. Indeed, a number of studies have suggested that the children of employed women compare favorably in intellectual and social development with the children of mothers at home.

A more precise answer than this is impossible without specifying what *type of behavior* on the part of children is likely to be affected by a mother's employment and the total *circumstances* surrounding her employment. A review of several studies on these questions will illustrate the general point.[14]

Early studies explored the presumed association between maternal employment and juvenile delinquency. They found that boys from lower-income families who were inadequately supervised were more likely to be delinquents, and that the sons of employed women were more likely to be inadequately supervised. But it was the quality of supervision, rather than employment per se, that contributed to delinquency. In general, these early reports linking juvenile delinquency to maternal employment have since been qualified, as researchers have taken into account such critical factors as how the children were cared for in the mother's absence, the socioeconomic group studied, and the emotional health of the family.

It is often assumed that children of working women do poorly in school because their mothers have less time and energy to help the children with homework and other intellectual pursuits than mothers at home and because the working mothers may be disinterested in, or even rejecting of, their children. In fact, children of working women do not seem to suffer impaired academic performance. Several studies have even found a positive relationship between I.Q. scores and maternal employment, although one study did find that middle-class sons of working women received lower grades than those with mothers at home. In lower-class families, maternal employment is positively associated with academic performance for children of both sexes.

Children of working women have been found to be higher in achievement motivation and more likely to plan to attend college. Both these effects are slight, however, and researchers have often failed to apply appropriate controls. (For example, college aspirations may be linked to maternal employment because mothers are working to pay for tuition or because children from two-income families perceive college as economically feasible.) It does seem clear, though, that employed mothers provide their children, especially their daughters, with achievement models. (See the next section of this chapter and Carol Ireson's chapter above.) Predictably, college-educated daughters of employed mothers have higher career aspirations and achievements than the daughters of nonemployed mothers.

Employed mothers also tend to stress independence in their children. For example, the children of working mothers typically have more household responsibilities than the children of full-time homemakers. This stress on independence appears to be less true among well-educated women and women who enjoy their work, however. The latter seem to compensate for their employment by being especially nurturant toward their young children.

The natural maturation of the child may hold less threat for a woman with alternative satisfactions and commitments than for a mother who has invested all her time in home and family. Betty Friedan decries the softness and passivity of children raised by full-time housewives who are living vicariously through their children.[15] She argues that the child of a woman with a sense of self, with interests and a life of her own, will grow up to be a stronger and more resilient adult. A study by M. R. Yarrow and others illuminates this point.[16] Mothers were divided into four groups: satisfied homemakers, dissatisfied homemakers, satisfied employed women, and dissatisfied employed women. Satisfied homemakers scored highest on a measure of adequacy of mothering. Dissatisfied mothers scored lower, especially the dissatisfied homemaker. Women who stressed duty as the reason for being a full-time homemaker had the lowest scores on mothering. We might speculate that the children of dissatisfied homemakers would be better off if their mothers were employed.

The Yarrow study illustrates the importance of considering labor force participation as more than a simple employed–nonemployed dichotomy. A woman's motivation for working, her satisfaction with her job, the duration of the employment, her husband's opinion of her employment, the adequacy of child care, the amount of help received with housework, and the family's socioeconomic status all seem likely to influence the consequences of maternal employment for children. Further studies should control for these differences. In addition, the date when a study was conducted can affect the results. Research on women who worked during the 1950s, when public opinion generally held that women should be home with their children, may not apply to the 1970s. Finally, little attempt has been made to follow the longer-term achievements and mental health of children, as they are revealed over the life cycle, and their possible association with the mother's employment and other early influences. Until more research is done on this vital and complex question, it is difficult to come to firm conclusions.

Sex-Role Attitudes

Whatever the effects of a mother's employment on her children's welfare, the transmission of attitudes or values from one generation to the next is likely to be affected by the life-styles of today's parents. In this regard, one set of research findings from several studies shows that the children of employed mothers have a different concept of women's role than those whose mothers do not work.

In a study by Philip Goldberg, college students were presented with short professional articles on topics ranging from city planning and law to art history and dietetics. In some cases, a particular article was attributed to a female author and in other cases to a male author. In every instance, students evaluating the quality of the work rated the manuscripts attributed to male authors higher than the manuscripts attributed to female authors, whatever the topic.[17] These findings were later qualified by a replication of the original study by G. K. Baruch, which showed that the daughters of employed women were significantly less likely to devalue the articles attributed to women than were the daughters of full-time housewives.[18]

Another group of researchers studied sex-role stereotypes in an attempt to learn which traits were seen as masculine and feminine.[19] They developed a list of characteristics, such as "active" and "dependent," and asked samples of men and women to evaluate which traits typified males and which females. Traits categorized as typically male tended to reflect competence (independent, objective, active, competitive, logical, etc.) while those characterized as female tended to form a warmth and expressiveness cluster (gentle, sensitive, tactful, religious, etc.). When describing themselves, women conformed to the female stereotype, even to the point of saying that they were more passive and less rational and competent than men, as well as warmer and more expressive. Daughters of employed women were expected to have a different view of women, however. The researchers reasoned:

> A person's perception of societal sex roles, and of the self in this context, may be influenced by the degree of actual role differentiation that one experiences in one's own family. Maternal employment status appears to be central to the role differentiation that occurs between parents. If the father is employed outside the home while the mother remains a full-time homemaker, their roles tend to be clearly polarized for the child. But if both parents are employed outside the home, their roles are more likely to be perceived as similar—not only because the mother is employed, but also because the father is more likely to share child-rearing and other family-related activities.[20]

Daughters of working women did indeed perceive significantly smaller differences between males and females, compared to daughters of nonemployed women. In addition, while they did not differ from daughters of nonemployed women in describing women as warm and expressive, they did differ in describing women as relatively competent. Sons of working women also perceived smaller differences between men and women in warmth and expressiveness.

What these findings imply, of course, is that new experiences of women working tend to generate new attitudes about women that may significantly influence the sex-role behavior of the next generation of adults. This interaction between experiences and attitudes can become a powerful basis for a cumulative movement toward more equality between the sexes in the future. In the past, attitudes and experiences tended to reinforce one another to create a kind of cumulative inertia, but once the system has been disrupted, a return to the previous status is quite unlikely.

Some of the research we have discussed on sex-role attitudes showed that boys as well as girls were influenced by the example of a working mother. This is significant because, as we have seen, one area in which the status quo appears rather firmly entrenched is the amount of household work—including child care—that husbands are willing to undertake. But if young boys are growing up with a different set of attitudes from their fathers', they may behave differently when they become husbands and fathers.

If women continue to move into the labor force and a greater sharing of domestic responsibilities does not come about, then there are two other possible outcomes. One is a much greater delegation of child care and other personal services to public or private institutions outside the family. Another is that families will simply have fewer children. Just as employed women have cut back on the number of hours they devote to housework, they may choose smaller families to accommodate their need to supplement the family income or their interest in careers outside the home.

Employment and Family Size

Raising children and being employed are both extremely demanding in terms of time and energy. Women involved in both activities at the same time may find themselves stretched and drained to the point where they wonder whether they are succeeding at either role. In fact, work overload is such a serious problem for the mothers of preschool children that most of them do not seek paid work. Women with large families are also much less likely to work for pay than those with small families. The association between labor force participation and small families has been consistently documented and is illustrated in 1974 Census Bureau data for women aged thirty-five to forty-four who have ever been married: nonemployed women had an average of 3.3 children; women employed part-time had an average of 3.1 children; and women employed full-time had an average of 2.8 children.[21] Moreover, when asked about how many children they would like to have, or what they consider the ideal family size to be, women who work outside the home mention fewer children than other women.[22] A variety of reasons have been suggested to explain the association between female employment and small families. For one, women who are unable to have children may find compensating satisfactions in a job or career. Alternatively, women who enjoy working may deliberately limit their family size to enable them to work. Working may fulfill needs for self-expression, creativity, accomplishment, and social identity that childbearing has previously satisfied.

In addition, the cost of having a child is substantial, especially if a couple counts the value of the wages that a full-time homemaker could be earning in the paid market place. Ritchie Reed and Susan McIntosh have calculated the cost of rearing a single child through college: they estimated $33,000 for direct costs such as food and medical care, and then added the value of the wife's forgone earnings; the total cost was $84,000 for a woman with an elementary school education, $99,000 for a woman with a high school degree, $122,000 for a woman with some college or a four-year degree, and $143,000 for a woman with five or more years of college.[23] Second children are a bargain by comparison, since they simply lengthen the time the mother spends out of the labor force. The extra cost depends on how closely they are spaced; for example, the cost of a second child born two years after the first, is (depending on the mother's education) $47,000, $49,000, $53,000, or $56,000.

Clearly the cost of not working is highest for well-educated women, and this may be one reason why better-educated women have smaller families. However, there are other reasons why such women may wish to limit their family size. The jobs they hold tend to be more interesting, pleasant, and stimulating than the opportunities available to unskilled women. In addition, they are more likely to use effective contraceptives.

While the association between a woman's education, employment, and family size has been consistently documented, and many reasons have been proposed to explain the relationship, the cause-and-effect pattern is unclear. Do women have small families because they wish to work or need to work? Or do they have small families for other reasons, and then find that they simply have more time to work? If a significant number of women are limiting their fertility because of the practical difficulties of combining motherhood with work, then increasing the availability of day-care facilities and husbands' participation in housework and child care could reduce the barriers to childbearing and bring about a rise in fertility. On the other hand, if women who work have smaller families because working satisfies needs that they would otherwise meet by having babies, then it is unlikely that changes in day care and in the division of labor between husbands and wives will affect the birth rate much. Linda Waite and Ross Stolzenberg argue that women develop their plans for employment and child bearing jointly and simultaneously—that is, plans for work affect plans for having children and vice versa. They find there is a reciprocal causation, but women's employment plans have somewhat more influence on fertility than fertility has on employment plans.[24] If this is so, it is an important finding.

If women's employment plans are an important determinant of family size, and if women's participation in the labor market continues to increase, the current fertility rate, which is already at an all-time low, may drop still further. Provision of more social supports, such as day care, could modify this by enabling women to combine work and family responsibilities more easily. On the other hand, emerging attitudes about women's roles, about the economy, and about population and environment may diminish people's preferences for having children compared to other possible uses of scarce time and resources.

One distinct possibility is that many families will continue to have strong positive feelings about children but will be forced to curtail childbearing so that wives can contribute to family income. Having a second earner in the family often makes the difference between just getting by and establishing a solid position within the ranks of the middle class. Thus, it may become increasingly difficult for women to *choose* to stay home and to forgo the standard of living that two-career families enjoy. Americans have always judged their economic well-being not by the absolute value of their income but rather by their position relative to other families in the income structure. If most families have two incomes, families with one earner may feel disadvantaged by comparison. This brings us, then, to still another interesting question about the future: What will happen to the distribution of family income if more and more women choose, or feel required, to work?

CHANGES IN THE DISTRIBUTION OF FAMILY INCOME

Although real incomes and standards of living have risen quite dramatically over the past three decades, the distribution of income among families has hardly changed at all. In 1972, for example, the 20 percent of families at the top of the income pyramid received slightly more than 40 percent of aggregate family income while the 20 percent at the bottom received only 5 percent. The total economic pie has been divided about that way ever since the end of World War II.

How does the participation of women in the labor force affect the income distribution of families? If all wives worked and women had the same earning potential as men, then the answer would depend only on who married whom. A tendency for high-income men to marry high-income women would exacerbate the degree of income inequality relative to a world in which only husbands worked.

Of course, at present, less than half of all wives work, and this fact complicates the analysis, because the labor force participation of women tends to be negatively related to their husband's income but positively related to their own income prospects. The net result is that the labor force participation of wives increases as husbands' earnings rise up to the average earnings for all husbands, but then it falls at higher levels. Overall, this causes the current distribution of income to be somewhat more equal than it would be if wives did not work at all. Moreover, according to Lester Thurow and Robert Lucas, the increased participation of women in the labor force over the past twenty-five years has tended to reduce the relative inequality of family income.[25] The stability of the overall income distribution among families, noted above, evidently reflects offsetting influences of other factors; if more and more wives had not gone to work, those factors would have led to greater inequality. So, the desire to keep up with the Joneses and to reduce disparities in income may indeed have been a potent force in bringing more women into paid employment.

An example of how this phenomenon has worked in the past is provided by an analysis of the income differentials between black and white families. Because a greater proportion of black wives than of white wives have traditionally been in the labor force, differences in the income status of black and white families have not been as great as the racial inequality in individual earnings. More recently, however, the labor force participation rate of white wives has surpassed that of black wives for the first time, causing a decline in the relative income position of black families.

This recent development may be a harbinger of greater inequality in family income distribution generally. If there is an influx of relatively well-educated, high-earning women into the labor force—women who in the past married high-earning men and worked less frequently than wives in lower-income families—family incomes will become more unequal in the future. People might then react with demands for more egalitarian tax policies to offset the greater disparity in standards of living.

CONCLUSIONS AND POLICY IMPLICATIONS

In most of the preceding sections, we have not given explicit attention to the policy issues raised by the changes we have reviewed. But policy questions are lurking just below the surface of the discussion.

Clearly, the potentially profound repercussions on home and family life of women's greater work attachment necessitate a rethinking of public policies in such diverse areas as Social Security, divorce, alimony, child support, welfare, and income tax laws. These laws are based on the assumption that the vast majority of women are homemakers financially dependent on their husbands.[26] (See also Mary Eastwood's chapter above.) Such laws need to be retailored to fit a world in which that assumption is false at least as often as it is true. Already working wives are pressing for a revision of Social Security and income tax laws that discriminate against two-earner families; if they succeed, someone else will have to bear the cost. And we may yet see a backlash if highly paid men and women pool income through marriage and exacerbate the disparities in family income.

Women's market participation also has implications for fertility and marital stability that will change the shape of the future. For example, we have seen that improvements in women's economic opportunities appear to be a significant factor increasing divorce rates, currently the highest in the history of this country and the industrialized Western world. This, in turn, has contributed to an unprecedented increase in female-headed families. Indeed, the absolute increase in the number of children living in single-parent homes exceeded the increase in the number living in two-parent homes during the decade of the sixties. In part, this is an indictment of our welfare system, which, according to recent research, may well contribute to the growth of single-parent homes. But given the size of the female-headed family population and the poverty these families often face, we need to reevaluate our present alimony and child support laws. Evidence suggests that these laws are working very poorly.[27] Reform might entail designing a national child support policy, establishing a fund to which all absent parents would contribute and from which all eligible children would draw; or, it might take the form of a system of divorce insurance, an idea that the New York State legislature is already considering.

While these are all interesting questions, the most critical issue is how the essential work of a household, especially child care, can be organized, as women move increasingly into the labor market. The possibilities run the gamut from wholly private, nonmarket arrangements, through increasing market organization, to substantial public involvement in the financing and provision of services. Will husbands and wives work out a new division of

> ❝ The potentially profound repercussions on home and family life of women's greater work attachment necessitate a rethinking of public policies in such diverse areas as Social Security, divorce, alimony, child support, welfare, and income tax laws. ❞

labor on a voluntary partnership basis? Certain women are agitating for this, but, as we have suggested, the record on male–female sharing of home tasks is quite thin. Does the lack of sharing result from ingrained attitudes or the absence of appropriate financial incentives? Will either attitudes or incentives shift enough in the future to produce new behavior patterns?

In the event that husbands do not come to share home responsibilities equally with working wives, how will the work of the home sector get done? Will the private market organize ways to carry out these functions, as it already has with capital goods for the home, paid domestic help, household maintenance organizations, and day-care services? Before these private mechanisms can develop, will they be overtaken by plans to socialize household work and to pay some or all household workers out of public funds— for example, a trust fund to which all parents or all adults contribute to

FIGURE 1   Percentage of Women and Men
Thirty-five to Forty-four Never Married and Divorced, by Income

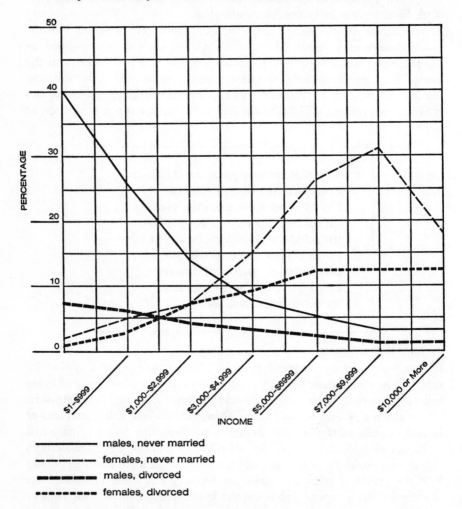

———————— males, never married

— — — — — — females, never married

▬▬ ▬▬ ▬▬ males, divorced

▪▪▪▪▪▪▪▪▪▪ females, divorced

Source: Drawn from Census Bureau data tabulated in E. Havens, "Women, Work and Wedlock: A Note on Female Marital Patterns in the United States," in *Changing Women in a Changing Society,* ed. Joan Huber (Chicago: University of Chicago Press, 1973), p. 217.

pay for individual or group care for all children? Will public involvement go beyond paying people to do household tasks and develop large-scale direct programs to provide household services, with child care as the leading element?

These are some of the policy issues we need to examine. At the present time most individuals or couples are making their decisions and plans alone, with little counseling or social support. The rules are changing, and the final outcome, as well as much about the intervening process, is unclear.

Few social scientists think the family is going to disappear. However, the lower birth rates and increased labor force participation of women will almost certainly continue to change their personal rewards, their power relationships, their role expectations, and ultimately perhaps the definition and prevalence of marriage. More research, discussion, and debate are needed if social scientists and government decision makers are to plan intelligently for the future and if individuals are to embark on that future confidently.

TABLE 1   Women's Divorce Rates, Marriage Rates, Average Age At Marriage, and Childbirth Rates, 1940–73.

	1940	1950	1960	1970	1971	1972	1973
Divorces per thousand married females aged fifteen and over	9	10	9	15	16	17	18
Marriages per thousand unmarried females aged fifteen and over	83	90	74	77	76	78	74
Average age of females at marriage	21.5	10.3	20.3	20.8	20.9	20.9	21.0
Births per thousand women aged fifteen to forty-four	79.9	106.2	118.0	87.9	81.8	73.4	69.2

Sources: U.S. Department of Commerce, Bureau of the Census, *Statistical Abstract of the United States, 1974* (Washington, D.C.: Government Printing Office, 1974); U.S. Department of Health, Education, and Welfare, National Center for Health Statistics, *Vital Statistics Report,* various issues (Rockville, Md.: Health Resources Administration, various dates).

NOTES

1 William Goode, "Family Disorganization," in *Contemporary Social Problems,* ed. Robert Merton and Robert Nisbet (New York: Harcourt Brace Jovanovich, 1971), pp. 467–544.

2 E.g., Hugh Carter and Paul C. Glick, *Marriage and Divorce: A Social and Economic Study* (Cambridge: Harvard University Press, 1970).

3 Heather L. Ross and Isabel V. Sawhill, *Time of Transition: The Growth of Families Headed by Women* (Washington, D.C.: Urban Institute, 1975), chap. 3.

4 Stephen Bahr, "Effects on Power and Division of Labor in the Family," in *Working Mothers,* ed. Lois Hoffman and Ivan Nye (San Francisco: Jossey-Bass, Inc., Publishers, 1974), pp. 167–85.

5 Robert Blood and Donald Wolfe, *Husbands and Wives: The Dynamics of Married Living* (New York: Free Press, 1960).

6 David Heer, "The Measurement and Bases of Family Power: An Overview," *Marriage and Family Living* 25 (1963): 133–38; Constantina Safilios-Rothschild, "The Study of Family Power Structure: A Review 1960–1969," *Journal of Marriage and the Family* 32 (1970): 539–52.

7 Otis Dudley Duncan, Howard Schuman, and Beverly Duncan, *Social Change in a Metropolitan Community* (New York: Russell Sage Foundation, 1973).

8 Joann Vanek, "Time Spent in Housework," *Scientific American,* November 1974, pp. 116–20; see also her chapter below in this volume.

9 Mirra Komarovsky, "Cultural Contradictions and Sex Roles: The Masculine Case" in *Changing Women in a Changing Society,* ed. Joan Huber (Chicago: University of Chicago Press, 1973), pp. 111–22.

10 Matina Horner, "Toward an Understanding of Achievement-related Conflicts in Women," *Journal of Social Issues* 20 (1972): 157–75.

11 Kristin A. Moore, "Fear of Success: Antecedents, Consequences and Correlates of Fear of Success Imagery among Females in a Metropolitan Survey Sample" (Ph.D. diss., University of Michigan, 1975).

12 Joseph Pleck, "Work and Family Roles: From Sex-patterned Segregation to Integration" (paper presented at the 70th American Sociological Association Meeting, San Francisco, August 1975).

13 U.S. Senate, Committee on Finance, *Child Care Data and Materials* (Washington, D.C.: Government Printing Office, 1974).

14 Lois Hoffman, "Effects on Child" in *Working Mothers,* ed. Lois Hoffman and Ivan Nye (San Francisco: Jossey-Bass, Inc., Publishers, 1974), pp. 126–66.

15 Betty Friedan, *The Feminine Mystique* (New York: Dell Publishing Company, 1963).

16 M. R. Yarrow, P. Scott, L. DeLeeuw, and C. Heinig, "Childrearing in Families of Working and Non-working Mothers," *Sociometry* 25 (1962): 122–40.

17 Philip Goldberg, "Are Women Prejudiced against Women?" in *And Jill Came Tumbling After: Sexism in American Education,* ed. Judith Stacey et al. (New York: Dell Publishing Company, 1974), pp. 37–42.

18 G. K. Baruch, "Maternal Influences upon College Women's Attitudes toward Women and Work," *Developmental Psychology* 6 (1972): 32–37.

19 Inge Broverman, Susan Vogel, Donald Broverman, Frank Clarkson, and Paul Rosenkrantz, "Sex-Role Stereotypes: A Current Appraisal," *Journal of Social Issues* 28 (1972): 59–78.

20 Ibid., p. 73.

21 U.S. Department of Commerce, Bureau of the Census, "Fertility Expectations of American Women, June 1974," Series P-20, no. 277 (Washington, D.C.: Government Printing Office, 1975), p. 35, table 16.

22 E.g., Jeanne Clare Ridley, "Number of Children Expected in Relation to Non-familial Activities of the Wife," *Milbank Memorial Fund Quarterly* 37 (1958): 227.

23 Ritchie Reed and Susan McIntosh, "Costs of Children," in *Economic Aspects of Population Change,* ed. Charles Westoff and Robert Parke, Jr., Report of the Commission on Population Growth and the American Future, vol. 2 (Washington, D.C.: Government Printing Office, 1972), pp. 333–50.

24 Linda Waite and Ross Stolzenberg, "Intended Childbearing and Labor Force Participation of Young Women: Insights from Nonrecursive Models," *American Sociological Review,* in press.

25 Lester Thurow and Robert Lucas, *The American Distribution of Income: A Structural Problem* (Washington, D.C.: Government Printing Office, 1972).

26 Martha W. Griffiths, "Requisites for Equality." in *Women and The American Economy: A Look to the 1980's,* ed. Juanita Kreps (Englewood Cliffs, N.J.: Prentice-Hall, 1976).

27 Carol-Adaire Jones, Nancy M. Gordon, and Isabel V. Sawhill, "Child Support Payments in the United States," Working Paper no. 992–03 (Washington, D.C.: Urban Institute, 1976).

Women's Labor Force Participation and the Residential Mobility of Families

Larry H. Long

Many young households give the impression of being on the basis of perfect equality. But as long as the man retains economic responsibility for the couple, this is only an illusion. It is he who decides where they will live, according to the demands of his work; she follows him from city to country or vice versa to distant possessions, to foreign countries; their standard of living is set according to his income; the daily, weekly, annual rhythms are set by his occupation . . .

This article attempts an empirical test of this statement by deBeauvoir (1949) as to place of residence—and changes in place of residence—on the part of married couples. The question is this: To what extent does the wife's work influence the residential mobility of families? If the wife's job is invariably subordinated to that of the husband, then there should be no difference in the likelihood and frequency of migration between families in which the wife works and those in which she does not work.

Reprinted from *Social Forces* vol. 52, March 1974. "Women's Labor Force Participation and the Residential Mobility of Families" by Larry H. Long. Copyright © The University of North Carolina Press. This article is from a larger study supported in part by the Center for Population Research of the National Institute of Child Health and Human Development.

The most reasonable alternative hypothesis is that families in which the wife works are less migratory than those in which she does not work. The basic reasoning behind this hypothesis is that an opportunity for the husband to move is seldom accompanied by one for the wife and that under such circumstances husbands make sacrifices by not moving out of deference to the wife's career. But finding only small differences in migration propensity between families in which the wife works and those in which she does not work could probably be taken as evidence that the employment of wives exercises only a small influence on the migration patterns of their husbands.

Also to be investigated is the effect of the wife's employment on short-distance moving. Little has been written about the subject, and in the absence of previous empirical investigation we test the hypothesis that there are no differences in the likelihood of short-distance mobility between families in which the wife works and those in which she does not work.

The hypotheses to be tested are part of a larger question as to the family contexts in which decisions are made about residential mobility. Researchers often point out that most analyses of migration are in terms of persons as units, although most moves are made by entire families (see Beshers, 1967; Glick, 1965). Furthermore, most migration analyses consider only men. The purpose of this article is to investigate the effect of one aspect of family structure—the wife's employment status—on the family's residential mobility and to encourage other research into the way family structure influences migration and how migration influences family structure.

HYPOTHESES AND DATA

The first hypothesis to be tested is that there are no migration differences between families in which the wife works and those in which she does not work. The alternative hypothesis is that families in which the wife works are less migratory than families in which she does not work. These hypotheses were tested with data from special tabulations of the March *Current Population Surveys* and with data from the 1970 Census.

Each month's *Current Population Survey* consists of about 50,000 households and is a representative sample of the United States population. The March questionnaire contains questions for each member of the household asking whether current (March) residence is the same as in the preceding March. If the answer is no, additional questions ascertain whether the move was across county or state boundaries. Movement between counties is often accepted as an operational definition of migration (Bureau of the Census, 1972). In order to produce the detailed tabulations needed for this study, the March samples from 1966 through 1971 were combined and treated as one large sample.

Table 1 shows rates of moving within counties, between counties (including moves between states), and between states for men at different age groups and with nonfarm occupations according to whether married and, if married, whether at the survey date the wife was in the paid labor force. "Other marital status" in the table includes men who are single (never married) as well as men who are divorced, widowed, or separated from their spouse.

Table 1 shows that at each age group except *20-24* married men have lower migration rates (rates of moving between counties) than men in other marital statuses. Furthermore, beyond age *30* married men also have lower rates of local moving (within counties) than men in other marital statuses. It appears, therefore, that there is a good deal of both short- and long-distance moving associated with getting married and setting up a household, but thereafter married men are more residentially stable than unmarried men.

These findings are pointed out because it is frequently observed that family life sometimes entails residential movement. For example, Petersen (1969:266) states that

In the United States today not only do married couples move about
as well as single persons, but they are often motivated to do so precisely
because of their family life—in order to have a larger house for an
increasing number of children, in order to live in a "nicer" neighborhood
or close to a better school, and so on.

While it is true that families often move for these reasons, it should be emphasized that married couples make significantly fewer residential changes over the course of a lifetime than persons who never marry or who experience marital disruption.

The original question was: Are married men with working wives as migratory as married men whose wives do not work? Based on the evidence in Table 1, the answer appears to be no. Except at ages *20-24*, men whose wives were working at the survey date were consistently less likely to have moved between counties during the preceding year than men whose wives

TABLE 1   Men 20 to 64 Years Old with Nonfarm Occupations—Percent Geographically Mobile During Preceding Twelve Months, According to Type of Mobility, Age, Marital Status, and (if Married) Whether Wife Was in the Paid Labor Force at the Survey Date

	Number (000)	Percent moving within counties	Percent moving between counties	Percent moving between states
20 to 24 years old				
Married, wife present	14,099	39.8	19.2	8.8
Wife in paid labor force	6,405	42.0	19.7	8.5
Wife not in paid labor force	7,694	38.0	18.8	9.0
Other marital status	13,561	14.9	13.5	8.5
25 to 29 years old				
Married, wife present	24,994	23.5	12.4	5.8
Wife in paid labor force	9,653	27.1	10.8	5.1
Wife not in paid labor force	15,341	21.3	13.3	6.3
Other marital status	31,635	20.4	13.1	7.4
30 to 34 years old				
Married, wife present	24,230	14.7	7.8	3.6
Wife in paid labor force	8,429	17.0	6.3	2.7
Wife not in paid labor force	15,801	13.5	8.5	4.1
Other marital status	4,256	20.9	10.0	4.8
35 to 44 years old				
Married, wife present	52,817	8.9	4.9	2.5
Wife in paid labor force	21,398	9.5	3.8	1.8
Wife not in paid labor force	31,419	8.5	5.7	3.0
Other marital status	7,295	17.0	7.2	3.5
45 to 54 years old				
Married, wife present	49,931	6.2	2.7	1.3
Wife in paid labor force	22,623	6.5	3.0	0.8
Wife not in paid labor force	27,308	5.9	3.3	1.7
Other marital status	7,021	14.4	4.9	2.4
55 to 64 years old				
Married, wife present	32,571	4.6	1.9	0.7
Wife in paid labor force	13,119	4.6	1.4	0.3
Wife not in paid labor force	19,452	4.5	2.2	1.0
Other marital status	4,771	10.7	3.9	0.8

Source: March *Current Population Surveys,* summed from 1966–71.

were not working at the survey date. For moves of longer distance (between states) there were no exceptions, for at every age men with working wives were less likely to have undertaken interstate migration during the preceding year than men whose wives were not working at the survey date.

The alternative hypothesis, therefore, receives some support, but there is a possible bias because the above evidence relates only to the wife's employment at the end of the migration interval. A more definitive test will be given in the next section, where the wife's employment status at the beginning and end of a five-year migration interval will be considered. For the moment, we simply note that men whose wives were working at the survey date were less migratory during the preceding year than men whose wives were not working at the survey date.

On an a priori basis there seemed little reason to think that the employment of wives would have any effect whatsoever on short-distance moving. But Table 1 shows that at every age group men whose wives were working at the survey date were *more* likely to have moved within counties during the preceding year than men whose wives were not working. Thus, having a wife who works may inhibit long-distance movement but appears to promote short-distance movement.

Additional tabulations were prepared (but are not shown) controlling for occupation. These tabulations supported the same conclusions as those emerging from Table 1. Controlling for occupation (ten nonfarm groups) revealed that: (1) beyond age 25 or 30 married men had lower rates of moving within or between counties than men who were not married, and (2) married men whose wives were working at the survey date were more likely to have moved within counties but less likely to have moved between counties or states during the preceding year than men whose wives were not working at the survey date.

Tabulations of mobility status according to age, occupation, and marital status were also prepared for women but are not shown. These revealed the expected pattern, namely, that beyond age 25 and for each occupation, married women were appreciably less likely to be mobile (either within counties or between counties) than unmarried women.

Thus there is a clear demonstration that marriage ties people to a given locality. To return to the initial quotation, there is reason to believe that wives who share in the economic responsibility of the household by holding a job influence both the short-distance mobility of their families (increasing it) and the long-distance mobility (decreasing it). But up to now the evidence has been limited to characteristics after moving.

EMPLOYMENT STATUS AT THE BEGINNING
OF THE MIGRATION INTERVAL

With the above information, it is impossible to differentiate clearly the effects of employment status on migration and the effects of migration on employment status (see Goldscheider, 1971; Masnick, 1968; Miller, 1969). During the years in question, the *Current Population Survey* did not include questions on characteristics of persons before moving, but the 1970 Census obtained information on residence in 1965 and activity in 1965 (working, going to college, or being in the Armed Forces).

These data are not ideal for our purposes because the five-year migration interval (in contrast to a one-year interval) may mask several changes of residence and entries to and withdrawals from the labor force, and considerable time may elapse between the time of a move and the time of enumeration. Nevertheless, the census data can be used to test the hypotheses previously offered. Table 2 shows rates of moving within counties and between states for the 1965–70 period according to the husband's age and the wife's employment status in 1965.

These data reinforce earlier conclusions about a wife's employment raising local mobility rates. Column 1 shows that at each of the five age groups men whose wives were working in 1965 were more likely to move within counties during the subsequent five years than men whose wives were not working in 1965. Thus it is quite clear that at all ages a working wife raises her family's local mobility rate.

How might a working wife promote short-distance moving? Part of the answer may be that most short-distance moves are undertaken for reasons connected with housing (Bureau of the Census, 1966; Lansing and Mueller, 1967). In the Census Bureau study, about two-thirds of married men *18–64* years old who had moved within counties during the preceding twelve months said that the desire for a better house or a house located in a better neighborhood or in a more convenient location (to work, schools, shopping, etc.) was the reason for their having moved. Thus housing considerations can be said to account for about two-thirds of within-county moving on the part of families.

Finding that families with a working wife are more likely to undertake within-county moving than other families may suggest that an important motivation for married women working is the desire for a better house, a better neighborhood, or a more convenient location. The income earned by

TABLE 2   Married Men 20 to 59 Years Old in 1965 with Nonfarm Occupations in 1970—Percent Moving Within Counties and Between States Between 1965 and 1970, According to Age and Wife's Employment Status in 1965

			Percent of wives employed in 1970			
	Percent moving within counties, 1965–70*	Percent moving between states, 1965–70*	Non-movers†	Movers within counties	Movers between counties within a state	Movers between states
Husbands 20 to 24 in 1965						
Wife employed in 1965	46.6	18.8	54.0	48.2	42.0	41.0
Wife not employed in 1965	42.6	18.8	25.7	31.7	34.0	35.4
Husbands 25 to 29 in 1965						
Wife employed in 1965	41.6	13.9	63.6	55.3	46.3	41.7
Wife not employed in 1965	34.9	13.1	23.6	25.4	23.7	23.4
Husbands 30 to 39 in 1965						
Wife employed in 1965	29.4	7.7	78.9	70.8	60.8	54.7
Wife not employed in 1965	23.8	9.0	25.4	26.3	25.4	23.9
Husbands 40 to 49 in 1965						
Wife employed in 1965	19.7	4.1	83.7	78.5	69.6	61.7
Wife not employed in 1965	16.6	5.4	21.9	23.6	24.2	22.8
Husbands 50 to 59 in 1965						
Wife employed in 1965	16.1	2.5	80.9	76.6	67.9	57.4
Wife not employed in 1965	14.3	3.1	12.9	15.9	16.7	16.8

Source: Bureau of the Census (1973: Table 11).

*Percent based on total reporting residence in 1965.

†Persons living in the same house in 1965 and 1970.

working wives appears to enable the family to upgrade its housing, and the fact that at each age men with working wives were more mobile within counties suggests repeated moving over the family life cycle to successively more desirable housing.

The general effect, therefore, of the wife's employment on short-distance movement appears about the same whether one considers employment only at the end of the migration interval (Table 1) or at the beginning of the migration interval (Table 2). But the effect of her employment on long-distance migration appears somewhat less when one considers employment at the beginning rather than at the end of the migration interval.

Column 2 of Table 2 shows that for men *20–24* years old there were no differences in 1965–70 interstate migration rates between families in which the wife was, and was not working in 1965. At ages *25–29* men whose wives were working in 1965 were actually slightly more likely to move between states during the subsequent five years than men whose wives were not working. Only after her husband is past *30* does a working wife decrease the likelihood of her husband's interstate migration.

A working wife thus appears to have little effect on her husband's long-distance migration in the early years of his career—the years when long-distance migration is most likely to occur. Only after her husband has become established in his career does a wife's employment reduce the readiness with which he relocates to a new job in a different state. Of course, this conclusion applies only to the general case. It is possible that a professionally employed wife has a greater effect on her husband's long-distance migration than do other working wives.

Columns 3, 4, 5, and 6 of Table 2 show the conditional probability of the wife's being employed in 1970, given her employment status in 1965. These columns were included to show the probability of the wife's continuing her employment when moves of increasing distance are made. For example, among women employed in 1965 and married to men who were *20–24* in 1965, *54.0* percent of those who did not move were still employed in 1970. With increasing distance of move this percent is steadily reduced to *41.0*. The same pattern holds true for all later ages shown.

It would appear, therefore, that any geographical movement is unfavorable to the wife's continued participation in the labor force. And the greater the distance moved (at least up to a point), the greater the likelihood of her dropping out of the labor force.

ENTERING AND LEAVING THE LABOR FORCE

Table 3 shows rates of moving within counties and between states for married men according to age and wife's employment status in 1965 and 1970. For the wife's employment status, there are four possible combinations: (1) employed in 1965 but not 1970, (2) employed in 1970 but not in 1965, (3) employed at both dates, and (4) employed at neither date.

Of course such data do not reveal all entries to and withdrawals from the labor force. Some women could have entered and left the labor force many times during the five-year period, but only the difference between activity in 1965 and activity in 1970 would have been counted. Similarly, not all geographical moves are counted; some persons may have moved several times, but only the difference between place of residence in 1965 and place of residence in 1970 would have been counted. Furthermore, a good

TABLE 3   Married Men 20 to 59 Years Old in 1965 with Nonfarm
Occupations in 1970—Percent Moving Within Counties and
Between States Between 1965 and 1970, According to Age and Wife's
Employment Status in 1965 and 1970

	Age of husband in 1965				
	20 to 24	25 to 29	30 to 39	40 to 49	50 to 59
*Percent moving within counties, 1965–70**					
Wife employed in 1965 only	45.0	40.6	31.6	22.3	18.0
Wife employed in 1970 only	42.1	36.4	24.5	17.4	16.6
Wife employed at both dates	48.4	42.4	28.6	19.1	15.6
Wife employed at neither date	42.9	35.4	23.6	16.4	14.0
*Percent moving between states, 1965–70**					
Wife employed in 1965 only	20.7	17.7	12.9	8.2	5.0
Wife employed in 1970 only	20.7	12.6	8.4	5.4	3.7
Wife employed at both dates	16.6	10.7	5.8	3.1	1.8
Wife employed at neither date	17.8	13.2	9.2	5.3	2.9

Source: Bureau of the Census (1973: Table 11).

*Percent based on total reporting residence in 1965.

deal of time may have elapsed since migrating, allowing some wives to have reentered the labor force after dropping out when the move took place. Nevertheless, these data provide to date the best test of the sort of questions addressed in this article.

Note first the migration patterns of men whose wives were employed at both dates and those whose wives were employed at neither date. Men whose wives were employed at both dates invariably had higher within-county rates of moving and lower interstate migration rates than men whose wives were employed at neither date. Continued participation of wives in the labor force, therefore, produces high (but not always the highest) rates of within-county moving and low rates of interstate migration (the lowest shown in Table 3). Nonparticipation of wives in the labor force is associated with low (usually the lowest) rates of within-county moving and high (but not the highest) rates of interstate migration.

Wives who were employed in 1965 but not 1970 indicate a withdrawal (at least temporarily) from the labor force. By dropping out of the labor force wives increase both the short-distance mobility and long-distance migration of their husbands. Men whose wives were employed in 1965 but not 1970 had high rates of within-county moving (the highest beyond age 30) as well as the highest rates of interstate migration.

Finding that a wife who drops out of the labor force increases her husband's mobility is in accord with interpretations offered by other studies. Miller (1966) offered the tentative conclusion that interstate migration generally raised labor force participation rates among men but often lowered labor force participation rates for women. She suggested that this was because many wives gave up their jobs when their husbands moved over long distances and were unable to find new jobs by the survey date. Her study has been criticized (Goldscheider, 1971; Masnick, 1968) because the data referred only to labor force participation at the end of a five-year migration interval and did not control for marital status. The data in Table 3, however, do have the necessary controls and support her interpretation.

Miller's chief interest was in the possible effects of the husband's migration on the wife's labor force participation, whereas the present article has been more interested in considering the effect of the wife's labor force participation on the husband's migration. Quite obviously, either variable can and should be considered dependent as well as independent. In fact, we may say that occurrence of either event lowers the likelihood of occurrence of the other: participation of wives in the labor force decreases the likeli-hood of the family's migration (at least when the husband is over *30*), but migration, when it occurs, lowers the likelihood of the wife's continued par-ticipation in the labor force.

The effect of wives entering the labor force during the mobility interval is difficult to account for. Men whose wives were employed in 1970 but not 1965 generally had low rates of within-county moving but fairly high rates of interstate migration. The high migration rates may reflect some moves specifically undertaken to aid the wife's entry into the labor force, as when the move is from places with few job opportunities for women (e.g., rural areas) to places with greater job opportunities (e.g., metropolitan areas).

DISCUSSION

The evidence presented above shows that a working wife gives a couple more freedom of choice as to which neighborhood to live in but less freedom of choice as to whether to move to a different city. But because a working wife reduces her husband's long-distance migration by a rather small amount, we conclude that the migration of husbands interferes substantially with the formulation and achievement of clear occupational goals among women—a point that is frequently acknowledged (Holmstrom, 1972; Poloma and Garland, 1971; Rapoport and Rapoport, 1971; Weissman and Paykel, 1972; Wolfle, 1971).

Such disruptions in women's careers brought about by the migration of their husbands seem certain to lower women's earnings. It has been ade-quately demonstrated that women earn less than men at the same age and with the same educational level, occupation, and years in the labor force (Suter and Miller, 1973). At least some of the income differences between men and women arise from the interruptions of women's careers caused by the migration of their husbands and the inability of many (if not most) wives to use migration to further their careers in the same ways that most men do. Any effort at quantifying the degree of economic discrimination against women should consider this as one component of income differences between men and women.

Good evidence that the husband's migration may not only result in the wife's dropping out of the labor force (at least temporarily) but often low-ers earnings among wives who are able to continue working is given by

Gallaway (1969a; 1969b). Gallaway found that for men interregional migration was, on the average, accompanied by an increase in earnings. But for women interregional migration was associated with no change, or a decrease in earnings. His study did not control for marital status, but the most likely explanation of his findings is that interregional migration is most often purposive among men but resultant among women.

It might even be argued that the husband's migration influences not only the career development of the wife but also the initial choice of career. Such

> **❝ The migration of husbands interferes substantially with the formulation and achievement of clear occupational goals among women. ❞**

occupations as elementary school teaching, nursing, and secretarial work are traditional occupations of women. They are also fairly readily transferred from one area to another and can be practiced in almost any part of the country. It may be that the geographical transferability of these occupations has played a part in their perpetuation as favorite career choices of women.

REFERENCES

Beshers, James. 1967. *Population Processes in Social Systems.* New York: Free Press.

Bureau of the Census. 1966. "Reasons for Moving: March 1962 to March 1963." *Current Population Reports.* Series P-20, No. 154. Washington: Government Printing Office.

———. 1972. "Mobility of the Population of the United States: March 1970 to March 1971." *Current Population Reports.* Series P-20, No. 235. Washington: Government Printing Office.

———. 1973. "Census of Population: 1970." *Mobility for States and the Nation.* Final Report PC(2)-2B. Washington: Government Printing Office.

deBeauvoir, Simone. 1949. *The Second Sex.* New York: Bantam Books, 1970.

Gallaway, Lowell E. 1969a. "The Effect of Geographic Labor Mobility on Income: A Brief Comment." *Journal of Human Resources* 4 (Winter): 103–9.

———. 1969b. *Geographic Labor Mobility in the United States: 1957 to 1960.* Washington: Government Printing Office.

Glick, Paul C. 1965. "Census Data as a Source for Theses and Dissertations in the Field of Sociology." *Milbank Memorial Fund Quarterly* 63 (January): 17–30.

Goldscheider, Calvin. 1971. *Population, Modernization, and Social Structure.* Boston: Little, Brown.

Holmstrom, Lynda Lytle. 1972. *The Two-Career Family.* Cambridge: Schenkman.

Lansing, John B., and Eva Mueller. 1967. *The Geographic Mobility of Labor.* Ann Arbor: Institute for Social Research, University of Michigan.

Masnick, George. 1968. "Employment Status and Retrospective and Prospective Migration in the United States." *Demography* 5: 79–85.

Miller, Ann R. 1966. "Migration Differentials in Labor Force Participation: United States, 1960." *Demography* 3: 58–67.

———. 1969. "Note on Some Problems in Interpreting Migration Data from the 1960 Census of Population." *Demography* 6 (February): 13–16.

Petersen, William. 1969. *Population.* New York: Macmillan.

Poloma, Margaret M., and T. Neal Garland. 1971. "The Married Professional Woman: A Study in the Tolerance of Domestication." *Journal of Marriage and the Family* 33 (August): 531–40.

Rapoport, Rhona, and Robert Rapoport. 1971. *Dual-Career Families.* Middlesex, England: Penguin Books.

Suter, Larry E., and Herman P. Miller. 1973. "Components and Differences between the Incomes of Men and Career Women." *American Journal of Sociology* 78 (January): 962–74.

Weissman, Myrna, and Eugene S. Paykel. 1972. "Moving and Depression in Women." *Society* 9 (July/August): 24–8.

Wolfle, Dael. 1971. *The Uses of Talent.* Princeton: Princeton University Press.

Working in Mid-Life

Evelyn R. Rosenthal

Persons who experiment with novel patterns of living and innovative forms of social relations are the pioneers of social change. In some cases they become the daring few whose names are remembered because their lives illuminate new paths and possibilities for us. Sometimes they are remembered only as warnings against imprudent attempts at innovation. Most often they are forgotten as individuals, and we interpret their novel recombinations of existing social forms as the beginnings of long-term, seemingly inexorable, trends. These are the reluctant pioneers, who never intended to change broad existing social patterns by their individual behavior. Their actions in the aggregate, however, bring about sweeping changes because many individuals try similar solutions to similar life dilemmas. Population migrations in response to famine fall into this last category, as does the adoption of contraception by married women. The work activity of mature women in the United States since 1940 is another instance.

Women who work in mid-life are for the most part reluctant pioneers. They are pioneers in two ways: often they are working at jobs traditionally held by men, and it is a novel pattern for them to be working at all. They are reluctant pioneers because their labor force activity does not signify a renunciation of the traditional roles of mature women as homemakers, child-rearers, and wives, or a desire to switch roles with men. On the contrary, their work for pay outside the home can be viewed as a novel means to attain traditional female goals. These "new" workers, women who are pioneers in spite of themselves, went to work in a society inhospitable to the employment of older women who are wives and mothers. The opportunity structure provided by employers, the norms of family life, and contemporary social policies have all helped to shape their work experiences and occupational choices into novel forms.

The recent work experience of mature women differs in several respects from that of men and from that of younger female workers. The kinds of jobs they do, the rewards they seek from work, and the manner in which work is woven into the patterns of their lives indicate a special set of constraints that circumscribe the work decisions of women in mid-life.

CONSTRAINTS IMPOSED BY SOCIALIZATION

As Carol Ireson pointed out in her chapter above, early socialization is one source of these constraints. Young girls learn culturally appropriate behavior orientations and by adolescence exhibit what McClelland calls a "typical female interest" in people as opposed to things, interdependence rather than assertiveness, the structure of relationships, and sensitivity to context as opposed to concentrated focus on single aspects of a situation.[1] However, the culturally appropriate attitudes of young girls do not translate directly into the work decisions of mature women. Early socialization simply provides a framework for later behavior, including occupational behavior, and the effects of this general orientation are mainly indirect. One aim of this analysis is to show how younger and older women workers respond differently to traditional "typical female interests," and how different patterns of work activity result.

Sex-specific socialization shapes ambitions and goals, but the available and preferred means for realizing these ambitions vary according to an individual's current social position. The social structural factors that influence the work decisions of the mature woman are her current family situation, the opportunities offered by employers, and the effects of social policy.

As these factors vary, so do the costs and benefits of particular work activities. Widespread changes in the characteristics and work patterns of the female labor force can be analyzed in terms of changes in family situation, opportunity structure, and social policy, even though early sex-role socialization remains relatively constant. The influence of feminist thinking on early sex-role socialization is too recent for the most part to have had clear effects on the work patterns of American women and men, and the dramatic changes in the aggregate work activities of American women since 1940 generally preceded that influence. Moreover, recent research shows that today's older women have ambitions and goals for themselves that are consonant with a traditional view of women's roles. Surprisingly, neither the presence nor the age of children in the home is related to the views of married women on the propriety of being employed outside their homes. Only a small minority of married women report disliking child care, and a slightly larger percentage are unenthusiastic about housework. Background characteristics, such as race, rural–urban residence, and the respondent's mother's employment status when the respondent was growing up are not related to these attitudes. Significantly, women with the most education have the most acceptant attitudes toward the employment of women with small children: 30 percent of women with college degrees express permissive attitudes compared to 17 percent of women with fewer than nine years of schooling.[2]

While older women have traditional goals and ambitions, the means chosen for attaining those goals and ambitions are often novel, such as entering the labor force at unpredictable times and assuming work roles uncharacteristic of women in the past. The novel means represent attempts to adapt traditional sex-role orientations to current needs, and in part explain the evolving patterns of older women's pioneering work activity.

One aim of this chapter, then, is to resolve the apparent contradiction of women with traditional concepts of their female roles exhibiting increasingly nontraditional behavior with respect to work decisions. A brief overview of the recent patterns of stability and change in women's work activity will provide the necessary frame of reference in which to view the experiences and choices of women working in mid-life.

Today the typical American working woman is a high school graduate, in her forties, married, and a mother. She works at a job that is done almost exclusively by women. Her wages are generally lower than those of working men with somewhat less education and experience than she.[3] Her less tangible rewards, in terms of the prestige attached to her work, are very likely to be lower than those of her own first job, two decades earlier: my own analysis of the national longitudinal study (NLS) data shows that 61 percent of the working women experienced downward mobility from their first jobs to their current jobs. This sketch of today's working woman highlights important points of stability and change in woman's work patterns in recent years.

Some features of women's work patterns have changed very little since 1900: sex segregation of occupations has, if anything, become accentuated; the poor pay of women workers compared to men persists; the concept of a "career" remains quite useless in describing most women's work lives. Some features have changed dramatically: the median age of women workers, twenty-six in 1900, is now forty-two (about the same as that of men); marriage no longer signals a withdrawal from employment; mothers of school-age children are more likely to be working than not.

These changes and continuities have affected the experience of women working in mid-life, the kinds of jobs they enter, and the factors influencing their work patterns. The most persistent characteristic of female work activity is its sex-segregation (see Francine Blau's chapter above). Despite broad changes in technology, large increases in labor force participation rates of women, and the changed age structure of the female labor force, the percentage of women workers employed in jobs dominated by women has not declined since 1900 and in fact shows a slight increase.[4] In 1900, 60 percent of women workers were employed in jobs that were at least half female; by 1968 the proportion was estimated at 75 percent.[5]

In contrast to the persistence of sex-segregation in the labor force, the most remarkable change is the rapidly increasing heterogeneity of the female work force by age, marital status, and family status, as Blau pointed out above. The age groups least likely to be employed in 1900 have increased their participation rates most rapidly, so that today the female labor force duplicates the age distribution of women in general very closely up to the age of sixty-five.[6] Work patterns of married women and mothers have changed dramatically. Only 15 percent of women with husbands present were employed in 1940, but by 1969 their participation rate had grown to 40 percent. Mothers of children under eighteen had a 9 percent participation rate in 1940 compared to a 41 percent rate in 1973.[7] In sum, age, marital status, and parental status are no longer the strong factors they once were in determining which women work for pay and which do not.

These two patterns of women's work activity—persistence in entering occupations already dominated by women workers, and change in the characteristics of the female labor force—illuminate the experience of women working in mid-life. On the one hand, the new working women, who are older and often have family responsibilities, are in the labor force out of economic necessity. There are, of course, older single women workers and older women professionals who do not work out of economic necessity. These categories of women have always been in the labor force, and their relative representation has declined dramatically since 1940. But the new groups of older working women are likely to be the sole support of themselves and perhaps others: one in ten households now is headed by a woman, and a recent survey of working women showed one in three to be the sole household wage earner.[8] Most often they are important contributors to family incomes that would be desperately inadequate without their earnings.

> 〰 **The median age of women workers, twenty-six in 1900, is now forty-two (about the same as that of men).** 〰

On the other hand, the new working women are confronted by narrowly sex-segregated job opportunities that developed historically to attract young, single women with no long labor force commitment. Donald Bogue points out how traditional female jobs neatly fit the stereotype of the young woman seeking to fulfill her feminine role through work. These jobs require traditional housewives' tasks; patience, waiting, and routine; rapid use of hands and fingers; few or no strenuous physical activities; a welfare or cultural orientation; contact with young children; and sex appeal.[9] In light of these job characteristics, it should not be surprising to find many women in mid-life seeking novel ways of meeting their economic needs.

We are accustomed to associating novel behavior with the young, and indeed many young women in school today are planning long work lives in sex-atypical careers. But older women were (and continue to be) pioneers out of traditional motives. Studies of girls who were adolescents in the 1950s—today's mid-life women—clarify the aspirations they developed through early socialization.[10] The jobs these young girls wanted for themselves represented "typical female interests"—they emphasized glamor, helping others, and pleasant coworkers. Marriage and children were highly valued. Yet ambition was strong: one study concluded that the status ambitions of young girls were at least as high as and perhaps higher than those of young boys.[11] The girls typically expected to fulfill their status ambitions through their choices of spouses, however, not through their own activities. "The desire for social status and for a middle-class life style is the key to understanding the girls' picture of married life" concluded the authors of one nationwide interview study of teenagers in the fifties.[12] Only one in ten girls said she would be satisfied if her future husband were a blue-collar worker, while a majority would settle for nothing less than a professional-level job for him.

Given the realities of stratification in the United States, many of these girls could not realize their status ambitions through their choices of husbands. In time, either their picture of a satisfactory married life had to be altered, or they had to seek other means to attain it. Pioneering older women have chosen a novel means, paid employment, to achieve traditional goals. One in five of these older women workers is employed for the first time, after marriage and child rearing, but a majority had worked when younger, before the birth of their children.

CONSTRAINTS IMPOSED BY EMPLOYERS

Older women workers have to compete with young women for traditional female jobs, and employers prefer the young women. In addition, these jobs have a high ratio of costs to rewards for the mature women: employers shape the requirements of jobs to attract particular categories of workers, and for several reasons traditional female jobs are made less attractive to middle-aged women workers.

Employers succeed in attracting young women into low-paying, monotonous, dead-end jobs by obvious means, such as sex-exclusionary hiring practices,[13] or by subtler means, which focus on making extrinsic features of the jobs more attractive without raising wages or modifying the intrinsic nature of the work itself. The appeal of the job is manipulated by building on the motives and ambitions of the particular categories of workers an employer wishes to attract.

If the employer's goal is to attract young, high-status men, one manipulation is to "professionalize" the job by creating a career ladder and redefining job specifications so that the more routine aspects of the work are relegated to subordinate workers at lower wages. If the employer's aim is to secure a loyal, dependable, and productive professionally skilled work force at the lowest cost, this stratification of jobs so that top level positions are created for men makes sense. Employers can also manipulate the extrinsic features of a job to fit the motives and ambitions of young women. From the employer's point of view, it is much less costly than raising wages to enhance a job with an aura of glamor, a sense of service to others, and opportunities for the worker to have congenial relationships with coworkers and clients. If these features are combined with systematic opportunities for the worker to meet high-status men, a job will attract a stream of skilled young women despite low wages, no advancement opportunities, and grueling or monotonous tasks. One of the more successful examples of this "glamorization" process is the job of waitress at "key" clubs and ski resorts, where, if magazine accounts may be believed, employers turn away women willing to work for no wages at all.

Aspects of a job intended to appeal to young women may be seen as drawbacks by a forty-year-old woman with family responsibilities. A young woman may enjoy the downtown location of many office jobs, while the older woman sees this feature as a time-consuming and costly inconvenience. Dressing up, commuting back and forth, and lunching out are drains on her meager financial resources. She prefers to work closer to home, and home for mature women workers is likely to be in a working-class or middle-class suburb. The glamorization of low-paying jobs attracts young women workers, and an important feature is the opportunity for casual conversation and flirting with high-status men.[14] Older women may also be attracted by jobs with this particular feature, but they may find it difficult to compete with younger women for such positions. Employers' preferences are clear, especially in stewardess, receptionist, and cocktail waitress jobs.

How may employers manipulate the extrinsic features of a job to entice the mid-life working woman without offering an attractive wage? One way is to locate the job near her home, arrange the hours to facilitate child care and husband care, and set a tone of casual dress. or inexpensive uniforms. If close supervision by superiors is not required, all the better, since older women are often used to setting their own task sequence and pace of work. The intrinsic features of the job should build on the competence that the worker has developed during her years of caring for children, shopping for consumer goods, and managing her home.

In the 1940s very few jobs with these characteristics existed for women workers: private household work, practical nursing, and the female-dominated professions of teaching, nursing, and interior decorating. The jobs that now employ older women and also seem well-suited to their traditional concerns have emerged in recent decades. These jobs existed in the past, but for the most part they were held by men. Opportunities for mature women to do these jobs have resulted from structural changes in the nature of the work itself and from extrinsic features that now make the jobs unattractive to men and to many younger women workers. At the same time, they appear to be "tailor-made" to the needs and interests of older women workers.

Many of the jobs have emerged as a result of the "professionalization" of male jobs. Employers have created the new jobs as spin-offs of masculine service careers, and often the pay is better and the work less monotonous than in more traditional female jobs. Women who are meter maids, school crossing guards, medical technicians, and dental technicians fall into this category.

A second category consists of jobs that once provided men the chance to earn high wages on a commission basis. Since 1940, many large organizations have expanded the lower ranks of their pyramidal commission sales forces so much that direct client-contact jobs no longer promise good dependable returns for the hours worked. Women now have new "opportunities," and underemployed men can moonlight, as real estate agents, insurance salespeople, and travel agents.

A third group of new opportunities for women with family responsibilities consists of jobs specially designed with great managerial ingenuity to accomplish a triple task: keeping overhead low, offering earnings that can rise as high as the worker's ambition, and encouraging increased consumption of the product by the same category of persons for whom the jobs were designed. These are door-to-door (or living-room-to-living-room) sales of female-interest products and "home party" hostessing.

These jobs all have extrinsic features that make them attractive to the new working women, but they employ a relatively small share of today's older female labor force. I strongly suspect that, if the increasing numbers of women workers with family responsibilities suddenly shrank, these jobs would either disappear altogether (as the housemaid position has), or be filled by teenagers or senior citizens. The jobs that have succeeded most in attracting the new middle-aged workers are not jobs designed to suit their special needs and experiences but rather jobs that are particularly unattractive to other categories of workers.

Blue-collar jobs at low skill levels employ the largest proportion of older women workers, including many whose earlier jobs were in clerical positions. These jobs often pay higher wages than sales, service, or clerical jobs at comparable skill levels, but they have low appeal for most young women. The availability of factory operative jobs for women has not resulted from industrial expansion, prosperity, or technological breakthroughs, as analyses of government groups predicted. For example, the National Manpower Council optimistically assumed that opportunities for women in industry would follow the expansion of jobs and changes in technology.[15] These analyses erroneously assumed that folk traditions of job assignment by sex and unautomated strenuous operations were the major barriers to women's expanded job opportunities in production work. Although job opportunities for women in industry expanded at the same time that many industries were automating their operations and opening new types of jobs that bore no traditional sex labels, a close analysis by type of industry reveals that the new jobs went mainly to men. Opportunities for older women arose in industries that were long established, declining in numbers of jobs, and little influenced by technological reorganization.[16]

Blue-collar jobs open to women in these declining industries, such as furniture upholstering and book manufacturing, illustrate the same general process described earlier in reference to higher-status employment: older women are kept out of jobs not because of folk traditions of the work place, but because employers manipulate the attractiveness of jobs to appeal to preferred categories of workers. In low-level factory jobs, mature women workers are again pioneers in spite of themselves. They enter sex-atypical jobs when employers are unable or unwilling to compete for higher-priced male labor, or where the structure of the jobs has been changed dramatically.

CONSTRAINTS IMPOSED BY THE FAMILY

The story of the working woman's "double duty" is told by Kristin Moore and Isabel Sawhill above and Joann Vanek below. Women work in paid employment, child care, and other home tasks for a total workweek that averages ten hours longer than that of employed men or housewives (longer if the working women are employed full-time).[17] Work-and-leisure time studies highlight the traditional nature of most working women's responses to their home roles. Less often studied than the role overload and workweek of employed wives and mothers are the aspects of traditional home role relationships that limit women's choices of jobs and potential market wages.

The social relations of the prevalent male-centered nuclear family require that the wife primarily support her husband's well-being and provide the services he cannot afford to purchase with his meager wages. The median income of full-time male workers in 1972 was $10,202, as estimated by the United States Department of Labor. Home economists estimate the current annual market value of a wife's services at $4,500 to $7,000. Some labor force analysts, noting that higher wages are paid to married men than to single men and to all categories of women, interpret this as the employers' recognition that a married man will be a more loyal and dependable employee, and therefore a more productive worker, because of his family responsibilities; others see the husband's higher wage rate as recognition that hiring a married man puts two workers on the job for the (slightly higher) price of one. Few stress the effects of the wife's unpaid household work on her own potential market wage.

Household work demands do not reduce a working woman's market wage by increasing her days off from work or her quit rate. Quit rates are not much higher for women than for men, and time lost from work is related to the nature of the work, not the sex of the worker.[18] A woman's home role affects her wages primarily because it traditionally allows other family members a prior claim on family investments in human capital.

Human capital, the potential value of a person as a commodity exchanged for wages, can be enhanced in many ways. Education, experience, personal development (for instance, to improve health and attractiveness), and geographic migration can all increase an individual's lifetime income potential and may be viewed as investments in human capital. The norm in the American family is for the husband's and children's claims on the family's human capital investment resources to have priority over the wife's claims. Young families often invest a wife's wages in her husband's education and training, thereby increasing his potential lifetime earnings while reducing hers. Older women often work to invest in the education, health, and attractiveness of their children.

Seldom does a family invest its resources to enhance the potential market wage of the older woman who plans to work. The norm of others' prior claims to family resources is so powerful that practically none of the families of mature working women invest in the women's training before or during their employment. The few women whose families do invest resources in this way choose the briefest training programs from available options, and these prepare them for the least rewarding jobs.[19] The calculations of human capital economists, intended to show the returns to the worker of investments such as education and training, do not take into account that the investment often enhances one person's earning potential at the expense of another's (see Carolyn Bell's chapter above).

Geographic migration is undertaken in much the same way as investment in education and job training. A family move may enhance the earning potential of one family member at the expense of others. The overwhelming majority of intercounty moves in the United States are undertaken because of the work-related needs of a male wage earner,[20] but the costs of the move fall heavily on the working woman (see Larry Long's chapter above). Even if others do all the (unpaid) planning, packing, and house-hunting chores, the wife pays heavily in time lost looking for new employment, loss of job seniority and pension rights, and loss of valuable contact networks. Geographic migration as an investment in male human capital is one factor that inflates women's quit rates and unemployment rates and contributes to women's erratic labor force attachment. At the same time, it reduces their potential market wages. Ironically, the more highly skilled and specialized the woman's work, the less likely it is that she will be able to find satisfactory employment in a new location. And currently even the traditionally female, transferable jobs such as teaching and social work are becoming hard to get. One of the ironies of the sex-segregated labor force is that it does protect many women's jobs in times of rising unemployment, since men are socialized to avoid such jobs and therefore are not trained to fill them. However, the more desirable jobs do attract men, after a time-lag for male workers to perceive the opportunities. These jobs then are often doubly desirable for the men who prepare for them, since a disproportionate number of the top posts will go to the men in a woman's field.

The role structure of the nuclear family also limits a woman's choice of jobs. Labor force analysts assert that the older woman has fewer job possibilities because her skills are obsolete, as a result of her withdrawal from work to attend to family needs.[21] This is sometimes true, but it makes two assumptions that may not be true for the majority of older women workers:

that the women had job skills in the first place, and that the jobs open to them require some skill. The obsolete skills argument seems to have a middle-class bias; it applies to the relatively small group of college-educated older women who did have job skills earlier. However, teachers, nurses, physicians, scientists, and other professionally trained women are the workers least likely to be out of the labor force for extended periods of time.

Most jobs open to women require no prior skills. Typing and shorthand are exceptions, but other clerical and production tasks can generally be learned in a few days. Older women tend to stay away from office jobs, but this is because of the competition and convenience reasons outlined above more than because their skills are obsolete. The factor that has become obsolete for mature women workers, and that tends to limit their job choices, is their network of personal contacts in the world of work. Most older women hear of their jobs through interpersonal contact. The privatization of home life within the nuclear family often reduces a woman's interpersonal contacts to neighbors (in the working class), her husband's job associates (in the middle class), and service workers. The older woman's knowledge of available employment options is directly related to the extent of her interpersonal contacts outside the family circle. The lower her socioeconomic level, the narrower those contacts tend to be.

The privatization of family life affects mature women's work experiences in other ways as well. The desire to work at all is sometimes related to the psychological effects of privatization—which produces a sense of alienation from community life. More importantly, privatization requires each single-family unit to purchase the "standard package" of consumer items needed to maintain an acceptable level of living. The woman with family responsibilities seeks work in response to economic need, created in part by this privatization of family life. At the same time, she commands a low market wage and finds limited opportunities partly because she accepts the traditional norms institutionalized in the nuclear family (for example, that the needs of her husband and children come first).

CONSTRAINTS IMPOSED BY SOCIAL POLICY

The main effect of much social policy is to discourage women with family responsibilities from working: zoning laws keep most workplaces away from home sites; federal income tax rules, as presently constructed, penalize the family in which father and mother both earn a living wage; and many employed women whose husbands are covered by Social Security are not entitled to benefits from their own contributions. In addition, mothers who receive AFDC benefits often suffer a financial loss when they go to work, because their wages are low, and free or cheap day-care facilities are scarce.[22] So much of social policy seems designed to keep mothers at home that we may well marvel at how ineffective it is. Women with family responsibilities

> 👀 **The main effect of much social policy has been to discourage women with family responsibilities from working.** 👀

continue to work in increasing numbers, although the social policy effects mentioned above make working more costly for them. Perhaps other current social policies, often implemented with no intent to influence women's work patterns, create a counterforce that encourages wives and mothers to work.

The social policies that most obviously encourage older women to work are those that promote an inflationary economy, making it difficult for families to maintain a satisfactory level of living on the earnings of a single breadwinner. Other, more indirect forces created by social policy decisions also contribute to women's employment. For example, compulsory education and school centralization reduce the need for an adult at home and permit mothers to enter paid employment with minimal strain on their home role obligations, especially if their work time is coordinated with school hours. Mothers living outside urban areas generally have more flexibility in arranging work time because their children's school day is lengthened by a bus ride and a cafeteria lunch. Urban school districts increasingly provide lunchtime meals and supervision in response to community needs and the availability of state and federal subsidies for these programs. Urban school busing will also lengthen the school day of city children and unintentionally increase the work time flexibility of urban mothers of school-age children. Simultaneously, these educational policies increase the number of desirable jobs for women—as teachers, classroom aides, school bus drivers, and cafeteria workers.

Educational policies have affected women's work experiences in more direct ways as well. For example, most of today's pioneering mature women workers attended school at a time when a student's pregnancy or marriage was sufficient cause for school dismissal. Few of these "dropouts" completed high school later on, as the prior claims on family resources of other family members took precedence over those of the wife and mother.

Policies in other areas also encourage women to work. Laws that relax the requirements for divorce, abortion, and distribution of contraceptives contribute indirectly to the labor force participation of mature women. Perhaps one of the strongest indirect influences on women's work activity stems from immigration policies. Early in this century, most nonfarm working women with family responsibilities were immigrants. They were the service workers and the factory operatives, along with young girls and boys. Immigration restrictions combined with compulsory education laws and child labor laws to dry up this supply of cheap, low-skilled factory and service labor. These are the jobs that older women now fill.

I see no unified effort to achieve consistency in the effects of public policy decisions on women's work experience today. Many feminists desire social policies that will unequivocally facilitate the employment of women. Advocates for the poor fear that such policies will coerce impoverished mothers to enter the labor force. The most encouraging social policies may be those that facilitate civil rights and provide protection for the least powerful. The creation of the Equal Employment Opportunities Commission was a start, since employer discrimination in hiring and wages is still the single most constraining influence on the experiences of the new female labor force.[23]

The work and family experiences of women will change along with changes in early socialization patterns. But socialization is a lifelong process. I have tried to show that early socialization is only one factor shaping the experiences of working women. The privatization of social relations within the nuclear family and the power of employers to manipulate the rewards and costs of work are two major influences. Social policy, in attempting to support both family relations and employer prerogatives, often works in contradictory ways; it seeks incompatible goals and creates both social and personal disorder for women who work.

NOTES

1 David C. McClelland, "Wanted: A New Self-Image for Woman," *Daedalus,* spring 1964, reprinted in *Dialogue on Women,* ed. Robert Theobald (Indianapolis: Bobbs-Merrill Company, 1967), pp. 35–55.

2 These and other data reported in the text that describe older women's work behavior and attitudes are from a national longitudinal study directed by Herbert Parnes of Ohio State University (hereafter referred to as the NLS data). Where the results have been previously published, the source is noted; otherwise the results are from my own reanalysis of the data. For a complete description of the sample, interview schedule, and preliminary data analyses, see U.S. Department of Labor, Manpower Administration, *Dual Careers,* Manpower Research Monograph, no. 21 (Washington, D.C.: Government Printing Office, 1970). Women's attitudes toward work and home are reported at pp. 44–52 of the monograph.

3 A discussion of mature women's earnings, based on the NLS data, appears in Larry E. Suter and Herman P. Miller, "Income Differences between Men and Career Women," *American Journal of Sociology* 78 (1973): 962–74.

4 Valerie Kincade Oppenheimer, *The Female Labor Force in the United States,* Population Monograph Series, no. 5 (Berkeley: University of California, Institute of International Studies, 1970), p. 69.

5 Ibid., p. 71; U.S. Department of Labor, Women's Bureau, *1969 Handbook on Women Workers,* Bulletin no. 294 (Washington, D.C.: Government Printing Office, 1969). Data from 1968 surveys by the Department of Labor are used in preference to the 1970 census reports because recategorizations of occupations in the most recent decennial census have made comparison to earlier reports difficult.

6 *1969 Handbook on Women Workers,* p. 22.

7 Ibid., p. 26; U.S. Department of Labor, Bureau of Labor Statistics, *Children of Working Mothers,* Special Labor Force Report no. 165 (Washington, D.C.: Government Printing Office, 1974), p. 52.

8 "Facts and Fictions about Working Women Explored: Several Stereotypes Prove False in National Study," *ISR Newsletter,* autumn 1972, pp. 4–5.

9 Donald Bogue, *The Population of the United States* (Glencoe, Ill.: Free Press, 1959), pp. 491–92.

10 Elizabeth Douvan and J. Adelson, *The Adolescent Experience* (New York: John Wiley and Sons, 1966).

11 Ralph Turner, "Some Aspects of Women's Ambition," *American Journal of Sociology* 70 (1964): 271–85.

12　Douvan and Adelson, *Adolescent Experience, p. 42.*

13　The extent of complaints against employers for sex-exclusionary hiring practices is one indicator of those practices. These complaints are tabulated in the United States Equal Employment Opportunity Commission's *Annual Reports* (Washington, D.C.: Government Printing Office, annually).

14　"Sexy talk" between bank tellers and customers is commented on by Jane Prather in "When the Girls Move In: A Social Analysis of the Feminization of the Bank Teller's Job," *Journal of Marriage and the Family* 33 (1971): 778–82, and is illustrated by the interview reported by Studs Terkel in *Working* (New York: Random House, 1972), pp. 257–63.

15　National Manpower Council, *Womanpower* (New York: Columbia University Press, 1957).

16　Dale Heistand, *Economic Growth and Employment Opportunities for Minorities* (New York: Columbia University Press, 1964).

17　"Time Use Studies Reveal Plight of Working Women; Everyday Life in 12 Countries Has Common Design," *ISR Newsletter,* autumn 1973, pp. 6–7.

18　Carolyn Shaw Bell, "Age, Sex, Marriage and Jobs," *The Public Interest,* winter 1972, p. 87.

19　B. N. Seear, *Re-entry of Women to the Labour Market after an Interruption in Employment* (Paris: Organisation for Economic Co-operation and Development, n.d.).

20　Alden Speare, "Home Ownership, Life Cycle Stage and Residential Mobility," *Demography* 7 (1970): 449–58.

21　Seear, *Re-Entry of Women,* pp. 96–107.

22　For a feminist interpretation of current social policy and how to change it, see Constantine Safilios-Rothschild, *Women and Social Policy* (Englewood Cliffs, N.J.: Prentice-Hall, 1974).

23　EEOC, *Annual Reports.*

THREE

SPECIFIC OCCUPATIONAL EXPERIENCES OF WOMEN

EDITORS' INTRODUCTION

Most previous case studies of occupations have focused on men and their work, as we noted earlier. Here we present a collection of papers on women in various occupations. These chapters analyze some of the jobs women hold, particularly ones that are often overlooked even in studies of women—clerical, blue-collar, and service occupations and the female-dominated professions. These contributions reveal the wide diversity in women's occupational experiences and delineate experiences women workers have in common.

The chapters in this section cover a variety of white-collar, blue-collar, and service occupations. The Bureau of the Census lists eleven major occupational categories:

White-collar

Professional workers
Proprietors, managers, officials

Clerical workers
Sales workers

Service

Private household workers
Other service workers

Blue-collar

Craftsmen
Operatives
Laborers

Farm

Farmers and farm managers
Farm laborers and foremen

We would have liked to present an analysis of an occupation from each, but because of space limitations and, in some cases, a dearth of research, we have not been able to include discussions of women in management, retail sales, skilled crafts, and farm management and labor, for example. Neither have we been able to present a chapter on stigmatized occupations, such as prostitution and stripping, although these occupations have been more thoroughly discussed elsewhere than many of the more commonplace occupations in which women are concentrated. We have, however, included a selection on the work of housewives. Although this job is not a paid occupation in the same sense as the others discussed here, it is the single most common type of women's work, and it is certainly deserving of careful analysis.

The chapters in this section illustrate the status, experiences, and problems of women working at all levels of the occupational hierarchy. The authors' approaches vary considerably, but their contributions have some central themes in common. They discuss, for example, the sex-typing of jobs and women's lower earnings compared to those of men, the role of schools and training programs in preparing aspirants to enter an occupation, the opportunities and obstacles to mobility presented by the organization of the work place, and the informal relationships that develop among workers. The authors here are addressing, for specific occupational groups, the characteristics and explanations of women's work discussed in broader terms in sections I and II of this volume.

All the chapters in this section underscore the pervasiveness of occupational sex-typing, no matter how broad or narrow the occupational categories being analyzed. With only a brief glance at the eleven major categories named above we can quickly note how most of them are sex typed. Private household work and clerical work, for example, are dominated by women, whereas crafts and farm labor and management are men's fields. Occupational segregation by sex also occurs within these major categories. Within the broad group of the professions, for example, librarianship and nursing are associated with women while law and medicine are linked to men. Even within a specific occupational category, such as medicine, there is sex-typing of specialties. Women physicians, for example, are overrepresented in pediatrics and psychiatry and underrepresented in surgery. Within most occupations, women and men are segregated in other ways as well. Men are much more likely to be found in supervisory positions, for example, and they are often better remunerated than women doing the same tasks.

The process by which an occupation becomes sex-typed is a complex one. In studying some of the factors, demographer Valerie Kincade Oppenheimer found that female-dominated occupations are ones that expanded when their pay was

low and the supply of female labor high. They are
often jobs that require the skills women traditionally acquired as part of their female role (such as
sewing) or require traits that were believed to be
innately female (such as selflessness). The jobs that
became sex-typed for women also tended to require little on-the-job training, to demand little
career continuity, and to ensure that women would
not be placed in supervisory positions to men.[1]

A number of factors, including socialization and
education, women's statuses as wives and mothers,
and the structure of the marketplace help to maintain occupational sex-typing and underscore the
many ways in which men's and women's occupational experiences differ. In section two, Carol
Ireson described how boys and girls begin to be socialized for "appropriate" sex-role behavior almost
at birth. The authors in this section develop this
theme further in their discussion of the channeling
that occurs in educational and job-training programs that prepare men and women for specific
occupations.

Several of the authors also discuss women's traditional familial responsibilities as a factor that
influences their choices of jobs and their occupational achievements. They find that a wife's employment does not generally relieve her of any
household maintenance and child-care tasks, and
it is easy to see how this "double duty" may seriously limit what women can accomplish on their
jobs. Employed blue-collar wives often have little
free time to dedicate to the union activities that
might help to improve their working conditions,
upward mobility, and earnings. Married professional women may find themselves at a decided
disadvantage in competing with men who can give
"their all" to their jobs because their spouses are
full-time housewives.

A number of contributors discuss another source of men and women's different labor force experiences—how their occupations and work settings are organized. Male- and female-dominated occupations often differ in the extent to which they are professionalized or unionized, for example. Likewise, the hierarchical structures of their employing organizations, and their opportunities in them, vary in predictable ways. Several of the authors point out, for instance, that the career ladders are very short in many female-labeled jobs, such as clerical work, private household service, and certain blue-collar jobs. Even when women are in occupations that have more extensive career ladders, they often receive fewer opportunities for promotion than do men.

The informal side of the work world generally reinforces the system of power differentials between sex-typed formal positions in an organization. Luncheons, after-work cocktails, the club and athletic activities, for example, are usually single-sex activities, and they have the effects of reducing men's acquaintance with their women colleagues, excluding women from crucial information and contacts, and protecting those in power from confronting their own prejudices. In such settings, no one is likely to challenge male workers' and managers' assumptions about women's work behavior. Without contradictory voices, men perceive women workers, for example, as satisfied with jobs that lead to little in the way of position, power, and pay.

Many of the authors in this section conclude their analyses by looking to the future. They consider the demand for workers in the occupations they examine, and they speculate about changes in women's relative position. The contributors identify a number of factors that seem to bode well for women, but their discussions of occupational sex-typing, educational tracking, the household division of labor, and the nature of organizational hierarchies warn us not to be unduly optimistic.

The discussion of women in selected occupational categories begins with the chapter by Michelle Patterson and Laurie Engelberg on the male-dominated professions of medicine, law, and university teaching, and James Grimm's analysis of the female-dominated professions of social work, nursing, librarianship, and elementary school teaching. In both chapters the authors address the issue of what constitutes a profession, provide a broad overview of the status of women in these fields, and discuss for specific professions the process of entry, the paths to mobility, and factors contributing to the marked sex-typing of specialties. In examining the male-dominated professions, Patterson and Engelberg identify discrimination and women's difficulties in managing both their careers and their households as factors contributing to their marginality and concentration in particular specialities. Similarly, Grimm's discussion of the female-dominated professions sheds light on factors contributing to the sex-typing of specialties and the disproportionate representation of men in supervisory positions. The authors consider ways in which the professions could be more flexibly structured to expand opportunities for all practitioners.

Virginia Olesen and Frances Katsuranis deal with another white-collar occupation in which women predominate—clerical work. The authors begin with an overview of women in the clerical field as a whole and then present their own research on temporary clerical workers. In their open-ended interviews with temporary workers, Olesen and Katsuranis focused on the workers' sources of identity and job satisfaction. The authors found that, although their interviewees disliked certain features of their work, many of them had the sense of controlling their job assignments and their time. Among temporary workers, Olesen and Katsuranis distinguish two major types—transitional and permanent—according to the role temporary clerical work plays in their work histories.

Sally Hillsman Baker's article on women in blue-collar and service jobs is notable for the extent and depth of its coverage. After social scientists had neglected blue-collar working women for decades, several significant articles on this topic were published in the 1970s,[2] and Baker's chapter not only discusses them but also reports on her own major study of vocational training in New York City. Like other authors in this section, Baker examines job training, entry, and on-the-job experiences, and she shows specifically how occupational sex-typing and discrimination against women, especially black and Puerto Rican women, takes place in blue-collar jobs at all levels. Her analysis identifies employer preferences as one important factor influencing the sex-typing of jobs and the racial discrimination found in vocational training programs. Baker considers the efficacy of unionization as a solution to the problems of segregation experienced by working-class women.

David Katzman's chapter is concerned with another category of blue-collar work, private household service. In one of the first published analyses of its kind, Katzman, a social historian, traces the history and attempted reforms of this occupation. He also describes the nature of the work, including the private and isolated work setting and the highly personal employer–employee relationship in which, unlike most other jobs, both parties are generally women. Domestic service is an occupation deserving far more attention than it has received in the past; certainly it is one that sociologists should observe closely in the future, since it is now the object of both unionization and professionalization efforts. Should these efforts succeed, they might improve the working conditions and upgrade the social status of both paid and unpaid private household workers. Katzman notes several reasons why the prospects of success, unfortunately, are not too bright.

Unpaid household work is the work performed by more women than any other job, whether these women also participate in the labor force or not. Joann Vanek analyzes this job, describing historical trends in the nature of household tasks, the amount of time spent in housework by both employed and unemployed wives, and efforts that have been made to calculate the value of housework. One of her points is a sobering one: that the employment of wives has little effect on the amount of time husbands spend doing housework. Not only does the employed wife's "double duty" reduce the time she has for needed relaxation, but it also makes it very hard for her to assume more responsibility at her paid job when she wants to do so. Vanek's chapter gives us the basis for analyzing the housewife's work as an occupation, in terms of training, entry, career mobility, and informal on-the-job experiences, and for considering how this job resembles and differs from the other occupations discussed in this section.

NOTES

1   Valerie Kincade Oppenheimer, *The Female Labor Force in the United States,* Population Monograph Series, no. 5 (Berkeley: University of California, Institute of International Studies, 1970), pp. 96–116; see also James Grimm's chapter below.

2 Cf. Nancy Seifer, *Absent from the Majority: Working Class Women in America* (New York: American Jewish Committee, National Project on Ethnic America, 1973); Pamela Roby, *The Conditions of Women in Blue-Collar, Industrial and Service Jobs: A Review of Research and Proposals for Research, Action and Policy* (New York: Russell Sage Foundation, forthcoming); Barbara M. Wertheimer and Anne H. Nelson, *Trade Union Women, a Study of Their Participation in New York City Locals* (New York: Praeger Publishers, 1975).

Women in Male-Dominated Professions

Michelle Patterson
and
Laurie Engelberg

Although the past several decades have witnessed a striking increase in female labor force participation, the professions have not opened to women in substantial numbers. The professions are at the top of the American occupational hierarchy in terms of the power and prestige they confer on their practitioners. The major professions of medicine, law, and higher education have been in existence for centuries. Begun as medieval guilds reserved to men, they have remained bastions of male dominance.

This chapter explores the place of women in the traditionally male world of these three professions. Although the work performed by each profession is quite different, the general patterns and trends with respect to women in them are quite similar. The most significant fact about women in these three professions is that there are so few of them. Beyond this, women in these professions are likely to hold less desirable positions than men and to be paid less for equivalent work. In short, the position of women in the professions has traditionally been, and continues to be, a marginal one. The root causes, as we shall see throughout our examination of medicine, law, and higher education, lie primarily in overt and subtle discrimination and in the conflicting role-demands that are placed on women.

THE PROFESSIONS

Almost everyone knows what occupations are considered professions in the United States, and most people have a rough idea of the characteristics that describe the professions. These characteristics have as much to do with formalized privilege and power as with the type of training or work involved in the professions. The "professionalization" of an occupation allows practitioners to lay claim to an exclusive market for their particular service.

Sociological definitions describe an "ideal type" or model rather than any actual profession; a particular profession will only approximate the attributes of the ideal type. The traditionally accepted characteristics that are used to distinguish professions are: (1) a basis of systematic theory and wide knowledge of a specialized technique obtained by a long period of intensive training; (2) authority based on this knowledge and recognized by both the clientele of the professional group and the larger community; (3) autonomy (based on the claim of unique expertise) in the exercise of the skills, in the training of new entrants, and in the evaluation and control of practice of the profession; (4) a code of ethics and professional culture developed by formal professional associations, inculcated by professional schools, and regulating the relations of professionals with clients and with colleagues; and (5) an intense commitment to the profession based on the required long investment in professional training and on a strong sense of identification with the work.[1]

Although specialized knowledge and skill are frequently used to define the professions, the possession of special expertise also becomes an ideology when used by a group to advance its claim to be a profession.[2] Knowledge itself does not give power; however, exclusive knowledge does give power, particularly when government grants a particular group the exclusive right to use or to evaluate a body of knowledge or skill. A profession has to organize and act as an interest group first to pressure the government to convey this right to it and later to promote itself and protect itself from groups with competing aims that may threaten its exclusive authority.

In brief, then, a profession can be defined as an organized occupation that makes a claim to special, esoteric competence and to concern for the quality and benefits to society of its work. By virtue of this claim, it is given the exclusive right to perform a particular type of work, to control the training for and access to it, and to control the way the work is performed and how it is evaluated.[3] Professions thus have monopolies over particular markets for particular services.

Professions maintain their monopolies and their control partly by devising and promoting models of the professional practitioner. These models, which the professions seek to maintain at all costs, depict the practitioner as having the requisite knowledge, skill, and commitment to serve the community properly. The practitioner almost always has one other attribute (supported in recent years by media characterizations): he is male. In fact, men have continued to dominate the professions, in large part, as a result of this model of the practitioner. The public expects professionals to be men, and women professionals tend to be viewed as oddities. The near-monopoly of men over the professional monopolies contributes greatly to the dominant position of men in American society.

With these models of practitioners, the professions in the United States have traditionally been sex-typed. According to Robert K. Merton, "Occupations can be described as 'sex typed' when a very large majority of those in them are one sex and when there is an associated normative expectation that this is as it should be."[4] For example, at present about 97 percent of doctors and 93 percent of lawyers are male. The subordinate professions, such as nursing and librarianship, have traditionally been female-dominated (see James Grimm's chapter below). As Cynthia Epstein observes:

> The more nearly a profession is made up entirely of members of one sex, the less likely it is that it will change its sex composition in the future and the more affected will be the performance of those few members who are not of that sex. Sex-typing tends to be a self-perpetuating process operating according to the dynamics of the self-fulfilling prophecy.[5]

That such sex-typing is not the result of the inherent nature of the work performed is demonstrated by the fact, noted below, that in other countries women comprise the majority in professions that are considered "male" in the United States.

When an occupation becomes sex-typed, the sex of the members of the minority becomes occupationally salient. Those whose sex does not fit the model of the practitioner of their profession will be viewed as "deviant" and treated accordingly by patients or clients. R. Barker compares the uncertainty in social interactions experienced by these atypical practitioners with that of the physically disabled:

[Such people] can never be sure what the attitude of a new acquaintance will be, whether it will be rejective or accepting, until the contact has been made. This is exactly the position of the adolescent, the light-skinned Negro, the second-generation immigrant, the socially mobile person, and the woman who has entered a predominantly masculine occupation.[6]

A woman in a male profession, then, is forced to be self-conscious, burdened by the feeling that she is "on." She must calculate the impression she is making and counteract possible wrong assumptions about and misperceptions of her by others.[7] Behavior that would be viewed favorably in a male may be interpreted as demonstrating a woman's lack of suitability for her profession:

> Men, according to many attorneys, expect a woman to be emotional, so they read irrationality into her every word and gesture. "If a man gives the riot act to his secretary when she's made a mistake, he runs a tight ship," comments one female attorney. "Let a woman do the same thing and she's neurotic." Her female colleague agrees: "When a male attorney gets into a heated discussion over a point of law, he's a dynamic ball of fire. Should a woman attorney get equally excited, she's overwrought, easily agitated, and taking the matter personally."[8]

Displays of behavior that are thought to be "typically female" conflict with the woman's role as a professional. On the other hand, for many women exceptional professional competence may conflict with their role as "woman." Matina Horner found that women were much more likely than men to be disconcerted, troubled, or confused by the prospect of success in a typically male profession.[9] She found that women tend to see success as being accompanied by a loss of femininity, social rejection, and personal or societal destruction, and she concluded they may have an unconscious motive to avoid success. Later researchers have more clearly identified this phenomenon as a "fear of sex-atypical behavior" coupled with a motive to avoid the costs involved in violating sex-role norms. In any case, women see themselves as having to manage the effects of role deviation if they choose male-dominated professions.

The result is that women find it harder to get into and remain in the professions than men do. Problems of access to, entry of, and persistence in professional training are forerunners of difficulties faced by women in the professions. Once they have joined the professional ranks women must be far more conscious of competing demands on them than men, and problems of career management, including maintenance and advancement, come to the fore. The sections that follow explore these problems faced by women in three professions: medicine, law, and higher education.

MEDICINE

Only about 7 percent of American doctors today are women, and the proportion of women among active American physicians has remained essentially unchanged since the turn of the century.[10] A few comparisons demonstrate how small this proportion is. In Great Britain women constitute 24 percent of all physicians; in Germany they are 30 percent; in the Netherlands they are 20 percent; and in the Soviet Union medicine is a "female" profession—72 percent of the physicians are women.[11] The only Western country with a lower proportion of women in the medical profession than the United States is Spain, with approximately 3 percent.[12] On the other hand, women constitute approximately 70 percent of all health workers in the United States; they are 98 percent of all professional nurses and 96 percent of all practical nurses.[13] Thus, medicine in the United States has a clear, internal, sex-typed hierarchy, with male doctors on the top and women nurses and hospital workers on the bottom.

What accounts for the relatively small number of women physicians in the United States? In the beginning there was open discrimination against women. The first medical school in the United States was established in 1767, and no women were permitted to enroll. It was not until 1847 that the first woman was admitted to an American medical school, and she was admitted at least partially as a practical joke.[14]

Women could not join the American Medical Association until 1915. Harvard University maintained the tradition of excluding women from medical practice until 1945, when it first accepted a woman into its medical school; Jefferson Medical College in Philadelphia opened its doors to women only in 1960 and appears to be the last medical school to allow female entry.

In more recent years, the barriers to women entering medicine have been no less present, but they have been more subtle. One significant finding is that only 10 percent of the college women who declare premedical majors actually complete all premedical requirements, take the Medical College

Admission Test, and apply to medical school.[15] Thus, a lack of persistence at the college level contributes to a low rate of female medical school applicants. College vocational counselors have been identified as an extremely potent force steering women away from medicine.[16] Counselors tend to exaggerate the difficulty of medical school to women and play on women's fears and anxieties about engaging in conduct that is not "appropriate" for a female. Conversely, encouragement from others is one of the most significant factors influencing women who do decide to study medicine.[17]

Once women apply to medical schools they confront still another barrier. More than half the physicians surveyed in 1973 (50 percent of the men and 62 percent of the women) believed that women were discriminated against

> 〇〇 **Only about 7 percent of American doctors today are women, and the proportion of women among active American physicians has remained essentially unchanged since the turn of the century.** 〇〇

in admissions to medical school.[18] Testimony at 1970 hearings before the Special Subcommittee on Education of the House Committee on Education and Labor demonstrates that this belief is well founded. The testimony disclosed that many medical schools applied an "equal rejection" theory, by which applicants were separated according to sex and an equal proportion of each sex admitted.[19] This procedure was inherently discriminatory against women because their smaller applicant pool contained only the brightest and most determined women, who had succeeded in completing the premedical program despite college barriers. Indeed, the testimony showed that many of the women rejected were as qualified as or better qualified than men who were accepted; but for their sex, they would have been admitted. Another study found that, while medical schools have policies of formal equality, there are subtle prejudices against women, especially those with children.[20] Rather than openly rejecting applications on the basis of sex, these medical schools tend to question women applicants' motives more than men's. Women applicants are viewed as less dedicated to the ultimate practice of medicine and as presenting "higher risks" of failure to complete medical training. On these bases, rather than simply sex, women are prevented from entering medical schools.

In spite of the barriers, recent trends in women's medical school enrollments are upward. In 1965, only 7.7 percent of all American medical students were women. By 1976, this proportion had nearly tripled, rising to 20.5 percent. Even more encouraging, the proportion of first-year medical students who were women had grown to 24 percent.[21]

For women who are admitted to medical school the struggle is not over. Although women medical students perform academically at least as well as their male counterparts, their attrition rate is approximately double that of the men: 16 percent of the women drop out of medical school, compared to only 8 percent of the men. Half the women who drop out, or 8 percent of women medical students, leave for nonacademic reasons, while only 3 percent of the males leave for those reasons.[22] Lest these numbers be read to support the "high risk" rationale for discrimination against women, it should be pointed out that what appears to be going on in medical school is, at least in part, a self-fulfilling prophecy. Medical schools do not provide a welcoming or supportive atmosphere for the women they grudgingly admit. Most of the women who completed medical school were the daughters of doctors, who could find support at home.[23] Conversely, most women who dropped out of medical school had mothers who were housewives and provided no role-model for the ordeal they were enduring.[24]

Women who overcome the barriers to entering a medical career then confront problems of career management, which they must solve in order to continue in their chosen profession. Two of the major areas in which career management by women physicians is evident are choice of specialty and choice of type of practice.

Table 1 presents a breakdown of the specialties of practicing women physicians, based on the 324,942 doctors listed in the American Medical Association's "Physician Master List."[25] The table shows that more women—almost one-fifth of all women physicians—specialized in pediatrics than in any other area. In contrast, only about one woman in ten, compared to

TABLE 1   Specialization of Women Physicians

Specialty	Percentage		Ratio of actual to expected
	Actual (N = 20,304)	Expected*	
General Practice	12.1	19.4	0.62
Medical Specialties (subtotal)	31.9	23.7	1.35
Allergy	0.6	0.6	1.00
Cardiovascular	0.8	2.0	0.40
Dermatology	1.3	1.3	1.00
Gastroenterology	0.2	0.6	0.33
Internal medicine	10.2	12.6	0.81
Pediatrics	17.9	5.9	3.03
Pulmonary	0.9	0.7	1.29
Surgical Specialties (subtotal)	9.9†	27.4†	0.36
General surgery	1.4	9.4	0.15
Obstetrics, gynecology	6.2	6.0	1.03
Ophthalmology	1.5	3.2	0.47
Orthopedic surgery	0.2	3.0	0.07
Otolaryngology	0.3	1.7	0.18
Plastic surgery	0.2	0.5	0.40
Other surgery	0.2	3.5	0.06
Other Specialties (subtotal)	39.0	25.1	1.55
Anesthesiology	7.2	3.4	2.12
Neurology	1.0	0.9	1.11
Occupational medicine	0.4	0.9	0.44
Pathology	5.7	3.3	1.73
Psychiatry	13.7	7.3	1.88
Physical medicine	1.1	0.5	2.20
Preventive medicine	0.5	0.3	1.67
Public health	2.8	1.0	2.80
Radiology	2.9	4.1	0.71
Other specialty	3.7	3.3	1.12
Unspecified	7.1	4.4	1.61

Source: Josephine E. Renshaw and Maryland Y. Pennell, "Distribution of Women Physicians, 1969," *The Woman Physician* 26 (1971): 187–195.

*This is the percentage of women that would practice the specialty if the sex composition of each specialty reflected the sex composition of the profession as a whole.

†The sum of component specialities does not equal the subtotal because numbers were rounded.

three out of ten men, is found in any of the surgical specialties. In comparing the expected percentage to the actual percentage of women in each medical specialty, pediatrics again stands out: three times more women are found than would be expected according to their proportion in the profession. Other areas in which women are substantially overrepresented are anesthesiology, pathology, psychiatry, physical medicine, preventive medicine, and public health. Women are substantially underrepresented in nine fields, most of them prestigious specialties: cardiovascular, gastroenterology, general surgery, opthalmology, orthopedic surgery, otolaryngology, plastic surgery, other surgery, and occupational medicine. Obstetrics and gynecology are the only surgical specialties in which women are not underrepresented. Women are also underrepresented in general practice, where the actual number of women is slightly more than half the expected proportion. Overall, the seven fields in which women are overrepresented contain almost half of all practicing women physicians (48.9 percent), more than double the expected proportion (21.7 percent). Only one in twenty women physicians (5.2 percent) is in any of the nine specialties in which women are substantially underrepresented, compared to an expected proportion of one in four (24.8 percent).[26]

These figures imply that women's choices of specialty are determined, in part, by a conscious attempt to manage their careers in order to minimize both internally and externally perceived conflicts between their roles as women and their roles as doctors. One study of 525 doctors who had been public health doctors at some time in their careers showed similarly skewed results in the specialties of male and female doctors, and this led John Kosa and Robert Coker to suggest that "women doctors tend to manage their professional career by selecting for work those fields of medicine and that type of practice which are least likely to offer work duties incompatible with the female task."[27] By practicing pediatrics, women conform to the feminine role stereotype of caring for children. Psychiatry, another "caring" specialty, also draws large numbers of women. Perhaps not coincidentally, psychiatry was ranked lowest by medical students of both sexes who were asked to evaluate the relative standing of specialties within the profession.[28]

The conflict that is managed by women's choice of specialty in medicine is one that appears to exist primarily in the minds of the public and, perhaps, male doctors. For one thing, single women physicians, who do not experience the same family demands in their "female" role as their married counterparts, are not significantly more likely to practice the primarily male specialties. More significantly, the specialties in which women do cluster conform more to the *idea* of the woman's role than to the practical demands of that role. For example, the reality of the practice of pediatrics is that it is "incompatible with the female task" in many ways. It is a specialty that involves many house calls and calls late at night and would interfere with a woman doctor's ability to manage tasks at home. Likewise, obstetrics, the only surgical specialty in which women are not underrepresented, probably causes more interruptions of the doctor's personal life than any other surgical specialty. Pediatrics and obstetrics, however, conform more closely to the stereotypical view that "children's problems" are the province of women, and women physicians may have found that the public is more likely to bring its children than its general medical problems to them.

A recent study of internal labor market distribution lends further support to the view that women's choices of specialty in medicine may result from career management decisions prompted by popular prejudices. Jill Quadagno's study found that women's specialty choices may be the result of a subtle discrimination that encourages them to enter certain specialties, while discouraging them from others.[29] She notes: "Rejection in some areas, encouragement in others and a tendency to avoid open confrontations all work to affect the specialty choice of women physicians and ultimately their distribution in the labor force."[30] Thus, the consequence of increased numbers of women in medicine may not be the eradication of differences between male and female physicians, but an increasing differentiation of specialties on the basis of sex.

The second area in which women doctors tend to manage their careers in order to maintain them is in their choice of type of practice. Women physicians are far more likely than men to be salaried and less likely to be in private practice (particularly as sole practitioners) than their male counterparts.[31] While 31 percent of the women are in salaried positions (compared to 15 percent of the male physicians), only 48 percent of the women are self-employed (compared to 75 percent of the men). Similarly, only 52.5 percent of the females are in full-time practice, compared to 79.1 percent of the males.[32] Again, the choice involved in this aspect of career management is not altogether a free one. It is likely that the public's "Marcus Welby" model of the physician deters many women who would otherwise wish to enter private practice on a full-time basis.

Marriage and family have a significantly different impact on the careers of male and female physicians. An early marriage or engagement among male physicians is associated with a tendency to select private practice. Among women, on the other hand, marriage or engagement is associated with a tendency to take a salaried position.[33] Similarly, although marriage and family have no noticeable effects on the career development of male physicians, they have the effect of lessening or interrupting the practice of female physicians. Harold Kaplan found that 38 percent of women doctors removed themselves from professional activities for four years or more due to pregnancy and/or family responsibilities.[34] Single women physicians fall between married women and men in their degree of professional involvement and level of achievement; those who are in academic medicine actually publish more than both married women and men.[35] In spite of the fact that marriage and family may interrupt the careers of women physicians, at any given time approximately 90 percent of women doctors are professionally active (at least part-time),[36] thus demonstrating the high commitment of these women to their careers.

Another method of career management that allows women to deal with competing family and societal demands is simply restriction of their professional involvement. Thus, women physicians work fewer hours per year on the average, see fewer patients on the average, and spend fewer total hours in professional activities than do men.[37]

Partly as a consequence of managing their careers by choice of specialty and type of practice and partly as a result of patient and employer discrimination, women physicians earn less income than their male counterparts for the same number of hours of work. According to a 1972 report, women working 1,000 hours per year or more had a median income of $8,635, compared to $19,791 for men. The median income of women working 2,000 hours or more was $16,132, compared to $25,879 for men.[38]

LAW

The situation of women in law is remarkably similar to that of women in medicine. Only about 3 percent of the more than 300,000 practicing attorneys in the United States are female.[39] Again, international comparisons are instructive. For example, more than 30 percent of the lawyers in the Soviet Union are women.[40] On the other hand, in this country more than 98 percent of the secretaries, stenographers, and typists working in the legal field are women.[41] Women and men in law, like those in medicine, are sex-segregated in an occupational hierarchy: the lawyers and judges are almost invariably men, while the clerks, paralegal workers, and secretaries who work for them are usually women.

The low participation of women in law too had its genesis in open discrimination on the basis of sex. As late as 1869, when the Illinois State Bar refused to admit a woman, the United States Supreme Court upheld this action, with one justice declaring that "the natural and proper timidity and delicacy which belongs to the female sex evidently unfit it for many of the occupations of civil life."[42] Ironically, that same year the first American woman was admitted to the bar association in the state of Iowa. A year later, in 1870, the first woman graduated from an American law school.

> 🙶 Only about 3 percent of the more than 300,000 practicing attorneys in the United States are female. . . . On the other hand, more than 98 percent of the secretaries, stenographers, and typists working in the legal field are women. 🙷

However, Harvard Law School, venerating tradition, waited more than 130 years from its founding, before it began to admit women in 1950. As late as the fall of 1969, neither Notre Dame University nor Washington and Lee University had ever admitted a female student to its law school.[43]

In recent years less open forms of sex discrimination, many of them apparently operating before a student even applies for law school, have kept women from becoming lawyers. In the academic year 1969–70, women constituted only 1.7 percent of all law school applicants. By 1972–73 this proportion had risen to a still low 7.4 percent.[44] Beatrice Dinerman found that law schools admitted they scrutinized women's applications with greater care in evaluating ability, motivation, and the effects of marital status.[46] Another survey, conducted about the same time as Bysiewicz's, found that one-half of all lawyers, both male and female, felt that women encountered resistance at the point of admission to law school.[47]

Perhaps one reason that women seem to be deterred from applying to law school in the first instance is a widely held conception of law as a masculine field—a conception supported by the fact that only 3 percent of American lawyers are women. Many lawyers, both male and female, believe that there is something inherently masculine about the practice of law. The argument, related by Dinerman, runs like this:

> The law is born of conflict, and its practice, almost by definition, must be aggressive and warlike in nature. To be successful an attorney must have a fighting disposition. He should have mental alertness, unusual self-confidence, a logical mind and a non-retiring personality. These qualifications, many contend, are not the type of traits normally associated with the feminine personality. Female attributes, such as softness, gentleness and pacifism, just aren't characteristics that make for effective lawyers.[48]

Whatever the reasons for women's traditionally low participation in law schools, once the schools, under the impetus of the women's movement, began actively to encourage women to apply, their participation increased substantially. The proportion of women law students more than quadrupled in ten years: women constituted 23 percent of all law students in 1975, compared to 5 percent in 1965. The increase in women among first-year law students was even more dramatic, with three law schools having 1975 entering classes that were more than half women.[49]

James White's major study found that, once in law school, women were at least equal to men scholastically.[50] A survey of Columbia Law School students found that women received proportionately more academic honors than men, surpassed men in class rank, and surpassed men in law review participation. Indeed, law schools generally report that women outperform men scholastically.[51] In contrast to medicine, the dropout rates for male and female law students are virtually identical, as are the reasons for their attrition.[52]

After completing law school, women confront another barrier to the practice of law: finding a job. In a 1969 study, law schools reported difficulty convincing law firms to interview their finest female graduates, and female attorneys agreed that the most serious roadblock to a legal career was the difficulty of finding a first job.[53] In a matched sample of male and female Harvard Law School graduates, Dorothy Glancy found that women had more job interviews than men but men received a significantly greater number of job offers.[54] The position of women in law was well summarized by Professor Frederica Lombard of Wayne State University Law School, chairperson of the Committee on Women in Legal Education of the Association of American Law Schools:

> The real problem facing women lawyers is getting a job. The discrimination is somewhat less blatantly stated now than it was seven years ago when I got out of law school, but that is the only change. And if law firms do hire women, they still shunt them into estates and trusts. They tell us we're good at working with widows and orphans.[55]

A United States government publication advises women planning to make a career in the law:

> Women's opportunities seem best in those law specialties where their contributions to the field have already been recognized. Some of these are real estate and domestic relations work, women's and juvenile legal problems, probate work (about a third of all women judges are probate judges), and patent law for those who have the required training in science.[56]

Women lawyers do tend to cluster in the specialties where their "opportunities seem best." Like women physicians, they seem to manage their careers in two major ways: by choice of specialty and by choice of type of practice (discussed below). Table 2 shows the specialties indicated by White's sample when respondents were asked to describe their legal work at the time of the survey. The most striking finding concerns the relative proportions of men and women in general practice. Nearly half the men characterized themselves as general practitioners, while less than a third of the women did so. A similar avoidance of general practice and a greater tendency to specialize was noted among women in medicine. There may be fewer women generalists in both law and medicine because general practitioners are in the front line of their profession in terms of initial consultation by the patient or client and initial decisions about the legal or medical problems. It is the general practitioner who refers the person to a specialist. The bias against a woman lawyer or physician may be undercut somewhat if she receives clients or patients after initial introductions or referrals from a male lawyer or physician, who fits more closely the model of the professional practitioner.[57] White suggests that:

The woman makes a conscious choice to avoid general practice because she believes that a special skill will reduce or overcome sex discrimination. Or, the relative absence of women in general practice may mean only that some employers hire women for specialized positions in probate, tax and other fields.[58]

Table 3, which presents data on the type of work actually performed by lawyers, gives a better idea of the specialties attorneys actually practice. According to White's study, men dominate litigation and corporate work. Women predominate, to a significant degree, in trusts and estates and domestic relations—and these are the traditional female domains in the profession.[59] White found a surprisingly high proportion of women engaged in litigation, given the common belief that women are rarely trial lawyers, but his data reveal nothing about the type or size of the litigation they handle. Women may try only cases of relatively little importance, and, therefore, of low visibility. On the whole, women lawyers are engaged either in low-prestige specialties, such as domestic relations, in which there are large proportions of female clients, or in specialties such as trusts and estates where firms

TABLE 2   Specialties of Attorneys by Sex

	Percentage	
Specialty in law	Women (N = 654)	Men (N = 1115)
General practice	31.4	49.0
Litigation	7.0	7.2
Corporate	5.2	3.8
Tax	4.8	3.5
Trusts and estates	4.1	1.1
Criminal	4.1	2.1
Labor	1.8	2.2
Real estate	1.5	1.7
Domestic relations	0.3	0.0
Other (including nonlaw)	39.8	29.4

Source: James J. White, "Women in the Law," *Michigan Law Review* 65 (1967): 1064, exhibit 7. Reprinted by permission of the publisher and the author.

can put them in "back rooms," making sure they do not have contact with big clients who, the firms claim, would find it unacceptable to deal with women.

The second area in which women lawyers, like their medical counterparts, engage in career management is in their choices of type of practice. There is a smaller proportion of women than men in the private sector—71 percent of all women lawyers compared to 82 percent of all men lawyers.[60] Among those in private practice, women are much more likely to practice alone than are men: 41 percent of the women attorneys are sole practitioners, compared to 35 percent of the men. Conversely, only 20 percent of the women are in law firms, while 35 percent of the men are. Among those in firms, fewer women are partners (joint owners of the firm rather than employees): only 65 percent of the women are partners, while 79 percent of the men are. Women are least represented in middle-sized firms. White found that one-fifth of the men (21.7 percent) were in firms of five to thirty people, but only one-tenth (10 percent) of the women were.[61] It seems that women must either "go it alone" (or virtually so) in a very small practice or

TABLE 3   Type of Work Performed
by Attorneys by Sex

	Percentage	
Type of work	Women ($N = 575$)	Men ($N = 952$)
Trusts and estates	60.0	52.7
Real estate	51.0	52.8
Domestic relations	49.8	38.6
Litigation	45.6	58.5
Corporate	42.0	53.8
Tax	31.0	27.9
Criminal	27.7	28.0
Labor	7.3	11.8

Source: James J. White, "Women in the Law," *Michigan Law Review* 65 (1967): 1063, exhibit 6. Reprinted by permission of the publisher and the author.

join the extremely large firms that can more easily tolerate "deviant" practitioners and where they may remain anonymous.

Finding private practice less inviting than their male colleagues do, a slightly higher proportion of the women turn to government positions: 14 percent of female attorneys are employed by the government at one level or another, compared to 10.5 percent of males.[62] But, while men tend to use government employment as a stepping-stone into private practice, a large proportion of women make it a career.[63]

Finally, a much higher proportion of female attorneys (13.2 percent) than males (4.7 percent) are inactive or retired, despite the fact that there are no significant age differences.[64] For the most part, the inactivity of women attorneys is attributable to child rearing. A 1970 study of Harvard Law School graduates found that at the time of the survey 98 percent of the men but only 84 percent of the women were employed.[65] Of the women who were not employed, 90 percent had left the profession because they had very young children. White found that 85.5 percent of the males who responded to his survey were employed full-time and none said that they were not working.[66] Among women attorneys, 65.3 percent were working full-time, another 12.1 percent were working part-time, and 12.9 percent were not working at the time of the study. The record for women without children, however, was remarkably similar to that of the men: 83.5 percent of the single women and 74.5 percent of the married women without children were employed full-time and an additional 5.5 percent and 4 percent, respectively, were employed part-time. It was married women with children who had to bear the primary burden of child rearing and who found that career and family were incompatible. Only 44.5 percent of the married women with children were employed full-time, although another 22.2 percent were employed part-time. More than one-quarter of the married women with children (25.7 percent) were not working at the time of the study.

That women attorneys are discriminated against in salaries as well as hiring is almost universally recognized by practicing lawyers of both sexes (88 percent of the women and 80 percent of the men believe this).[67] Women attorneys are clearly paid less than men. The average annual salary differential between females and males the first year out of law school is $1,500. Within ten years this discrepancy grows to between $9,000 and $18,000 a year.[68] Dinerman and White found differences even when they controlled for variations in the amount of time worked, experience, class rank, participation on the law review while in law school (an honor), and type of work performed.[69] The differences in income that remain, after accounting for these factors, are simply a function of sex discrimination.

HIGHER EDUCATION

The situation of women in higher education is probably the most researched and best known among female situations in the professions. In 1972–73 a major effort was undertaken to investigate and to compile in one place the data and analyses pertaining to all aspects of women in higher education. The results of this effort were published in *Academic Women on the Move*, edited by Alice S. Rossi and Ann Calderwood.[70] The book contains "an overview of the major research findings on differences between women and men students in higher education; . . . a summary of the major results of research on the career development and status of women faculty compared to that of men; . . . a discussion of the current economic and political scene in academe as it bears upon the future status of academic women;" and "a brief overview of the political revolt of academic women during the past five years and the direction this movement may take in the coming years."[71] Since the situation of women differs by type of institution (university, four-year college, two-year college), institutional control (public or private, sectarian or nonsectarian), and discipline (physics, English, etc.), to mention only a few of the major differences, our discussion can give only a brief and general overview.

The proportion of women faculty in higher education in 1975–76 was 21.7 percent. This reflected a decline from the proportion a year earlier, 22.5 percent (see table 4), and only a minimal increase (from 19.1 percent) over the period seven years earlier, 1968–69.[72] The role women play in academe is even somewhat less equitable than these figures suggest. In universities, where graduate training and research take place and, accordingly, where the highest pay and prestige are found, only 16.4 percent of the faculty were women in 1975–76. This proportion, too, declined from the preceding year's 16.8 percent and has risen only slightly (from 14.8 percent) since 1968–69. The decline both overall and in universities was greatest at the highest ranks (see table 4).

Higher education, like the other professions, was begun on a "male only" basis. It traces its origins in this country to the founding of Harvard University in 1636. Not until 200 years later, in 1837, did Oberlin College admit the first woman to higher education in the United States.[73]

Institutional barriers to women's entry into higher education, like those in law and medicine, have become less overt and more subtle. Women applicants to colleges and graduate schools are better qualified scholastically than their male counterparts, yet differential admissions policies disadvantage women; these facts have been well documented.[74] More women undergraduates than men are dependent upon their families for financial support because of sex discrimination in the allocation of financial aid.[75] Proportionately fewer high-ability girls from lower income families attend college than boys from all ability groups, and this is a clear waste of some of our brightest students; the availability of financial aid for these young women might bring them into higher education.

For the relatively few women who make it to graduate school, the endurance contest is far from over, and deviant status, competing demands, socialization, and discrimination continue to take a toll. The mean time for completion of the doctorate ranges from 11.7 years in the humanities to 7.3 years in the physical sciences.[76] More than three-fifths of women graduate students do not make it, compared to about two-fifths of the men. A study by Michelle Patterson and Lucy Sells showed that among the rela-

TABLE 4   Proportion of Faculty Members Who Are
Women (by Rank), 1974–75 and 1975–76

Rank	All institutions (Percentage)			Universities (Percentage)		
	1974–75	1975–76	Change	1974–75	1975–76	Change
Professor	10.1	9.1	−1.0	6.1	5.6	−0.5
Associate professor	17.3	16.6	−0.7	12.7	12.3	−0.4
Assistant professor	27.9	27.9	0.0	23.9	24.5	+0.6
Instructor	48.0	49.3	+1.3	46.8	48.3	+1.5
Lecturer	41.4	41.2	−0.2	36.1	39.6	+3.5
All ranks	22.5	21.7	−0.8	16.8	16.4	−0.4

Source: Computed from "Nearly Keeping Up: Report on the Economic Status of the Profession, 1975–76," *AAUP Bulletin* 62 (1976): 220, table 20.

tively elite graduate students who received Woodrow Wilson Fellowships, 64 percent of the women dropped out—and this rate was 20 percent higher than that for men.[77] Although the attrition rate varied across disciplines (for men, from a high of 52 percent in the humanities to a low of 26 percent in the physical sciences; for women, from 66 percent to 54 percent, respectively), the rate was always significantly lower for men. Moreover, while marriage had no effect on male graduate students (the dropout rate was 45 percent for single men and 44 percent for married men), it hindered women graduate students (the attrition rate for married women was 9 percent higher than that for single women).

After the many years of training for academic work, the career that women can expect is still not equal to that of men. Women are disadvantaged most obviously in faculty rank. Table 5 presents the actual and expected (proportional) ranks of women in higher education careers. Women are most underrepresented at the full professor rank: there are substantially less than half the number who would hold this position if sex were not a factor. At universities it is a meager one-third. Women are also significantly underrepresented at the other tenured rank, associate professor. More than one-fourth of all women faculty are in the instructor and lecturer ranks—

TABLE 5   Rank of Women in Higher Education, 1975–76

Rank	All institutions			Universities		
	Percentage		Ratio of actual to expected	Percentage		Ratio of actual to expected
	Actual	Expected*		Actual	Expected*	
Professor	11.5	28.3	0.41	12.0	34.9	0.34
Associate professor	21.2	28.0	0.76	20.6	27.4	0.75
Assistant professor	42.4	32.7	1.30	43.4	29.3	1.48
Instructor	22.5	9.8	2.30	19.5	6.6	2.95
Lecturer	2.3	1.2	1.92	4.4	1.8	2.44

Source: Computed from "Nearly Keeping Up: Report on the Economic Status of the Profession, 1975–76," *AAUP Bulletin* 62 (1976): 219, table 18.

*This is the percentage of women that would hold each rank if the sex composition of each rank were the same as the sex composition of the institutions or universities as a whole.

temporary academic appointments that do not provide the salary or job rights of regular faculty positions. Most women in academe (67.2 percent, compared to less than 40 percent of the men) hold the three lowest positions—positions that have no job security and little prospect for career advancement.

Given the struggle for jobs and advancement, many women have apparently concluded that the only way to manage the competing demands of an academic career and a family is to shun marriage. Less than one-half the women academics (48.1 percent overall and 47.8 percent of universities) are married, compared to nine-tenths of the men (87.4 percent overall and 89.7 percent at universities).[78] Even fewer women are able to combine career and children: about one-third of the women in academe (33.6 percent overall and 34.8 percent at universities) have dependent children, compared to more than two-thirds of the men (70.4 percent overall and 71.1 percent at universities). Married women are substantially less likely to achieve tenure than unmarried women, who are still less likely to earn tenure than are men.[79]

Finally, women receive far less pay in academe than men. Indeed, sex differentials in salary have been found to be greater than sex differentials in rank.[80] Between 1974-75 and 1975-76 the percentage difference between the average compensation of men and that of women in higher education increased from 4.5 percent to 5.2 percent, although at universities it declined from 5.8 percent to 5.1 percent.[81]

CONCLUSION

Because their monopolies are repositories of significant economic and political power, the professions have been slow to yield to women. As we have seen, women in professions do not share the same situations as their male colleagues. Women face a host of problems—from initial, and sometimes continuing, overt discrimination to lower pay, less prestigious positions, and circumscribed specialties. They represent a very small minority, and their role in the professions can be characterized as marginal. Confronted with these barriers and with conflicting sex-role demands throughout their careers, professional women have resorted to individual strategies of career management.

Women have to be far more conscious about managing their careers than men. All professionals manage their careers to some extent, but for men career management is generally part of a larger process of career development. A man's career is managed not to maintain his position as a professional, but to develop and improve his opportunities. For a woman, career management may overshadow career development. She is forced to manage her career simply to maintain it, not only to improve it. The perceptions of fellow professionals and the public at large as to appropriate "female" behavior and specialties must be taken into account and managed by women, often by choosing types of practice that will be more readily accepted.

Events that may be of no consequence to male career development become problems to be managed by women professionals. For example, marriage and family are part of or at least consistent with a male professional's career development. For a woman, they constitute potential conflicts with career development and problems to be managed. The predominant structure of the contemporary American family and its accompanying sex-role differentiation create a double standard of expectations whereby the family and home are assumed to be the primary responsibility of the woman, even if she also holds a professional position. As long as women are primarily responsible for running the household and rearing the children, they will have to work at managing their careers in order simply to maintain them, much less make it to the top. Changes in the direction of an equal sharing of familial responsibilities will allow greater opportunities for the participation of women in the professions and reduce somewhat the need for career management. But such individual solutions are not enough.

In the late 1960s increasing numbers of professional women began to see their "private troubles" as public issues. They began to document their marginality in the professions, demonstrating that the paucity of women was a result both of real social constraints and of conscious and nonconscious discrimination. The need for constant career management on the part of women came to be seen as stemming directly from the fact that the structures of the professions were designed over the course of time to accommodate the work needs of the male professional routinely. Narrow, inflexible, and resistant to change, these structures are major impediments to the full participation of women. Higher education well illustrates this:

> Leaves of absence for research, reduced teaching loads upon the assumption of large administrative responsibilities, joint appointments for persons with expertise in two fields, and part-time appointments for senior faculty—these are just some of the adjustments men have built into the system to allow for the demands upon their time and energies.

Increasingly, requirements and expectations are being made flexible to accommodate militant minority groups, yet no provisions are made in academia for the added burdens of married career women. The academic man is not expected to make a choice between his family and his work; indeed, he is not expected to "raise" a family or be a "helpmate" to his spouse in the same sense that a woman is. But it is this choice—between family and career—that men routinely thrust upon married women by requiring them to comport themselves as though they were men—men who have molded the work structure to suit their gender.[82]

Suggestions for changing the professions to produce greater flexibility include the additions of routine leaves of absence for "nonprofessional" reasons, and split and part-time positions.

Joining together in professional organizations and activist groups, women professionals began to focus public attention on these inequities and to exert pressure to bring about change. Their efforts to open up the professions to women, coupled with the attention they drew to the low-paying, low-prestige, dead-end nature of most women's jobs, led more young women to break away from the ghetto of traditional women's occupations. A national survey of freshmen entering college in the fall of 1975 found that one woman in six (16.9 percent) is planning a career in business, engineering, law, or medicine.[83] This figure represents a 2-percent increase over 1974 and nearly triple the proportion in 1966, when only 5.9 percent of women college entrants planned such careers. A substantial influx of women into the professions will of itself end the marginality of women's roles and will go a long way toward making women's career management a normal part of their career development.

NOTES

1   See e.g., William J. Goode, "The Theoretical Limits of Professionalization," in *The Semi-Professions and Their Organization,* ed. Amitai Etzioni (New York: Free Press, 1969), pp. 266–313; Ernest Greenwood, "Attributes of a Profession," *Social Work,* July 1957, pp. 44–45; Edward Gross, *Work and Society* (New York: Thomas Y. Crowell Company, 1958), p. 77; Robert Perrucci and Joel E. Gerstl, *Profession without Community: Engineers in American Society* (New York: Random House, 1969), pp. 10–14.

2   Eliot Freidson, "Professions and the Occupational Principle," in *The Professions*

and Their Prospects, ed. Eliot Friedson (Beverly Hills: Sage Publications, 1973), p. 30.

3 Cf. Ibid., pp. 19–38.

4 Correspondence quoted in Cynthia Fuchs Epstein, *Woman's Place: Options and Limits in Professional Careers* (Berkeley and Los Angeles: University of California Press, 1971), p. 152. Also see Cynthia B. Lloyd, ed., *Sex, Discrimination, and the Division of Labor* (New York: Columbia University Press, 1975).

5 Ibid., p. 165.

6 R. Barker, "The Social Psychology of Physical Disability," *Journal of Social Issues* 4 (1948): 33.

7 Erving Goffman, *Stigma: Notes on the Management of Spoiled Identity* (Englewood Cliffs, N.J.: Prentice-Hall, 1961), p. 14.

8 Beatrice Dinerman, "Sex Discrimination in the Legal Profession," *American Bar Association Journal* 55 (1969): 953.

9 Matina F. Horner, "Fail: Bright Women," *Psychology Today,* November 1969, pp. 36–38; idem, "Femininity and Successful Achievement: A Basic Inconsistency," in *Roles Women Play: Readings toward Women's Liberation,* ed. Michele H. Garskof (Belmont, Calif.: Brooks/Cole Publishing Company, 1971), pp. 97–122.

10 R. J. Ruben, "Women in Medicine: Past, Present and Future," *Journal of the American Medical Women's Association* 27 (1972): 251–59; Maryonda Scher, "Women Psychiatrists in the United States," *American Journal of Psychiatry* 130 (1972): 1118–22.

11 Harold Kaplan, "Women Physicians: The More Effective Recruitment and Utilization of Their Talents and the Resistance to It," *Women Physician* 25 (1970): 561–70; John Kosa, "Women and Medicine in a Changing World," in *The Professional Woman,* ed. Athena Theodore (Cambridge, Mass.: Schenkman Publishing Company, 1971), pp. 709–19; Carol Lopate, *Women in Medicine* (Baltimore: Johns Hopkins University Press, 1968); John B. Parrish, "Women in Medicine: What Can International Comparisons Tell Us?" *Woman Physician* 26 (1971): 352–61.

12 The figures for women in dentistry are very similar: United States—2 percent; Soviet Union—85 percent; Denmark—75 percent; Israel—33 percent. Epstein, *Woman's Place,* p. 158; Parrish, "Women in Medicine"; Judith T. Shuval, "Sex Role Differentiation in the Professions: The Case of Israeli Dentists," *Journal of Health and Social Behavior* 11 (1970): 236–44.

13 U.S. Department of Labor, Women's Bureau, *1969 Handbook on Women Workers,* Bulletin no. 294 (Washington, D.C.: Government Printing Office, 1969).

14 Lopate, *Women in Medicine,* pp. 3–5.

15 Beverly C. Morgan, "Admission of Women into Medical Schools in the United States: Current Status," *Woman Physician* 26 (1971): 308.

16   Ibid., pp. 305–9; Minerva S. Buerk, "Career Status of Women Physicians," *Woman Physician* 26 (1971): 216–17.

17   Lopate, *Women in Medicine;* Nancy A. Roeske, "Women in Psychiatry: Past and Present Areas of Concern," *American Journal of Psychiatry* 130 (1973): 1127–31; Scher, "Women Psychiatrists."

18   Bradley Soule and Kay Standley, "Perceptions of Sex Discrimination in Law," *American Bar Association Journal* 59 (1973): 1145.

19   Pamela Roby, "Institutional Barriers to Women Students in Higher Education," in *Academic Women on the Move,* ed. Alice S. Rossi and Ann Calderwood (New York: Russell Sage Foundation, 1973), pp. 43–44; Alice S. Rossi, "Summary and Prospects," in *Academic Women,* pp. 511–12.

20   Kaplan, "Women Physicians."

21   "Medical Education in the United States, 1975–1976," *Journal of the American Medical Association* 236 (1976): 2962.

22   Morgan, "Admission of Women"; Scher, "Women Psychiatrists."

23   Lopate, *Women in Medicine.*

24   Morgan, "Admission of Women."

25   Josephine E. Renshaw and Maryland Y. Pennell, "Distribution of Women Physicians, 1969," *Woman Physician* 26 (1971): 187–95.

26   Michelle Patterson, "Sex and Specialization in Academe and the Professions," in *Academic Women on the Move,* Ed. Rossi and Calderwood, p. 316.

27   John Kosa and Robert E. Coker, Jr., "The Female Physician in Public Health: Conflict and Reconciliation of the Sex and Professional Roles," *Sociology and Social Research* 49 (1965): 295–96.

28   Robert K. Merton, Samuel Bloom, and Natalie Rogoff, "Studies in the Sociology of Medical Education," *Journal of Medical Education* 31 (1956): 552–65.

29   Jill S. Quadagno, "Occupational Sex-Typing and Internal Labor Market Distributions: An Assessment of Medical Specialties" (Ph.D. diss., University of Kansas, 1976).

30   Ibid., p. 31.

31   Kosa, "Women and Medicine."

32   Ruben, "Women in Medicine."

33   Kosa and Coker, "Female Physician in Public Health."

34   Kaplan, "Women Physicians."

35   Lopate, *Women in Medicine.*

36   Scher, "Women Psychiatrists"; Morgan, "Admission of Women."

37   Ruben, "Women in Medicine"; Scher, "Women Psychiatrists."

38   Ruben, "Women in Medicine."

39 Gail McK. Beckman, "A Comparison of Women in the Legal Profession in Scotland and America," *New York State Bar Journal* 42 (1970): 20–24; Arlene M. Simolike, "Ladies Create a New Trend in Legal Practice," *New York State Bar Journal* 45 (1973): 15–18; Soule and Standley, "Perceptions of Sex Discrimination."

40 Beckman, "Comparison of Women"; Doris L. Sassower, "Women in the Law: The Second Hundred Years," *American Bar Association Journal* 57 (1971): 329–32; Simolike, "Ladies Create a New Trend."

41 *1969 Handbook on Women Workers.*

42 Bradwell v. State, 83 U.S. 130, 141 (1972) (Bradley, J., concurring).

43 Beckman, "Comparison of Women"; Dorothy J. Glancy, "Women in Law: The Dependable Ones," *Harvard Law School Bulletin* 21 (1970): 23–33; Anne Thornton and Linda Davis, "Women at Harvard Law School," *Harvard Law School Bulletin* 21 (1970): 34–35.

44 Shirley Raissi Bysiewicz, "1972 AALS Questionnaire on Women in Legal Education," *Journal of Legal Education* 25 (1973): 503–13.

45 Ibid.

46 Dinerman, "Sex Discrimination."

47 Soule and Standley, "Perceptions of Sex Discrimination," p. 145.

48 Dinerman, "Sex Discrimination," p. 953.

49 James P. White, "Legal Education: A Time of Change." *American Bar Association Journal* 62 (1976): 335–358; Martha Grossblat and Bette H. Sikes, eds., *Women Lawyers: Supplementary Data to the 1971 Lawyer Statistical Report* (Chicago: American Bar Foundation, 1973).

50 James J. White, "Women in the Law," *Michigan Law Review* 65 (1967): 1051–122.

51 Dinerman, "Sex Discrimination."

52 Bysiewicz, "1972 AALS Questionnaire"; Dinerman, "Sex Discrimination."

53 Dinerman, "Sex Discrimination."

54 Glancy, "Women in Law."

55 *New York Times*, October 22, 1971, p. 25.

56 Verna E. Griffin, *Employment Opportunities for Women in Legal Work* (Washington, D.C.: Government Printing Office, 1958), p. 12.

57 Patterson, "Sex and Specialization," p. 320.

58 White, "Women in the Law," p. 1064.

59 Epstein, *Woman's Place;* Glancy, "Women in Law"; White, "Women in the Law."

60 Grossblat and Sikes, *Women Lawyers, p. 8.*

61   White, "Women in the Law," p. 1058.

62   Grossblat and Sikes, *Women Lawyers,* p. 8.

63   White, "Women in the Law," p. 1059.

64   Grossblat and Sikes, *Women Lawyers,* pp. 4, 8.

65   Glancy, "Women in Law."

66   White, "Women in the Law," p. 1065.

67   Soule and Standley, "Perceptions of Sex Discrimination," p. 1145.

68   Beckman, "Comparison of Women"; White, "Women in the Law," pp. 1055–56.

69   Dinerman, "Sex Discrimination"; White, "Women in the Law."

70   Published by Russell Sage Foundation, New York, in 1973.

71   Rossi, "Summary and Prospects," p. 505.

72   Alan E. Bayer, *Teaching Faculty in Academe: 1972–73* (Washington, D.C.: American Council on Education, 1973), p. 14.

73   Saul D. Feldman, *Escape from the Doll's House* (New York: McGraw-Hill Book Company, 1974), p. 21.

74   See Roby, "Institutional Barriers," pp. 38–44.

75   See ibid., pp. 44–50.

76   Allan Tucker, David Gotlieb, and John Pease, *Attrition of Graduate Students at the Ph.D. Level in the Traditional Arts and Sciences,* Publication no. 8 (East Lansing: Michigan State University, Office of Research and Development, 1964).

77   Michelle Patterson and Lucy Sells, "Women Dropouts from Higher Education," in *Academic Women on the Move,* ed. Rossi and Calderwood, pp. 84–89.

78   Bayer, *Teaching Faculty,* p. 27.

79   See Michelle Patterson, "Alice in Wonderland: A Study of Women Faculty in Graduate Departments of Sociology," *American Sociologist* 6 (1971): 229.

80   Helen S. Astin and Alan E. Bayer, "Sex Discrimination in Academe," in *Academic Women on the Move,* ed. Rossi and Calderwood, pp. 342–46.

81   "Nearly Keeping Up: Report on the Economic Status of the Profession, 1975–76," *AAUP Bulletin* 62 (1976): 221.

82   Patterson, "Alice in Wonderland," p. 233.

83   Alexander W. Astin, Margo R. King, and Gerald T. Richardson, *The American Freshman: National Norms for Fall 1975* (Los Angeles: University of California, Laboratory for Research in Higher Education, 1975), p. 32.

Women in Female-Dominated Professions

James W. Grimm

This chapter deals with several "helping" professions that women have entered in large numbers for some time now.[1] They include elementary school teaching, librarianship, nursing, and social work. I refer to them as "female-dominated professions" only in the sense that their membership is mostly female, not in the sense that women hold the most desirable jobs or positions of power in these fields. In fact, I attempt to demonstrate that men and women prepare for, enter, and progress within these professions in very different ways, and I argue that the sex-typed nature of work in elementary school teaching, librarianship, nursing, and social work makes women second-class citizens in their own professions.

The Bureau of the Census classifies these four occupations as *professional and technical* fields, those of highest prestige within the white-collar sector of the occupational structure. They are among the most prestigious occupations that employ large numbers of women, and the census classification clearly, and quite correctly, reflects this fact. However, sociologists who study occupations have tended to classify these four as "semiprofessions."[2] Most of these sociologists have attempted to develop a detailed model of higher status fields, in order to learn how and to what degree "professions" differ from each other and from "occupations." Without attempting to deny that the careers discussed here are less "professionalized" (according to the criteria of those sociologists) than medicine and law, for example, this chapter uses the term *profession* for librarianship, nursing, social work, and elementary school teaching. This is consistent with the idea that differences between established and developing professions are those of degree, not kind, and the notion that a given profession may be more or less professionalized, depending on which aspect of professionalization is under consideration.[3]

By professionalization I mean the process by which an occupation claims and receives the legal autonomy to exercise a monopoly over the delivery of an important service.[4] One of the major arguments of this chapter is that female-dominated professions have not obtained the power to professionalize themselves fully. Typically, as in medicine and law, a profession's legal monopoly includes training and licensing members to practice and prohibiting other occupations from encroaching on the service being delivered.[5] Later in this chapter I explore in some depth the idea that none of the female-dominated professions has been very successful in professionalizing. I believe this failure to professionalize fully stems primarily from the absence of a clear link between training, licensing, and practice in the female-dominated professions. The point is that the mere presence of large numbers of women in these fields cannot explain why female-dominated professions are less powerful than male-dominated professions.

Before evaluating the reasons for this lack of power, the chapter explores several questions: (1) What are the proportions of female workers in the occupations under discussion? (2) What are the processes by which people enter these fields? (3) What experiences characterize the careers of women and men in these occupations? (4) What future trends in employment may affect these fields?

EXTENT OF FEMALE DOMINATION

The most obvious characteristic of workers in the four occupations under consideration is that a large majority of them are women. In 1973 women constituted 82.1 percent of librarians, 97.8 percent of registered nurses, 60.8 percent of social workers, and 69.9 percent of elementary and secondary school teachers.[6] In this last category women are much more likely to be found as kindergarten and prekindergarten teachers (97.9 percent) and as elementary school teachers (84.5 percent) than as secondary school teachers

(49.5 percent).[7] The figures show clearly that the occupations are not just somewhat more female; they are predominantly female. This has been true for some time. Since before 1900, at least 70 percent of all librarians, nurses, and elementary school teachers have been women.[8] In all three cases, the occupation quickly became and has remained a major source of employment for women.

Several explanations have been given for the early and consistent female domination of these occupations.[9] First, many professions in which women now predominate, especially teaching, nursing, and social work, did not pay enough to attract men and became monopolized by women early in the 1900s.[10] Secondly, female-dominated professions have grown rapidly during this century, and the increased demand for workers enabled ever larger numbers of women to secure employment in them.[11] Thirdly, the supply of highly educated women qualified for and motivated to seek careers in these professions has increased as the pool of educated women has grown and as these women, including wives with children, have entered into paid employment outside the home in rapidly increasing numbers.[12] Fourthly, the work activity in these fields is closely linked with aspects of the traditional female role, including nurturance, caring, and socialization, especially of young children.[13] The cultural factors that have made such work seem appropriate for women are beyond a doubt a major explanation of why women have been socialized to enter these fields consistently.[14]

Professional and technical fields are sex-typed in terms of aggregate membership.[15] In 1973, approximately 14 percent of women (4.7 million) were in an occupation classified by the Bureau of the Census as professional or technical, yet about 60 percent of these women were employed as noncollege teachers and nurses. Excluding the other two female-dominated professions, librarianship and social work, women comprised fewer than one-third of the workers in all other professional and technical fields. For example, women were 12.2 percent of physicians, 27.1 percent of college and university teachers, 10.2 percent of engineers and scientists, 21.6 percent of accountants, and 19.5 percent of computer specialists.[16]

The overall occupational distribution of nonwhite women is considerably different from that of white women, and representation in the female-dominated professions also varies by race. From 1962 to 1974, the proportion of women in professional and technical occupations who were black rose from 7 to 10 percent. The figures for black men, incidentally, rose from 3.6 to 6.6 percent, confirming the idea that black women have greater opportunities in higher-status fields than do black men.[17] The increases in black female employment in this sector of the labor force, however, have occurred primarily in fields identified as female, not in other professions. In 1973 about 60 percent of all minority women in occupations classified as professional and technical by the Bureau of the Census were noncollege teachers and registered nurses.[18] As of 1974, black women were 9.8 percent of all registered nurses, 21.7 percent of all social workers, and 10.5 percent of all elementary school teachers. Only in social work does the proportion of black females exceed their proportion in all jobs (12.2 percent in all jobs in 1974).[19] Between 1962 and 1974 the proportion of registered nurses who were black women doubled (from 5 to 10 percent) and the proportion of black women in social work increased by half again (from 14 to 22 percent).[20] While the increase in black female librarians is not known, the number of blacks in librarianship doubled from 1960 to 1970 (from 4,000 to 8,000), and most of these new entrants were undoubtedly women. The proportion of black female elementary school teachers has remained stable at around 10.5 percent during the last thirteen years. At that time the proportions of black female professional and technical workers employed as registered nurses (17.9 percent), social workers (8.2 percent), and elementary school teachers (23.7 percent), exceeded the corresponding proportions for white females (17.7, 3.2, and 19.6 percent, respectively).[21] In general, then, the proportion of black women in most of the female-dominated professions has increased recently.

Within a given profession work may also be sex-typed. Many studies have demonstrated that women in male-dominated professions tend to be clustered in specialties—real estate law, pediatrics, residential architectural design —traditionally considered feminine, and in practice settings such as public health and government where earnings are based on salaries instead of fees for services.[22] Studies of men in female-dominated professions though few in number, indicate that men tend to be clustered in positions traditionally viewed as male—supervisor, director, administrator, principal, and so forth.[23] This sort of sex-typing within female-dominated professions is discussed further later in this chapter.

Some sociologists have concluded that it is the presence of disproportionate numbers of women in sex-typed fields such as librarianship, nursing, and social work that prevents these fields from progressing toward full status as professions. Indeed, an article widely cited in the literature on the occupations discussed here treats the presence of and presumed attitudes of women in these fields—deference toward men and lack of long-range am-

bition, among others—as characteristics that diminish the professionalization of the occupations.[24] This conclusion ignores the many other aspects
of work in the female-dominated professions that would limit professionalization irrespective of the gender of the workers.[25] Moreover, even if many
women in the professions had the traits implicitly ascribed to them by the
article, a body of growing literature clearly shows that women who have
demonstrated career commitment and productivity in these fields have been
thwarted by discrimination.

The tendency for professions to be sex-segregated is, however, important
in explaining the inequalities in employment opportunities and rewards

> 🎭 **Studies of men in female-dominated professions indicate that men tend to be clustered in positions traditionally viewed as male—supervisor, director, administrator, principal, and so forth. 🎭**

that exist between women and men in higher status fields. As noted above,
both white and nonwhite women continue to find jobs in occupations that
are dominated by females, maintaining society's labeling of certain occupational activities as female. Do these employment patterns help produce
the lower levels of education, income, and power held by women in these
fields?[26] To explore this question, the next section reviews the occupational
characteristics of female-dominated professions.

CHARACTERISTICS OF FEMALE-DOMINATED PROFESSIONS

Educational Requirements

For men, and to a somewhat lesser extent for women, close relationships
exist between duration and type of schooling, on the one hand, and choice
of a career, earnings, and unemployment, on the other. Women's educational backgrounds often reflect anticipated entry into female-dominated

professions. For example, women earning bachelor's and master's degrees are disproportionately represented in the fields of education, health, library science, and social sciences (including social work). In the 1970–71 school year, for example, the proportions of female baccalaureate earners in those fields were 74.4 percent, 77.2 percent, 92.2 percent, and 37.0 percent respectively. These fields accounted for approximately 58 percent of all the bachelor's degrees conferred on women that year. Among master's degree recipients in 1970–71 the concentration of women in preparatory work for female-dominated professions was even more pronounced. Over two-thirds of female master's degree recipients received them in education (53.8 percent), health (3.5 percent), library science (6.1 percent), and social science (including social work) (5.1 percent).[27]

Furthermore, the proportion of women earning degrees decreases as the level of education increases, from 43.5 percent for bachelor's to 40.1 percent for master's and 14.3 percent for doctoral degrees in 1970–71.[28] This phenomenon is obviously related to the fact that most female-dominated professions do not require a doctorate or professional degree requiring six or more years of higher education, as most male-dominated professions do. Few female-dominated professions require more than a fifth-year master's, and in many cases, such as nursing, the bachelor's degree suffices. A large proportion (46 percent in 1970–71) of degrees received by women are below the bachelor's level—associate degrees and other certificates.[29] Many of these degrees prepare and qualify recipients to work in female-dominated professions (registered and practical nurses in the health field, for example).

The disparity between the educational attainments of women and men is, of course, subject to alteration. It will decrease to the extent that more women prepare for and enter fields requiring six-year professional degrees or more—dentistry, law, medicine, veterinary medicine, and optometry among others, all of which have in the past been dominated by men. A recent analysis of data on women earning professional degrees indicates that, from 1960 to 1973, a steadily increasing proportion were earned in fields such as pharmacy, veterinary medicine, and optometry.[30] Less noticeable increases occurred in fields such as engineering, dentistry, and law. In many fields the number of women is so low, however (for example, 23 female optometrists in 1970 and 126 female veterinarians in 1973), that *any* increase is proportionally substantial.[31] In general, male domination of the professions that larger numbers of women are now entering is so great that it will be decades before a more balanced sex ratio is attained. (For further discussion of the male-dominated professions, see the chapter by Michelle Patterson and Laurie Engelberg above.)

Control of Entry and Licensing

In any profession the patterns of training and entry are shaped by the degree to which the placement of entrants is controlled by the profession itself, rather than outside forces, such as employing organizations. An important difference between male-dominated professions, such as law and medicine, and female-dominated professions, such as librarianship, school teaching, nursing, and social work, is that the employment of new recruits in the latter often is not contingent on acquisition of a professional degree. Multiple channels of entry into female-dominated professions continue to exist, because there are fewer legal regulations requiring those entering the field to hold a license, as in medicine, or to be certified, as in public accounting and clinical psychology.[32] Unless laws and rules governing employment require all practitioners to have professional degrees, women and men in the female-dominated professions will be less motivated to obtain formal and extended professional training.

While all the female professions have actively sought to upgrade the accepted requirements for practice through their professional associations, a master's degree is not required for practice by state law in most situations. For example, in almost all states the minimum educational requirement for school librarians—who comprised nearly half of all librarians in 1970—is a bachelor's degree and a state teaching certificate.[33] Only 15 percent of school libraries in a 1973 Bureau of Labor Statistics survey required a graduate degree in librarianship, compared to 70 and 95 percent of public and academic libraries respectively.[34] Within librarianship, men hold a disproportionate share of the specialized positions that, in general, require five or more years of higher education. While men were only 16 percent of all librarians as a whole in 1970, 60 percent of male librarians were employed in academic or special libraries, while only 26 percent of women librarians were similarly employed.[35] These disparities in employment reflect the fact that a higher proportion of the men (52 percent) than the women (39 percent) in librarianship have completed five or more years of higher education. The educational backgrounds of female librarians compare less favorably with those of women in other professional and technical fields than those of male librarians do with other male professionals.[36]

Nursing, like librarianship, does not necessitate advanced levels of training before entry. A degree in nursing is not a prerequisite for work in the settings that employ most registered nurses. In 1972, a large majority of nurses worked in hospitals (64.2 percent) and nursing homes (6.9 percent).[37] In both these settings only a small minority of registered nurses had baccalaureate or higher degrees in nursing (12.3 percent in hospitals and 7.8 percent in nursing homes). Similar figures on the proportion of nursing degree holders are found among private duty, industrial, and office nurses, while the percentage is somewhat higher among public health nurses (32.4 percent hold nursing degrees). Only in schools of nursing do a majority of registered nurses (58.1 percent) have baccalaureate or higher degrees in nursing.[38] While separate data on the education of male registered nurses are not available, it is doubtful that their training differs markedly from that of their female colleagues, since the vast majority of the men in nursing also work in hospitals and nursing homes (82.9 percent in 1972).[39]

Thus, in nursing, perhaps more than in any other female-dominated profession, formal training in the discipline is not tied to a license to practice. The absence of both a well-developed theoretical body of knowledge and a period of extended training over which practitioners claim control and monopoly keeps fields such as nursing from gaining the power and influence enjoyed by male-dominated professions.[40] The absence of such a monopoly over knowledge in the health field, which is clearly controlled by physicians, is, of course, intimately linked to the subordinate status of nurses (women) in the major settings where health care is delivered. Thus, the lack of a requirement of formal training for licensure in nursing is, in my opinion, of crucial importance. It illustrates why this female-dominated profession and others like it have less power than fields in which the profession itself rigidly controls licensure and the training or knowledge required for it. This fact, I believe, is far more important in denying practitioners autonomy and power in female professions than the practitioners' gender and the fact that females are stereotyped as "subordinates."

Unlike nurses, most school teachers are certified by and through state regulations governing public education. Nevertheless, elementary education is another profession in which the connection between formal training and entry into practice can be described as tenuous. Historically, many teachers began teaching without certification, particularly in times when the demand exceeded the supply of qualified teachers.[41] Private preparatory schools have hired teachers without regard to certification criteria, when they could.[42] In addition, the length and content of the specialized education required for certification in school teaching is not as extensive as for many other occupations requiring college training.[43] It has been estimated that education undergraduates spend between one and two years' worth of full-time study on specialized courses, primarily in standardized classroom instruction, such as lecture and discussion. The field of education lacks a "theory" of its own, and various attempts to integrate it with fields such as psychology have not fully succeeded.[44] In fact, much of the professional training in education takes place after a practitioner begins to teach and returns to college for continued study.[45] For these reasons it should come as no surprise that the vast majority of elementary school teachers (74.5 percent in 1970–71) hold no more than a baccalaureate.[46]

Social work resembles nursing in that the period of training is short and rather loosely linked to practice. In 1970 the National Association of Social Workers (NASW) redefined its educational qualifications for membership, in effect broadening the definition of a professional social worker to include those receiving undergraduate training in approved programs. Previously, only the two-year master's degree in social work (M.S.W.) had been recognized by the NASW as differentiating social work professionals.[47]

A number of developments led to this expansion of recognized professional training. First, only a minority of those doing social welfare work have had M.S.W. degrees.[48] Secondly, the NASW and other social work groups failed in an attempt to set consistent salary and employment standards in agency work—the type of work employing three-fifths of the NASW members in 1969.[49] Thirdly, undergraduate social work programs expanded throughout the 1960s, and by 1967 an estimated 16,000 students were in such programs; about half the graduates with social work majors entered social work employment directly. Undoubtedly many direct service positions were therefore filled by both persons who had M.S.W. degrees and those who did not.[50] Fourthly, during the 1960s increasing numbers of nonprofessionals (including the poor themselves) and people trained in social and behavioral sciences who did not have social work degrees became involved in agency work.[51]

New NASW membership criteria also provide for eventual entry of a person with a baccalaureate degree in any field, if employed (for two years) in a social work position.[52] Therefore, in the years ahead it is likely that entry into social work will be tied increasingly to college-level work rather than graduate professional training. Moreover, in 1970 only seven states had legal regulations for the licensing of social workers. It is apparent that social work has not always sought a monopoly over the training and placement of its recruits, and has not always been successful when it *has* sought this control.

Sex-typing within Professions

Sex-based patterns of entry exist within each of the female-dominated professions. This means that the career experiences of men and women differ in the female-dominated professions. Because the pathways of entry into various types of teaching are sex-typed, most women in teaching (two out of three in 1973–74) work in noncollege settings.[53] The concentration of women teachers at the elementary level explains some of the discrepancies between male and female teachers when different levels of instruction—elementary versus secondary—are lumped together and aggregate data analyzed. For example, among public school teachers in general, a much higher proportion of men (42.6 percent) than women (19.0 percent) have master's degrees or at least six years of higher education.[54] Male public school teachers earn more than their female colleagues ($9,854 compared to $8,953 in 1970–71).[55] Most women teach at the elementary, not secondary, level; as might be expected, the average salary of elementary school teachers was $10,541 in 1973–74, whereas for secondary school teachers it was $11,011.[56] Thus, adoption of standard pay schedules in schoolteaching based on subject taught, educational background, etc., has not and will not equalize the pay levels of male and female teachers.

The sex-based differences between teachers in education, income, and other professional traits do not necessarily reflect differences in aspirations, abilities, performance, or career commitment. Rather, men and women have traditionally prepared for and entered different types of teaching. In addition, differences in subject taught and size of school district also probably affect incomes of male and female teachers.[57] Among public secondary school teachers in 1970–71, a much higher proportion of the men taught science, social studies, and industrial arts, and a much higher proportion of the women taught English, home economics, and foreign languages.[58] These data support the conclusion that both level and type of school teaching are sex-segregated. The result is that employment markets in teaching explain differences between men and women teachers in preparation for and experience in teaching. For example, although male teachers appear to work longer hours than women, that difference merely reflects the difference in level of instruction taught between men and women.[59] I am arguing, then, that differences in employment markets—not motivation or "professionalism"—explain why many women appear to be less "committed to" and "successful in" female professions.

In social work, too, men and women tend to enter different areas of specialization. This is true even though the ratio of women to men in social work (two to one for at least the last two decades)[60] is lower than in librarianship, elementary school teaching, and nursing. Social work is divisible into two major levels: direct service (including casework, group work, and community organization functions) and supervision.[61] The last major survey of National Association of Social Workers membership found that, in 1968, a much higher proportion of women (43 percent) than men (25 percent) were engaged in direct services and a much lower proportion were involved in some form of administration (43 percent of women compared to 58 percent of men).[62] These sizable differences in position and responsibility are reflected in the fact that female social workers earn less, on the average, than their male colleagues: men consistently earned between $1,000 and $1,500 more than women in NASW membership surveys since 1961.[63] Such salary differences cannot be accounted for by differences in educational attainment.[64] This 1968 survey found that men were employed a shorter time in their present positions than women, indicating that men have greater career mobility than women in social work.[65] I shall return to this point later.

The limited available evidence on patterns of entry into segments of direct services suggests that here, too, social work is sex-typed. A 1967–68 survey of students enrolled in Columbia University School of Social Work found that males constituted a much higher proportion of those preparing for work in community organizations (44 percent) than group work (26 percent) and casework (14 percent).[66] And, consistent with data on the other fields discussed above, the segment of direct services in which men predominate, community organization, has the highest median salary—about $3,000 more than casework and $2,000 above group work in 1968.[67] Furthermore, community organizers are more likely than other social work practitioners to encounter executives, officials, and other professionals who are influential in community affairs. Many students preparing to work as community organizers anticipate executive positions in social work in the future.[68]

My previous research has shown that men tend to progress to the higher echelons of nursing and librarianship, as well as social work, at rates that exceed their overall representation in these occupations. Furthermore, I found no evidence to suggest that the disproportionate entry of men into such positions is declining.[69] Evidence on the entry of women into administrative positions in business organizations is similar, suggesting that in general women's careers do not lead them to and through the doors of power.[70] The proportion of female elementary school principals *declined* from 1960 to 1970 (from 37 to 21 percent), as did the number of female superintendents (from a total of ninety to eighty-four).[71] The proportion of top administrative positions held by male librarians increased from 1950 to 1970 in public, academic, and state libraries.[72] The proportion of administrative nurses who are male is increasing, although men still form a small minority of such nurses.[73] Trend data on the sex composition of status levels in social work are not available, although, as I noted, men were disproportionately represented in such positions in 1969. Unless some change occurs in the internal structure of female professions, increased numbers of men will probably mean increased male *control*.[74]

An adequate explanation of the different rates at which men and women progress in female professions has yet to be developed. It should recognize that men and women prepare for and enter different segments of these fields, with different preparation requirements and rewards. Beyond this, women's work experiences in the female-dominated professions, like other occupations, reflect a conflict between work and family that women continue to confront. They have traditionally been socialized to give child care priority over work, and this is reflected in both their work attitudes and their behavior. Many women who enter female-dominated professions expect their careers to be interrupted by marriage and child care. Those who do leave their jobs give family reasons most frequently as the basis for interrupting their employment.[75] Married women employed in female professions are more likely than men to work part-time, in their attempt to balance the commitments of home life and career.[76] For further discussion of this conflict, see the chapter by Kristin Moore and Isabel Sawhill above. Data on the quit rates of men and women in female-professions is sketchy. Available evidence indicates similar rates of exit for both sexes, although men are more likely to quit for reasons of professional advancement and women for family reasons.[77]

Remaining single is one way in which professional women may reduce conflicts between involvement in a career and the demands of a family. The proportion of single women is higher in librarianship and social work than in elementary school teaching and nursing.[78] It may be that the more flexible hours of work in nursing and the shorter workday and longer vacations in teaching are more compatible with married women's family obligations. Many women do mention the work schedule as a major attraction of elementary school teaching.[79]

Career interruption and the conflicting loyalties it represents cannot, however, explain away discrimination in promotion within female-dominated professions. Career discontinuity may be and undoubtedly has been used as a rationalization for the failure to promote *any* woman. This explains why in elementary school teaching, for example, the only variable significantly related to the hiring of administrators is sex—not age, length and type of experience, or type of position.[80]

I have sought to demonstrate that avenues of preparation and entry segregate and differentiate the activities of men and women in female-dominated professions. Differences in women's opportunities for employment within these fields affect their success substantially. Lack of success cannot be explained simply by such factors as women's lesser motivation and aspirations, as some previous analysts have implied.[81]

Income Differentials

Most work in the female-dominated professions involves a salary from an employing organization, often a public agency. The proportion of social workers in private practice is minuscule (1.3 percent in 1969),[82] and only about 10 percent of elementary school teachers were employed in private schools in 1973–74.[83] Public institutions employ all public librarians, of course, plus three out of five academic librarians, most school librarians, and the largest proportion of special librarians (subject area specialists employed by organizations).[84] In 1970 only 5 percent of registered nurses were employed in private duty; the vast majority were employed in hospitals, nursing homes, and public health agencies.[85] This predominance of the public agency work setting in the female professions certainly provides a partial explanation for the lesser economic rewards in these fields. Typically, public salary schedules are lower than salary scales in the private sector of occupations requiring similar levels of training.

The median earnings of women in female professions are relatively high compared to those of women in other fields, but the earnings of men are relatively low compared to those of men in other fields. Of 380 occupations ranked high to low on median salary, the numerical rank in 1969 for men in social work was 180, public elementary school teaching 182, librarianship 222, and nursing 269. Of 391 occupations ranked for women, public elementary school teaching was 61, social work 78, librarianship 96, and nursing 126.[86] Higher educational levels do not "pay off" for either men or women in female professions, however.[87] The average salaries in these fields place both sexes behind employees in many other occupations requiring far less education.

Furthermore, salary increases in the female professions are only moderately tied to years of experience. In elementary school teaching, for example, each pay increase is typically a smaller percentage of the salary base than the previous one.[88] Social work salaries are affected more by the type of position held—administrative or nonadministrative—than by years of experience.[89] The salaries paid nurses also seem rather insensitive to differences in years of experience. Data collected in the most recent survey of registered nurses in hospitals indicate that differences between the starting and the maximum median wage rate for any status level within nursing, from staff nurse to director of nursing services, did not exceed 20 percent.[90] While data on salaries by years of experience are unavailable for librarianship as a whole, information on segments of the field indicates that the salaries of women and men compare unfavorably with those in other professional fields that require comparable training.[91]

Thus, comprehensive studies of income by economists conclude that the lower wage levels in female occupations, for both women and men, result primarily from the effects of noncompetitive markets, which segregate entire fields as either male or female (see the discussion of the crowding hypothesis in Mary Stevenson's chapter above). On the whole, there are greater differences in income between sex-typed fields than within them.[92] Men and women in female professions will therefore suffer economic losses as long as sex-segregated markets in higher-status fields continue to exist, resulting in lower levels of income for all in the female-dominated professions.

As noted above, however, income differentials also exist within these professions between men and women. If women's family commitments sufficiently explained the salary differences between the sexes in female professions, then women with training and experience equal to men (often single women) should be earning comparable salaries to men. Available data suggest that this is not the case in social work[93] or librarianship.[94] Women in these fields earn less than men, regardless of their marital status, education, and experience. Even though the rate of pay in teaching is determined by experience and training, there is a sizable difference ($2,000 in 1970–71) in the average salaries of men and women teachers, and the average salary for female school administrators was almost $5,000 less than that for male administrators in 1970.[95] Salary data for nursing are not complete enough to assess the effects of sex and marital status.

Are women in female professions simply less interested in salary and status than men in these fields? Current data on the career motivations of these

> **The predominance of the public agency work setting in the female professions provides a partial explanation for the lesser economic rewards in these fields.**

women are, unfortunately, virtually nonexistent. However, it appears extremely unlikely that "deference to men" and "lack of ambition" accurately characterize the responses of most women who are subjected to career disparities. The impact of the women's liberation movement, legislation governing equal employment opportunity, and the increasing labor force participation of married women with small children, among other recent developments, challenge the conclusion that women's work values discourage their career advancement in the female professions.

Some differences in attitudes toward employment between women and men in the female professions may be gathered from a recent study of registered nurses in Kansas.[97] While a large majority of male nurses (72.4 percent) believed that women preferred male supervisors, a substantial majority of female nurses (60.3 percent) disagreed.[98] While 52 percent of male nurses agreed that men exhibited a higher level of professional dedication than women, only 15.3 percent of female nurses had similar views.[99] Asked whether female nurses usually have lower aspirations for advancement than male nurses, 71.4 percent of male nurses said yes but only 38.3 percent of female nurses agreed.[100]

The same study found further evidence of differing attitudes between men and women nursing administrators. Fewer female (39.1 percent) than male (56.1 percent) administrators agreed that entry of men into nursing would upgrade the profession.[101] More male administrators (64.1 percent) than female (41.3 percent) felt females had lower aspirations for advancement than male nurses.[102] More female (35.5 percent) than male (14.4 percent) administrators agreed that men tended to be paid more than women for basically the same work.[103] While a sizable minority of male administrators (38.0 percent) agreed that men were better suited than women for administrative positions in nursing, only 19.5 percent of female administrators had similar views.[104] An even greater disparity of opinion existed on the statement that male nurses were generally more effective than female nurses in supervising other members of the nursing team; 45.1 percent of the men agreed while 65.2 percent of the women disagreed.[105]

Future research on the female professions must pursue the line of questioning raised by this Kansas study of nurses. Do females believe males are better supervisors? Do the attitudes of male administrators in female professions sustain the traditional sex stereotyping of jobs? Will female administrators acquiesce to traditional patterns of promotion or seek to change them? The Kansas data suggest potential conflicts and changes in sex-segregated work within the female-dominated professions. It is quite possible that the changing attitudes of women in female professions will lead them to challenge the traditional disparities in careers between the sexes.

FUTURE PROSPECTS

Today, careers in the professions that women dominate provide both male and female practitioners with relatively fewer rewards than other high-status fields. Public work settings, smaller salary increments with advancement, and the economically depressing effect of sex-segregated markets help explain why. Women, however, fare less well than men even when their experience and qualifications are similar, and discrimination certainly contributes to this.

It is probable that employment opportunities for women in the female-dominated professions will continue to expand through 1985, although not as rapidly as from 1960 to 1972.[106] The overall rate of increase will slow, in part as a result of the decrease in jobs for elementary school teachers. As the pupil population declines, fewer women with primary education degrees will be able to find employment. This problem could be exacerbated as more and more women with older children attempt to reenter elementary school teaching. Growth of librarianship is also expected to slow, particularly in school librarianship because of declining enrollments and budget cutbacks. This will mean that female librarians who interrupt their careers to have children and then seek reentry will have difficulty finding jobs.[107] The growth of both nursing and social work will probably continue at somewhat higher levels, reflecting the continuing demand for these human services in the future.[108]

Women's status in female-dominated professions will be shaped, I have argued, by the degree to which traditional sex-typed patterns of preparation and entry persist. Since these patterns are firmly established and supported by social conditioning, it seems likely that specialties within all these fields will continue to be distinguishable by sex and that women will cluster in the less prestigious and rewarding areas of each profession. Promotions of women within specialties then can have only limited effects in equalizing men's and women's payoffs in a profession as a whole. Whether more and more women will be promoted to higher administrative positions within female professions is an open question. The implementation of recent legislation prohibiting discrimination in hiring and promotion on the basis of sex and age may help,[109] but traditional barriers still hinder the movement of women up organization ladders and outside female-typed specialties.[110] The continued growth of collective bargaining for public employees in general and for teachers in particular may help to equalize and increase the salaries and promotional opportunities for unionized men and women in the female-dominated professions.[111]

In conclusion, prospects for changes in the status of women in female professions resemble the outlooks for women in the labor force as a whole. While an increasing number of women are willing and able to participate in these careers, they will continue to encounter many barriers to equal entry and progress.

NOTES

1   Margaret Adams, "The Compassion Trap," in *Women in Sexist Society*, ed. Vivian Gornick and Barbara K. Moran (New York: Basic Books, 1971), pp. 402–6.

2   Extended discussions of the term *semiprofession* appear in Amitai Etzioni, ed., *The Semi-Professions and Their Organization* (New York: Free Press, 1969); George Ritzer, *Man and His Work, Conflict and Change* (New York: Appleton-Century-Crofts, 1972), pp. 205–20.

3   Richard H. Hall, "Professionalization and Bureaucratization," *American Sociological Review* 33 (1968): 92–104; Ronald M. Pavalko, *Sociology of Occupations and Professions* (Itasca, Ill.: Peacock Publishers, 1971).

4   Eliot Freidson, *The Profession of Medicine* (New York: Dodd, Mead and Company, 1970), pp. 71–84.

5   William Goode, "Encroachment, Charlatanism and the Emerging Profession: Psychology, Medicine, and Sociology," *American Sociological Review* 25 (1960): pp. 902–14.

6   U.S. Department of Labor, Women's Bureau, *1975 Handbook on Women Workers*, Bulletin no. 297 (Washington, D.C.: Government Printing Office, 1975), p. 89.

7   Ibid.

8   Valerie Kincade Oppenheimer, *The Female Labor Force in the United States*, Population Monograph Series, no. 5 (Berkeley: University of California, Institute of International Studies, 1970), pp. 77–80.

9   What follows is my own selective summary of points made in much of the literature on the female-dominated professions. To pursue any or all of these ideas further, consult these major sources: Oppenheimer, *Female Labor Force*, chap. 3; Athena Theodore, ed., *The Professional Woman* (Cambridge, Mass.: Schenkman Publishing Company, 1971), chap. 1; and Etzioni, *The Semi-Professions*, chap. 5.

10 Valerie Kincade Oppenheimer, "Demographic Influence on Female Employment and the Status of Women," *American Sociological Review* 78 (1973): 951–52.

11 Ibid.

12 For detailed discussion of the factors related to the entry of women, especially wives, into employment, see James A. Sweet, *Women in the Labor Force* (New York: Seminar Press, 1973); Juanita Kreps, *Sex in the Marketplace: American Women at Work* (Baltimore: Johns Hopkins University Press, 1971); and Glen G. Cain, *Married Women in the Labor Force* (Chicago: University of Chicago Press, 1966). See also the chapter by Kristin Moore and Isabel Sawhill above.

13 Theodore, *Professional Woman*, pp. 4–5.

14 For an extensive discussion of the cultural, economic, and ideological factors defining traditional female employment, see Harold L. Wilensky, "Women's

Work: Economic Growth, Ideology, Structure," *Industrial Relations* 7 (1968): 235–48.

15 Cynthia Fuchs Epstein, *Woman's Place* (Berkeley: University of California Press, 1970), pp. 151–66.

16 All figures in this paragraph were derived from data appearing in *1975 Handbook on Women Workers*, p. 89, table 38, "Employed Persons in Selected Occupations, by Sex, 1973 Annual Averages."

17 Cynthia Fuchs Epstein, "Positive Effects of the Multiple Negative: Explaining the Success of Black Professional Women," *American Journal of Sociology* 78 (1973): 150–73.

18 *1975 Handbook on Women Workers*, p. 104.

19 Stuart H. Garfinkle, "Occupations of Women and Black Workers, 1962–74," *Monthly Labor Review*, November 1975, p. 31.

20 Ibid., pp. 31–34.

21 U.S. Department of Labor, Bureau of Labor Statistics, *Library Manpower: A Study of Demand and Supply*, Bulletin no. 1852, (Washington. D.C.: Government Printing Office, 1975), p. 14.

22 Jean Lipman-Blumen and Ann R. Tickamyer, "Sex-Roles in Transition: A Ten-Year Perspective," in *Annual Review of Sociology*, ed. Alex Inkeles et al. (Palo Alto, Calif.: Annual Reviews, 1975), pp. 297–337, especially pp. 307–8; Ritzer, Man and His Work, pp. 101–6. See the chapter by Michelle Patterson and Laurie Engelberg above.

23 James W. Grimm and Robert N. Stern, "Sex Roles and Internal Labor Market Structures: The 'Female' Semi-Professions," *Social Problems* 21 (1974): 690–705.

24 Richard L. Simpson and Ida Harper Simpson, "Women and Bureaucracy in the Semi-Professions," in *The Semi-Professions*, ed. Etzioni, pp. 196–265.

25 For a similar observation, see Richard H. Hall, *Occupations and the Social Structure*, 2d ed. (Englewood Cliffs, N.J.: Prentice-Hall, 1975), p. 119.

26 For a general discussion of sex typing in the labor force, see Elizabeth Waldman and Beverly J. McEaddy, "Where Women Work—an Analysis by Industry and Occupation," *Monthly Labor Review*, May 1974, pp. 3–13.

27 *1975 Handbook on Women Workers*, pp. 203–6.

28 Ibid.

29 Ibid., p. 203.

30 John B. Parrish, "Women in Professional Training," *Monthly Labor Review*, May 1974, pp. 41–43.

31 Ibid., p. 43, table 3.

32 For a similar observation on female-dominated professions, see Nina Toren, "Semi-Professionalism and Social Work: A Theoretical Perspective," in *The Semi-Professions*, ed. Etzioni, p. 146.

33 *Library Manpower: A Study of Demand and Supply*, pp. 16–17.

34 Ibid., pp. 19–20.

35 Ibid., pp. 12–13.

36 Ibid., p. 19.

37 *Facts about Nursing, 1972–73* (Kansas City, Mo.: American Nursing Association, 1974), pp. 6–7. These data are the most recent available at this writing.

38 Ibid., p. 10, table I–A–3, "Registered Nurses Employed in Nursing, by Highest Educational Preparation and Field of Employment, 1972."

39 Ibid., p. 17, table I–A–9, "Employed Registered Nurses, by Field of Employment and Type of Position, 1972."

40 Etzioni, *The Semi-Professions;* Ritzer, *Man and His Work*, pp. 207–19.

41 For a brief review of the history of professionalization in elementary school teaching, see Dan C. Lortie, "The Balance of Control and Autonomy in Elementary School Teaching," in *The Semi-Professions*, ed. Etzioni, pp. 16–22, especially pp. 20–22.

42 Lortie, "Balance of Control and Autonomy," p. 25.

43 Dan C. Lortie, *School-Teacher: A Sociological Study* (Chicago: University of Chicago Press, 1975), p. 58.

44 Ibid., pp. 58–59.

45 Ibid., pp. 60–61.

46 U.S. Department of Health, Education, and Welfare, Education Division, *Digest of Educational Statistics*, 1975 ed. (Washington, D.C.: Government Printing Office, 1976), p. 52. table 47, "Selected Characteristics of Public School Teachers, by Level and Sex: United States, 1970–71.

47 Henry J. Meyer, "Profession of Social Work: Contemporary Characteristics," in *Encyclopedia of Social Work*, 16th issue (New York: National Association of Social Workers, 1972), 2:959–72, especially pp. 963–64.

48 Ibid., p. 962.

49 Ibid., pp. 964–65.

50 Ibid., p. 966.

51 Ibid., pp. 966–67.

52 Ibid., p. 967.

53 *1975 Handbook on Women Workers*, p. 149.

54 *Digest of Educational Statistics*, 1975 ed., p. 52, table 47.

55 Ibid.

56 *1975 Handbook on Women Workers,* p. 150.

57 Ibid., p. 151.

58 *Digest of Educational Statistics,* 1975 ed., p. 52, table 48, "Public Secondary School Teachers, by Teaching Field and by Sex: United States, 1970–71."

59 Lortie, *School-Teacher,* p. 90.

60 Meyer, "Profession of Social Work," p. 962.

61 Ibid., p. 964.

62 Alfred M. Stamm, "NASW Membership: Characteristics, Deployment, and Salaries," *Personnel Information,* May 1969, p. 40, referred to in Janet Saltzman Chafetz, "Women in Social Work," *Social Work,* September 1972, p. 14.

63 Meyer, "Profession of Social Work," p. 962.

64 Chafetz, "Women in Social Work," p. 14.

65 Meyer, "Profession of Social Work," p. 962.

66 George Brager and John A. Michael, "The Sex Distribution in Social Work: Causes and Consequences," *Social Casework* 14 (1969): 596.

67 Stamm, "NASW Membership," p. 42, cited in Brager and Michael, "Sex Distribution in Social Work," p. 596.

68 Brager and Michael, "Sex Distribution in Social Work," pp. 596–97.

69 Grimm and Stern, "Sex-Roles and Internal Labor Market Structures," pp. 696–702.

70 Rosabeth Moss Kanter, "Women and the Structure of Organizations: Explorations in Theory and Behavior," in *Another Voice,* ed. Marcia Millman and Rosabeth Moss Kanter (Garden City, N.Y.: Anchor Press, Doubleday and Company, 1975), pp. 34–77.

71 Suzanne S. Taylor, "Educational Leadership: A Male Domain?" *Phi Delta Kappan* 53 (1973): 124.

72 Schiller, "Women in Librarianship," pp. 120–21.

73 Grimm and Stern, "Sex Roles and Internal Labor Market Structures," pp. 696–99; *Facts about Nursing, 1972–73,* p. 7.

74 Wilensky, "Women's Work," p. 241.

75 Lortie, *School-Teacher,* pp. 86–87; Simpson and Simpson, "Women and Bureaucracy," pp. 207–16.

76 Meyer, "Profession of Social Work," p. 962; *Facts about Nursing, 1974–75,* p. 2.

77 Simpson and Simpson, "Women and Bureaucracy," pp. 219–21.

78 Ibid., pp. 212–13.

79 Lortie, *School-Teacher,* pp. 31–32.

80   Taylor, "Educational Leadership," p. 125.

81   Simpson and Simpson, "Women and Bureaucracy," especially pp. 220–47.

82   Meyer, "Profession of Social Work," p. 965.

83   *Digest of Educational Statistics*, 1975 ed., p. 10, table 7, "Number of Teachers in Elementary and Secondary Schools, and Instructional Staff Members in Institutions of Higher Education: United States, 1929–30 to 1973–74."

84   *Library Manpower*, pp. 1–3.

85   *Facts about Nursing, 1972–73*, pp. 6–7 and p. 9, table I-A-2, "Estimated Number of Employed Registered Nurses, by Field of Employment, Selected Years 1960–72."

86   Dixie Sommers, "Occupational Rankings for Men and Women by Earnings," *Monthly Labor Review*, August 1974, pp. 35–47.

87   Valerie Kincade Oppenheimer, *Female Labor Force*, pp. 100–101.

88   Lortie, *School-Teacher*, p. 84.

89   Meyer, "Profession of Social Work," p. 965.

90   Marjorie A. Godfrey, "Nurses' Salaries Around the Country: Where Can You Earn the Most (and the Least)?" *Nursing '74*, June 1974, pp. 54–55, cited in *Facts about Nursing, 1974–75*, p. 106, table III-B-2, "Hourly Salaries of Registered Nurses in Hospitals, by Type of Position and Region, December 1973."

91   Anita R. Schiller, "Women in Librarianship," in *Advances in Librarianship*, vol. 4, ed. Melvin J. Voight (New York: Academic Press, 1974), pp. 103–47, especially pp. 116–20.

92   Janice Fanning Madden, *The Economics of Sex Discrimination* (Lexington, Mass.: D. C. Heath and Company, 1973), pp. 90–95.

93   Martha Williams et al., "Career Patterns: More Grist for Women's Liberation," *Social Work* 19 (1974): 464–66.

94   Schiller, "Women in Librarianship," pp. 108–12.

95   Taylor, "Educational Leadership," p. 125.

96   For a discussion of how traditional attitudes limit women's involvement in female professions, see Simpson and Simpson, "Women and Bureaucracy," pp. 225–44.

97   Naomi B. Lynn et al., "The Challenge of Men in a Woman's World," *Public Personnel Management*, January–February 1975, pp. 4–17.

98   Ibid., p. 7.

99   Ibid., p. 11.

100 Ibid., pp. 10–11.

101 Ibid., p. 13.

102 Ibid., pp. 13–14.

103 Ibid., pp. 14–15.

104 Ibid., p. 15.

105 Ibid.

106 *1975 Handbook on Women Workers,* pp. 254–55.

107 Ann Kahl, "What's Happening to Jobs in the Library Field?" *Occupational Outlook Quarterly* 18 (1974): 24–25.

108 Neil F. Bracht, "Health Care: The Largest Human Service System," *Social Work* 19 (1974): 532–42.

109 For a useful summary of this and other types of legislation affecting the employment of women, see *1975 Handbook on Women Workers,* pp. 285–357. See also Mary Eastwood's chapter above.

110 Joan Acker and Donald R. Van Houten, "Differential Recruitment and Control: The Sex Structuring of Organizations," *Administrative Science Quarterly* 19 (1974): 152–63.

111 David B. Lipsky and John E. Drotning, "The Influence of Collective Bargaining on Teachers' Salaries in New York State," *Industrial and Labor Relations Review,* October 1973, pp. 18–35.

Urban Nomads: Women in Temporary Clerical Services

Virginia L. Olesen
and
Frances Katsuranis

In fact, if you really have a boring job, it's nice to switch from one boring job to another.

—A temporary services employee

The deepest problems of modern life derive from the claim of the individual to preserve the autonomy and individuality of his existence in the face of overwhelming social forces, of historical heritage, of external culture, and of the technique of life.

—Georg Simmel

Grants from the Center for the Study of Metropolitan Problems (NIMH 230399-01A1) and the University of California, San Francisco, School of Nursing Research Committee to Virginia Olesen funded the research on which the paper is based. Sheila Krasow, Jane Tabata Usami, and Victoria Peguillan provided helpful bibliographic and technical assistance. Our colleagues Rose Coser, Elvi Whittaker, Cynthia Nelson, and Anne Davis helped sharpen our ideas. The participation of four temporary services firms and their employees is also gratefully acknowledged.

Social scientists have generally tended to obscure, overlook, or misinterpret the topic of women and work.[1] Their view of the market as an exclusively male arena explains part of this neglect; another contributing factor is the scholarly imagery of devalued work: many analysts have not found the types of work most women do—housekeeping and clerical work, for example—as attractive to investigate as the so-called women's professions or the women who work in traditionally male professions.[2] Some researchers argue that surveys and interviews of women clerical workers exploit them, since they, unlike self-assured or powerful women lawyers, physicians, and business executives, are less likely or less able to refuse to participate. While this criticism reflects a legitimate concern, it should not be allowed to deter such studies. The lack of research on clerical workers already deepens the obscurity that surrounds this occupation and thus denies social scientists and other audiences the opportunity to understand it. Rather, the criticism should spur researchers to attend scrupulously to the rights of these respondents and to secure their meaningful informed consent to participation.

An inquiry into clerical work, the sector of American occupational life where most working women earn their paychecks, is long overdue.[3] This chapter focuses on one part of that sector—female temporary clerical workers. These women, and all other clerical workers, have entered the American labor force in increasing numbers during the twentieth century. They encounter all the clerical worker's problems that are engendered by a low status occupation and additionally face the difficulties of being highly transitory participants in the urban work force. It is this transitory element, the factor of impermanence, that we analyze in depth, after reviewing the growth of clerical work and of the temporary services industry.[4]

HISTORY OF CLERICAL OCCUPATIONS

Since the earliest times, when scribes committed the affairs of literate groups to written record, the clerk has been a figure of importance in commercial, ecclesiastical, and literary fields.[5] With the Industrial Revolution, literacy and bookkeeping increased, and clerks proliferated. This growth accelerated during the twentieth century. From 1950 to 1974, for example, the number of clerical workers in the United States doubled, from 7,632,000 to 14,845,000.[6] This surge was matched only by that of professional, technical, and sales workers, whose growth also reflects the shift to a postindustrial society based on communication, consumption, and service.

While the number of clerks has increased, their prestige has declined. Genteel respectability was once accorded the occupation, when "the clerk was the real factor in the entity of the British firm."[7] Some analysts claim that the decline in prestige came about because increased numbers of women entered clerical work. "The loss of economic privilege of white-collar employees can be explained in large measure by the progressive invasion of white-collar occupations by women, whose level of compensation is distinctly lower across the board in all industries."[8] Cause and effect are doubtless mingled in a complicated cycle: women by virtue of their second-class status in the labor force are granted access to declining occupations vacated by males moving on to more prestigious and more remunerative work; the occupations then decline further in prestige because they are predominately filled by workers accorded second-class status—women.

In the quarter century between 1950 and 1974, the number of male clerks rose slightly, from 3,035,000 to 3,382,000, whereas the number of females jumped from 4,597,000 to 11,462,000.[9] This continued a trend begun as early as 1870.[10] Women accounted for more than 95 percent of the total increase in clerical workers during the 1950–74 period. At the same time, many more minority women came into clerical services, decreasing their heavy concentration in personal service work. In 1963, for instance, 10.2 percent of employed minority women were clerical workers; by 1973 the figure had increased to 24.4 percent. By comparison, the proportion of white working women in clerical jobs rose from 33.8 percent to only 35.7 percent during that decade.[11] These changes occurred in an era when increasing numbers of women were leaving their homes to take up paid employment in the job market. For instance, in the brief period between 1960 and 1973, the proportion of the adult female population in the labor force rose from 37.1 to 44.2 percent.[12]

By 1973, 76.6 percent of all clerical workers in the United States were women, and some experts have predicted the figure will surpass 90 percent by the end of the century. Most of these women are bank tellers, bookkeepers, cashiers, counter clerks, enumerators and interviewers, field clerks, office machine operators, payroll and timekeeping clerks, receptionists, and similar workers; a minority are stenographers, typists, and secretaries.[13]

In summary, the occupational category with the largest proportion of women is clerical work. Within the clerical field there are three women workers for every man. Clerical work is where most working women find jobs (one-third of all working women are clerical workers).

These comparisons reveal some of the inequalities and strains in the American occupational structure and illustrate the sexual division of labor, which limits opportunities for working women in general. Among the factors that have produced these statistics are early sex-role socialization, the organization of the educational systems, and the narrow opportunity structure for women (see Carol Ireson's and Mary Stevenson's chapters above). Women have been socialized to play submissive roles in which their career motivations are stunted and marriage is the dominant goal. They have been deflected from career preparation at almost every level in the educational system by counselors who hold traditional views of sex roles. Eventually they are drawn to clerical work, where both low and high levels of education can be marketed, and where the demands of the job do not threaten to disrupt marital obligations as more challenging work might do (see the chapters by Kristin Moore and Isabel Sawhill and by Evelyn Rosenthal above). While male networks govern entry to and ascent in many occupations, clerical work offers job access to women excluded from other opportunities. These points bear on why and how women enter temporary services work. How they see themselves in that work is analyzed more fully later in this chapter.

One other observation points up the devaluation of women in this and other fields. As James Grimm noted above for professionals, in all female-dominated occupations male workers are more handsomely rewarded than female workers. The median annual earnings of full-time clerical and kindred workers in 1973 were $10,811 for white males and $9,241 for black males. Black females earned $6,522, while white females received $6,462, a reversal for these two groups.[14] Thus, within this low-prestige occupational group American working women are paid at least one-third less than their male colleagues.

Despite these appalling figures, labor organizers have not found willing recruits for unions among women clerical workers. Although organized white-collar women in general, not merely clerks, receive better salaries than unorganized women, clerical workers have not affiliated with unions in significant numbers historically or at present. Whether the new militance of some women in other occupations will spread to women clerical workers remains to be seen. Women workers for the telephone company, for example, failed to organize effectively to combat deplorable work situations.[15] Perhaps least susceptible of all to unionization are temporary clerical workers, because of the characteristics of their type of employment. We examine these characteristics next.

THE TEMPORARY SERVICES INDUSTRY

Temporary services firms provide industrial, technical, and clerical workers to businesses, industries, hospitals, and schools on short-run assignments. The services firm receives a fee, part of which is returned to the worker as wages. These firms differ from employment agencies in that they are legally enjoined from placing employees in positions for permanent hire. Both the temporary services firm and the employee may be fined if this occurs. The largest sector of the temporary services industry, as the firms call themselves, is the clerical sector, supplying 70 percent of all temporary employees.[16] Most temporary clerical workers are women, but in recent years, because of affirmative action programs and the depressed economic conditions of the mid-1970s, more men have sought such assignments.

Temporary services clerical workers constitute only 1.25 million of the 9.58 million American clerical workers, but their importance in the urban work scene is growing.[17] The industry is not new, for this type of business was known in London before World War I. The growth of temporary services firms in the United States, however, has occurred primarily since the 1940s, and it gives no sign of abating. In 1970 there were more than a thousand such firms (several with international branches); they placed more than a million employees and grossed approximately $1.5 billion.[18] Every indication is that these firms will continue to grow and that they will place increasingly large numbers of employees in a wider variety of jobs. It is also predicted that more businesses will rely on temporary help firms more frequently both to provide clerical assistance when work overloads occur or regular employees are absent and to reduce costs, since temporary employees do not receive regular staff fringe benefits.

Temporary services firms hire clerical workers after face-to-face interviews conducted by supervisors (called *counselors*), who eventually assign jobs to the workers. The counselor evaluates the employee's dress, demeanor, and clerical skills (typing, spelling, fundamental mathematics). Psychological testing, once done routinely, is no longer in vogue, though interviewers may record their impressions of the applicant's personal qualifications. (On employee cards we saw phrases such as, "She/he is an attractive, well-groomed young woman/man.") Once the "temporary," or "temp," to use the British term for such workers, is listed in the files of the firm, he or she either waits for the counselor to call with an appropriate job assignment, or calls to ask for assignments. After the initial interview, telephone rather than face-to-face contact between employee and counselor is the rule, but in some firms employees come into the office to ask for assignments or to pick up their checks for previous work done.

The temporary services firm receives calls from client businesses describing to the counselor the tasks to be done, working conditions, length of the assignment, and locale. When the counselor assigns a job to a temporary, the worker goes to the client's offices and does the assignment under the direction of someone in that firm.

The temporary services firm pays the employee's wages and then charges the client for those wages plus a fee for its services. It may charge a client $5.00 an hour while paying the employee an hourly wage of $3.50. The employee's personal attributes and skills are "the means of production" through which the temporary services firm makes its (often substantial) profits.[19]

A job assignment may last as little as a day or as long as several months. The employee may terminate the assignment if working conditions are very poor, the work is too difficult, or the area of the city is dangerous. Employees who encounter problem conditions are urged to call their counselor at the temporary services firm immediately so that the difficulties can be mediated. The counselor may pull the complaining employee off the job and attempt to find a replacement for that job, reassigning the employee to another place.

A client firm may terminate the job if the employee's performance is unsatisfactory, for such reasons as personality conflicts or tardiness. If the client firm calls that morning to discontinue the employee by noon of the first day's work, there is usually no charge to the client and the employee receives a day's pay. If the firm calls subsequently, it must pay for as much employee time as it used. Client businesses agree not to hire temporaries to fill permanent job openings within six months of the time the temporary begins working for the client, for this would place the temporary services firm in competition with employment agencies, an illegal practice. A client business that nevertheless hires a worker directly is fined, and sometimes the employee is fined by the temporary services firm as well.

The temporary services industry thus must delicately balance several interwoven factors to offer its service to business. The services firm must have enough reliable employees on file to fill clients' calls for help. The industry is highly competitive, and other temporary firms are always eager to pick up clients' unfilled work demands. Some counselors double as sales agents for their firms, persuading large corporations and businesses that their firms' services are the best and most reliable. On the other hand, if the temporary firm has too many highly skilled workers on its roster, employees will not receive enough assignments and will, as many employees do, register with and seek assignments from other temporary firms or take other part-time jobs. In some urban areas firms face the further problem of trying to keep track of a transitory employee population. Rosters of employees who can be called for assignments are constantly becoming out-of-date. Many temporary workers, particularly younger people, spend only a brief time in an area before they move on. (This very transience constituted a methodological problem for us in sampling and locating enough employees for interviews.)

EXPLORING TEMPORARY WORK FROM THE WORKER'S PERSPECTIVE

Background of the Study

This chapter is part of an exploratory study of the temporary services industry from the worker's standpoint. The perspective of the study is crucial both conceptually and methodologically. It means that our discussion derives from statements made to us by workers concerning their views of their work and their lives. Our inquiries were guided by our interests in women and work rather than by a series of theoretically generated hypotheses. Our conceptualizations are predicated on the workers' constructions of their own world. Our guiding questions were: What is the meaning of this transitory occupational world for the employee? How does it relate to crucial questions about work, work styles, and women? To what extent are alienating factors such as powerlessness, meaninglessness, isolation, and self-estrangement[20] found in temporary services work? The temporary clerical worker in many situations seems to be merely another type of movable office equipment. When work is characterized by such alienating qualities, what place does it have in the lives of the workers?[21] Can temporary workers develop otherwise important audiences to whom their claims for esteem and worth are addressed? If not, what is the effect on their self-images? Can a married woman temporary worker sustain apparently alienating work because of her commitments in other (family) sectors of her life?[22] In sum, what is the impact of impermanence on the meaning of work to the employee in this occupation?

Though impermanence seems to characterize much of American life, the temporary services industry presents an extreme and hence useful case of it for analysis. Many Americans, in the military or business elite, for example, do change jobs or move from work setting to work setting (itinerant farm laborers or academics, for instance) but the temporary services employee experiences change more frequently—sometimes having five different jobs in five different settings in five working days.

> ❝ **The temporary clerical worker in many situations seems to be merely another type of movable office equipment. When work is characterized by such alienating qualities, what place does it have in the lives of the workers?** ❞

To explore these questions, we selected a sample of temporary workers from four firms in the San Francisco Bay Area. Because the industry is highly competitive, information about employees is jealously guarded. We therefore encountered a long delay in gaining access to subjects for our study. Finally we received help from an official in the statewide association of temporary services firms. Her appeal to member firms brought cooperation from four in the San Francisco area, two with national offices. Since there are sixty such firms in the area, this was a very small response, further indicating the closed quality of the industry.

For this reason we left to the cooperating firms the decision of how to provide us with employee names. This is not a desirable sampling technique, but the access problem was so difficult that we settled for what we could obtain, believing that this was preferable to a lengthier "snowball technique." In only one case were we invited to select as we wished from the company's files; in the other three, names were given to us with no information on how they had been selected. Where we were allowed to select the names, we took every other name in the file of two hundred.

In all, we obtained some two hundred names from the four firms and pared them down to one hundred eighteen from whom we thought we could most likely obtain interviews. We sent letters to all these, requesting participation in our study. We received no reply from sixty-nine, fourteen came back as "addressee unknown," thirteen persons refused, and twenty said they would be interested. These sampling problems reflect the transience of temporary clerical workers.

We conducted face-to-face interviews with these twenty men and women during the winter and spring of 1974. (As this chapter went to press, a further series of interviews was underway, with additional respondents.) We also interviewed counselors in the four cooperating firms and in the New York, Chicago, Detroit, and New Orleans offices of one firm. Of the twenty respondent workers, sixteen were women, ten were thirty years of age or older, and fourteen were unmarried, although several were living with a person of the opposite sex. Almost all had attended college, and several had graduated. The composition of this small sample in these respects was similar to that of other studies of clerical temporary services workers.[23]

Guided by the questions above, we analyzed the interviews to see what themes emerged around the issues of transience and work alienation. Our analysis here is based on the women's responses. We did not compare women's and men's answers, because we had such a small sample. Men were included in the study, however, since their numbers are increasing in this type of work, although they are still clearly a minority. The men's answers on questions related to the themes at issue were not greatly different from those of the women.

This type of analysis is properly used when the usual sampling procedures cannot be followed, when the nature of the study topic itself is relatively unknown, and when the analysts are particularly interested in the respondents' own views of the topic.[24] Experimental or survey research procedures would not have been appropriate for our study topic or sample.

Several themes emerged from this analysis, and we discuss each in turn: control of work, social relationships at work, and work attitudes.

Control of Work

From the standpoint of the temporary clerical employee (which, again, is the perspective of this paper), there is an exquisite series of balanced dilemmas, ambiguities, and obscurities to be encountered that are linked to the problems of the industry that we have already outlined. The temporary clerical employee may accept or refuse job assignments offered by the counselor, and therefore seems to exercise a fair amount of control over her work. She must carefully weigh the consequences of refusal, however. The counselor may be irritated by an employee's refusal, since, unless she can find another employee to do the job, the refusal must be relayed to the client and makes the firm look unprepared. This may lessen the refusing employee's chances for a later assignment. The temporary must try to assess in a telephone call the counselor's mood on that day. To compound the problem, she does not know what, if anything, previous clients have revealed to the counselor about her on-the-job performance. Another factor to be weighed is the length of the assignment. The employee may not wish to work an entire week, or she may prefer a longer assignment than the counselor is offering. Most of the elements for an informed choice are unknown to the employee when she weighs acceptance of the assignment. She is not told the range of assignments available that day, the merits of each, or the consequences of refusal or acceptance.

Our interviewees acknowledged a great deal of uncertainty and lack of information about how they received or failed to receive specific job assignments. Nevertheless, they did not consider themselves powerless with respect to their work assignments or conditions on the job. Indeed, when we asked who among the involved parties (employee, firm, or client) they thought had the upper hand, some said the employee—a view some counselors shared. Workers believed they could negotiate for better assignments, although they knew there were limits on the possibilities for better work assignments and better pay. They could not, for example, refuse certain assignments too often without risking that they would not be called again. Some reported that their earlier refusal to take assignments or their demands for better assignments seemed to explain later slack periods when they did not receive work assignments from their counselors. One of the strategies these workers adopted was to accept some undesirable assignments so that at another time they could refuse jobs or demand work more suited to their schedules and abilities. As one employee put it, "In my kind of [work] life you don't have much power, but one of the powers you do have is the right to give yourself where you want and give or take yourself away."

Many employees also alternated refusal of assignments with bargaining, negotiating, or compromising so as not to eliminate the possibilities for further assignment. An older woman who spent two days on a job she thought meaningless illustrated this:

They [the client firm] had me doing the exact same letter over and over and over and over eight hours a day which was really ludicrous to me because right across the street was IBM and I know that IBM has computers that do that. I kept making mistakes. All they had to do is spend a little money and IBM would do this job better than me. That was the only temporary job that I ever had that after I had it for two days I called up the agency and said, "Look, I am so sick I can barely move, but if you can find me another job I'll go today. I cannot handle that." That was the only one that really made me feel really insane.

It seems that temporary workers could and did influence the assignments offered to them and in so doing gained a sense of control of their work assignments. Certainly the fact that they could and did say no to certain assignments gave them a feeling of greater control than many other workers have. Permanent employees who refuse work assignments risk dismissal, censure, or at least their supervisor's displeasure. Temporaries could say no with less risk. Autonomy was thus not absent from the temporary worker's life. This contrasts sharply with findings of powerlessness among clerical workers.[25] In light of earlier themes on alienation in work, it was an unexpected finding. Some, of course, would argue that such refusals, bargains, and influences do not constitute control of work.

Social Relationships

Many interviewees reported that they found their work sites isolating and lonely. They were not welcomed into groups of permanent employees, and the attitudes of those employees were sometimes corrosive of the temporary's self-esteem. One interviewee told us, "I'm just the temporary employee, not to be taken seriously and not even known by name, just 'that's one of the temporaries.' They don't show me things they show regular employees." Another older woman said she was expected to know the names of the permanent staff, but none of them bothered to learn her name. The brevity of the assignments also made the effort of getting to know people burdensome to her: "I reach a saturation point of names and places. You know when I move around I'm in a different place every week or every other week and just to remember the different Lindas and Sallys and who had priority and where to find things is very difficult." Her comment was echoed by that of a younger woman: "If you're here for three days and here for a week plus doing jobs you don't like, which doesn't put you in a very good frame of mind anyway, you don't feel any warmth, probably because . . . I'm not putting any out also, because I know I'm only going to be there three days."

The longer assignments seemed to provide more chances for social contact. In brief assignments, however, the temporary employee's impermanence hindered social relationships initiated by the permanent staff. Some of them preferred not to become acquainted with temporaries because the contacts were so fleeting, and social relationships were difficult to build and sustain.

The temporary workers are conscious that they represented different things to different permanent staff members, not the least of which was a reminder of the regular staff's expertise and stability. One temporary stated:

> You can be an ego boost to the people, the other people that work in the place, you know, 'cause, oh, here you are this little temporary and they're being nice to you, you know, they know so much and can tell you where the bathroom is and where so and so's office is and stuff like that. Some people get off on that, I guess. I think you, naturally, as a temporary, feel—I don't know if "inferior" is the word—humble. The position is not as sturdy as theirs and you're always just the little temporary.

On the other hand, fear of job loss, jealousy of the seemingly easier schedules of temporary workers, and worry that the temporary worker would be a "rate buster" (produce more for lower pay than others) were experienced by some permanent employees dealing with temporaries. Such feelings could produce extreme reactions; for example, a counselor in the Chicago office of a firm reported that the permanent employees of one client business had refused to share the key to the restroom with the temporary employee.

Isolation and negative responses in social relationships at work locales led many interviewees to having feelings of inferiority. Both temporary and permanent employees felt isolated from each other, a characteristic of alienating work.

Some temporaries, however, formed lasting social relationships through their work. They made friends while on temporary assignments and maintained those contacts later, participating in office parties after they had left the client site. Others lunched or had coffee occasionally with other temporaries, with whom the usual topic of conversation was comparison of wage rates. One young woman reported she made acquaintances more quickly because the impermanence of her assignment forced her to speed up the usual processes of establishing relationships. For inexperienced newcomers to the area, temporary assignments also provided a way to learn the ways of the city and gain the experience and references needed to find satisfying permanent jobs that would offer them more enduring social contacts.

Attitudes toward Work

Few respondents said their work was "meaningless" in the sense that they could not see a fit between their particular assignment and the larger whole of the work setting they were temporarily joining. While some were bored with repetitive assignments or work they did not find interesting or challenging personally, "meaningless" was not a term they used to describe their jobs.

In fact, contrary to the predictions of some analysts that cynicism and lack of loyalty would characterize temporary workers,[26] most of our interviewees held traditional work ethic attitudes. These views were, however, tempered for some with recognition that they could stand temporary work and even do it well only because they knew it was temporary. None of the interviewees indicated any attempt to slack off or gouge the temporary firm or the client. On the contrary, a number of employees prided themselves on being able to do the work well even though it was sometimes boring: "I always work at my top pace wherever I am. . . . I think one should do one's best." These attitudes sometimes caused trouble for temporary employees who worked efficiently and quickly. They might then be left without tasks, and, what was worse, permanent employees became displeased at their show of productivity.

While temporaries expressed a willingness to work hard, many made it clear that they did not want to take responsibility in assignments. Indeed, in their view, one of the advantages of temporary work was that it gave them jobs without saddling them with responsibility. Some also declared that the temporary services world offered certain safeguards to them and their employers that are not available elsewhere. If the employee walked off the assignment or the client firm released her, the consequences were not disastrous: "Nobody seems to be losing anything. If the client company doesn't like you, they can get rid of you and the temporary firm will send out someone else. If you don't like it, you can change to another job assignment."

Respondents expressed different stances on how to bargain for adequate or better pay. Several of them accepted demanding work assignments with little or no awareness of the discrepancy between their rate of pay and the cost to the client or of the possibility that they could negotiate for better wages. They lacked a sense of their own value to the firm and to the client.[27] One militant interviewee thought temporary workers should be unionized, because they "don't have a feeling of their own worth."

Some workers, however, realized the discrepancies between their own salaries and the firm's earnings when they became more knowledgeable about the industry's operations. Ironically, some employees got glimpses of the facts when they were given temporary assignments in their firms' head offices. One young woman who had been sent for a day to her firm's headquarters to help with bookkeeping reported:

> I realized what a rip-off it was and how much money they were making off me and I got really upset after a while. 'Cause I would be making $2.50 an hour and the company would be paying $4.50 an hour for me, so that meant they [the temporary firm] were making $2.00 an hour profit and I didn't like that.

On the strength of this insight, she began to offer her services directly to client companies for a fee higher than $2.50 an hour but less than $4.50. Eventually, however, she stopped this practice for fear of being discovered by the temporary services firm for which she had worked.

Bargaining for better wages varied according to the employee's skill level. Those with long work records, top stenographic ability, and statistical typing skills could and did ask for more pay on specific assignments. File clerks, unskilled typists, and general office helpers could not make these demands successfully.

To summarize, the world of the temporary employee is complex—both more and less alienating than other types of clerical work in terms of control, isolation, and estrangement from self. While some of the temporaries reported dull work and little chance to meet or know fellow employees, others found they could control their assignments and develop permanent employment and social relationships on the sites. Respondents differed on the degree to which they could and would bargain for wages and the amounts they thought they were worth. They all took pride in doing the work well, however.

We concluded that the means of establishing a sense of self as a worker was both enhanced and stunted in the temporary world. Ways did exist for employees to develop self-esteem on the job, valuing themselves as good workers and as hard bargainers for what they were worth, for example.

IMPERMANENCE IN LIFE AND WORK

Two types of employees emerged in the analysis of the interviews, exhibiting different orientations to temporary work for different reasons, based on the temporal features of their lives. We called the first group *transitional temporaries*, since their tenure in this occupational field was limited. The second group, which apparently engages in the work on a longer or continuing basis, we called *permanent temporaries*. Persons in the first group seemed to lack resolution in their life situations, whereas the second group included persons whose work and life roles had stabilized in a variety of ways.

The transitional temporaries included persons entering the labor force for the first time, those coming back to work, those already in the labor force but looking for different work, and those seeking to find themselves (rather than to find a job or career) through the avenues of temporary work.[28] Typically, respondents who were just entering the labor force were young college graduates who had migrated to San Francisco. They heard of the temporary work field from their friends and decided to enter it. They saw it as a way to begin work life, to gain experience, to establish themselves in a city where they had few acquaintances, and eventually to find permanent occupations.[29] In the words of one young woman, "It just so happens we know a lot of people who aren't settled, and temporary is a good way to make some money until you are settled. There seems to be a large body of unskilled kids running around, and for us it's really good to be able to get a job so fast."

For those just entering the labor market, the very nature of temporary work combines favorably with their lack of skills: "As long as I have to work and I'm dealing with jobs that are really nothing, no challenge, no interest, it's better to do it on a temporary basis." Some younger workers, however, saw that temporary work could become a way of life and expressed misgivings that it would deflect them from serious pursuit of careers in their own fields of interest, binding them instead to jobs in the temporary field.

Two transitional temporaries in our sample were older women returning to work, one after remarriage and the other when her children had left home. One turned to the temporary field as a way to refurbish her out-of-date clerical skills. The other was seeking diversion in a life that had grown quiet as her family patterns changed:

> I started out in a temporary agency to get my feet wet because it is difficult to get back in when you've been out of it for so long. I didn't go back to work for 18 years, and I had to bluff through a lot of my

return because I thought things hadn't changed, but they have. That was before electric typewriters and instead of that nice Selectric, it was the old Edison II where you erased by grinding it . . . it was like sanding.

In a society where older women are devalued as persons, temporary work offers these women a reentry path to active work life that might otherwise be closed to them, particularly if they were not highly trained or educated prior to marriage.[30]

Some of the other transitional temporaries had held clerical jobs in the past and were using temporary assignments to tide them over until they could find a more satisfying job. Others hoped to find work in a different field:

You know, I realized I can't make a living as a musician . . . you know, I really don't know what I want to do. You know, I don't have a career, and . . . temporary work is really the solution for now. . . . You know it's tolerable work. . . . I mean it's income. . . . I certainly hope I find some permanent work I enjoy, because I don't want to be a typist all my life.

The latter type of employee did not have a firm preference for any one work style, and could mark time in temporary jobs until the uncertainties were resolved.

In sum, transitional temporaries used the work as a way station to another occupational or personal niche. They were often looking for a permanent job in another field and used the temporary work to earn money, to assess the job market, or to up-date their skills. Some also used temporary work as a means to find themselves, not necessarily as workers but as persons.

By contrast, the permanent temporaries seemed fixed in this occupation for various reasons. Several younger women were active in theatrical, craft, or artistic pursuits. For some, these activities were diversions that filled out their lives; for others, they were serious career efforts that could be supported by earnings from temporary assignments. In short, the work and life interests of these employees did not lie in temporary work, but they were content to engage in temporary jobs in order to support those other aspects of their lives. Indeed, they acknowledged that their pursuit of these crafts or talents was made possible by the fact that temporary work supported them without engulfing them.

Some permanent temporaries in our sample liked temporary work for its own sake and claimed they found it exciting.[31] They echoed French temporary workers in a study in the Paris region,[32] who said they enjoyed the constantly changing elements in this work and followed it for this reason, as well as to earn a living. Said one of our respondents:

> It's the challenge I want. . . . I'm making myself go to these different places, take on these different jobs and see if I can do it and I found out that I can. . . . It's convincing myself. I enjoy being transferred from one office to another and staying a few months and then going on to something different, because every job is a challenge. And to myself I think that's what you should be faced with at this time of your life and to enjoy that.

Another type of permanent temporary also pursued this work in its own right: this group, according to the counselors who placed them, included persons unable to pursue other full-time work, such as alcoholics, mentally ill persons, and those with other limitations. Temporary employment thus provides these persons with the sporadic employment they can manage.[33] Finally, there was one employee without definite goals for work or self, who seemed content to pursue temporary work not as a means of finding something better or learning more about herself, but as a way of earning a living for an indefinite period of time in the future:

> I don't think I'll ever have a career that I'll pursue. It'll just constantly be different jobs here and there, you know, which is kind of . . . which kind of depresses me when I think about it, but I can't really think of anything I want to devote a bunch of time to for the rest of my life. . . . I can't think of anything. . . . I can't see any other way than working off and on. Temporary jobs I'll call them, even if they're permanent, you know, for the rest of my life 'cause I don't plan on getting married and being supported. That's kind of depressing when you think about it.

Thus, temporary employees differed from each other with respect to the place temporary work held in their lives. Some used it as a means to other ends—gaining work experience, finding better jobs, changing careers, or sorting out other parts of their lives. These workers were passing through temporary employment. Other workers seemed to consider temporary work a way of life, but their reasons also varied greatly. Some used it to support artistic pursuits that do not provide a full-time living, except for those who are very successful. Others, suffering disabilities that made them incapable of full-time employment, found temporary work tolerable in a work force that does not easily accept disabilities. Some pursued temporary jobs because they liked the constant change of tasks and settings, finding this diversity challenging. Some had no further ambitions and thus no intention to change to permanent work.

CONCLUSIONS

This exploratory study of temporary services employees touched on the meaning and place of work and work styles in life as a whole.

Concerning the meaning of work, despite earlier research on the alienation of clerical workers, our study of temporary workers does not give evidence that these women are alienated. They do not have an acute sense of powerlessness, meaninglessness, isolation, and self-estrangement in their work. In fact, the temporary worker may have a greater sense of control over self and work than clerical workers who spend their lives in a single job or a series of related jobs. The temporary employee retains some control over her job assignments because she can request removal if a job is too difficult or odious. In our analysis these women emerged not as creatures adrift in a rapacious business world, but as individuals exercising critical judgments for themselves and for the industry they made possible. Some, though not all, could and did bargain for themselves, gaining a sense of at least partial control of their assignments. The stereotype of clerical workers in American society as individuals without choices, who have no variety in their work and no autonomy in their job situations, did not characterize the temporaries in our study. (It may not characterize clerical workers generally, for all we know.)

Our respondents did experience varying degrees of social isolation. Some, however, welcomed this, while some managed to form lasting social relationships through work.

Self-estrangement was not prevalent among these workers. They saw themselves as highly competent employees who did their very best. While it is arguable that this is a manifestation of false consciousness (that is, that these workers are fooling themselves with such high self-evaluations while they receive very low wages), some of the workers did in fact bargain effectively for work assignments and in some cases better wages, indicating they were not oblivious to the realities of their situation.

To turn to the theme of the place of work in the lives of temporary workers, we did not find a profound *commitment* to work among them. Even those we characterized as permanent temporaries did not manifest a deep, personal investment in work, self, situation, and setting that commitment to a job implies. They did, however, give evidence of *involvement* in temporary work. These women selected degrees of involvement according to their disabilities, temperaments, economic situations, and other commitments (to artistic or craft endeavors, for instance). Moreover, temporary work relieved them of the drudgery, dehumanization, and alienating features of housework. It allowed them a range of levels of involvement in work.

Numerous work assignments and roles offer temporary employees highly varied circumstances, in contrast to the homogeneous world of the clerk on a continuing job. In this respect, temporary work allows for individualism,[34] experience in different social arenas, and relationships with a variety of people. Even though those relationships may be less than satisfactory in some settings, they present diversity not similarity. The degree of challenge, type of work, and work setting vary much more in temporary services work than in the general field of clerical work. Indeed, temporaries may experience more variety than workers in more prestigious occupations in which tasks have largely become routine.

C. Wright Mills urged social scientists to describe the "larger economic and political situation in terms of its meaning for the inner life and external career of the individual."[35] Our limited study has tried to do this in part. While our findings seem to suggest that temporary workers are exploited, our study has not addressed this issue in depth; rather it has focused on the experience and meaning of temporary work for individual workers as they describe themselves and their world. In a society like that in the United States, where opportunities for women are profoundly limited and where the marketplace channels women into clerical work, the temporary services worker finds variety and a chance for individualism that women in other pursuits may not. Some analysts predict that temporary work is the wave of the future in many occupations, including professional fields. If that is the case, the lives of these urban nomads will be quite instructive. This limited portrait provides us with preliminary understandings of a world too little explored. We need to know a good deal more if we are to comprehend work in the lives of both men and women. Studies of work exploitation must take into account not merely industries, such as temporary services, but the functioning of American sex-role socialization patterns, opportunity structures, and market operations, how these factors lead women, and more and more men, to temporary or transitory work, and the differentiation between commitment to and involvement in work. The temporary services industry is but part of this larger configuration of factors in American occupational life.

NOTES

1 See Marcia Millman and Rosabeth Moss Kanter, eds., *Another Voice: Feminist Perspectives on Social Life and Social Science* (Garden City, N.Y.: Anchor Press, Doubleday and Company, 1975).

2 An exception would be, of course, C. Wright Mills, *White Collar* (New York: Oxford University Press, 1951), especially chap. 9. pp. 189–212. On the professions, see Carol Lopate, *Women in Medicine* (Baltimore: Johns Hopkins University Press, 1968); Sarah Bentley Doely, ed., *Women's Liberation and the Church* (New York: Association Press, 1970); Amitai Etzioni, *The Semi-Professions and Their Organization: Teachers, Nurses, Social Workers* (New York: Free Press, 1969); Ronald G. Walton, *Women in Social Work* (London: Routledge and Kegan Paul, 1975); Margaret Cussler, *The Woman Executive* (New York: Harcourt, Brace and Company, 1958); Eli Ginzberg and Alice M. Yohalem, *Corporate Lib* (Baltimore: Johns Hopkins University Press, 1973); Alice S. Rossi and Ann Calderwood, eds., *Academic Women on the Move* (New York: Russell Sage Foundation, 1973); Jessie Bernard, *Academic Women* (New York: Meridian Books, New American Library, 1966).

3 Pamela Roby, "Sociology and Women in Working-Class Jobs," in *Another Voice,* ed. Millman and Kanter, pp. 203–37, notes that there is little research on blue-collar women, another neglected area. See Sally Hillsman Baker's chapter below.

4 See Francine D. Blau, "Sex Segregation of Workers by Enterprise in Clerical Occupations," in *Labor Market Segmentation,* ed. David Gordon (Lexington, Mass.: Lexington Books, 1975), pp. 257–96.

5 J. R. Dale, *The Clerk in Industry* (Liverpool: Liverpool University Press, 1962); Mary Kathleen Benet, *The Secretarial Ghetto* (New York: McGraw-Hill Book Company, 1972), especially chap. 2, "The Rise of the Secretary"; David Lockwood, *The Blackcoated Worker* (London: Allen and Unwin, 1958).

6 U.S. Department of Commerce, Bureau of the Census, *Statistical Abstract of the United States: 1974,* 95th ed. (Washington, D.C.: Government Printing Office, 1974), p. 350, table 568.

7 J. B. Priestley, *Angel Pavement* (London: William Heinemann, 1930).

8   Michel Crozier, *The World of the Office Worker* (Chicago: University of Chicago Press, 1971), p. 15. See also Lockwood, *Blackcoated Worker,* p. 67; Jane Prather, "When the Girls Move In: A Sociological Analysis of the Feminization of the Bank Teller's Job," *Journal of Marriage and the Family* 33 (1971): 777–82; and Etzioni, *The Semi-Professions.*

9   *Statistical Abstract of the United States: 1974,* p. 350, table 568.

10 Margery Davies, "Woman's Place Is at the Typewriter: The Feminization of the Clerical Labor Force," in *Labor Market Segmentation,* ed. Gordon, pp. 279–95.

11 U.S. Department of Commerce, Bureau of the Census, *The Social and Economic Status of the Black Population in the United States, 1973,* Current Population Reports, Series P–23, no. 48 (Washington, D.C.: Government Printing Office, 1974), p. 55.

12 *Statistical Abstract of the United States: 1974,* p. 337, table 542. A useful analytical model on this type of occupational segregation may be found in Blau, "Sex Segregation of Workers."

13 U.S. Department of Labor, Women's Bureau, *1975 Handbook on Women Workers,* Bulletin no. 297 (Washington, D.C.: Government Printing Office, 1975), pp. 89–90, table 38.

14 U.S. Department of Commerce, Bureau of the Census, *Money Income in 1973 of Families and Persons in the United States,* Current Population Reports, Series P–60, no. 97 (Washington, D.C.: Government Printing Office, 1975), p. 140, table 65.

15 See Edna E. Raphael, "Working Women and Their Membership in Labor Unions," *Monthly Labor Review,* May 1974, p. 27; Virginia Olesen, "Militants in a Woman's Profession: Psychological Characteristics of Partisans and Critics of a Nurses' 'Strike,'" *Psychological Reports* 32 (1973): 171–77; Stanley Aronowitz, *False Promises* (New York: McGraw-Hill Book Company, 1973), especially pp. 296–300; Elinor Langer, "Inside the New York Telephone Company," in *Women at Work,* ed. William L. O'Neill (Chicago: Quadrangle Books, 1972), pp. 307–60.

16 Martin J. Gannon, "A Profile of the Temporary Help Industry and Its Workers," *Monthly Labor Review,* May 1974, pp. 44–49; Mack A. Moore, "The Role of Temporary Help Services in the Clerical Labor Market" (Ph.D. diss., University of Wisconsin, 1963); idem, "The Temporary Help Service Industry: Historical Development, Operation and Scope," *Industrial and Labor Relations Review* 18 (1965): 554–69.

17. John D. Griswold, *The Temporary Help Industry* (San Francisco: Arthur D. Little Company, 1969).

18 Leonard Sloane, "Part-Time Help: A Permanent Industry," *New York Times,* January 4, 1970, Business Section, pp. 1, 26.

19 One source notes that the after-tax return on net worth for some firms averages 20 percent and is sometimes much greater. Griswold, *Temporary Help Industry*. For an indictment of profit-taking in the industry, see Anthea Ballam, "The Temp Racket," *New Statesman*, August 13, 1971, p. 203.

20 Robert Blauner, *Alienation and Freedom* (Chicago: University of Chicago Press, 1964).

21 Ibid.; Barbara A. Kirsch and Joseph J. Lengermann, "An Empirical Test of Robert Blauner's Ideas on Alienation in Work as Applied to Different Type Jobs in a White-Collar Setting," *Sociology and Social Research* 56 (1972): 180–94.

22 Virginia Olesen and Elvi Waik Whittaker, *The Silent Dialogue: The Social Psychology of Professional Socialization* (San Francisco: Jossey-Bass, Inc., Publishers, 1968), especially pp. 213–18.

23 Gannon, "Profile of the Temporary Help Industry," p. 46.

24 The method is described by Barney G. Glaser and Anselm L. Strauss, *The Discovery of Grounded Theory: Strategies for Qualitative Research* (Chicago: Aldine Publishing Company, 1967), especially pp. 36–43.

25 Kirsch and Lengermann, "Empirical Test of Robert Blauner's Ideas."

26 Sloane, "Part-Time Help," p. 26. See also *Work in America*, Report of a Special Task Force to the Secretary of Health, Education, and Welfare (Cambridge, Mass.: MIT Press, 1973), especially p. 38.

27 C. Wright Mills, *White Collar* (New York: Galaxy Books, Oxford University Press, 1946), p. xx.

28 For a more detailed study of the reasons for short or long employee tenure in the temporary help industry, see Martin J. Gannon and Uri Brainin, "Employee Tenure in the Temporary Help Industry," *Industrial Relations* 10 (1971): 168–75. The key variables used by Gannon and Brainin—salary, personal characteristics, availability, and perceptions of hiring interviewers—provide a different analytic perspective than that in this chapter. They focus on work patterns, while we examine the phenomenon of temporality in work *and* in life.

29 The distributive function the temporary services industry performs in integrating new, inexperienced workers and those with impaired job prospects into the work force was discussed by Virginia Olesen in "Temporary Workers and Occupational Integration: A Little Explored Sector of the Urban Struggle" (paper presented at the panel "The Urban Struggle: Alienation, Poverty and Work," American Psychiatric Association meeting, Detroit, May 9, 1974).

30 Inge Powell Bell, "The Double Standard," *Transaction*, November-December 1970, pp. 75–80.

31 It may be that this sense of challenge derived from the feeling of achievement these women gained as they entered the labor market and worked successfully

at such jobs. The relationship between achievement and challenge has been demonstrated by Donald D. Bowen, "Work Values of Women in Secretarial-Clerical Occupations," *American Journal of Community Psychiatry* 1 (1973): 83–90. The importance of the challenge some workers find in filling a number of part-time assignments is noted in Douglas T. Hall and Francine E. Gordon, "Career Choices of Married Women," *Journal of Applied Psychology* 58 (1973): 42–48.

32 Madeleine Guilbert, Nicole Lowit, and Joseph Creusen, *Le Travail Temporaire* (Paris: Centre National de la Recherche Scientifique, Centre d'Études Sociologiques, 1970).

33 Olesen, "Temporary Workers and Occupational Integration."

34 See Georg Simmel, "The Metropolis and Mental Life," in *George Simmel on Individuality and Social Forms,* ed. Donald N. Levine (Chicago: University of Chicago Press, 1971), pp. 324–39.

35 Mills, *White Collar,* p. xx.

Women in Blue-Collar and Service Occupations

Sally Hillsman Baker

AN OVERVIEW

Over 12.5 million American women are currently employed in manual industrial and service occupations, generally as unskilled or semiskilled workers. They constitute 38 percent of all employed women. Women are almost one-fifth (18 percent) of all workers in blue-collar craft, operative, and nonfarm laboring jobs in the American economy, and they are over three-fifths (63 percent) of all workers in service occupations, including domestic employment. While the majority of these women are white, almost three out of five employed black women (57 percent) work in blue-collar industrial or service jobs.[1] We know very little about these women workers, their job experiences, their lives, and their struggles as some of the lowest-paid, least skilled, unorganized workers in the United States. Very recently interest in these women has awakened, encouraged by their own rising activism, growing concern about them in the women's movement, and the increasing economic importance of all women workers. Until now they were virtually forgotten members of the work force.

Women in American society have always done "manual" work, paid or not. Before the economy became highly industrialized, men and women were both engaged largely in manual work centered around the family or household as the production unit.[2] With industrialization and the accompanying separation of work from the family, many women not only continued their manual labor in the home but also became manual workers in the paid labor force. Between 1900 and World War II, most women working outside their homes were unmarried and employed in private household service, factories, and sweatshops. While the number of white-collar clerical and sales jobs grew during this period, 50 percent or more of all working women remained employed in manual blue-collar and service jobs. Among them were migrants from rural areas, many of whom were black, and urban immigrant women of various ethnic and religious backgrounds.

World War II was an important turning point for these working women, and the changes it brought had a substantial impact on the composition of the urban industrial working class. For the first time, many minority and women workers were admitted to its ranks. As war production increased and men left their jobs for military service, the need for civilian workers rose rapidly. Many women, particularly married women from lower-income families, were forced back into the labor market by the loss of their family's male wage earners. The availability of new industrial opportunities encouraged other women to resume working, often after long periods of unemployment brought by job shortages during the depression. Along with these reentrants to the labor force, poorly paid women workers in service, domestic, and factory jobs also gained access to more remunerative industrial skills, training, and jobs previously available only to men. The number of women employed in manufacturing industries more than doubled during the war years, especially in war industries, where the pay, working conditions, and access to new skills were particularly good. In heavy industry, for example, the number of women rose from 340,000 to over 2 million.[3] Women "ran lathes, cut dies, read blueprints, and serviced airplanes. They maintained roadbeds, greased locomotives, and took the place of lumberjacks in toppling giant redwoods. As stevedores, blacksmiths, foundry helpers, and drill-press operators, they demonstrated that they could fill almost any job, no matter how difficult."[4]

During this period, therefore, a major transformation took place in the structure of work for women accustomed to manual employment. First, largely because of economic necessity, the number and proportion of married women workers rose appreciably, beginning a trend. Secondly, many women workers, married and single, benefited from expanded job opportunities in more skilled and higher-paying industries and were able to leave lower-quality manual jobs as waitresses, domestics, and sweatshop workers. Thirdly, black women had an unprecedented opportunity to escape domestic service. Before the war, 72 percent of all employed black women had been household workers; by the war's end, the proportion had dropped to 48 percent, and it has continued to decline.

After the war, returning servicemen successfully sought to regain their industrial jobs. Their efforts were generally supported by employers, unions, and the government, often at the expense of women workers. At the national level, for example, pressure on women to relinquish their industrial jobs was reinforced by withdrawal of federal funds for child-care centers. Of the 3,102 facilities that had offered care to 1.5 million children at the end of the war, 2,800 were closed.[5] Yet there is evidence that many blue-collar women did not want and could not afford to return to full-time unpaid housework. One historian reports, for example, that 81 percent of the women employed at the Springfield Arsenal in Massachusetts hoped to continue working after the war, yet every woman employee was fired within one week of V-J Day.[6]

Certainly some women manual workers voluntarily left their jobs to bear children they had postponed having because of the war or just to recuperate from having carried the full burden of jobs and families alone. But women who had held good industrial jobs during the war and the increasing number of married women rejoining the labor force after 1950 often had to take other, less-desirable jobs. For women manual workers, this generally meant returning to the low-paying factory jobs they had traditionally held or taking equally low-level work in the rapidly expanding service sector, as waitresses, hospital attendants, laundry workers, and beauticians. Although the *proportion* of the female work force employed in manual occupations declined in the decades following the war, the *absolute number* of women in manual jobs increased appreciably, because the total number of women working rose so steadily. The proportion of women in blue-collar industrial occupations dropped from 21 percent in 1950 to 16 percent in 1974, but their numbers increased by more than a million to 5.3 million women workers. Yet by the mid-1970s, only about 2 percent of all employed women were holding more skilled craft jobs.

This chapter explores several very basic questions about women nonhousehold manual workers: Who are the women in blue-collar industrial and service occupations, and what are their life situations? What are the characteristics of their jobs? How do they get into such work? What are their attitudes toward their jobs and work experiences?

Several themes are evident throughout these discussions. The most obvious and frequent is the woeful lack of information available about these 12.5 million women.[7] This absence of data suggests an extremely unfortunate lack of concern. Not only have researchers overlooked the problems and needs of a sizable group of women workers, but also our ignorance in this area inhibits our understanding of many central social issues, including poverty, racial discrimination, and sexual discrimination. Our failure to explore fully the situation and needs of women in manual jobs is a virtual disregard of the lives of minority working women, since three out of five are employed in these occupations.

A second recurring theme is the vast amount of change that has occurred in the lives of women manual workers over the last several decades. While most American women have certainly experienced change, those from working-class backgrounds have been particularly affected by the rapid social, political, community, and normative changes in the urban United States. Barbara Mikulski, a political leader and Baltimore city councilwoman, describes this profound disruption:

[In the 1950s] in my community in Baltimore, women participated in philanthropic community activities like the Mothers March of Dimes or bingo parties to raise money for the Polish Day Nursery. . . . We dreamed of marrying white collar organization men and moving up and out. . . . Then came the age of the two Johns—Kennedy and Pope John the XXIII. . . . [W]orking class women were propelled during this period into complicated and confusing roles which generated anxiety. . . . Our lives were changing faster than our own self-image or basic values. The new social forces of civil rights, the Ecumenical Council, Watts, Washington, Selma, Viet Nam; issues like birth control and busing; new categories of people like hippies, hard hats, and militants; new problems like drugs, inflation, crime, the urban crisis—all frightened, confused and astounded us. Our world would never be the same.[8]

Although this chapter focuses primarily on the *work* experiences and attitudes of working-class women, the discussion cannot ignore their general life situation. How do larger economic forces structure their need to work and the jobs available to them? How do the resulting problems intersect with other aspects of their lives? For example, rising inflation has had important effects on the work and family lives of working-class women. Over the last decade, inflation has eaten away at the ability of working-class people to improve or even maintain their life-styles. While all economic groups have suffered, this phenomenon has affected the lives of women in lower- and moderate-income families more than those of middle-class women. As Judith Blake points out, blue-collar husbands' incomes peak earlier in their careers than do those of more highly paid men. Their financial situation, therefore, is deteriorating just when family expenses are the highest.[9] The economic pressure on working-class wives and mothers to return to work is thus substantial. The decision to do so is often received with resentment by their husbands, and, as Mikulski indicates the women themselves do not tend to react initially with the positive feeling that work will enrich their personal lives and increase their self-control:

> It was a shock to be 34 years old and out of the labor force for 14 years. No counselling, advice, or re-entry help. For many it was part-time work selling, "rent-a-girl" temporary office help, or back to the assembly line. . . . We looked at our mothers. They worked off and on for 60 years and have no (portable) pensions.[10]

Part of the reason for their lack of enthusiasm about returning to work is that a very narrow range of jobs is available to working-class women. This is the third theme of our discussion. The sexual, racial, and class segregation that is characteristic of American labor markets has been an important restrictive factor in women's employment at all levels of the occupational system and one that has resisted change (as Francine Blau points out above). It affects social processes beginning in childhood and continuing throughout the educational and labor market experiences of Americans, assuring that those of middle-class and working-class origins, men and women, blacks and whites are rarely in the same occupations or hold the same jobs. For many working-class women, this has meant restriction to manual jobs that are among the lowest-paying, least desirable, and most marginal work in the marketplace. For the woman who is stigmatized and constrained not only by her class background, her age, and her triple role as wife, mother, and worker but also by her race, the labor market limitations are most severe (see the chapter by Elizabeth Almquist and Juanita Wehrle-Einhorn above).

BLUE-COLLAR WOMEN AND WHY THEY WORK

In speaking of men, the question, "Why do they work?" seems odd indeed. Men work primarily because they must. Women holding blue-collar and service jobs also work because they must. Yet United States society strangely clings to the notion that married women should not work outside their homes, particularly if they have children, and the myth that if their work is necessary this is merely a temporary phenomenon.[11] The fact is that even when there are preschool children in the family, employment is necessary for 57 percent of the women whose husbands make between $5,000 and $10,000, and for 32 percent of wives whose husbands earn more. Rising inflation has created great economic pressure on women in low- and middle-income families to remain in the labor force or to return shortly after the birth of their children. While women's employment rates have increased steadily at all levels of education and family income and at all stages of the life cycle, the biggest increase since the early 1950s has occurred among married women whose husbands earn between $3,000 and $10,000, especially between $7,000 and $10,000.[12]

Many women from these low- to middle-income families find employment in blue-collar and service jobs. Complex economic factors since the 1950s have increased the market demand for women's labor, expanding "female" jobs, which are avoided by men because of their low pay. Many of these working women are "ethnic whites" (white women from distinct ethnic minority groups) or urban blacks. Their husbands are also likely to be blue-collar workers earning less than the federally established "intermediate" level of living ($11,446 for an urban family of four in 1973). As working wives, these women contribute an estimated average of 30 percent of their family's total annual income, which for marginal families is likely to be the one factor keeping them above poverty.[13]

For the less fortunate women, blue-collar or service employment is one of the factors contributing to poverty. About 20 percent of female domestic workers, 12 percent of female service workers, and 9 percent of female operatives and laborers were living below the official government poverty level in 1973. By contrast, only 4 percent of female clerical and sales workers and 2 percent of female professional and managerial workers were living in poverty.[14] Manual women workers are often the sole support of themselves and their families. The divorce, illness, death, or desertion of a spouse leaves women who are already struggling economically even more vulnerable. With little education, training, or job experience, they are unable to secure better-paying jobs in other sectors of the economy. In 1973, 45 percent of all families living in poverty were headed by women, the majority of whom worked. For minority women, the probability of being caught in poverty is more than three times as great as for white women. Of the 12.5 million women holding manual blue-collar and service jobs, approximately 1.4 million (11 percent) are part of the "working poor," black and white, and many are supporting their families alone.[15]

Like the men studied in the sociological literature on the inheritance of social class, women tend to follow the class patterns of their fathers. Many women currently employed in manual jobs were born into working-class or poor families; they are the daughters of blue-collar and service work fathers. This pattern of class inheritance is partly related to the influence of both race and class factors on their educational attainment, a subject I discuss

> **In speaking of men, the question, "Why do they work?" seems odd indeed. Men work primarily because they must. Women holding blue-collar and service jobs also work because they must.**

more later. A recent study of working women from thirty to forty-four years old shows that *regardless* of their educational attainment, a majority of black women whose fathers were manual workers also became manual workers. White women from manual labor backgrounds, however, were somewhat more successful at securing white-collar employment, if they completed high school. Among those who did not finish high school, 51 percent of the white women and 74 percent of the black women were employed in manual jobs even if their fathers had been white-collar workers.[16] Although far more research is necessary to explore fully the problems of social mobility among women, powerful class inheritance factors seem to persist even among younger groups of women.[17] It must be noted here that, in 1973, 80 percent of all American women over the age of twenty-five had no more than a high school education. Almost two out of five white women had less than a high school education and another two of the five had completed high school but no more. Among black women, three out of five had not completed high school.[18] It is not surprising, therefore, that at least half the female blue-collar and service workers, white and black, have less than a high school education.[19]

In summary, women manual workers tend to be from working-class or poor families, to have less than a high school education, to marry working-class men, and to be employed because of financial need, which they may well be meeting alone. Many live in urban areas, about 20 percent are black, and a good many of the others are "ethnic whites."

CATEGORIES OF WOMEN'S
BLUE-COLLAR AND SERVICE JOBS

Blue-collar women do not hold the same jobs as their male counterparts. Like women at other levels of the occupational hierarchy, they are crowded into a relatively narrow range of blue-collar and service jobs in comparison to male workers. Valerie Kincade Oppenheimer has estimated that between 1900 and 1960, 60 to 73 percent of the female labor force was employed in occupations filled primarily (50 percent or more) by female workers.[20] While exceptions to this pattern among manual workers have become somewhat more visible in recent years (the occasional woman cab driver or plumber), there is no evidence that the structural processes creating this labor market situation have changed.[21] Since the end of World War II, women have rarely "run lathes, cut dies, read blueprints, and serviced airplanes." Instead, they work in those blue-collar and service occupational categories and industries that have traditionally hired women. They are machine operators, particularly in apparel manufacturing, textile, and knitting mills; operators in laundries and dry cleaning establishments; dressmakers outside of factories; assemblers in certain manufacturing industries such as electrical component manufacturing; packers and wrappers in all kinds of establishments; operators in telephone and other communications industries; beauticians, especially in small firms; waitresses, particularly in small and fast-food restaurants; hospital aides and orderlies; chambermaids; and, of course, household domestics.

Male manual workers are typically employed in other occupational categories and industries. They are craftsmen in the construction and other industries, foremen, mechanics, repairmen, and printers; transportation equipment operators, including bus, taxi, and truck drivers; protective service workers, including police and fire officers and guards. When they are in the same *occupational* category as women, such as factory operatives, they are rarely found in the same *industries* as women, such as apparel or textile manufacturing; instead, male operatives work in steel mills and automobile manufacturing, for example. When both sexes are employed in the same industries, men rarely hold the same jobs as women (for example, in apparel manufacturing firms, men are usually skilled cutters and pressers, while women are mass production sewing machine operators). (See Francine Blau's chapter above.)

This occupational, industrial, and job segregation by sex reflects a general pattern of employment referred to as *labor market segmentation* (see Mary Stevenson's chapter above). Basically, this means that different groups of workers are typically found either in different industries or in different occupations within an industry, and that workers in one industry or occupation rarely compete for jobs in other industries and occupations. It is important to note that sex is not the only personal characteristic that distinguishes the separate groups of workers. Race is another obvious distinguishing characteristic, and one that bears on the segmentation of manual women workers, since many racial minority women are employed in blue-collar occupations.

Working-class women, like most American workers, experience the phenomenon of labor market segmentation as a progressive pattern of segregation occurring at all stages of their education and career preparation. This was illustrated in the lives of a group of young working-class women I studied in New York City. They had all graduated from a good New York vocational high school and had received substantial training for jobs in the apparel manufacturing industry. In examining their educational experiences and their early careers after high school graduation, I found that step by step they were separated and segregated by class, sex, and race, in preparation for the segmented structure of employment dominating the local labor market.[22] It is instructive to see exactly how this occurred.

Like many school systems, the New York schools make several curriculum tracks available to high school students. Girls from working-class backgrounds are more likely to be tracked into the nonacademic (non-college-preparatory) tracks, including the vocational track, than are girls from middle-class backgrounds.[23] Those who enter the vocational track are typically isolated from students in other high school programs. This is because vocational programs are often located in entirely different school buildings.

Within the vocational track, men and women are further tracked into different occupational training programs, and comparatively few programs are allocated to women.

In New York, 94 percent of the students enrolled in the apparel manufacturing program are women. While they are frequently led to believe they are preparing for glamorous "fashion" careers, the reality is starkly different. The apparel industry is one of New York's lowest-paying industries, and the majority of its workers are semiskilled, mass production sewing machine operators working in ancient, dingy, dirty factories. These workers are predominately women and increasingly minority women.

Within the special vocational school for apparel trades, tracking occurs again. The girls are tracked into classes preparing them as sewing machine operators for mass production work or somewhat more specialized sewing tasks. In contrast, the comparatively small number of boys are trained for other, traditionally "male," jobs in the apparel industry, the higher-paying, higher-skilled trades such as cutter, presser, and tailor.

This is not the end of the progressive educational and training segregation, however. Most black and Puerto Rican girls entering the apparel school are assigned to the least skilled, least prestigious "female" classes, while the white girls predominate in the more "elite" classes. During the years I studied the students, almost half the white girls in the school were placed in "fashion design" classes, where they studied machine and hand sewing, design, and the construction of complete garments. Only 12 percent of black and 19 percent of Puerto Rican girls were assigned to these classes. In contrast, 57 percent of the black girls were tracked into "garment operating" classes, where they learned almost exclusively to do routine, mass production sewing. Only 29 percent of the Puerto Rican girls and 20 percent of the white girls were tracked into these less desirable classes.

At the completion of their high school academic and vocational training, male and female, black and white graduates were referred to very different jobs in workplaces that were virtually sexual and racial ghettos. For example, among the girls, white graduates were more likely to leave the apparel trades and be placed in higher-paying, higher-status white-collar jobs (for which they had received no special training) than were their minority classmates who participated in exactly the same vocational program. Minority women were placed in the less well-paying apparel factory jobs for which they had been trained. This outcome is not surprising in light of the data cited earlier from the national study of women thirty to forty-four years old: white women from manual backgrounds who are high school graduates tend to have greater mobility into white-collar jobs than similar minority women. In the New York study this pattern emerged from the normal operations of a school and a local labor market even when white and minority girls were given exactly the same manual vocational training and general high school education—in the same school and even the same classrooms.[24]

CHARACTERISTICS OF WOMEN'S BLUE-COLLAR JOBS

The economic consequences of the class, racial, and sexual segregation of women into specific occupations, industries, and jobs are substantial. Men and women, blacks and whites do not even compete for the same manual jobs. Minority women particularly tend to be isolated in some of the poorest quality jobs available in the labor market. Many labor force analysts are now discussing the existence of multiple labor markets and relating this phenomenon to problems of poverty and poor working conditions. Peter Doeringer and Michael Piore were among the first to formally identify two distinct labor markets and to note that the workers rarely experience mobility from one to the other. They describe this "dual labor market" as follows:

> Jobs in the primary market possess several of the following characteristics: high wages, good working conditions, employment stability, chances of advancement, equity, and due process in the administration of work roles. Jobs in the secondary market, in contrast, tend to have low wages and fringe benefits, poor working conditions, high labor turnover, little chance of advancement, and often arbitrary and capricious supervision.[25]

The types of firms within which women typically find employment have been described as small, marginal, nonunion enterprises with low capital investments, low profit margins, irregular personnel practices, high turnover, and low pay.[26] Manual jobs in such firms are clearly part of the secondary labor market of which Doeringer and Piore write. The discussion above of the blue-collar and service jobs that women traditionally have occupied, showed that many are low-level occupations in industries characterized by marginal firms. For example, apparel manufacturing firms tend to be small, and their capital investment amounts to little more than sewing machines, cutting equipment, and stocks of fabric. Their profits tend to be low and unstable because of intense competition and the unpredictability of tastes in fashion. Most jobs in these firms are semiskilled operative occupations, characterized by low pay, little advancement, and seasonal employment. While firms in urban areas are likely to be unionized, the threat that these businesses will move to rural areas where cheaper, nonunion, female labor is available keeps existing unions from making strong wage demands.

Many of these economic features characterize other firms employing women, as manufacturing operatives, beauticians, waitresses, laundry and dry-cleaning workers, and dressmakers. Even in larger, less marginal firms, the blue-collar and service jobs held by women often have the characteristics of the secondary labor market: poor wages, poor fringe benefits, unstable employment, and exploitive part-time work. As Mary Stevenson has pointed out, a steady or growing supply of women workers willing to take (or unable to avoid taking) such jobs encourages employers to keep their wage levels below those of men's jobs.[27] In 1974, full-time female operatives received a median wage of $107 weekly, or about 63 percent of the median for full-time male operatives. Full-time female service workers earned a median of $92 per week, about 61 percent of male workers' wages. Even when women worked full-time and year-round, they earned only about $5,360 annually as operatives and about $4,590 as service workers in 1973, both less than 60 percent of the wages of men similarly employed and less than those of women in white-collar clerical jobs ($6,470 annually).[28]

These financial problems typify employment in the secondary labor market, and they create particular hardships for the woman who is the sole support of her family. Comparing the earnings of *family heads* who were employed in production and nonsupervisory jobs between 1963 and 1973, the real increase in earnings among male heads was 21 percent, but among women heads it was only 8 percent.[29] Since little change has occurred in the segregation of women in the secondary labor market, there is no evidence that these male-female wage differentials are narrowing; if anything, they are widening.[30]

Additional financial problems are reflected by the higher unemployment rates among women in craft, operative, and service jobs compared to men in these occupations and to women in white-collar employment.[31] Since 1950, an increasing proportion of those looking for work at all occupational levels has been female, ranging from 30 to over 45 percent of the total unemployed.[32] Unable to obtain full-time employment, because it is either not available or made impossible by their home responsibilities, almost half the women in craft and operative jobs and seven out of ten in service jobs are employed only part-time. A growing number of women need part-time employment. Yet part-time jobs tend to be among the most exploitive in the secondary labor market, because workers are generally denied the benefits accruing to full-time employees: health insurance, pension contributions, seniority, on-the-job training, and promotion. Unionization tends to be quite difficult in industries that rely heavily on part-time workers, so the working conditions remain poor.

Whether they work full- or part-time, female manual workers have not generally embraced labor unions. Their poor economic conditions can be explained partly by the general lack of unionization characteristic of jobs in the secondary labor market. Whereas three out of ten male workers in the United States are unionized, only one out of seven female workers is.[33] In 1952, over 15 percent of all working women were active union members. The figure for 1972 was 12.6 percent.[34] The absolute number of women union members is increasing, however, despite a general decline in the growth of unions in recent years, yet women's employment gains have far exceeded their growth in union membership. Union growth among women workers is particularly poor in the occupations historically associated with the union movement—manual jobs. Membership among women in service occupations has increased by only 0.4 percent, and it has actually declined by 8 percent among women operatives, a decline that unfortunately exceeds that among male blue-collar workers.[35]

There is no question, however, that unionization improves wages for both men and women no matter what their occupation. In most occupational categories where comparisons are possible, male and female union workers earn higher wages than nonunion workers of the same sex. In 1970, for example, nonunion women in blue-collar occupations averaged $647 per year less than their unionized counterparts.[36] Yet in comparable occupations, union *men* uniformly earn more than union women.[37] Furthermore, while unionization *narrows* the earnings gap between the sexes in both white-collar and service work, this is not true for blue-collar workers. Among non-unionized service workers women earn 120 percent less than men; the gap is reduced to 70 percent among unionized workers in these occupations. The gap for blue-collar workers, however, is 90 percent among nonunionized workers and 100 percent among unionized workers![38] These figures clearly reflect a lack of concern by many blue-collar unions about their female members.

Nonetheless, increased unionization is vital if the quality of female manual workers' jobs is to improve and if their earnings are to rise both absolutely and relatively to those of men. According to Paul Ryscavage, across all occupational categories, union membership means an improvement of 22 percent in income for white women, 19 percent for black women, 27 percent for black men, and only 8 percent for white men.[39]

In addition, unions already representing women workers need to be more responsive to the needs of these members. This means that women must increase their participation in central decision-making roles. Women are rare at the higher levels of union organization in all 177 American unions, and their numbers have increased only slightly in the last twenty years.[40] This is true even of unions whose membership is predominately female. In a 1972 survey, the Clothing Workers (75 percent female), the Ladies' Garment Workers (80 percent female), and the Electrical Workers (40 percent female) reported only one woman official each; the Textile Workers (40 percent female) had two.[41]

In spite of such dismal figures, union activism among women manual workers is on the rise. Although detailed data are sparse, it appears that the number of women in leadership positions at the *local* level is increasing, that women unionists are more vocal, and that more union locals are holding women's conferences to examine their problems. While enormous structural and attitudinal barriers block women's participation, both are undergoing change.[42] Gloria Johnson of the International Union of Electrical, Radio, and Machine Workers offers the following observation on the changing attitudes of women manual workers:

> My own feeling is that there are strong similarities to attitudes that blacks used to have: a fear of losing, or rejection, if a woman does step forward to take an active role; a feeling of "I've never done it before so I might fail"; a feeling that one's husband might object; and always, of course, the problem of time, because of domestic responsibilities as well as work. But, judging by an IUE survey, these attitudes are changing. In our opinion, we have women in what we call social-action programs, we have women's committees in the locals, and the districts are beginning to have their own women's conferences.[43]

It is important, however, that unionization also spread to the women in unorganized industries and workplaces. This extremely difficult task is a major goal of the newly created national women's labor organization, the Coalition of Labor Union Women (CLUW), as indicated in its statement of purpose:

Of the 34 million women in the work force—little more than 4 million women are members of unions. It is imperative that within the framework of the union movement we take aggressive steps to more effectively address ourselves to the critical needs of 30 million unorganized sisters and to make our unions more responsive to the needs of all women, especially the needs of minority women who have traditionally been singled out for particularly blatant oppression.[44]

If CLUW is successful, it could bring about major improvements in the quality of work experienced by women in blue-collar and service occupations.

An important barrier to improving the job quality, wages, wage progressions, and union strength of classically female blue-collar and service jobs is

> ❝ An important barrier to improving the job quality, wages, wage progressions, and union strength of classically female blue-collar and service jobs is their systematic underrating in terms of skill, compared to male jobs. ❞

their systematic underrating in terms of skill, compared to male jobs. Norma Briggs, for example, has pointed out that the federal government's *Dictionary of Occupational Titles* grossly underrates the skill levels of many women's jobs. A Home Health Aide who "cares for elderly, convalescent or handicapped persons" is given virtually the lowest possible skill rating, slightly below that given Delivery Boy (Newspaper Carrier) and the same as Public Bath Maid, which is rated as "not quite as skilled as . . . Pet Store Attendant." Practical Nurse, Nursemaid, Nurse Mid-Wife, and Homemaker (who is cross-referenced with Maid—General) are all rated *lower* in skill than Hotel Clerk and Barber and at the *same* skill level as Parking Lot Attendant![45]

One important consequence of these low skill ratings, and the one with which Briggs is particularly concerned, is that they block many women's jobs from becoming part of the formal apprenticeship system. "Apprenticeship is the training ladder from unskilled to skilled work," she notes in her report on women in the Wisconsin Apprenticeships Project.[46] According to the United States Department of Labor, a job that can be apprenticed must involve manual, mechanical, or technical skills that are developed over time and that require at least two years of on-the-job training for competence (for example, plumbers, electricians, cooks, barbers, draftsmen, and bakers are apprenticed). Apprenticeship is almost invariably accompanied by unionization and reaps its benefits: skill progression, wage progression, and transferability of skills from one job to another. Briggs makes the point that

> apprenticeship is the major employment mobility channel for people
> with a limited formal educational background. It is through appren-
> ticeship that one with no college training, and with no money to attend
> college, can earn while learning one of the 350 recognized skilled trades
> or crafts and eventually command a wage that is substantially above
> the legal minimum and sufficient to maintain a family well above the
> poverty level. . . . [However,] analysis of apprenticeable jobs and
> industries led to the observation that of the multitude of potentially
> apprenticeable occupations . . . those that had been recognized and
> approved for formal apprenticeships had, with only one or two out-
> standing exceptions [cosmetology] happened to fall into the "tradi-
> tionally male" occupational category. There appeared to be large
> numbers of skilled and paraprofessional jobs that fit apprenticeable
> criteria equally well, most of which fell into the "traditionally female"
> employment areas that had been overlooked.[47]

As Briggs indicates, many of the jobs working-class women enter are inaccurately considered too unskilled to be apprenticed. The Wisconsin project is a hopeful effort to bring women into apprenticeships and upgrade their occupations. There are, however, still many barriers to surmount. Very few women enter already apprenticed manual and service occupations: less than 1 percent of all registrants for apprenticeship opportunities are women.[48] Many of the reasons for this arise in women's vocational preparation and patterns of labor market entry. Women are often discouraged from preparing for such male jobs; they lack the information they need to enter apprenticeships; and many enter the labor market with serious career intentions at an age past the usual limit for applicants (ranging from twenty-four to twenty-seven).[49]

PROCESSES OF JOB TRAINING
AND LABOR MARKET ENTRY

To understand fully how working-class women become segregated in poor-quality manual and service jobs, it is necessary to examine the vocational socialization they undergo, the training available to them, and their experiences on entering the labor market. Although socialization for adult roles obviously starts early in childhood, there are also two particularly crucial later periods for working women: the high school years, when early career plans are made, and the period of reentry into the labor force during or after marriage and childbearing.

While it is somewhat exaggerated to say that young working-class girls are their own worst enemy when it comes to career preparation, their traditional aspirations, self-images, and adult role expectations do not help them face the realities of a long work life and the possibility of supporting a family alone. Working-class girls have traditionally married young, had relatively large families, rarely thought about further education, and not challenged the cultural emphasis on their role as homemakers. While recent data indicate these patterns are changing, this is not always fully understood by the very women whose lives are reflected in the data. Although many more are being encouraged to plan for longer, steady careers, most still share the ideology that their work is "temporary" and not a major life role for them. Briggs found that these patterns remained particularly strong for the average young woman who was not college bound:

> She has been shortchanged into believing that if she is a normal American girl she will only be in the paid labor force for a while, marking the time until she marries and solves life's problems by becoming a full-time wife and mother, and that a wholesome girl starting out in life does not plan seriously for extended paid employment any more than she plans on a divorce. She has been shielded from the cold statistics of life.[50]

In a recent survey of women eighteen to twenty-four years old who were no longer in school, fewer than one out of five white women and not many more black women were favorably inclined to the idea of a mother going to work. Over half of both groups, however, expressed ambivalent rather than fully negative feelings.[51] This ambivalence probably indicates that their actual adult experiences have made inroads on the traditional role expectations of adolescence. Nevertheless, many still cling to the old images. Pamela Roby reports:

> West Coast organizers for the United Electrical Workers express heart-ache from hearing dozens of women electrical workers in their twenties echo their employers saying assuredly, "I won't be working long—only until we pay for the washer and dryer (the car, our vacation, etc.,)—I don't need to worry about how this job's treating me." The organizers know many women workers in their forties and fifties who held the same belief 10 years ago.[52]

Unfortunately, these young women's parents and spouses, the mass media, and even their schools continue to reinforce rather than help correct these images. In a 1959 study of working-class wives, many of whom are the mothers of today's young women in blue-collar and service work, Lee Rainwater and others found that most mothers wanted their daughters to follow traditional role definitions: to be good wives and mothers and to continue to be loving, respectful daughters. Encouraging their daughters to prepare for paid employment was, in their view, inimical to these central goals.[53] This pattern is further reinforced by the negative attitudes of working-class fathers and husbands toward married women working. In spite of the economic realities of recent decades, there is evidence that working-class men remain less favorable to having women work than middle-class men.[54] Harold Sheppard reports, "Blue collar males do not feel that they have really succeeded if they cannot, all by themselves, provide their families with the necessary income to pay for the level of living they aspire to."[55] Yet, as noted above, this is becoming increasingly difficult to achieve.

These attitudes are undergoing some change, however, as the daughters of Rainwater's 1959 working-class wives experience the increasing problems of the 1960s and 1970s. Inflation, divorce, and the community and cultural changes described earlier by Mikulski have forced reality on these women. According to Seifer,

> even among working class girls who say they identify strongly with tradition and expect their lives to be much the same as their mothers' were, there are perceptible differences (even if only slight) in some of their values and aspirations. Nevertheless, low self-esteem, low expectations and relatively few options still impose limitations on their lives, much as they constricted their mothers', and to a far greater degree than they impede their middle class counterparts in the 1970's.[56]

Despite the importance of these changes and the number of people they affect, we have devoted little attention to them. It is clearly time for new, extensive, and thoughtful research on the attitudes, self-images, aspirations, and problems of working-class women. Such research should be designed both to inform public policy and to aid working-class women in their own personal and social struggles.[57]

More often than not, high schools accept and reinforce these young women's aspirations, self-images, and beliefs that employment will be only "temporary." One former junior high school guidance counselor told me that the vocational interest test used for years in her school was constructed so that any interest in marriage or motherhood expressed by a girl automatically lowered her scores in all other areas of vocational interest. This was not the case for the boys' version of the same test. The consequence was serious. Virtually all girls not pressing to go to college were encouraged to take a noncollege general curriculum supplemented by minimal skill-preparation courses, which was considered suited to their "short-term" employment outlook!

> In 1973, 98.5 percent of the enrollees in Wisconsin high school industrial classes were male. The girls are given home economics or, if they are not on the college track, business subjects. In most schools, girls are either overtly forbidden or subtly discouraged from seriously experimenting with shop courses that lay the foundation for work in the skilled trades; too great an interest in, or proficiency at, things technical are considered "unfeminine." This puts most women at a disadvantage when taking selection tests that examine familiarity with the tools and terms of the trade.[58]

This example is not uncommon. It reflects the two-pronged pattern operating in many, indeed most, school systems. First, working-class women are tracked out of college-preparatory and serious, career-oriented vocational programs, as noted in the New York vocational school study. In the second place, they are socialized to believe this is appropriate. This subtle form of discrimination runs very deep in many institutions but its day-to-day forms are often difficult to identify and measure.[59]

In many school systems, serious vocational training is not even available to women, despite continued increases in funds for public vocational education and laws against sex discrimination in education. While in 1972 over half the students in vocational courses were women (almost 6.5 million), only 55 percent of the women were enrolled in courses preparing them for gainful employment. The remainder were in non-wage-earning consumer and homemaking programs within home economics curricula. Of the women in job-oriented courses, 51 percent were in office and business programs, often preparing them for low-level, dead-end jobs. Although many female high school students enter blue-collar and service jobs and could begin training in high school for higher-paying, skilled trades, only 9 percent of women vocational students were enrolled in technical programs (such as electrical, mechanical, or automotive technology), trade and industrial programs (such as carpentry, masonry, plumbing, cosmetology, and drafting), or health service training (such as dental or medical assistance and occupational or physical therapy).[60]

Even when extensive technical, trade, and industrial training is readily available in school systems, women are generally denied access to the full range of opportunities. By formal (and blatantly illegal) or, more often, informal means, women are virtually excluded from training for all manual occupations except the narrow range of jobs they have traditionally held. Roby writes:

> Despite the federal law against sex discrimination in vocational education, tracking of girls often occurs because schools are for boys only, or because male teachers simply refuse to allow girls in their classes. Peter Holmes, Director of the Office of Civil Rights of the U.S. Department of Health, Education and Welfare recently reported findings of his office's survey of area vocational schools. These showed that . . . [a] chronic problem . . . is the separation of programs and courses by sex. Even more serious is the existence of vocational schools that accept only students of one sex. . . . The other aspect of sex discrimination in vocational schools has to do with segregation by course.[61]

The largest public school system in the country, that of New York City, offers a clear example of these patterns. Extensive and reasonably good vocational training is widely available through a system of special vocational schools. In 1974, male students were enrolled in fifty-three different trade curricula, women in thirty-six. Forty-five of the trade courses available contained students of one sex only, fifteen for women, twice as many for men. An enormous 91 percent of the women trained in New York City vocational programs other than home economics were in traditionally female, low-paying, low-skilled areas, including office skills, cosmetology, health occupations, retailing, and apparel construction. Only 3 to 4 percent of the male students were enrolled in these programs. Instead, four-fifths of the boys were enrolled in programs training for a wide range of mechanical, technical, and repair skills (such as computer technology, television broadcasting technology, and radio-television mechanics), skilled crafts (such as carpentry, plumbing, and printing), and other skilled trades (such as sheet metal work and computer programming). Only about 2 percent of the girls were enrolled in these courses.[62]

Since there is no evidence of ability differences as the basis for sex and race segregation in training for blue-collar and service jobs, why do schools track women and particularly minority women into poor quality jobs and

> ❝ Even when extensive technical, trade, and industrial training is readily available in school systems, women are generally denied access to the full range of opportunities. ❞

reinforce other socialization experiences that encourage them to accept and even desire such jobs? The answers are not simple. School personnel often do what they genuinely believe to be in the best interests of young women. Yet their judgments may not always be good ones. For example, several New York City teachers and guidance counselors told me that they believed working-class black and Puerto Rican girls were not really interested in careers or good jobs. (They did not report the same belief about whites.) But, because they believed minority girls were more likely than white girls to find themselves with children to support, school personnel tried to help them avoid the "welfare trap" by encouraging them to train for a trade that was easy to learn and in which employment was readily available. Consequently, they tracked minority girls into training for mass production apparel manufacturing—one of the lowest-paying, most seasonal, dead-end jobs in New York City, as noted above. Instead of acting to change the social realities that encouraged their initial assumptions about working-class minority girls, school personnel acted to reinforce these conditions. Being tracked into training for dull, repetitive work actually drained many girls of their interest in employment. School personnel could not see that preparing minority girls (and boys) for only poor quality jobs helped assure that they would find it difficult as adults to overcome poverty and discrimination.[63]

School systems have also shown little interest in opening training opportunities to help reduce sex and race segregation in jobs. This is partly organizational inertia. Such changes would mean considerable reorganization of very traditional educational programs, and there has been little local or national political pressure on schools to do so. While reform of vocational education has sparked considerable interest in recent years, according to Roby, few of the suggested changes even mention the special problems of women.[64] Roby also points out that little of the multimillion-dollar funding by the federal government since 1968 for research in this area has been devoted to women's needs.

To understand more fully the general lack of interest in change, we need to take another analytical approach. It is hardly a novel idea that schools are the selectors of talent or the society's "gatekeepers" to a *highly stratified* occupational hierarchy. It is also well documented that, despite the rising educational attainment of most groups, the relative positions of women versus men, blacks versus whites, and working-class versus middle-class people have altered little in the last few decades. There is also growing evidence that schools play a part in this process by not fulfilling their *ideologically* defined function of helping disadvantaged groups overcome their relative disadvantage.[65] In practice, the mechanisms schools and other gatekeepers use to screen and select candidates for preferred occupational slots tend to advantage already advantaged groups in the society. For example, as Briggs noted, selection tests used to screen applicants for skilled manual training programs measure familiarity with the tools and terms of the trade. There is no evidence that women cannot learn most of these skills, but they rarely have the opportunity to do so *before* applying for formal training. Yet the screening tests are considered appropriate selection devices, because they measure job-related traits. They are, therefore, generally defined as legitimate prerequisites for admission to training.

The consequence is obvious. Since the number of highly desirable positions at the top of any occupational hierarchy (blue-collar, white-collar, or professional) is always small, selection and screening patterns tend to maintain the existing rank order of various social groups occupying positions along that hierarchy. That is, the advantaged pass on their advantage wherever possible. White males have traditionally dominated skilled blue-collar and service jobs. One way they maintain their individual and collective competitive advantage is by blocking the access of other groups to formal and informal training. Brigid O'Farrell provides a very good example of this process from her research on craft jobs in an industry put under a court approved affirmative action program.

> The foreman was a fairly new foreman with a recently appointed second line boss [above him]. . . . He had no senior rated craftpersons and his semi-skilled crew was now almost completely female. . . . He knew the women needed more training but at the same time, by making top pay, they could earn more money working over-time at the semi-skilled level than he did as a foreman. He was ambitious and had hopes of becoming a second liner himself. He was aware, however, that under the new affirmative action program the next several openings might well go to the very woman he was training. . . . In reaction he seemed to have decided that women just couldn't do the work and he told them so.[66]

Employers have a variety of reasons for wanting to hire particular groups of workers. Some certainly fear that the introduction of new groups will upset traditional status hierarchies (putting blacks over whites, women over men) and disrupt the work place. Probably a more important factor, however, is that employers select people they *believe* to be the most "trainable" or in other ways most "suitable" for the job. Since formal education or training is not always related to performance on the job, employers often have little to go on in making their decision other than their own images, stereotypes, and personal or social preferences.[67] It is no wonder, then, that traditional groups of workers are generally judged most suitable. They are believed not only to have the technical skills required but also to fit the more subjective estimates of a job's particular "personality" or social requirements.

This can be seen in the restaurant business. New York City waitresses have recently challenged the hiring practices of some "elite" restaurants. Owners claimed that the "atmosphere" of their exclusive establishments would be disturbed by the presence of female employees who allegedly "distracted" the predominately male customers. Such distractions, however, do not worry the owners of less expensive restaurants, who *want* waitresses instead of waiters because they can be hired for less money or because the owners can capitalize on their employees' sex by requiring the waitresses to wear revealing uniforms.

Why do educational and training programs tend to pattern their decisions about students on employers' unstated preferences for different social categories of workers? The answer lies in the fact that educational and training organizations are directly or indirectly dependent on the business (employing) community. While this dependence is most visible for explicitly vocational schools, it occurs at all levels of the educational system. Since this chapter is concerned with the career preparation of women manual workers, however, I confine my discussion to vocational programs.

Many vocational schools and training programs rely on business organizations and unions for technical assistance, personnel, equipment, supplies, and on-the-job training positions for their students. In addition, since most are supported by public funds, they are accountable to the political system. The "effectiveness" of most public training programs is evaluated by the number or proportion of graduates who enter training-related employment. While this seems quite logical, it has some important consequences for women. Program personnel naturally want their own jobs and programs to be positively evaluated. If employers do not want women workers, or if apprenticeships are virtually closed to women, the proportion of training-related job placements among women graduates will be low. This is likely to erode support for their programs. Consequently, as long as criteria such as training-related employment are used (and they are used extensively), "effective" training programs for women will continue to be those that prepare women for traditionally female blue-collar and service jobs.[68]

The training and selection systems, therefore, are mutually reinforcing. Schools provide the most access and encouragement to those social groups considered desirable for higher-level positions by employers, unions, or co-workers. Employers find that the social characteristics they want are indeed found among the applicants with higher educational attainment, training, and skill! Employers then have "legitimate" grounds for selecting traditional, already advantaged groups for these positions.

Many of the training and hiring problems discussed here are compounded for the "older" working-class woman seeking to reenter the labor market. I place the word in quotation marks because such women tend to be between thirty and forty, hardly old by either biological or cultural standards in the United States. They are old by employment standards, however, because they are out of phase with males of their age who started their steady work lives a decade earlier. Age becomes a handicap particularly in male-dominated jobs that require apprenticeships or other forms of training. Employers consider such training uneconomical for workers with "shorter" work lives. While this may be a valid factor for jobs requiring heavy physical labor, which is difficult for older workers to do, it is not necessarily valid for other jobs. Women beginning work between thirty and forty are likely to have careers for twenty-five to thirty-five years. This is as long as employers expect of male workers, who may start younger but may also leave a particular job sooner to move to a second career. A woman's "second" career (motherhood) simply comes first in her long work life, but this is used as a reason to deny her access to higher-quality manual jobs.

The "older" woman worker is also disadvantaged in seeking female-dominated jobs where a youthful appearance is considered a prerequisite (see Evelyn Rosenthal's chapter above). Her confidence in herself is eroded by failure to secure a job, by her years as "just" a housewife, and by finding her previous manual skills out of date. She desperately needs retraining or further education. Yet programs for her are rare, child-care arrangements needed during the training period are too costly, and when programs are held at night she cannot get away from home obligations. She is cut off from familiar formal sources of job referral, such as her high school employment office, and has no idea where to find other help. So she seeks a job in a factory, hospital, or restaurant near her home, where she finds other neighborhood women like herself employed in low-quality, poorly paid work.

WORK ATTITUDES AND EXPERIENCES ON THE JOB

While women in blue-collar and service jobs, like most workers, work because they have to, it would be wrong to assume that they do not want to work. Paid work often offers a socially valued challenge to their abilities and talents. It also gives women an opportunity to escape the isolation and boredom of housekeeping, if not its manual drudgery. Little research has been done on the noneconomic meanings that blue-collar and service women attach to their employment—how they feel about it and themselves in very personal ways.[69] It is clear, however, that many employed working-class women, like men, have a substantial commitment to work. When asked whether they would continue working if they could afford not to work, 56 percent of white women service workers from thirty to forty-four answered yes, 45 percent of blue-collar workers said yes, and 40 percent of domestic workers did the same. The proportions were higher among their black counterparts: 59 percent, 74 percent, and 66 percent respectively.[70]

Work has such psychological and social importance for these women that, in one group of workers, unemployed women reported almost four times more stress (psychosomatic and depression–withdrawal symptoms) than unemployed men from the same communities.[71]

The majority of working-class women also say they like their work. However, caution must be used in interpreting all job satisfaction literature. In our culture, people's self-images and the society's evaluation of their individual worth are deeply related to the work they do. Acknowledging job dissatisfaction, therefore, may be tantamount to admitting personal failure. The common procedure of simply asking respondents how satisfied they are elicits high levels of positive responses from all groups of workers.[72] Yet indepth research among male workers has raised serious doubts about the actual levels of satisfaction, particularly among blue-collar workers.[73] Unfortunately, women have rarely been included in discussions of alienation or the so-called "blue-collar blues."[74] We know only that women's job satisfaction, like men's, is related to their occupational status: those in low-status blue-collar and service jobs are the least satisfied.

Given the nature of their jobs and economic circumstances, it is not surprising that when women manual workers were asked which was "the most important thing about any job—good wages or liking the kind of work you are doing?" they pointed to good wages more frequently than women in other jobs.[75] Nevertheless, like most workers, these women are not concerned only with wages and other extrinsic job characteristics. Nearly half of blue-collar women report that what they like best about their jobs are the "intrinsic" aspects (the work itself, its interest, the potential for self-development, the promotion possibilities, etc.). Yet women manual workers are more likely than white-collar women to mention liking "extrinsic" factors as well, particularly wages and fringe benefits, the nature of supervision, and enjoyment of their coworkers.[76] The salience of extrinsic factors may stem from the more pressing economic needs of blue-collar women, their particularly acute need for interaction with other adults outside their homes, or the strength with which they cling to the myth that their jobs are "temporary." Whatever the case, it is unwarranted to assume that their concern with the extrinsic aspects of their jobs *excludes* concern with more challenging and interesting employment. A recent national sample of workers indicates no difference between men's and women's desires for jobs providing an opportunity for self-development.[77]

As I noted above, little systematic in-depth research is available on manual women workers' subjective feelings about their jobs and meanings of work to them. Furthermore, far too little is known about the specific day-to-day experiences and problems of women in these jobs. Before the early 1930s, considerable research was done on the blue-collar woman's working conditions and her physical, psychological, and social problems as an employee and family member.[78] Since that time, however, research by industrial and occupational sociologists, psychologists, and manpower experts has focused on men to the virtual exclusion of this group of women. In the last few years, a small resurgence of interest has provided more up to date, largely anecdotal, material on the problems and issues today's blue-collar and service women face daily on the job.

An interview with a young woman auto assembly worker, for example, in Stanley Aronowitz's book *False Promises: The Shaping of the American Working Class Consciousness,* gives a sensitive and informative description of a woman factory worker in contemporary society. It draws heavily on her own statements about and reactions to working in a male-dominated plant, and it is particularly interesting because the plant recently received national attention when workers actively protested the dehumanizing nature of the assembly line.

> Mary, a young woman of twenty, worked on the motor line, a sub-assembly operation that is not part of the main [auto assembly] line. Mary was also out on sick leave but her ailment was not physical. She was suffering from nervous tension and dreaded the day when she would have to decide whether to go back to Lordstown [the plant] or quit for another job. Mary's complaints were not focused on the pace of the work but on its content. She wished that she had a job, "where you could use your brain instead of the monotony of just standing there doing the same thing over and over," but she was compelled by the need for money so she remained on the motor line for more than two years. Her main complaint at Lordstown was the men. "Most men out there are perverted, dirty old men." Her special target for criticism was the foremen. "They can be real nasty," she said. Since she had been there, "I had one good foreman." The foreman on her line had sexual designs on her. She told him, "I don't want to hear it." Mary is a pretty woman with a ready smile and a friendly way about her. "People come up and talk to me. He [the foreman] comes up right away. 'What are those men doing here?' he would say. I'd be snotty and

missin' work and he'd DLO [disciplinary layoff] me and get me kicked out for two weeks." Mary got tired and angry at the men who "slapped me in the rear," or were mad at her for being able to do a job they thought should be reserved for them. She was frustrated because she felt impotent to complain about the problems on the job. "When I get a job I don't complain about it. I hired on sayin' I could do it. If I complain they say: 'Look you can't ask for special treatment because you're a woman. If you can't do the work we'll get a man to do it.' Most men just don't want the women there. They think they're just comin' out there to miss work and collect money. The older men are really down on the women." Mary had little confidence that the union could help her. "As for the [union] committeemen it's all men. They should have women committeemen. I don't think the women have too much say-so."[79]

In these reactions to her work, Mary clearly identifies several key issues faced by many women manual workers, including those in male-typed jobs. The lack of satisfying work is a problem women share with men. Women, however, also face their coworkers' hostility and undesired sexual advances by male workers, superiors, customers, or clients. Hostile reactions can cost women more than personal discomfort. Male coworkers may not share vital information women need to do the work, as they would with new men on the job. This puts women at a severe disadvantage, since the specific tasks in many manual and service jobs are often taught to younger workers by more experienced ones on the job. O'Farrell's research on women entering nontraditional craft jobs observes:

[I]t was estimated that as much as 80% of the job was learned informally from other workers on the job. Because of strong group norms, cliques, status, job satisfaction, and generally negative attitudes, women were excluded from the informal peer group training. Consequently they did not learn the job as well as men thus reinforcing negative attitudes about women not being able to do craft work. One woman said, "The guys won't help. They help each other but then criticize because you're not learning all on your own." In general, men agreed that it was fine for women to work there but they would not get any help. In principle, men agreed that women should be able to do the work. They doubted, however, that the women they currently worked with could learn the skilled tasks and certainly "their wives never could."[80]

It would be a mistake, I think, when reading statements like this last one, to forget that working-class men, like working-class women, may have a very precarious sense of self-worth. The status system of the larger society does not value manual work no matter who does it. It is unfortunate, however, that these men assert their worth and achievement in job-related definitions of masculinity that inhibit women's attempts to secure greater financial security and occupational identity.

Another key issue raised by the interview with Mary on the assembly line was fear that her legitimate complaints about work problems would label her a "problem" worker and ultimately cause her to lose her well-paying "man's" job. Her feeling that the union representative offered no support is a far from uncommon experience.[81] Lack of concern by the union can exacerbate women's problems on the job. The formal mechanisms created by

> ❝ The lack of satisfying work is a problem women share with men. Women, however, also face their coworkers' hostility and undesired sexual advances by male workers, superiors, customers, or clients. ❞

union agreements to help workers deal with unfair supervision, arbitrariness in the exercise of power, management's failure to provide equal opportunities to upgrade skills, etc., are often not effectively available to women. Moreover, blue-collar women may not know how to, or even that they have the right to, file an official sex-discrimination complaint under federal laws. If they do know, they are likely either to doubt their ability to initiate such actions or to fear the repercussions.

This situation makes even more poignant the lack of mutual support among women workers in Mary's plant. Aronowitz writes:

[T]here are about three hundred women at Lordstown working on the production lines. Most of the older women work on the first shift. Mary believed they resented her for her youth and ability to attract young men. The trouble was that the women were not supportive of one another because they were scattered throughout the plant, and there was a considerable amount of friction between the older and the younger women. Mary thought that if she had more women on her line she could have more "say-so" in dealing with her problems on the job.[82]

As noted above, interaction with coworkers is a particularly important aspect of working-class women's personal lives on the job. Cohesiveness among them is a strategic issue in women's fight for equality and opportunity in the workplace. If work groups do not contain other women, as in nontraditional work settings, women are not likely to find the support they need. Male coworkers do not offer them this support, not only because of competition on the job, but also because in working-class communities traditional friendship patterns rarely extend across sex lines outside the workplace.[83] Lack of support and understanding both in and out of work may be a major barrier to career success for working-class women, particularly those trying to break down the sex-segregation of the labor market.

This is not to suggest that women in more traditional blue-collar and service jobs do not also face tremendous problems of mutual support even though they have many female coworkers. Limited friendship networks, even with members of their own sex, tend to be the rule rather than the exception for working-class women.[84] In a study of several urban communities, Rachelle Warren found that employed blue-collar women reported more problems and received less help than either white-collar women or blue- or white-collar men.[85] In short, their relative isolation at home and in the community continues in the work place. Lillian Rubin has also noted this isolation and the serious personal problems it can create: "unaware that their friends and neighbors often share the same feelings, several women confessed both the conflict and the guilt: 'My friends, they all seem happy to take care of the house and the kids. What's the matter with me?'"[86]

It is evident that the orchestration of home and work life is extremely difficult for working-class women both emotionally and structurally. In other words, the way manual jobs are organized adds problems to the long list they share with other working mothers. All working mothers suffer from the lack of child care, the inflexibility of work schedules, and the exploitiveness of part-time employment. Manual jobs also impose lack of time off for personal business and the absence of telephones, both of which are generally available in white-collar work settings. Many industrial and service jobs also have swing shifts and forced overtime, so that the working mother must readjust her home and child-care arrangements week after week to accommodate the demands of the work place.

On the emotional level, working-class women may be undergoing more change than any other group of women. As Nancy Seifer has very sensitively discussed, the new role of working wife and mother is creating both grave difficulties and exciting new opportunities for women who have traditionally married early, stayed close to home and neighborhood, and been isolated from participation in major political and social movements.[87] In light of these changes, it might seem strange that they are still isolated from the women's movement, which has sought to provide emotional support and concrete assistance to other women seeking to broaden their lives. There are many complex reasons for this, some stemming from the movement itself. Lillian Rubin has pointed out, however, that the movement is known to working-class women not through experience but rather through the negative stereotypes of the mass media. She suggests, therefore, that these women perceive the movement's views as a potential threat to their already vulnerable marriages:

> For instance, a major demand of the Movement is that women be free to work outside the home—a demand about which many working class women, even those who work and enjoy it, are ambivalent. For one thing, most believe that no *married* woman should take a job from a married man. For another, there is a great reluctance to identify with the women's struggle, partly, I believe, for fear of alienating their men, because working class women, indeed, have fewer options than their more educated middle class counterparts. For a third, a wife may feel angry and deprived because her husband refuses to permit her to work; but at some level, she understands what it must be like for him to have his wife working outside the home when his sole definition of his manhood rests upon his ability to provide for his family, and when the slim skills he brings to the world of work do not permit him to do that very well. Add to that, her knowledge that he was an abandoned child who grew up in several not very charitable foster homes, and his insistence that, "It's her *job* to stay home and take care of me, and the kids, and the house," is at least comprehensible, even if the conflict is not readily solvable.[88]

CONCLUSION

Despite their doubts and ambivalences about their positions at home and at work, women manual workers are moving forward to secure better, nontraditional jobs, to improve the conditions of their present jobs, to become active in their unions, to fight for child care, and to improve their community lives. As in most complex social changes, progress is slow. In order to support their struggles, we need to do far more policy-oriented research based on detailed information on these women's career patterns, experiences, and own interpretations of their needs and concerns.

These issues warrant attention. Valerie Kincade Oppenheimer's labor force projections for the near future indicate that the demand for women workers in traditional, poor quality, blue-collar and service jobs will continue to be greater than their supply.[89] The absolute number of women manual workers is not expected to decrease, although their proportion of the total female work force will probably decline to about 35 percent by 1980. These projections reflect expected changes in the educational attainment and age structure of the female population but assume that their occupational distribution will remain unchanged; that is, women with less than a high school diploma are projected to be restricted to manual jobs. However, Oppenheimer's projections also show that, even though more women from working-class backgrounds will attain a high school education or more, their expectations of entering better-paying white-collar work rather than manual work will become more difficult to fulfill. This is because there is no evidence of an equivalent increase in the number of clerical jobs that will be available.

A key question is how women will respond to these conditions. Withdrawal from the labor market is one possibility, but many economic, social, and cultural developments appear to reduce the likelihood of this option. Alternatively women can exert tremendous pressure to break down sex and race segregation of the labor market and give themselves greater access to traditionally white male jobs. This will certainly occur to some extent. Finally, women can accept the available blue-collar and service jobs. Their occupational status will suffer a general deterioration as a result, and those who must work will continue to face serious financial difficulties.[90]

Each of these options has important social and personal drawbacks. In considering directions for social action, I believe it is important to see that the particular difficulties faced by women manual workers reflect problems operating in the larger social system. Securing better-quality work and greater economic opportunity for working-class women must be seen as an important part of a general effort to overcome systemic societal problems. These include the dehumanizing quality of work at many levels of the occupational system, widespread lack of opportunity, institutional discrimination, the irrelevance of education to people's lives, and integration of work and nonwork life for both men and women (see Constantina Safilios-Rothschild's chapter below). For example, full equality of opportunity for this particular group of women workers is unlikely to occur as long as the economy does not provide sufficient employment for all those who need and desire it and as long as occupational and income structures are so unequal that gains for women threaten some male workers with losses. Under such conditions, for many manual workers, male and female, the breakdown of sexual and racial segregation merely means equality of opportunity to compete for relatively poor quality jobs. Furthermore, since men and women of about the same skill and income-generating capacity are likely to marry, equalizing male and female wages at each level of the class system would probably widen the substantial inequality of family incomes *across* classes that is so characteristic of American society today.

NOTES

1 U.S. Department of Labor, Bureau of Labor Statistics, U.S. *Working Women: A Chartbook*, Bulletin no. 1880 (Washington, D.C.: Government Printing Office, 1975); U.S. Department of Labor, Bureau of Labor Statistics, *Handbook of Labor Statistics*, Bulletin no. 1790 (Washington, D.C.: Government Printing Office, 1973); U.S. Department of Commerce, Bureau of the Census, *The Social and Economic Status of the Black Population of the United States*, Current Population Reports, Series P-23, no. 48 (Washington, D.C.: Government Printing Office, 1973).

2 Judith Blake, "The Changing Status of Women in Developed Countries," *Scientific American*, September 1974, pp. 137-47.

3 Paddy Quick, "Rosie the Riveter: Myths and Realities," *Radical America* 9 (1975): 115-31; Sheila Tobias and Lisa Anderson, *What Really Happened to Rosie the Riveter*, Module no. 9 (New York: MSS Modular Publications, 1974), pp. 1-36; Mary P. Ryan, *Womanhood in America: From Colonial Times to the Present* (New York: New Viewpoints, Franklin Watts, Inc., 1975), pp. 313-22.

4 William A. Chafe, *The American Woman: Her Changing Social, Economic, and Political Roles, 1920-1970* (London: Oxford University Press, 1972), pp. 137-38. See also excerpts from several firsthand narrative accounts by women workers during the 1940s reprinted in *Radical America* 9 (1975): 133-61.

5 "The Economics of Day Care," *Dollars & Sense*, summer 1975, pp. 6-7.

6 Chafe, *American Woman*, pp. 179-81.

7 For a much fuller discussion of current research activities and an excellent overview of key research topics and issues for the future, see Pamela Roby, *The*

Conditions of Women in Blue-Collar, Industrial and Service Jobs: A Review of Research and Proposals for Research, Action and Policy (New York: Russell Sage Foundation, forthcoming).

8   Barbara Mikulski, Introduction to *Absent from the Majority: Working Class Women in America,* by Nancy Seifer (New York: American Jewish Committee, National Project on Ethnic America, 1973), p. ix.

9   Blake, "Changing Status of Women," p. 143.

10   Mikulski, Introduction to *Absent from the Majority,* p. ix.

11   Karen Oppenheim Mason and Larry L. Bumpass, "U.S. Women's Sex-Role Ideology, 1970," *American Journal of Sociology* 80 (1975): 1212–19; Herbert Parnes, John Shea, Ruth Spitz, and Frederick Zeller, *Dual Careers: A Longitudinal Study of Labor Market Experience of Women,* Manpower Monograph no. 21, vol. 1 (Washington, D.C.: Government Printing Office, 1970), pp. 44–45, 176; Sookon Kim, Roger D. Roderick, and John R. Shea, *Dual Careers,* Manpower Monograph no. 21, vol. 2 (Washington, D.C.: Government Printing Office, 1973), pp. 39–42; John Shea, Roger D. Roderick, Frederick Zeller, and Andrew I. Kohen, *Years for Decision: A Longitudinal Study of the Educational and Labor Market Experience of Young Women,* Manpower Monograph no. 24, vol. 1 (Washington, D.C.: Government Printing Office, 1971), p. 43.

12   Juanita Kreps, *Sex in the Marketplace: American Women at Work* (Baltimore: Johns Hopkins University Press, 1971), p. 21.

13   Sar A. Levitan, ed., *Blue-Collar Workers: A Symposium on Middle America* (New York: McGraw-Hill Book Company, 1971), p. 22.

14   *U.S. Working Women,* table 44.

15   Kathleen Shortridge, "Working Poor Women," in *Women: A Feminist Perspective,* ed. Jo Freeman (Palo Alto, Calif.: Mayfield Publishing Company, 1975), pp. 242–53.

16   Parnes et al., *Dual Careers,* pp. 147–48.

17   Shea at al., *Years for Decision,* p. 176.

18   U.S. Department of Commerce, Bureau of the Census, *Statistical Abstract of the United States, 1974* (Washington, D.C.: Government Printing Office, 1974), table 187. The government estimates that between 59 and 70 percent of the female population over the age of twenty-five in 1990 will still have no more than a high school education and that approximately 28 percent will have less than a high school degree. Ibid., p. 90, table 189.

19   *Handbook of Labor Statistics,* p. 90, table 33.

20   Valerie Kincade Oppenheimer, *The Female Labor Force in the United States,* Population Monograph Series, no. 5 (Berkeley: University of California, Institute of International Studies, 1970), p. 71.

21 Ryan, *Womanhood in America,* p. 384; Oppenheimer, *Female Labor Force,* pp. 66–77.

22 Sally Hillsman Baker, "Job Discrimination—Schools as the Solution or Part of the Problem? Some Research on the Careers of Working Class Women," in *Women in the Workplace,* ed. Pamela Roby (forthcoming).

23 Christina Tree, "Grouping Pupils in New York City," *Urban Review,* September 1968, pp. 8–15.

24 Sally Hillsman Baker and Bernard Levenson, "Job Opportunities of Black and White Working Class Women," *Social Problems* 22 (1975): 510–33.

25 Peter B. Doeringer and Michael J. Piore, *Internal Labor Markets and Manpower Analysis* (Lexington, Mass.: D. C. Heath and Company, 1971), p. 165.

26 Robert W. Smuts, *Women and Work in America* (New York: Columbia University Press, 1959).

27 Mary Stevenson, "The Determinants of Low Wages for Women Workers" (Ph.D. diss., University of Michigan, 1974).

28 *U.S. Working Women,* tables 34 and 36.

29 Ibid., table 38.

30 Stevenson, "Determinants of Low Wages"; Ronald L. Oaxaca, "Male–Female Wage Differentials in Urban Labor Markets" (Ph.D. diss., Princeton University, 1971).

31 *Handbook of Labor Statistics,* pp. 148–50, table 67.

32 *U.S. Working Women,* tables 6, 14, 16.

33 Marilyn Steele, "Women in Vocational Education," in *Sex Discrimination and Sex Stereotyping in Vocational Education,* Hearings before the Subcommittee on Elementary, Secondary, and Vocational Education of the Committee on Education and Labor, House of Representatives, 94th Congress, 1st Session (Washington, D.C.: Government Printing Office, 1975), p. 275.

34 Virginia A. Bergquist, "Women's Participation in Labor Organizations," *Monthly Labor Review,* October 1974, p. 3.

35 Steele, "Women in Vocational Education," p. 275.

36 Bergquist, "Women's Participation," p. 4.

37 Lucretia M. Dewey, "Women in Labor Unions," *Monthly Labor Review,* February 1971, p. 44.

38 Edna E. Raphael, "Working Women and Their Membership in Labor Unions," *Monthly Labor Review,* May 1974, pp. 27–28.

39 Paul M. Ryscavage, "Measuring Union–Non-union Earnings Differences," *Monthly Labor Review,* December 1974, pp. 3–8.

40 Bergquist, "Women's Participation," p. 5.

41 Ibid., p. 7.

42 Barbara Wertheimer and Anne H. Nelson, *Trade Union Women* (New York: Praeger Publishers, 1975).

43 "Women Workers: Gaining Power, Seeking More," *U.S. News and World Report,* November 13, 1972, p. 104, cited in Steele, "Women in Vocational Education," p. 279.

44 Steele, "Women in Vocational Education," p. 280.

45 Norma Briggs, *Women in Apprenticeship—Why Not?* Manpower Research Monograph no. 33 (Washington, D.C.: Government Printing Office, 1974), pp. 18-19.

46 Ibid., p. 5.

47 Ibid., p. 17.

48 Steele, "Women in Vocational Education," p. 275.

49 Briggs, *Women in Apprenticeship,* p. 14.

50 Ibid.

51 Shea et al., *Years for Decision,* p. 34.

52 Roby, *Conditions of Women,* p. 64.

53 Lee Rainwater, Richard Coleman, and Gerald Handel, *Workingman's Wife* (New York: Oceana Publications, 1959).

54 Mirra Komarovsky, *Blue-Collar Marriage* (New York: Random House, 1964); Betty Yorburg, *Sexual Identity* (New York: John Wiley and Sons, 1974); Carol Tarvis, "Woman and Man," *Psychology Today,* March 1972, pp. 57-64, 82-85.

55 Harold L. Sheppard, "Discontented Blue-Collar Workers—a Case Study," *Monthly Labor Review,* April 1971, pp. 25-32.

56 Seifer, *Absent from the Majority,* p. 50.

57 Ongoing research in this area includes a study by the Work, Family Interaction and Child Development Project, Laura Lein, project director, Center for the Study of Public Policy, Cambridge, Massachusetts; Lillian B. Rubin's study of blue-collar wives as workers and homemakers, The Wright Institute, Berkeley, California; Patricia Sexton's current research on working-class women, Department of Sociology, New York University, New York City; and work by Victoria A. Steinitz, Prudence King, Ellen R. Solomon, and Ellen Deen Shapiro, in the Project on Social Class and Adolescent Ideology, Harvard Graduate School of Education, Cambridge, Massachusetts.

58 Briggs, *Women in Apprenticeship,* p. 13.

59 Baker, "Job Discrimination."

60 Steele, "Women in Vocational Education," p. 287.

61 Pamela Roby, "Vocational Education and Women," in *Sex Discrimination and Sex Stereotyping in Vocational Education,* Hearings, p. 107.

62 Statistics provided by the Division of High Schools, Board of Education of the City of New York.

63 Baker, "Job Discrimination."

64 Roby, "Vocational Education and Women."

65 Samuel Bowles and Herbert Gintis, *Schooling in Capitalist America: Educational Reform and the Contradictions of Economic Life* (New York: Basic Books, 1976); idem, "I.Q. and the U.S. Class Structure," *Social Policy*, November-December 1972, January-February 1973, pp. 65–96. Walter E. Schafer, Carol Elexa, and Kenneth Polk, "Programmed for Social Class: Tracking in High School," *Trans-action*, October 1970, p. 39; Colin Greer, *The Great School Legend* (New York: Basic Books, 1972).

66 Brigid O'Farrell, "Affirmative Action for Women in Craft Jobs: Change in the Small Industrial Workgroup" (paper presented at the annual meetings of the Society for the Study of Social Problems and the American Sociological Association, San Francisco, August 1975).

67 Lester C. Thurow and Robert E. B. Lucas, *The American Distribution of Income: A Structural Problem*, study prepared for the Joint Economic Committee, United States Congress (Washington, D.C.: Government Printing Office, 1972).

68 Baker and Levenson, "Job Opportunities."

69 For examples of such research on male workers, see Harold L. Sheppard and Neal Q. Herrick, *Where Have All the Robots Gone? Worker Dissatisfaction in the 70s* (New York: Free Press, 1972): Richard Sennett and Jonathan Cobb, *The Hidden Injuries of Class* (New York: Random House, 1972).

70 Parnes et al., *Dual Careers*, pp. 173–74.

71 Rachell Barcus Warren, "Stress, Primary Support Systems and Women's Employment Status," testimony before the Commission on Human Rights, City of New York, *Hearings on Women in Blue-Collar, Service, and Clerical Occupations*, April 1975.

72 Frederick Herzburg, Bernard Mausner, Richard Peterson, and Dora Capwell, *Job Attitudes: Review of Research and Opinion* (Pittsburgh: Psychological Services of Pittsburgh, 1957); surveys conducted by the Survey Research Center, University of Michigan, 1958, 1969, 1971, 1973; Robert P. Quinn, Graham L. Staines, and Margaret R. McCullough, *Job Satisfaction: Is There a Trend?* Manpower Research Monograph no. 30 (Washington, D.C.: Government Printing Office, 1974).

73 Sheppard and Herrick, *Where Have All the Robots Gone?*; Studs Terkel, *Working: People Talk about What They Do All Day and How They Feel about What They Do* (New York: Pantheon Books, 1972); Robert Blauner, *Alienation and Freedom: The Worker and His Industry* (Chicago: University of Chicago Press, 1964).

74 Myra Marx Ferree of the Department of Psychology and Social Relations, Harvard University, is doing her doctoral thesis on the satisfaction and dissatisfaction that working-class women experience in their jobs.

75 Parnes et al., *Dual Careers,* p. 180.

76 Ibid., pp. 191-92.

77 Jean Crowley, Teresa Levitin, and Robert Quin, "Seven Deadly Half-Truths about the American Working Woman," *Psychology Today,* March 1973, pp. 94-96.

78 Roby, *Conditions of Women.*

79 Stanley Aronowitz, *False Promises: The Shaping of American Working Class Consciousness* (New York: McGraw-Hill Book Company, 1973), pp. 36-37.

80 O'Farrell, "Affirmative Action," pp. 6-7.

81 Wertheimer and Nelson, *Trade Union Women.*

82 Aronowitz, *False Promises,* p. 37. See also Constantina Safilios-Rothschild's chapter below.

83 Komarovsky, *Blue-Collar Marriage;* Herbert Gans, *The Urban Villagers* (New York: Free Press, 1962).

84 Komarovsky, *Blue-Collar Marriage.*

85 Rachelle Barcus Warren, "The Work Role and Problem Coping: Sex Differentials in the Use of Helping Systems in Urban Communities" (paper presented at the annual meetings of the Society for the Study of Social Problems and the American Sociological Association, San Francisco, August 1975).

86 Lillian B. Rubin, "Blue-Collar Wives: Worker and Homemaker" (working paper prepared for the First National Working Conference on Research: Women in Blue-Collar Jobs, Ford Foundation, New York, December 1974).

87 Seifer, *Absent from the Majority.*

88 Rubin, "Blue-Collar Wives."

89 Valerie Kincade Oppenheimer, "Rising Educational Attainment, Declining Fertility and the Inadequacies of the Female Labor Market" in *Demographic and Social Aspects of Population Growth,* ed. C. F. Westoff and R. Parke, Jr., U.S. Commission on Population Growth and the American Future, Research Reports, vol. 1 (Washington, D.C.: Government Printing Office, 1972), pp. 307-53.

90 Ibid., p. 316.

Domestic Service: Woman's Work

David M. Katzman

In many respects private household employment is an anachronism in the second half of the twentieth century. While other forms of labor have experienced specialization and depersonalization and have shifted away from the home, domestic service is less specialized and more personal than it was one hundred years ago. These factors distinguish it from all other work in contemporary American society.

Private household employees include child-care workers, cooks, housekeepers, launderers, maids, servants, and cleaning women. All do tasks that a mother or housewife commonly performs without receiving formal wages—work traditionally relegated to women.

This chapter is part of a larger study of domestic service sponsored by a Ford Foundation Fellowship for Research on the Role of Woman in Society. The conclusions, opinions, and other statements in this chapter are those of the author and are not necessarily those of the Ford Foundation. The author is grateful to Sharyn Katzman, Regina Morantz, and the University of Kansas Women's Studies Sandwich Seminar for critiquing this work in various forms and offering valuable suggestions.

THE EVOLUTION OF HOUSEHOLD EMPLOYMENT

Historically, domestic service has been very low-status work in the United States. It has always been among the lowest paid, it has always been done by second-class citizens (first indentured servants and slaves, then immigrant and black women, and always primarily women rather than men), it offers no opportunities for mobility, and it is highly personalized in both tasks and employer-employee relationships. Only two groups of domestic workers escaped the stigma of extremely low status attached to this work: in the nineteenth century, native-born rural girls hired for domestic service by town families, and in the twentieth century European servants brought to the United States by wealthy American families emulating aristocratic European life-styles. The rural teenage girls lived and worked within the family environment of a home as apprentices acquiring household skills. The European servants carried on a tradition of cultivated service that had never developed in the United States and added to the prestige of the families they worked for.

Low status and poor working conditions have generally led women to shun household employment if they could. Since Daniel Defoe wrote about domestic servants in early eighteenth century England, the "servant problem"—the perpetual shortage of servants—has been a theme of the literature on household employment. Because domestic work was commonly done by women who could find no other kind of work, in the United States it became predominantly an immigrant and black occupation. In the late nineteenth century, day workers began to replace live-in servants in American homes, and by the end of World War I this form of private household work had been firmly established. A number of factors dictated the shift: the availability of other kinds of work for women and the resulting shortage of domestics willing to live in, the employment of more married women who refused to live apart from their own families, the general shortening of hours of work in all occupations, the smaller size of middle-class homes and apartments now employing domestic workers, and the introduction of labor-saving devices such as central heating, electricity, vacuum cleaners, washing machines, and clothes dryers. Thus, the hourly "cleaning lady," although often still a black or immigrant woman, replaced the uniformed maid who was part of the household.[1]

PROFILE OF THE DOMESTIC WORKER

In 1970 there were more than one million private household workers in the United States. According to the census for that year, nearly 97 percent of these workers were women. Among men in the paid labor force, only 8 out of 100,000 worked in private homes, whereas among women nearly 4,000 out of 100,000 were so employed, and among black women nearly 18,000 out of 100,000 did so. Overall, more than half of all private household

> ❝ In 1970 there were more than one million private household workers in the United States. According to the census for that year, nearly 97 percent of these workers were women. ❞

workers were black women, and they tended to be older women: the median age of black domestic workers was 49.2 years. This is ten years older than the median of all gainfully employed women and nearly twelve years older than that of all employed black women.

Private household employment draws women who have the least formal education. While 10.8 percent of all gainfully employed women in 1970 had completed four or more years of college, only 0.7 percent of domestics had reached this educational level. At the other end of the spectrum, 14 percent of employed women had completed no more than eight years of formal education, but among domestics, 50.5 percent had never gone beyond the elementary grades. Among black domestics, 60.9 percent had never completed the ninth grade.

Domestic servants also have the lowest earnings of any major paid occupational group, according to the Bureau of the Census. Median earnings in 1970 for all women in the labor force were $3,649, and, for those who worked at least fifty weeks, earnings were $4,715. For private household workers, the figures were $986 and $1,482 respectively. Among black women workers as a whole the median was $3,008, and for those who worked fifty weeks or more it was $3,812. For black women in domestic work, the figures were $1,152 and $1,500 respectively.

Private household work offers little occupational mobility. Of the 600,000 female private household workers who were twenty-five years old or older in 1970 and had been gainfully employed in 1965, 78 percent had worked in private service five years earlier. Another way of measuring occupational mobility is from the earlier to the later year of reference. Of the nearly 600,000 private household workers in 1965 who were still gainfully employed in 1970, 81.2 percent remained in private service five years later; 10.5 percent were service workers outside of private households; 3.9 percent had become operatives; and 1.7 percent had become clerks or similar workers. Private service working women, then, had only a small chance of moving into higher-status or better-paying occupations.

According to census data, a higher proportion of private household servants work in urban than rural areas and in the central city than on its fringes. Regionally, the greatest concentration of servants is found in the South. Approximately half of all female private household workers are there, and 76.6 percent of these southern women domestics are black. In the Northeast, 42 percent of the female domestic workers are black; in the North Central states, the figure is 27.1 percent; and in the West, it is 18.5 percent.

It should be noted that the census information on private household workers seriously understates the number of women involved. First of all, because this is an area of predominantly minority employment, it involves the population groups in which the census has the greatest undercounts.[2] Secondly, because more than half the workers are employed less than fulltime (that is, less than thirty-five hours per week), the census responses tend to be less accurate in categorizing this occupation even when they do not miss the household or person. Finally, the private household work system itself encourages false responses by employees on census and other official documents. It is a common practice among domestics to avoid paying Social Security and income taxes (federal and state) by taking their earnings in cash and not declaring them. In New York City in 1971, for example, the head of the Mayor's Committee on the Exploitation of Workers estimated that 90 percent of the city's domestics were not covered by Social Security.[3] This is an attempt by household workers to maximize the immediate gain from their low earnings, but it costs them important long-range benefits later in their lives. Employees do it because they need the money badly; employers cooperate because it saves them money (they would pay 5.85 percent of the employee's wages as their share of the Social Security tax) and "red tape" (the paperwork of filing). It is unlikely that domestic workers evading taxes will place themselves in jeopardy by declaring their occupation to a state or federal agency such as the Census Bureau, regardless of that agency's claim of confidentiality. Thus, the census figures are undoubtedly low. Nonetheless they provide the best available estimate of the number of household workers in the United States.

PROFILE OF THE WORK

In Hollywood and television scripts, domestic service is often romanticized. "Hazel," a long-running television comedy series about the exploits of a housekeeper-domestic servant, portrayed her as the most dominating, powerful, and wise role model in the family. While she permitted her employers to feel that they ran the house and raised the children, the viewer witnessed Hazel acting as head of the household. Similarly, in Norman Lear's television series "Maude," about a suburban family, Florida, the maid, often displayed a wisdom lacking in the family. In fact, Florida was even more independent than Hazel; conflict frequently arose between maid and employer in this series, and it was presented as a dispute between equals. These television programs perpetuate long-held traditions about the presentation of domestic servants in Hollywood musicals and comedies.

For most private household workers, nothing could be farther from the truth. A "girl"—usually a mature woman, most often black—is hired to come into a private home to do the most physically demanding chores in an isolated environment, under complete subordination by the employer, for low hourly wages. The structure of domestic work is different in many respects, not only from fictional portrayals, but also from other job categories.

In the first place, hiring does not follow normal job patterns. Usually the worker gets a position through the recommendation of a friend—another domestic—or a current employer. Interviews are rare, and, when they do occur, they are generally by telephone. No special education is required by employers, and they assume that whatever skills are needed have been acquired by all women who work as domestics.[4]

Private household work is highly personal. In most other occupations a worker is hired to perform individual work tasks; in domestic employment a personal relationship is part of the job, and the worker is hired not for her labor alone but also for her personality traits. The employer-employee relationship is an anachronistic carryover from the traditional mistress-servant relationship when the domestic was an intimate member of the family's household. Today, too, the domestic works in the private domain of the family and is involved in the intimate and personal life of its members, or at least with the artifacts of that private life. If the employer does not regularly work outside the home herself, there is often sustained personal contact between employer and employee during the workday.

For more than a century employees and reformers in the domestic service field have described the inconsistencies and conflicts inherent in this relationship. Intimacies may pass back and forth between employer and employee, but whenever the employer feels that the servant is becoming too personal or forgetting her subordinate role, the mistress invokes her authority over the servant. The employee has no control over this process; it is solely at the whim of the employer. While some domestics develop warm relationships with their employers over the years, most complain that personal relationships interfere with their work and create a potential area of tension. They also dislike the fact that they are evaluated on this personal rapport with their employers rather than on the quality of the work they perform.

A private household worker, especially in a middle-class home, is usually the only employee in the house. Her sole contact during the day is with her employer. This isolates the worker from colleagues and other peers.

This isolation has several important consequences. Not only does it produce a certain degree of alienation and loneliness among domestics, but it also contributes to their powerlessness in the marketplace. Geographically isolated private household workers have little opportunity to organize as a group to control hiring and placement practices or to establish minimum working conditions and wages. The ease with which newcomers can enter the work and acquire the necessary skills further inhibits unionization. Yet this is a field with a severe labor shortage, which implies that employees potentially have tremendous power in the market. Nonetheless, domestics who have the ability and security to organize to improve their working conditions and the like often use their power to leave private household employment.

Another factor depriving domestic workers of power is their exclusion from much of the beneficial modern social welfare legislation. Although private service workers are covered by Social Security if they earn more than $50 from any one employer in a calendar quarter, hundreds of thousands of domestic servants remain uncovered either because they do not meet this minimum or because they or their employers wish to evade the law. In 1974, private household workers were for the first time brought under federal minimum wage standards, after nearly forty years of exclusion. To be covered, however, a domestic worker must earn more than $50 from one employer in a calendar quarter or work more than eight hours in one week. Thus, many part-time or occasional workers remain uncovered by minimum wage benefits. Other legislation, such as workers' compensation, often excludes domestic workers from coverage. California, however, voted to extend workers' compensation coverage to domestics beginning in 1977. A few states include domestics in their state protective labor laws, such as maximum hour limits (Washington's sixty-hour-a-week law and Montana's eight-hour-a-day law, for example, apply to domestics), but generally this legislation excludes domestic workers. In Wisconsin, domestic servants are covered by minimum wage laws if they are employed at least fifteen hours a week by the same employer; in Arkansas, an employer who has five or more employees at the same time must pay minimum wages; and in Michigan, those who have four or more employees must meet the minimum. Since the typical employer has one "cleaning lady" one day a week, it is obvious that these laws were never intended to cover most private household workers.[5]

WOMEN BOSSES, WOMEN WORKERS

One of the most interesting facets of domestic service is that in nearly all cases both employer and employee are women. In a society in which work is dominated by male-male or male-female relationships, domestic service breaks the normative pattern. Consistent with the society's norms, however, this occurs in the traditional female arena, the private household.

Some of the problems of domestic workers emanate from this unusual aspect of the work. Many employers are unused to hiring workers; indeed, this may be their first and only venture into the employer role. Unfamiliar with employer-employee relations, many try to relieve their discomfort by further personalizing an already personal employment relationship. Others, particularly full-time mothers and housewives, are used to viewing their homes as creative expressions of their own personalities, and they want the domestic worker to be an extension of themselves—an extra pair of hands to perform the most physically demanding work. They expect more than fulfillment of the work tasks; they want a level of performance that will give them the psychological rewards accruing to a homemaker who can display her house as a showcase. A household employee can rarely satisfy such demands, and the rewards to the worker are not commensurate with the effort required.

For other women, employment of a household worker fulfills needs unrelated to the work itself. The ability to employ servants is still a mark of social status and class position to some, although this attitude is less prevalent than in the past. In the South a black cook, maid, or children's nurse is considered obligatory by many upper middle-class white women.[6] Some women (like some men) find fulfillment in exercising power over another woman's life. Rather than seeking an intelligent, resourceful, and independent worker, they may want a servant to whom they can feel superior and dominating. Employing a domestic offers them a position of power not otherwise available to housewives.[7]

On the other hand, many women are uncomfortable about hiring and supervising another woman. They find the role incongruent with their own socialization to play a powerless or passive role in the economic system. Others experience discomfort because they hold egalitarian values. They feel ambivalent about exercising power as employers, paying low wages, or demanding heavy physical labor of black or minority women often older than themselves. Some employers respond by building good working relationships with their employees; others try to increase the personal relationships between them and often make the job more difficult for the worker in the process.

While women are the most common employers, private household employment is not always exclusively a woman's world; wives and mothers may not have the same degree of independence and authority over their households as, for instance, a businesswoman has over her firm. The initial decision to employ a household worker is sometimes made by the husband—to have his wife assume a more prestigious life-style, to release her from what he perceives as household burdens, or to induce her to engage in other activities for his benefit. The wife may initiate the idea of employing a domestic, but the husband may control the decision to do so or not. The wage-hour structure may also be determined by the male head of the household, although he may have no direct contact with (and never even meet) the domestic worker. The conditions of employment often reflect the husband's values and goals as much as the wife's.

The intrusion of men into this basically female world can create many problems. The husband of the employing family represents power: the au-. thority to fire, to reduce privileges, to make the work more difficult, etc. The employee's lack of countervailing power is reflected in the sexual and erotic themes of the literature and folklore about private household workers. Two common themes are the servant as sexual initiator for the young males in the family, and the servant as object of the fantasies of the more mature males. In the United States, especially in the South, interracial sexual tensions heighten the problems of black women in domestic work. One such worker writes: "Many times, growing up, I've heard women say I ain't gonna let my daughter work in no white man's kitchen."[8] The powerlessness of the private household worker facilitates her sexual exploitation by members of the employer's family.

There is an increasing need today for domestic help, because more and more women are seeking paid employment outside their homes. Many middle-class women wish to hire private household workers to do their child-care and housecleaning tasks, so that they can develop their interests, do more creative tasks, or earn a living. Much of the literature on women in the last few years has stressed the monotony of household work and the lack of intellectual intercourse in child-care activities. These are contrasted to the excitement and fulfillment possible in careers outside the home. But the "liberation" of middle-class women entering the labor force often demands the "subjugation" of lower-class women—those who replace them in doing the tasks they are rejecting. The career and employment opportunities opening up for college-educated women are not available to most private household workers. Thus it is possible that the gains emanating from the feminist movement in the 1960s and 1970s may expand rather than reduce the class gap between most women workers and private household workers. On the other hand, the number of service workers does not seem to be expanding—private household workers dropped nearly 50 percent between 1960 and 1970 according to census figures—and the absence of lower-class women willing to work as domestics may restrain the career options of many married women with children.

ATTRACTIONS OF HOUSEHOLD SERVICE

Despite the disabilities and disadvantages of domestic service—long hours, low wages, demeaning status, and blocked occupational mobility—household workers manage to survive and sometimes even flourish. Entry into the work is relatively easy because of the eternal shortage of domestic servants. A woman seeking work can simply tell a friend who is a domestic of her availability, and this is generally sufficient to get her a job offer. If she wishes to be covered by Social Security, she need only register at the state employment office. The work is familiar to most women, who have been socialized to run their own households. While for some women this set of tasks represents oppression—that is, confinement to traditional women's roles—for others the congruence with expected female behavior offers comfort.

Many domestics develop a personal pride in their work that transcends the physical fatigue they suffer from maintaining two households—their employer's and their own. They are aware that they perform tasks beyond the physical capabilities of their employers, and this satisfies their need to accomplish in a competitive, achievement-oriented society. Moreover, they do not necessarily internalize the low status accorded by others to domestic service.

Within their working-class world, where occupational opportunities for women are generally severely restricted, regular income from household service work keeps many families above the poverty line. Although a significant number of working-class women still prefer not to work—viewing the role of full-time housewife and mother as a symbol of middle-class attainment—for those who must work, steady employment in domestic service can be psychologically and monetarily satisfying when contrasted with the irregularity of other available jobs. Indeed, the ability to "hold a job" is another characteristic that divides the respectable working class from the poor.

Domestic service also offers some women greater control over their working conditions than most other occupations they could enter. They can often choose a short workday, from four to seven hours long, to be home when their children return from school or to have more time to maintain their own households. Employment by the day permits them to choose a shorter workweek as well. Frequently a domestic has four, five, or as many as ten regular employers, but she can choose the number herself and keep one or two weekdays free. Women in factories and offices do not have this flexibility. They must work according to a time schedule established without consideration of their individual needs.

Within the employer's home, many domestics have full control over their tasks. Some employers, particularly those holding full-time jobs themselves, simply define the work to be done and leave. The domestic herself determines how the tasks will be accomplished without further interference. However, since the employer provides the work tools, the employee's choices take place within a framework most suited to the employer.

REFORM EFFORTS

In the mid-1960s, reform of private household employment became a topic of interest. The Women's Bureau of the Department of Labor sponsored conferences in 1964 and 1965 on household employment, and as a result the National Committee on Household Employment (NCHE) was formed to coordinate national organizations interested in upgrading domestic service. The NCHE sponsored academic research, initiated training programs, and introduced management principles into private household employment.[9]

In 1968, under a grant from the Department of Labor, the NCHE sponsored demonstration projects in seven cities to upgrade the occupation. Many of the projects were designed to improve the skills of household employees and to depersonalize the employer–employee relationship. In Boston, education was the major tool used. A twelve-week training period was given to employees, and classes for employers were established. In Chicago the Household Employment Project (HEP) introduced courses for "household technicians" and "home-management specialists" (domestics and housewives, respectively), and attempted to establish minimum working conditions—hours, wages, and fringe benefits—as part of its goal to improve the image of the occupation. Certified graduates of the Chicago household-technician course were given a button-insignia and an HEP hatbox. In Pittsburgh, the program hoped "to persuade industrial firms to hire trainees to provide emergency household help as a fringe benefit for their executives." A nonprofit corporation employed the domestics, giving them the benefits and work relationships ordinarily found in commercial or industrial work, and billed the corporations for the services performed. Similar programs were introduced in other cities—Alexandria, Virginia; Manhattan, Kansas; New York; and Philadelphia.[10]

The demonstration projects incorporated reforms to upgrade domestic service that could be found in the pages of *Good Housekeeping* and other popular magazines in the 1890s and 1900s: skill improvement, professionalization, rationalization and specialization of tasks, employer education, contractual agreements, and industrial or commercial employment standards. Only two major reforms attempted in the nineteenth century were lacking in the 1968 demonstration projects: individually focused programs to uplift servants morally and utopian cooperative proposals for abolishing the household. The mid-twentieth-century demonstration projects, however, like their predecessors, have had no major impact on household employment. The NCHE introduction of a standard employee–employer contract represents a potentially significant step. But the latter-day reformers seemed to be unaware that their approaches had been attempted many times before.

This failure of the demonstration projects to upgrade the occupation does not lie in their ideas—many of which are good—but rather in their basic perspective, which essentially approaches the problem from the employer's point of view, as nearly all reformers of domestic service have. For example, one woman involved in the Boston project expressed concern with the fact that the high turnover in domestic help interrupted an employer's work outside her home, drawing her back into household tasks until another domestic could be hired. Similarly, the Pittsburgh project was designed to cut down on executive absenteeism and mental distraction by solving the executives' problems of household maintenance. Nearly all the programs included training courses to teach women to be better employers by using management principles, communication skills, and human relations techniques.

This approach continues to place domestic service outside the normative employer–employee relationship in the American economy. It stresses the personal, woman-to-woman approach. Implicit in the programs is the notion that problems in the work can be solved by goodwill, sympathetic understanding, and a protective attitude by the employer. The reforms explicitly reject the economic basis of employer–employee relationships that prevails in American industry: the concept that performance of the tasks and level of skill are the criteria for job tenure, not the worker's personality.

The NCHE correctly stresses the need for adoption of a standard labor contract guaranteeing minimum working conditions and explicitly specifying works tasks. But a contract alone cannot change the basic employee–employer relationship and the conditions that make the work so undesirable. Probably the best solution lies in making the tasks, rather than the employee, the central focus of domestic service. This is the principle involved in commercial janitorial services: a firm hires a janitorial service to perform certain specified tasks, and the hiring firm has no formal contact with the janitorial firm's employees. A focus on the tasks leads naturally to specialization, which in turn encourages greater skill development. However, the introduction of a profit-making intermediary third party in household services, such as the janitorial service firm, would only add to the exploitation of workers.

Another model that has been proposed is the hiring hall, which has long been used in the building trades and longshore work and is now being introduced in California agricultural fields. Employers needing help come to the hiring hall and are assigned available workers under principles established by the workers through their labor organizations. Usually workers are put on a priority list for assignment according to seniority or the number of hours they have already worked during a given time period. The hiring hall has exclusive control over union jobs, and the workers control the hiring hall by participating in union decision making.

A union would give domestic workers the collective power they lack as individuals—the power to establish minimum work rules and conditions. Past efforts to unionize domestic workers have not been able to overcome the atomization of workers and their sense of powerlessness, because they have not succeeded in creating hiring halls to control the work. If a hiring hall were established for this work, an employer would notify the hall that she wanted certain services done—cleaning a kitchen, two bathrooms, a living room, etc.—and the tools or appliances she wanted used. The hiring hall would send a team of workers to do the tasks, perhaps including a supervisor, and the employees would supply their own tools. The union hall might also rent tools to workers at cost.

This approach would depersonalize the work, introduce specialization, upgrade the skills, give employees greater control over performance of the work, and end the isolation most employees experience. It would still permit domestics to take only part-time or occasional work if they chose. It would offer employers a more efficient work team and remove the problems presently plaguing employee–employer relationships. Admittedly it would raise the cost of household labor, because it would stop private household workers from subsidizing employers, in a sense, by accepting such relatively low wages.

Establishment of a hiring hall, however, involves a radical restructuring of the power held by employers over employees in private household service. The rapid growth of household janitorial services in the last decade indicates that a number of employers favor such a step. By and large, however, women employers do not seem willing to relinquish their control over the employee and the work. It will take unionization of employees and supporting local legislation before worker-controlled hiring halls can gain a monopoly over the work. Without these shifts in power, domestic service will continue, as it has for the last 150 years, to be a low-status occupation, offering low wages, to virtually immobile workers, in an anachronistic employee–employer relationship based on personalities rather than job skills.

NOTES

1   For a brief history of domestic service, see Amy E. Watson, "Domestic Service," *Encyclopaedia of the Social Sciences* (New York: Macmillan Company, 1937), 5:198–206. For its history in the United States, see Lucy Maynard Salmon, *Domestic Service* (New York: Macmillan Company, 1897), and David M. Katzman, *Seven Days a Week: Women and Domestic Service in Industrializing America* (New York: Oxford University Press, 1977).

2   For an analysis of the census undercount, see National Academy of Sciences, National Research Council, Advisory Committee on Problems of Census Enumeration, "America's Uncounted People" (Washington, D.C.: National Academy of Sciences, 1971).

3   Susan Edmiston, "While We're at It, What about Maid's Lib?" *New York,* June 28, 1971, p. 24.

4   For employees' views of the conditions of domestic work, see Robert Coles, " 'I Am a Maid, and What Do I Know,' " *Atlantic Monthly,* August 1971, pp. 64–68; Verta Mae, *Thursdays and Every Other Sunday Off–A Domestic Rap* (Garden City, N.Y.: Doubleday and Company, 1972); Josephine Hulett as interviewed by Janet Dewart, "Household Help Wanted," *Ms.,* February 1973, p. 45; "Interview with Carrie King," *Women—A Journal of Liberation,* spring 1975, pp. 34–35.

5   For a summary of state and federal benefits denied private household workers, see Ethlyn Christensen, "Restructuring the Occupation," *Issues in Industrial Society* 2 (1971): 49.

6   C. Arnold Anderson and Mary Jean Bowman, "The Vanishing Servant and the Contemporary Status System of the American South," *American Journal of Sociology* 59 (1953): 215–30.

7   Lois W. Banner, *Women in Modern America: A Brief History* (New York: Harcourt Brace Jovanovich, 1974), p. 52.

8   Verta Mae, *Thursdays and Every Other Sunday Off,* p. 60.

9   U.S. Department of Labor, Women's Bureau, *1969 Handbook on Women Workers,*
    Bulletin no. 294 (Washington, D.C.: Government Printing Office, 1969), pp.
    240–41.

10 Duncan McDonald, "Arriving: The Household Professional," *House Beautiful,*
    March 1969, pp. 88–89.

Housewives as Workers

Joann Vanek

Housewives are women who are or have been married and who have the responsibility of running a home. For some it is a full-time occupation; others also work in the labor force. In total, more American women are in this occupation than in any other single type of work. In 1974, 32 million women were not employed in the labor force because of their responsibilities at home.[1] In addition 20 million employed wives[2] and an unknown number of the nearly 7 million employed widowed, divorced, and separated women also worked as housewives.

Since the qualifications for this work are only a person's sex and marital status, there is a great deal of diversity among the women in this occupation. Their ages range from the teens through the years of normal retirement from work. They represent all social strata. They have different skills, training, and interests. And the families they serve differ in size and composition. Yet housewives also share important similarities, although not always the similarities people believe they share.

There are several important misconceptions about housework. People often think that housewives work fewer hours, at a slower pace, and less strenuously than other workers. Many believe that housework has little productive value. And some believe the present assignment of tasks between husband and wife is equitable.

Do housewives work less than others? They clearly use many labor-saving goods and services, and they no longer produce as many goods for the family as they once did. Moreover, many married women have full-time paid jobs in addition to being housewives. These observations suggest that housekeeping in modern society must not be very time consuming. But facts contradict these surface impressions. The majority of housewives, particularly those not employed, continue to work as many hours at the job as women did fifty years ago.

Does housekeeping have productive value? It is not figured in national accounting systems and does not receive monetary rewards. Since no price is put on housework, people overlook its value. But housewives do contribute in important ways to both their families' economy and total economic output, although this contribution is not represented by the pricing system. (See Carolyn Shaw Bell's chapter above.)

Is the assignment of tasks between husband and wife equitable? In theory, although husband and wife work in different spheres, the labor of both is necessary to the family. The modern housewife, however, neither produces goods nor earns money, and her less tangible contribution to the family is often not recognized. This lack of appreciation creates strains on several levels: in a woman's self-esteem, in the relationship between husband and wife, and in the distribution of economic rewards.

This chapter considers how the occupational role of housewife has evolved during this century, what housewives do, and their status in relation to other workers.

TRENDS AFFECTING THE HOUSEWIFE'S WORK

Housekeeping has been changed by several modern developments: labor-saving devices, commercial goods and services, and urbanization. Housewives have had opportunities to reduce the length of their working day. If they do not now work shorter hours, are they illustrating Parkinson's law: Do women stretch out *the same work* to fill the time available to complete it? Undoubtedly housewives are no more immune to the Parkinson effect than other workers, but real additions have occurred in a housewife's workload. Many researchers have shown that housewives continue to work long hours because new tasks and new standards have been added to their job.[3]

Certainly the housewife's role at the turn of the century was quite different from what it is today.[4] Although her day started with preparation of breakfast for the family, she began by refueling and lighting the cookstove and carrying water from a tap outside the house. Whether breakfast was a hearty meal of meat and potatoes or a simple one of coffee and bread, the food was homemade.

After doing the breakfast dishes, the housewife turned to the family upkeep chores of the day. If it was Monday, she washed the clothing and linens by hand and hung them out to dry. On another day she ironed them with heavy irons heated on the kitchen stove. She had to filter the oil lamps and trim their wicks daily. The lamp chimneys and shades required washing every other day. She made the beds and fought to keep the house free of vermin. She emptied ashes from the cookstove and the water pan under the icebox. In addition, there were routine cleaning tasks that are still common today: dusting, sweeping, scrubbing, and emptying garbage.

If a family lived in the city and did not have an icebox, shopping for food was a daily task. The housewife cooked three meals a day, baking her own bread, cakes, and pies. After the evening meal, she turned to mending and sewing. Although most men's clothing was purchased, she made dresses and underwear for herself and her children. She also hemmed curtains and sheets and knitted scarfs, sweaters, caps, and stockings.

This routine was augmented by special tasks. For spring and fall cleaning, she had to wash windows, clean cupboards and closets, wash and iron curtains and drapes, take up and beat rugs and carpets and lay them down again. She also cared for the sick and the elderly among family members, neighbors, and boarders. Robert Smuts points out that these nursing tasks were far more extensive in the past then they are today.[5] Diseases such as diphtheria, malaria, and pneumonia occurred frequently in 1900, and without drugs illnesses lasted longer. Hospitals and homes for the aged were not reasonable alternatives for care; they were used only as a last resort by people without families or by the poor.

Changes in household technology have reduced the burdens of housekeeping enormously. In 1900 homes lacked electricity and running water; by 1930 about 60 percent of the nation's homes had electricity,[6] and by 1940 about 70 percent had indoor plumbing.[7] In the 1930s mechanical refrigerators, laundry appliances, gas and electrical cooking ranges, and a variety of canned and processed foods became widely available. In the 1950s automatic washing machines began to replace wringer-type machines. Automatic dryers and wash-and-wear fabrics were introduced in the 1960s.[8]

Where large rooms had been needed for cumbersome wood-burning stoves and metal washtubs, new appliances were more compact and allowed more flexible use of space. As Siegfried Giedion put it, homes in the 1920s and 1930s took on a streamlined appearance as bathrooms and kitchens became smaller, kitchen appliances were located in a compact space, and work areas combined continuous surfaces and easy-to-clean materials.[9] Modern households were consciously designed to save labor.

The migration from farms to cities also changed a housewife's work. In 1920 one-third of the nation's families lived on farms. Early farm families produced most of the goods they used. For example, in the 1920s they pro-

> 66 Housekeeping has been changed by several modern developments: laborsaving devices, commercial goods and services, and urbanization. . . . [Yet] housewives continue to work long hours because new tasks and new standards have been added to their job. 99

duced approximately two-thirds of the food they consumed.[10] Thus in earlier decades farm women tended gardens, kept poultry, gathered eggs, killed and plucked chickens, canned and preserved fruits and vegetables, cured meats, and made lard, cheese, and butter.[11] Urbanization removed these primary production tasks from the housewife's routine.

As the number of people living in the home declined, the housewife's work was reduced. In the early decades of the century, many families took in lodgers who added to the wife's burdens of cooking, cleaning, and laundry. As recently as 1930, 10 percent of the nation's families had at least one boarder.[12] Elderly relatives and adult children, even if they were married, often remained at home. Little by little these living patterns changed, and the "extra" adults left the family home.

Declining fertility also reduced women's work in the home. This trend was interrupted by the baby boom following World War II. But even during those years a change in childbearing occurred that reduced women's child-care and housekeeping responsibilities. Women began to concentrate childbearing into fewer years, spacing their children closer and often completing their families by age thirty. This new pattern together with the increased life expectancy for women meant that a smaller proportion of a housewife's life was devoted to caring for children.[13]

All these developments transformed a housewife's work, but the result did not always save labor. Although goods were no longer homemade, modern equipment was used, and people lived in cities, many new tasks took on importance. Shopping, servicing household equipment, and travel to do household errands became more time-consuming. Children could not be left to play unattended on city streets as they could on a farm. The smoke and grime of the city forced housewives to do laundry and housecleaning more frequently.[14]

The modern housewife had labor-saving equipment, but she was less likely to have paid help than her early counterpart. Between 1900 and 1970, the number of paid domestic workers dropped from one hundred to twenty-five for every thousand households.[15] Women were leaving jobs as domestics to take higher-paying jobs in industry.[16] (See David Katzman's chapter above.)

Attitudes about what a housewife should do were also changing. As machines eliminated drudgery, housekeeping could be more challenging and prestigious. Women were urged to raise their standards of home and family care, to provide for more than the basic needs of their families. Importance was put on making "homes a place of beauty, culture and spotless cleanliness; on keeping husbands contented and happy and on insuring the sound emotional development of children."[17] These ideas required new work, such as interior decorating, daily cleaning and laundering, planning varied and attractive meals, and supervising, entertaining, and educating children. Housekeeping continued to be a time-consuming job, and it became a great deal more complicated than it had been.

An important force in redefining the housewife's job, according to Barbara Ehrenreich and Deidre English, was the "domestic science movement."[18] In precise terms this was not a social movement. Its only organization was a series of conferences held at Lake Placid beginning in 1899.

The meetings were organized by Ellen Richards, a chemist, who, like many professional women of the day, was interested in alleviating the problems of modern family life, particularly the housewife's job. In the early decades of the century there was considerable interest in reformulating housework and educating women to do it well. Men and women in many different fields— academics, domestic science writers, social reformers—pursued this goal with crusading zeal. Their efforts are loosely referred to as the domestic science movement.

Its advocates saw housekeeping as a profession, one that required full-time work and considerable education and skill. They attempted to apply the principles of science and industry to the care of home and family. *Cheaper by the Dozen,* by Frank Gilbreth, Jr., and his sister Ernestine Carey, tells what it was like to be raised in a household organized according to these principles of efficiency.[19] Their parents, Frank and Lillian Gilbreth, were industrial efficiency experts, exponents of scientific management and an ideology called Taylorism that influenced industry in the early twentieth century. Taylorism advocated that managers analyze the work process and its component tasks in great detail and then reorganize jobs and work settings to achieve maximum speed and industrial efficiency from each worker.

The principles of Taylorism and scientific management were applied by the Gilbreths and others to the home. Housewives were urged to manage their homes as if they were modern industrial firms, calculating the most efficient way to do things. For example, they were told to count their steps as they went about daily routines, to measure the energy units expended in certain tasks, or to calculate the "happiness minutes" gained from various activities.[20] It is hard not to smile now at some of these instructions. The procedures did not in fact save labor or increase efficiency to the extent intended, because the household is too small a unit to benefit from a highly specialized division of labor. If the extreme aspects of scientific management did not take hold, others did. Housewives began to do a great deal of planning and record keeping. Today financial and medical records, recipe files, grocery lists, and scheduling of deliveries and repairs are routine work for housewives.

Domestic science also drew on scientific knowledge to improve home and family care. As Wesley Mitchell put it, progress in the art of housekeeping "rests upon progress in science—or rather waits upon progress in science. To secure the better development of our children's bodies we need a better knowledge of food values and digestive processes. . . . To secure the better development of children's minds we need better knowledge of the order in which their various interests waken."[21] Mitchell, whose credentials included the presidency of the American Economics Association, differed from most domestic scientists in that he saw the limits of what science could do for housekeeping. In his view, housework presented many unsolved problems and was often a matter of guesswork: "No doubt the sciences that will one day effect a secure basis of knowledge for bringing up a family are progressing but it seems probable that they will long lag behind the sciences that serve industry."[22]

The crusaders of the movement were determined to spread the principles of domestic science to housewives. The American Home Economics Association successfully lobbied for government money to educate women in principles of health, sanitation, and nutrition. Women's clubs organized centers to give advice to homemakers and to study and apply principles of scientific management.[23] Women's magazines devoted sections to the technical aspects of housekeeping. The popular press told housewives what their new role was and what environment they were to create in their homes. The *Ladies' Home Journal* declaimed:

> Home is a place of abode of persons bound together by ties of affection;
> a place where affection of parents for each other, for their children,
> and among all members of the family is nurtured and enjoyed; where
> genuine personal hospitality is extended; where the immature are
> protected and guarded. A place where one may have rest, privacy
> and a sense of security; where one may enjoy his individual kind of
> recreation and share it with others. A place where one may keep his
> treasures; where one may satisfy his individual tastes; where funda-
> mental culture, consisting of customs, language, courtesies and traditions
> is conserved and passed on to the young. A place where regard for others,
> loyalty, honesty and other worthy character traits are cultivated and
> enjoyed, a haven, a sanctuary and a source of inspiration.[24]

At a time when technology was reducing many of the traditional housekeeping functions, the domestic science movement provided an ideology that upheld the value of housekeeping and even gave it new importance. But raising the standards of home and family care required women to spend as much time in new housekeeping tasks as they saved by using technological advances.

Certain family-related values still pressure women to spend long hours in housework. The flowery quotation from the 1930 *Ladies' Home Journal* is not out of date in substance to many families. Home is seen as a haven from specialized, routine work outside, a place where family members may satisfy their emotional needs and individual tastes. Thus, the housewife is expected to provide more than the basic food, clothing, and shelter. It is not unusual for a woman to prepare several different menus for a meal: one for the dieter, one low in cholesterol, and one for the children. Nor would a housewife usually complain about the extra work required to entertain her husband's or children's friends. The amount of time she has to spend is considered less important than the goal of giving individual care and attention to family members. Efficient service is not of prime importance in housekeeping.

In the new definition of the housewife role, particular attention was focused on motherhood. Changes in the norms about child care made its duties more important and time consuming than they were in the past. Permissive, rather than programmed, child rearing was popularly advocated in the years after World War II, as Dr. Spock[25] and other experts told mothers not to depend on a set of rules but rather to be sensitive to subtle changes in their children so they could guide them. Children now required a mother's constant attention, and motherhood became more time consuming. Women were told that these efforts were worth the time, since being a mother was a woman's most important role.

Another factor adding hours to housework is our consumer-oriented economy. John Kenneth Galbraith[26] and Staffan Linder[27] point out that consumption is not entirely pleasurable but also requires work. Goods must be purchased, serviced, and maintained. These tasks become more complicated and time consuming as consumption levels increase, and they normally fall to the housewife.

In summary, many different trends have affected the housewife's job. Changes in the structure of society (such as technological developments, demographic changes, and urbanization) transformed housekeeping tasks, reducing some and adding others. Moreover, the very definition of a housewife's functions changed. New standards and new areas of care were added. Thus it is not surprising that time-use statistics reveal a uniformity in the time spent in housework for nonemployed women over the past fifty years.

TIME SPENT IN HOUSEKEEPING, 1920-70

Statistics of time on the job are abundant for most workers but not for housewives. Fortunately some information on the daily routine of house-wives exists for earlier years as well as today. The early information was compiled by home economists as part of the general attempt, discussed a-bove, to reformulate the housewife's job. Most of the studies were done in the 1920s and 1930s but a few were also conducted in the 1940s, 1950s, and 1960s.[28] The studies were done in land grant colleges under a set of guide-lines developed by the Bureau of Human Nutrition and Home Economics of the Department of Agriculture. The other source of data I use here is the "1965-66 United States Time Use Survey," a study directed by John Robinson and Philip Converse of the Survey Research Center of the Uni-versity of Michigan.

The Robinson-Converse survey is based on a national sample, but the early studies used limited, local populations and primarily rural women. The early data would normally be a weak basis for inferring national pat-terns, but there are grounds for believing that they can validly be used for such estimates. Even though the studies were dispersed over a wide area and over a forty-year period, the variations (that is, standard deviations) in time spent in housework turned out to be similar from study to study. In addition, since rural housewives worked under much less modern conditions than urban homemakers in their day, the studies with a rural composition could be taken as representing an even earlier period, extending the time span considered.

The records on homemaking activities are time budgets. A time budget is an accounting of everything a person does in some unit of time—a day, a week, or a month. It is difficult to study housework using other methods, such as direct observation of what people do or a woman's own description of her work. Direct observation is impractical because individual researchers would have to invade the privacy of subjects' homes for a long time period. And descriptions by homemakers cannot be controlled for exaggeration of the amount of work done. A time budget is more reliable because, although respondents construct it themselves, it lists all activities of a day, not just homemaking, and together they must total twenty-four hours.

Respondents in the Robinson-Converse survey kept a record of what they did in fifteen-minute intervals for a twenty-four-hour period. In the home economists' studies, logs were kept in five-minute intervals for a full week. I extracted housework from the listing of daily activities. Housework includes all activities connected with the care of a household and its members: food preparation and meal cleanup, clothing and linen care, home care, family care, shopping, household management, and travel connected with household errands. The original data of the home economists' studies are no longer available; only their published tabulations survive. I have compiled the early studies and tabulated the Robinson-Converse data to conform for comparison with the early research. Together these tabulations form a historical series on the time women spend in housework.[29]

The data show that American women continue to work long hours in housework (see figure 1). Full-time housewives (married women with no outside employment) have spent the same amount of time over the past fifty years. In the 1920s they spent about fifty-two hours a week doing housework and in 1966 they spent fifty-five hours. Throughout the period, the time spent has varied only between fifty-one and fifty-six hours.[30] All the changes affecting the household have not caused women to reduce their housework time. To take one specific change, urbanization, figure 1 shows that urban women spent no less time in housework than rural women, even though they worked with more modern equipment and produced fewer of the goods used by their families.

The data show that the nature of housework has changed, however (see figure 2). With labor-saving appliances and commercial products, food preparation and cleaning up after meals have become less time consuming. However, because of the consumption of commercial goods, the time spent in shopping and managerial tasks has increased. Time patterns in other tasks indicate higher standards. Housewives now spend more time on child care. An even more dramatic adoption of higher standards occurred in laundry work, but this change is muted by figure 2 because it traces the general category of clothing and linen care, which includes sewing and mending as well as laundry. The time spent in sewing and mending has decreased, undoubtedly because relatively cheap commercial clothing is now available. But the amount of time spent in laundry activities has risen even though modern housewives have running water, automatic equipment, and wash-and-wear fabrics. Families have more clothing and linens and wash them more frequently.

Of course, not all married women are full-time housewives. Married employed women spend much less time in housework. According to the Robinson-Converse data, they spend about one-half the time spent by women who are not in the labor force.[31] What accounts for this difference? Using the Robinson-Converse data, I explored whether the fact that employed women have smaller families and older children than full-time housewives makes for this much less housework. A type of regression analysis enabled me to see whether a difference between employed and nonemployed women remained if their families were identical in numbers and ages of children. These comparisons reduced the time differences to some degree, but the nonemployed women still spent much more time in housework.[32] I then examined whether employed women receive more household help either from paid workers or from their husbands. The Robinson-Converse data show no difference between employed and nonemployed women in the amount of paid household help or in the amount of assistance husbands gave their wives.[33] Kathryn Walker also found that husbands of employed women gave their wives no more help with housework than husbands of full-time homemakers.[34] (See the chapter by Kristin Moore and Isabel Sawhill above.) Thus, the time differences between employed and nonemployed women are not simply due to differences in their workloads.

The longer hours spent by full-time housewives must also reflect higher standards and lower efficiency. The argument I developed in the first section of this chapter stresses their higher standards. Social and cultural forces impose high standards of home and family care on modern housewives. Although these pressures affect all housewives, the time constraints of work outside the home prevent employed women from achieving the same quality of housework as nonemployed women. They must "cut corners." This explanation is overlooked in the popular view that employed women work with greater efficiency at home. Since it is difficult to detect the quality of care a woman gives her home and family, people see that married employed women have two jobs, not one, and conclude that they are simply more efficient workers.

THE VALUE OF A HOUSEWIFE'S WORK

Monetary values do not indicate the productive value of housework. Even though housewives are not paid, they contribute to the family economy and to the society's total economic output. A family could not live as cheaply and as well as it does if it did not have the services of the housewife. To purchase cleaning, meal, and child-care services is very costly. To forgo these services drastically lowers the family's standard of living. The work a woman does in the home stretches what the family's income will buy. Ismail Sirageldin estimates that about half of a family's disposable income comes from the unpaid work of its members, primarily the housewife.[35]

It is commonly recognized that the modern housewife is a consumer rather than a producer of goods, but it is not commonly acknowledged that this contributes to the total economic output. John Kenneth Galbraith asserts "It is women in their crypto-servant role of administrator who make an indefinitely increasing consumption possible. As matters now stand . . . it is their supreme contribution to the modern economy."[36] Galbraith argues

> ❝ It is commonly recognized that the modern housewife is a consumer rather than a producer of goods, but it is not commonly acknowledged that this contributes to the total economic output. ❞

that economic growth requires high levels of household consumption. Someone thus has to spend considerable amounts of time "to select, transport, prepare, repair, maintain, clean, service, store, protect and otherwise perform the tasks that are associated with the consumption of goods."[37] Lack of time to do these tasks is one important factor limiting consumption. Usually the costs of maintaining consumption are ignored, because they fall most heavily on an individual whose time is not monetarily valued, the housewife. In Galbraith's term, she is a crypto-servant to her family and the economy, because her economic contribution is not recognized.

A number of researchers have attempted to put a price on the housewife's work. The National Bureau of Economic Research estimated that the value of housewives' services would add an additional one-fourth to the gross national product in 1918, and Simon Kuznets estimated a similar figure for 1929.[38] Calculations by Juanita Kreps for 1960 show that the forgone earnings of married women would raise the gross national product by over one-sixth.[39] Recent figures from the Social Security Administration calculate the value of a housewife's work based on her age. The average value is $4,705 per year.[40]

One basis for these monetary estimates is replacement costs—that is, the cost of buying the housewife's services in the market. Another is opportunity costs—that is, the money a housewife forgoes by working at home rather than in the labor force. Unfortunately both methods give arbitrary, unrealistic estimates. The problem, as Carolyn Shaw Bell pointed out in her chapter above and in other writings, reflects "the basic premise of GNP—that its measuring rod consists of market prices and factor payments. It follows that where production—like housework or child care—occurs within a family rather than in a hotel or nursery school, there is no market price, no meaningful way to estimate one nor any valid wage estimate for the labor involved."[41]

Consider, for example, the replacement cost of a homemaker's services. This is usually based on the average market wage for persons employed as dishwashers, baby-sitters, seamstresses, maintenance workers, janitors, and the like. But an individual family needs too few hours of each service to hire substitutes easily, particularly at the low market wages it could offer. Moreover, a housewife contributes in intangible ways to her family. The personalized care she gives cannot be purchased.

Estimates based on forgone earnings are also unrealistic. The labor force under present economic conditions could not employ all the housewives who now work full-time at home. Labor statistics classify "women not in the labor force because of household responsibilities" as nonemployed. If this were not so, in 1974 some 30 million women might have joined the already swollen ranks of the unemployed.[42]

Although it is very difficult to determine the real worth of a housewife's services, these services do have productive value. Failure to recognize this value has important consequences for the housewife's self-esteem and for the equitable distribution of economic rewards and work within the marriage.

THE COSTS OF WORKING AS A HOUSEWIFE

If people are esteemed for the kind of work they do, or simply for working, on what basis should society value a housewife? Neither a wage nor a visible product results from her work. In fact housework is noticed more often for its absence than for being done well. Moreover many of the tasks—cleaning, doing laundry, and dishwashing—merit little esteem even when done for pay. Is it surprising, then, that women say, "I'm just a housewife"? The expression, according to women studied by Ann Oakley, implies that housekeeping is trivial and low-status work.[43] Women do not tend to get a sense of accomplishment or competence from working as housewives.

They also are deprived of economic benefits. Housewives are dependent on their husbands for the rewards the economic system routinely provides to workers. Money, Social Security benefits, insurance, and Medicare do

> ❝ All housewives confront problems arising from the way their work is rewarded—more precisely from the absence of certain rewards. ❞

not accrue directly to the housewife for her own efforts. Although the modern-day ideal of marriage is a relationship of equality and sharing, the wife's dependence in the important economic sphere is conducive to subordinate, not equal, status. The effects can be felt in family decision making, in the assignment of household work, in the feelings of esteem of family members, and in the distribution of monetary rewards. People commonly believe that a marriage is functioning equitably if husband and wife share income and other economic benefits. When marriages lasted until the death of one partner, this probably was equitable, or closer to it than today. But now divorce is common, and the consequent division of family resources is not always equal under current procedures.

Consider, for example, Social Security. Divorced women may receive Social Security benefits based on the earnings of their former husbands under certain conditions. The conditions, according to Bell, emphasize dependency: "The marriage must have lasted at least 20 years and the man must have been providing at least half the support of the wife when he became entitled to social security."[44] An employed wife can earn her own benefits, but these are usually lower than her husband's. The discrepancy reflects the differences in their employment histories. Generally a woman earns less than her husband and works for fewer years. All the time she has spent working in the home does not count in Social Security calculations.

Another inequality in marriage occurs in the amount of work done. Ideally, husband and wife work equally although traditionally in separate spheres. When the wife enters the labor force the traditional balance is upset. In the 1950s and 1960s many analysts predicted that the employment of married women would change the traditional distribution of household tasks.[45] Equality between the sexes and greater sharing of home duties were expected to result. Research findings by Lois Hoffman[46] and by Robert Blood and Donald Wolfe[47] showed that husbands of employed women were more likely to share housework than those of nonemployed women. As Oakley observed, certainly logic was on this side: one consequence of women's employment *should be* men's increased domestic responsibility.[48]

Recent studies have contradicted the early view, however. Oakley found that housework and child care were still women's responsibilities.[49] Walker's time-budget data showed that husbands averaged about 1.6 hours a day in housework whether or not their wives were employed.[50] My work with the Robinson-Converse data showed no difference in the time spent in housework by husbands of employed and nonemployed women.[51] My tabulations were based on women's responses to the question, "Last week, about how many hours did [your husband] help you with housework?" The question is important because the discrepancy in findings between earlier and more recent studies probably reflects differences in their methods of research. Hoffman and Blood and Wolfe asked respondents about only a few tasks not about a sizable proportion of the household routine. And they gave no detailed information about the frequency of performance. The recent studies asked about "the actual performance of specific tasks over a particular period of time," and this produces the information needed to reach a valid conclusion on the degree of equality.

The recent findings indicate that housekeeping continues to be women's responsibility in the division of labor in marriage. With paid employment, wives take on a second job and compress their housekeeping into fewer hours. Their total workweek averages about sixty-five hours.[53]

While this discussion has dwelt on the negative aspects of being a housewife, there are, of course, some very desirable features of the work. It is not highly regulated and is not competitive. The home is a pleasant work environment, and housekeeping is not segregated from other aspects of daily life. The housewives Helena Lopata studied found these aspects of their work satisfying.[54]

Some women prefer housekeeping to any other type of work. But all housewives confront problems arising from the way their work is rewarded— more precisely from the absence of certain rewards. The employed wife may suffer less from the deprivation of rewards, but the price she pays is holding down two jobs.

CONCLUSION

The role of the modern housewife is shaped by several dilemmas. Housewives work long hours, but they are not rewarded for doing so. Their labor has productive value, but it is very difficult to determine its worth in monetary terms. Solutions for these problems have been proposed for decades. The domestic science movement attempted to redefine the housewife's job, give it higher status, and make it professional. In the nineteenth century, Norway and Denmark included the housewife's work (at a very low valuation) in estimates of national productivity,[55] but they did not persist in this policy. In 1924, Dorothea Canfield Fisher's novel *The Homemaker* described a man who exchanged work roles with his wife.[56] It took a physical injury for the husband to stay home legitimately while his wife entered the labor force, even though, in the story, the role reversal benefited every member of the family. Early feminists also attacked the housewife role. Charlotte Gilman, for one, urged communal organization as a way to free women for the pursuit of more valuable and satisfying work.[57]

Although proposals to change the housewife's status are not new, they seem to have a new momentum today. Again efforts are being made to assign a dollar value to housework. Kreps provides one statement of why this is necessary and offers an estimating procedure.[58] Feminist groups such as the National Organization for Women have taken up this cause, and new groups have been organized solely for the purpose of securing "wages for housework."[59] There are proposals for changing the system of allocating the benefits routinely given to workers and for granting Social Security credits for work in the home. Other feminists feel that women's status will not be improved until the housewife role is abolished. For example, Jessie Bernard advocates equal sharing of home and labor market work by husband and wife,[60] and Carolyn Shaw Bell proposes that we create the new occupation of consumer maintenance.[61] By including the services traditionally called housework and child care in the classification of occupations, important changes result. First, the economic contribution made by this work is recognized. Secondly, human and consumer maintenance will no longer be seen as the responsibility of married women alone, but something that must be done by people for themselves and others whatever the family or household type.

FIGURE 1   Time Spent in Housework by Full-Time
            Homemakers, 1927–66

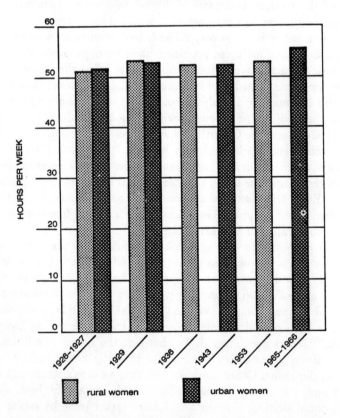

Women have worked as housewives for many generations. Modern life has changed this role, but it has not removed all the burdens and inequities. Certainly part-time jobs for men and women, day-care centers, fuller sharing of family responsibilities by husbands, and a reformulation of Social

FIGURE 2   Distribution of Housework Time by Task for Full-Time Homemakers, 1926–68

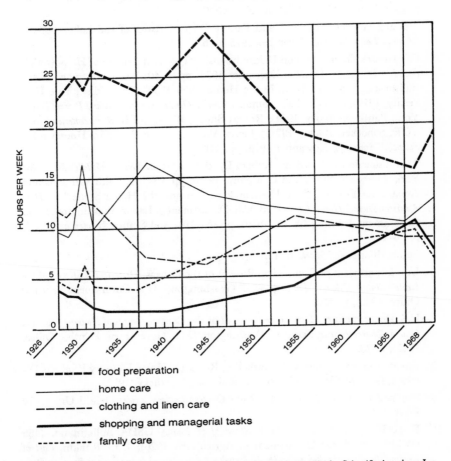

food preparation
home care
clothing and linen care
shopping and managerial tasks
family care

Security eligibility would benefit housewives. But, as all these proposals indicate, improvements in the housewife's life require considerable change in the economic and legal systems as well as in the family.

NOTES

1 U.S. Department of Labor, Bureau of Labor Statistics, *Handbook of Labor Statistics—1975*, reference ed., BLS Bulletin no. 1865 (Washington, D.C.: Government Printing Office, 1975), p. 46, table 9.

2 Howard Hayghe, "Marital and Family Characteristics of the Labor Force," *Monthly Labor Review*, November 1975, p. 53.

3 Cf. Barbara Ehrenreich and Deidre English, "The Manufacture of Housework," *Socialist Revolution*, October-December 1975, pp. 5–40; Heidi Hartman, "Capitalism and Women's Work in the Home, 1900–1930" (Ph.D. diss., Yale University, 1974); Ann Oakley, Woman's Work: *The Housewife Past and Present* (New York: Pantheon Books, 1974); Robert Smuts, *Women and Work in America* (New York: Schocken Books, 1971); Joann Vanek, "Time Spent in Housework," *Scientific American*, November 1974, pp. 116–20.

4 This discussion is based on Robert Lynd and Helen Lynd, *Middletown* (New York: Harcourt, Brace and Company, 1956), pp. 93–180; Faith Williams and Anna-Stina Ericson, "The Homemaker's Job and the Home Scene," in *How American Buying Habits Change*, ed. U.S. Department of Labor (Washington, D.C.: Government Printing Office, 1959), pp. 83–101; and Smuts, *Women and Work*, pp. 6–13.

5 Smuts, *Women and Work*, p. 13.

6 U.S. Department of Commerce, Bureau of the Census, *Historical Statistics of the United States: Colonial Times to 1957* (Washington, D.C.: Government Printing Office, 1960), p. 510.

7 U.S. Department of Commerce, Bureau of the Census, *Census of Housing*, vol. 11, *General Characteristics, Summary* (Washington, D.C.: Government Printing Office, 1942), p. 20.

8 Private correspondence with Marketing Research, Home Laundry Products Division, General Electric Company, Louisville, Kentucky, 1972.

9 Siegfried Giedion, *Mechanization Takes Command* (New York: Oxford University Press, 1948), pp. 607–27.

10 E. L. Kirkpatrick, *The Farmers' Standard of Living*, USDA Bulletin no. 1466 (Washington, D.C.: Department of Agriculture, 1926); J. O. Rankin, *Cost of Feeding the Nebraska Farm Family*, Nebraska Agricultural Experiment Station Bulletin no. 219 (Lincoln: University of Nebraska, 1927).

11 Inez Arnquist and Evelyn Roberts, *The Present Use of Work Time of Farm Home-makers,* Washington Agricultural Experiment Station Bulletin no. 234 (Pullman: State College of Washington, 1929), p. 15.

12 U.S. Department of Commerce, Bureau of the Census, *Population,* vol. 6, *Families* (Washington, D.C.: Government Printing Office, 1933), p. 25, table 32.

13 Jeanne Ridley, "On the Consequences of Demographic Change for the Roles and Status of Women," in *Demographic and Social Aspects of Population Growth,* ed. Charles F. Westoff and Robert Parke, Jr., U.S. Commission on Population Growth and the American Future, Research Reports, vol. 1 (Washington, D.C.: Government Printing Office, 1972), p. 293.

14 Smuts, *Women and Work,* p. 28.

15 Calculated from the following sources: David Kaplan and M. Claire Casey, *Occupational Trends in the United States, 1900 to 1950,* Bureau of the Census Working Paper no. 5 (Washington, D.C.: Government Printing Office, 1958); *Handbook of Labor Statistics—1975,* table 6; U.S. Department of Commerce, Bureau of the Census, *Census of Housing: General Housing Characteristics, Summary* (Washington, D.C.: Government Printing Office, 1972), p. 53, table 10.

16 George Stigler, "Domestic Servants in the U.S., 1900–1940," Occasional Paper no. 24 (New York: National Bureau of Economic Research, 1946).

17 Smuts, *Women and Work,* p. 28.

18 Ehrenreich and English, "Manufacture of Housework."

19 Frank Gilbreth, Jr., and Ernestine G. Carey, *Cheaper by the Dozen* (New York: Thomas Y. Crowell Company, 1948).

20 Lillian Gilbreth, *The Homemaker and Her Job* (New York: D. Appleton and Company, 1929).

21 Wesley Mitchell, *The Backward Art of Spending Money and Other Essays* (New York: McGraw-Hill Book Company, 1937), p. 11.

22 Ibid., p. 22.

23 Cf. Mary Pattison, *Principles of Domestic Engineering* (New York: Trow Press, 1915).

24 Lita Bane, "What's New in Homemaking?" *Ladies Home Journal,* March 1930, p. 29.

25 Benjamin Spock, *The Common Sense Book of Baby and Child Care* (New York: Duell, Sloan and Pearce, 1946).

26 John Kenneth Galbraith, *Economics and the Public Purpose* (Boston: Houghton Mifflin Company, 1973).

27 Staffan Linder, *The Harried Leisure Class* (New York: Columbia University Press, 1970).

28 These include the following studies used in my analysis: Inez Arnquist and
    Evelyn Roberts, *The Present Use of Work Time of Farm Homemakers*, Washington
    Agricultural Experiment Station Bulletin no. 234 (Pullman: State College of
    Washington, 1929); May Cowles and Ruth Dietz, "Time Spent in Homemak-
    ing Activities by a Selected Group of Wisconsin Farm Homemakers," *Journal of
    Home Economics* 48 (1956): 29–34; Ina Crawford, *The Use of Time by Farm Women*,
    Idaho Agricultural Experiment Station Bulletin no. 146 (Moscow: University
    of Idaho, 1927); Dorothy Dickens, *Time Expenditures in Homemaking Activities by
    White and Negro Town Families*, Mississippi Agricultural Experiment Station Bul-
    letin no. 424 (State College: Mississippi State College, 1945); Florence Hall and
    Marguerite Schroeder, "Time Spent on Household Tasks," *Journal of Home Eco-
    nomics* 62 (1970): 23–29; Hildegarde Kneeland, "What's New in Agriculture," in
    Yearbook of Agriculture, ed. U.S. Department of Agriculture (Washington, D.C.:
    Government Printing Office, 1928), pp. 620–22; Marianne Muse, *Time Expendi-
    tures on Homemaking Activities in 183 Vermont Farm Homes*, Vermont Agricultural
    Experiment Station Bulletin no. 530 (Burlington: University of Vermont and
    State Agricultural College, 1944); Jessie Richardson, *The Use of Time by Rural
    Homemakers in Montana*, Montana Agricultural Experiment Station Bulletin no.
    271 (Bozeman: Montana State College, 1933); U.S. Department of Agriculture,
    Bureau of Human Nutrition and Home Economics, *The Time Costs of Home-
    making* (Washington, D.C.: Department of Agriculture, 1944); Jean Warren, *Use
    of Time in Its Relation to Home Management*, Cornell University Agricultural Ex-
    periment Station Bulletin no. 734 (Ithaca: Cornell University, 1940); Grace
    Wasson, *Use of Time by South Dakota Farm Homemakers*, Agricultural Experiment
    Station Bulletin no. 247 (Brookings: South Dakota State College of Agriculture
    and Mechanic Arts, 1930); Margaret Whittemore and Bernice Neil, *Time Factors
    in the Business of Homemaking in Rural Rhode Island*, Rhode Island Agricultural
    Experiment Station Bulletin no. 221 (Kingston: Rhode Island State College,
    1929); Maud Wilson, *Use of Time by Oregon Farm Homemakers*, Oregon Agricul-
    tural Experiment Station Bulletin no. 256 (Corvallis: Oregon State Agricultural
    College, 1929).

29 Joann Vanek, "Keeping Busy: Time Spent in Housework, United States, 1920–
    1970" (Ph.D. diss., University of Michigan, 1973).

30 Ibid., chap. 4.

31 Ibid.

32 Ibid., chap. 5.

33 Ibid., chap. 4.

34 Kathryn Walker and Margaret Woods, *Time Use: A Measure of Household Produc-
    tion of Family Goods and Services* (Washington, D.C.: American Home Economics
    Association, Center for the Family, 1976).

35   Ismail Sirageldin, *Non-market Components of National Income* (Ann Arbor: University of Michigan, Survey Research Center, 1969).

36   Galbraith, *Economics and the Public Purpose,* p. 37.

37   Ibid., p. 33.

38   Discussed in Juanita Kreps, *Sex in the Marketplace: American Women at Work* (Baltimore: Johns Hopkins University Press, 1971), p. 67.

39   Ibid., p. 73.

40   Reported in Keith Love, "How Do You Put a Price Tag on a Housewife's Work?" *New York Times,* January 13, 1976, p. 39.

41   Carolyn Shaw Bell, "Social Security: Society's Last Discrimination," *Business and Society Review,* autumn 1972, p. 46.

42   *Handbook of Labor Statistics—1975,* p. 46, table 9.

43   Ann Oakley, *The Sociology of Housework* (New York: Pantheon Books, 1974), p. 183.

44   Bell, "Social Security," p. 46.

45   William Chafe, *The American Woman* (New York: Oxford University Press, 1972), p. 222.

46   Lois Hoffman, "Parental Power Relations and the Division of Household Tasks," *Marriage and Family Living* 22 (1960): 27–35.

47   Robert Blood and Donald Wolfe, *Husbands and Wives* (Glencoe, Ill.: Free Press, 1960).

48   Oakley, *Sociology of Housework,* p. 136.

49   Ibid., chap. 8.

50   Walker and Woods, *Time-Use.*

51   Vanek, "Keeping Busy," chap. 4.

52   Discussion of the research findings of M. Rutter and G. Brown, "The Reliability and Validity of Measures of Family Life and Relationships in Families Containing a Psychiatric Patient," *Social Psychiatry* 1 (1966): 38–53, quoted in Oakley, *Sociology of Housework,* p. 137.

53   Vanek, "Keeping Busy," chap. 4.

54   Helena Lopata, *Occupation: Housewife* (New York: Oxford University Press, 1971), p. 35.

55   Discussed briefly in Colin Clark, "The Economics of Housework," *Oxford University Institute of Statistics Bulletin* 20 (1958): 205.

56   Dorothea (Canfield) Fisher, *The Home-maker* (New York: Harcourt, Brace and Company, 1924).

57   Discussed in Smuts, *Women and Work,* pp. 135–36.

58   Kreps, *Sex in the Marketplace,* chap. 4.
59   Jean Grillo, "Wives Want Wages: Or the Great Housework War," *Soho Weekly News,* January 15, 1976, p. 13.
60   Jessie Bernard, *The Future of Marriage* (New York: Bantam Books, 1972).
61   Carolyn Shaw Bell, "A Full Employment Policy for a Public Service Economy: Implications for Women," *Social Policy,* September/October 1972, pp. 12–19.

FOUR

WOMEN'S WORK AND SOCIAL CHANGE

Many of the chapters in previous sections have raised thought-provoking questions about the future of women's work. Speculations are admittedly hazardous, given the marked changes that have occurred in women's work roles in recent decades and our still inadequate understanding of the complex forces underlying these developments. Even if we thoroughly understood these forces, we could not merely extrapolate from the recent past and present to the future because we cannot know what new social and economic factors will influence women's work at home and in the marketplace.

However, we should not be unwilling to consider the future possibilities because our knowledge is imperfect. Changes in women's work roles are well under way, and they have far-reaching implications for other social relationships and institutions. It is incumbent upon us to reflect on these changes, the benefits and difficulties they present, and the policies we can adopt to influence their direction and speed.

417

Constantina Safilios-Rothschild, author of a wide-ranging analysis of policies affecting women,[1] considers the future of women's work in the closing chapter of this volume. Enjoining all of us—individuals and institutions—to use flexibility and creativity in devising policies to solve some of the problems described in this volume, she takes the lead with several innovative suggestions in this piece. Perhaps the most thought-provoking issue Safilios-Rothschild raises is the question of the meaning of work. She criticizes the model of work in American society that demands that we "give our all" or "we are nothing." As an alternative, she proposes an intermingling of activities that we have categorically separated: labor force participation, leisure, and household work. From this overarching concern, she turns to more concrete recommendations for architects and city planners, employers in both public and private sectors, and governmental agencies charged with enforcing affirmative action policies. These changes would be difficult to implement, she admits, but they are worth considering. One goal of the policies would be recognition of the work women accomplish as individuals, reducing the tendency to belittle their labor by ascribing to them the status attained by their husbands. A broader effect of these social changes would be to enrich and integrate our lives on the job and in the home.

NOTE

1 Constantina Safilios-Rothschild, *Women and Social Policy* (Englewood Cliffs, N.J.: Prentice-Hall, 1974).

Women and Work: Policy Implications and Prospects for the Future

Constantina Safilios-Rothschild

Up to now the occupational system has been based on the assumption that all men had to work and that the majority of them had wives playing supportive traditional roles. These assumptions were decisive in shaping the structure of jobs, work requirements, and work-related policies and ethics. Once these basic assumptions no longer hold, some fundamental changes are in order.

There is little doubt that American women, including married women and mothers, are increasingly entering the labor force. Not only are more and more women seeking employment, but also their work behavior and career patterns are changing. More women have uninterrupted work patterns rather than occasional jobs that fit into the least demanding stages of family cycle; more women earn more in wages and salaries than before; women have entered many prestigious "masculine" occupations (even though still in small numbers); and more women are committed to their careers, have ambitions, and seek success, promotions, and responsibility.[1] Clearly, at present these are only emerging tendencies and are by no means widespread or consistent yet. They do, however, suggest what lies ahead.

Women's increasing and more continuous labor force participation raises a number of questions about the distribution of jobs and, indeed, the very nature of the work world because it occurs in a period of high unemployment and uncertain employment outlook. It is easy to say that available jobs should be distributed between prospective qualified workers, regardless of gender, age, religion, race, or ethnic background. However, on what basis will this distribution actually take place—merit and qualifications, need, or a combination of merit and need? In other words, selection of the criteria for equitable job distribution raises ethical and philosophical controversies. On an even more fundamental level, do we need to reexamine and reconceptualize the basic notions about work, its organization and scheduling, and its goals that are reflected in our economic and social policies?

THE "ALL OR NOTHING" MODEL
OF EMPLOYMENT AND ACHIEVEMENT

Up to now, a person who has a good employment record has been one who worked throughout adult life. A few interruptions—for military service, additional training or education, and perhaps illness—are considered legitimate (although illness or disability sometimes is viewed with suspicion and reflects negatively on the worker as a bad risk, unless his or her work achievements have already been considerable). The usual reasons for which women interrupt work—marriage, childbearing, child rearing, or caring for a husband or children who are seriously ill—were not considered legitimate and tended to stigmatize the woman worker as not serious and uncommitted to her work. Part-time work, which is mainly undertaken by women, tended to be viewed as temporary, auxilliary, and marginal employment. And the work records that led to raises and promotions in a factory or a profession often showed that the employee worked overtime and was as productive as possible.

In fact, an "all or nothing" model of employment and achievement has been operating, keeping workers from working and achieving to different degrees. Anyone not interested in working or able to work full-time and even overtime, throughout life, and to be as productive as possible is discriminated against and penalized.

It is exactly this all or nothing concept of employment and achievement that women are challenging more and more, and many of their policy suggestions seek to modify this monolithic model. Sweden has already institutionalized several policies that alter this model—a paid six-month parental leave (that can be taken by either the father or the mother); the acceptance of part-time work as having the same fringe benefits and rights to raises, promotions, and tenure as full-time work; and allowance of up to twenty-one days' leave per year for working fathers and mothers to stay home and take care of sick children.[2] Clearly, such policies are desperately needed in the United States.

NORMALIZATION OF THE DUAL-WORK FAMILY

These policies are not sufficient, however. Women's increasing labor force participation implies that dual-work families in all social classes are becoming almost the rule rather than the exception, and attitudinal studies find that Americans increasingly accept this arrangement. Recent surveys of college students and of well-educated, white, upper-middle- and middle-class adults show that the majority accept the employment of married women, especially when there are not small children at home, and the majority believe that household expenses and family responsibilities (child care and housework) should be shared equally by the spouses when the wife works.[3] It must be noted, however, that among noncollege populations, more women than men support these views. For example, two-thirds of the men and four-fifths of the women felt that most household chores should be shared equally except for household repairs and sewing; two-thirds of males and over three-quarters of females felt that both parents should share child-care responsibilities.[4]

In 1973 and 1974, two studies of college students in two different universities, with student populations ranging from working-class to upper-middle-class backgrounds, compared their beliefs with those of students in the early 1960s. The reported differences are significant. A much higher proportion of students in the 1970s believe that (a) the wife's career is of equal importance to the husband's career; (b) a woman's career and marriage or career and motherhood are (or should be) compatible; and (c) husbands should share housework and child-care responsibilities.[5]

It seems reasonable to expect, therefore, that dual-career families will increase among college-educated couples as these students start marrying and having children. The data from these studies suggest that some ideological changes have occurred among college-educated women, and to some extent men, leading them to expect the equalitarian, sharing marital relationship that is necessary for a dual-career family life-style. There are no similar data about changes in lower-middle- and working-class men and women. Probably some changes have taken place, but among blue-collar families there is more ambivalence and a tendency to prefer traditional roles for husbands and wives.

The "normalization" of dual-employment families creates new job-related and family-related problems, however. Both the labor force and the family need to offer more flexibility and options in order for men and women to participate actively in both systems without undue stress and strain. Much of the flexibility and many of the options needed within the family system can be influenced only indirectly by policies. Under new familial options a woman might marry a low-achievement-oriented man or a younger man at the beginning of his career or a man with a lower work commitment and achievement orientation than her own. These new options are emerging as women gradually become more confident in their own ability to secure income, status, and power.[6] The flexibility and options within the labor force are more subject to policy changes. Changes in ideology and cultural values are essential, however, for the successful implementation of innovative policies.

TOWARD A CONTINUUM BETWEEN EMPLOYMENT AND NONEMPLOYMENT

One much needed value change entails the recognition that high achievement and productivity are desirable but not mandatory for everyone or throughout life. When everyone who is qualified for and interested in employment has an equal right and equal access to work, it may be relatively easier to accept the notion that only some people will work hard, will work overtime, and will achieve highly throughout life and that many people will do so for some periods of their lives. The necessary work could then be carried out without everyone having to work hard and long throughout life. Men and women would both, thus, gain considerable work flexibility.

New policies could be introduced to allow people flexible schedules or time off work for a variety of reasons and to accept achievement at different levels at different stages of people's lives without undue penalties. Men and women might be allowed to trade a year or two of partially paid leave in their thirties or forties for a longer full-time work commitment in their fifties or sixties.[7] Economists could estimate under what conditions and for which categories of workers (in terms of health and skills) this risk can be taken by employers without unreasonable cost. At least some economists have recently acknowledged that the cost and benefits of flexible-time and part-time jobs must become the focus of economic studies.[8] A new institute, the Work in America Institute, has been established to examine through conferences and reports the effects of different types of part-time and flexible time programs on productivity.[9]

The fundamental purpose of all these policies would be to diminish the degree of discontinuity between work and nonwork, achievement and nonachievement, full-time and part-time work, and high and low work commitment. Thus, men and women workers would be allowed a smooth transition from employment to nonemployment, from one level of work commitment to another, and from one level of achievement to another.

How close are we to such policies? It is hard to tell. Their adoption depends partly on the men and women who are now living in dual-employment families and are paying a very high physical, psychological, and social cost, because social changes have not accommodated their occupational behavior and needs. These men and women must apply political pressure to convince labor unions and employers to incorporate such conditions in negotiated labor contracts. Workers must explore whether the introduction and acceptance of such conditions would not improve their lives more significantly than salary increases. Social scientists need to develop feasible and realistic policies and make these options known to the public through their writings and talks.

Until a significant degree of flexibility is built into the employment and achievement systems and into the family system, and until sex-role stereotypes are eradicated, women who like to work and to achieve will have to sacrifice love, fun, and enjoyment. They will have to choose between ambition and love; between achievement and fun. Men have faced similar dilemmas, and they will do so more as they marry working and ambitious wives and adhere to the principle of gender equality. Value changes and policies are needed that will allow people to shift their primary orientation, energy, and psychological investment from high work commitment and achievement, to family responsibilities, to the enjoyment of love relationships, to pleasure and fun, without entirely severing or seriously jeopardizing their occupational role during periods of low job commitment and achievement orientation.

The hard line between employment and nonemployment will also diminish when prevailing laws and social policies acknowledge household work as a legitimate occupation and regulate its pay and working conditions. When the person who does housework is classified as a household technician and paid according to the time put in and the quality of the work, the distinction between "working" women and housewives will become meaningless. Such policies also recognize that all work is valuable, regardless of the setting in which it is carried out and the gender of the person who performs it. These policies would actually help equalize the division of labor at home between husbands and wives more than any ideological commitment. However, it is difficult to evaluate the likelihood of their being adopted in the near future.

ACCOMMODATING DUAL-EMPLOYMENT FAMILIES

The spread of dual-employment families, especially in a period of high unemployment, highlights the need for hiring policies that help spouses find work in the same town.[10] Such policies are necessary for blue-collar workers, white-collar workers, professionals, technicians, and management specialists, since job opportunities for different employment categories differ widely from locality to locality. The essence of such policies would be preferential hiring of members of dual-employment families. This concept is unpopular, however, when some families have trouble finding even one job. Within certain business and academic settings preferential hiring policies are already practiced informally, but the problem is becoming acute for young professional couples. Emotional and familial relationships in dual-employment couples are often already strained because of lingering sex-role stereotypes and the lack of clear-cut norms. Splitting careers between two locations puts an additional burden on them. The notion that married women have less mobility (whether true or not) is a significant factor in occupational discrimination, because they are then not offered or cannot accept better job offers that require relocation.[11] A recent study of microbiologists showed, for example, that 93 percent of the women would move only if their husbands could find a satisfactory position in the new location, while only 20 percent of the men made the same condition about their wives' employment.[12] Some couples, especially those who have been married for several years and are comfortable in their relationship, can create enough flexibility in their marriage to maximize their work opportunities without jeopardizing their relationship. Some manage to live in different cities: they commute weekends or once a month, depending on the distance, and spend holidays and vacations together. A few enjoy this separate marital arrangement so much that they maintain it even when they could live in the same city. Many can accept such an arrangement for a year or two until, by making some compromises in their career involvements, they both manage to find work in the same area.

Another necessary policy concerns urban planning—housing, zoning laws, planning of communities, and relative distances between work places, residential communities, and shopping centers. It is becoming evident that urban planning must consider and accommodate the increasing numbers of dual-work families, in which neither spouse can travel long distances for shopping and family errands. Some cities and communities are responding to the new needs of dual-employment families by developing apartment complexes that center around major employers, such as universities and large companies; by developing large and varied shopping centers near residential areas; by extending shopping hours until late in the evening; and by providing special services facilities within large apartment houses or complexes. Such policies may spread more and more and could transform the American suburban style of living into an urban apartment style of living.

THE NORMALIZATION OF
EMPLOYED WOMEN'S CHARACTERISTICS

Two crucial social policies affecting working-class women's occupational choices would be the opening of all types of vocational training to women at all levels and in all settings and the provision of special grants to women for on-the-job training or for attending vocational schools. Vocational skills that for many years have been considered masculine would be attractive to low-income women if they were given special training grants and if women's involvement in such skills were made socially acceptable. This change in attitudes could be aided if the media, especially television and movies, showed a variety of "normal," "attractive," "happy" women in such jobs and if girls were exposed to a wide range of mechanical skills and crafts from an early age, starting in the first grade. Women commonly resist entering a masculine field for fear that they will be considered unfeminine and unattractive to men. This fear can be alleviated only when a sufficient number of attractive women enter the occupation to alter the image.

The increasing number of working women and presumably also successful women may help invalidate the assumption that high occupational achievements and attractiveness in women are incompatible. While a man's attractiveness and sex appeal increase in the eyes of women when he makes occupational achievements and wins success, a woman's attractiveness and sex appeal radically decrease in the eyes of men with these achievements.[13] When more and more highly attractive women start achieving success in work, it will become more difficult to see achieving women as unattractive, even though they exercise power and exhibit success. There are already some indications that women's occupational successes enhance their attractiveness in the eyes of at least a few "liberated" men.

Some changes are also taking place that free women from the compulsion to be physically appealing in order to qualify for a broad spectrum of "feminine" jobs. The increasing number of working women, coupled with pressures against open sex discrimination, have tended to broaden the range of physical appearances considered normal for working women. Auxilliary "decorative" employees, such as receptionists, secretaries, waitresses, and stewardesses, have up to now been hired by men often on the basis of which candidate is the most attractive rather than the most competent. These hiring criteria are now being scrutinized and challenged. Men now sometimes hire women for these jobs regardless of their physical attractiveness. This acceptance of the normal physical appearance of working women will have important consequences for the nature of work relationships between men and women. When women are not hired simply to be attractive, women workers in general will no longer be viewed as sex objects, and men will be able to relate to them in terms of their work contributions, their performance, their efficiency, their ideas, and their creativity as well as their sexuality. This process can also be expected to help free women from the agonizing compulsion to look attractive and be well-dressed at work day after day, since their career success will no longer depend heavily on looks. We know little about how women in power positions select men subordinates and especially about whether the physical attractiveness of these men enters the pictures. It is quite possible that at least some women may relate to male candidates and subordinates as sex objects and manipulate their power at work for sexual privileges and advantages from these men. It remains to be seen whether such practices are only transitory and will disappear gradually as men and women learn how to be good friends and colleagues.

Despite considerable gains made by women in the labor force the tendency still persists for employers to hire a woman candidate only when she is clearly superior to all male applicants.[14] This is especially true in male-dominated occupations and work settings. The only way that average women (in terms of ability, qualifications, and attractiveness) can be hired on an equal basis with men is if the pressures to hire substantial numbers of qualified women increase. The sheer numerical increase of women workers in occupations and work settings in which they are now scarce will normalize their employment there. Such a normalization would relieve women from the compulsion to be superwomen in order to qualify for ordinary jobs.

The importance of a numerical increase of women workers, especially in occupations and positions in which they are scarce, clearly underlines the

> **66 The only way that average women (in terms of ability, qualifications, and attractiveness) can be hired on an equal basis with men is if the pressures to hire substantial numbers of qualified women increase. 99**

need for affirmative action policies that are carried out energetically and conscientiously. Normalization of employers' demands of women (with respect to ability and physical appearance) is essential and cannot come about until considerable numbers of women work in occupations, positions, and settings that are still male bastions.

BREAKING THROUGH OCCUPATIONAL SEX DISCRIMINATION

One important attitudinal change that has already taken place is the increasing public confidence in women lawyers and doctors.[15] These women have broken the sex bias in two masculine and high-prestige professions. The trust they now command has significant implications for women's further involvement and performance in these professions and other masculine occupations. As more women become lawyers and doctors and are allowed to practice in increasingly visible and important positions, their image will become even more positive, and their clients' confidence will tend to increase. During the early transitional stages, women may come to trust women lawyers and doctors more than men practitioners, because they feel better treated, understood, helped, or defended by women. This is already happening to some extent with women psychiatrists and therapists and is beginning to spread to pediatricians, gynecologists, obstetricians, and even surgeons.

Employers' and managers' attitudes have not radically changed, however. Quite recent studies show that the present generation of graduate and undergraduate students in management hold traditional sex-role stereotypes that affect their evaluations of hypothetical job applicants. They tend to perceive women as applicants for clerical jobs and men as applicants for administrative management positions, even when both men and women indicate the same job aspirations.[16] It seems, therefore, that courses in business and management need to include education about sex-role biases, if future business executives and managers are to be less sexist than past and present ones.

Persons already working as employers and managers hold even more stereotyped views of women and women's work roles than students do.[17] They have been reported to feel that (a) the rules of etiquette, politeness, and deference that define interactions between the sexes in public can interfere in work interactions; (b) women do not make good supervisors because they cannot appraise the seriousness of a performance problem and because both men and women feel uncomfortable with a woman supervisor; and (c) women are not as dependable as men because of their biological and personal characteristics.[18]

Since the criteria of successful performance are not always clear-cut and precise, sex-role stereotypes can distort supervisors' perceptions of women's performances and belittle their achievements in comparison to men's.[19] Furthermore, managers' sex-role stereotypes may lead them to attribute women's high level of performance to luck,[20] unless it is repeated over a considerable time period.[21] Finally, because managers and supervisors stereotypically view women workers as less competent and dependable and as greater risks, they tend to have lower expectations of them and they tend not to assign them challenging and demanding duties that would give them the experience and self-confidence women need for higher positions.[22]

Affirmative action directives and policies have little if any impact on the stereotyped sex-role perceptions and attitudes of employers and managers. Business administration specialists, and sociologists, psychologists, and economists specializing in employment and sex-role issues, must find strategies and mechanisms for resocializing male managers, employers, and supervisors. It may also be necessary to resocialize women in these jobs, since the few women who are given top positions tend to be carefully selected antifeminists and "queen bees." Some of the resocialization process will take place informally through everyday interactions with colleagues, but this cannot be relied on to make a consistent and significant difference. Furthermore, the particular personalities of the men and women working together may tend to clash, producing negative rather than positive effects. Training in management and sex-role perceptions must be introduced not only in the regular college business administration curriculum for future managers but also in special management training programs and workshops for today's businesspeople. Strategies must be developed to make such training prestigious and desirable in the eyes of those hoping to qualify for top positions. Large companies and businesses can lead the way in giving the training this connotation.

THE "COLD WAR" AGAINST SUCCESSFUL WOMEN

Sensitization and resocialization of employers, managers, and supervisors are necessary to prevent the subtle types of occupational discrimination that take place as women move into top positions or what were exclusively male occupational territories. It has been documented, for example, that the more women perform well and aspire to top decision-making positions, the more informal sex discrimination increases; the higher women rise in an organization (in terms of rank, expertise, or authority), the more they tend to lose the friendship and respect of their colleagues, influence over peers, and access to information.[23] Experiments with college students show that competent women are granted the appropriate prestige but are not liked.[24] Women who want and manage to achieve a high status, experience a "cold war" and must have the psychology of long-distance runners to endure the loneliness that comes from rejection by their colleagues. Many talented and hardworking women have found the psychological cost of high occupational aspirations and achievements unbearable, and this has dampened their ambitions.

This cold war has been especially effective because women are socialized to seek and need the approval of others. A woman's early socialization experiences are reinforced when part of her job is to adjust to idiosyncratic rules in relationships with male bosses rather than dealing with impersonal work rules and regulations. The evaluation of her performance is often subjective, and her occupational rewards may be unrelated to promotions and raises. Instead they are small personal tokens of appreciation consistent with sex-role stereotypes, such as presents from the boss or being taken out to lunch.[25] These differential occupational rewards are clearly discriminatory, since they are granted only when the supervisor *likes* the woman, and what is more important these pleasant little rewards do not advance the woman occupationally. In fact, they condition women to seek and maintain the approval and friendship of men in high positions and to become psychologically dependent on such approval.

Some women now realize that they are being manipulated and exploited by this dependence and are trying to free themselves. They recognize that no man or woman should have to pay this psychological cost for competence and achievement. Awareness training of men and women in different settings and encouragement of open discussions at work between men and women may help end the ongoing psychological war against successful women. Personnel specialists should become sensitive to this issue during their training, and workshops should be given to train those already working to recognize and cope with manifestations of the problem. After all, the efficiency of companies and businesses is diminished when the women who are most competent, most capable of achieving, and most ambitious reduce their aspirations in order to keep the approval and friendship of colleagues.

Another type of subtle occupational discrimination is that directed against the first one or two women who enter masculine domains. Men resent that their all-male atmosphere is being disrupted and they tend to isolate the women. Male colleagues will prevent bona fide integration of a woman into the group, regardless of her characteristics and her efforts to break the barriers. To overcome this, affirmative action policies should require that more than one or two token women be employed in all-male occupational settings. Every effort should be made to ensure that at least three women are hired in the same department, unit, or team, so that they can rely on each other for psychological support until they are truly integrated into the male group of coworkers. When affirmative action policies are being carried out, they must be monitored to make sure that employed women are not scattered sparsely throughout a work setting so that they cannot form a mutually supportive and reinforcing group.

In addition to stronger and better enforced affirmative action policies, many of the strategies needed for the next ten to fifteen years must cope with various types of informal and subtle occupational discrimination against women. These strategies may in fact make affirmative action policies more effective. Increasingly, women may have to shift the focus of their policy efforts from equal opportunity and equal pay to policies that help women work, aspire, and achieve without paying excessive or unbearable psychological and social costs.

NOTES

1   Hilda Kahne and Andrew I. Kohen, "Economic Perspectives on the Roles of Women in the American Economy," *Journal of Economic Literature* 13 (1975): 1249–92.

2   Constantina Safilios-Rothschild, *Women and Social Policy* (Englewood Cliffs, N.J.: Prentice-Hall, 1974), pp. 20–22.

3   Betty Yorburg and Ibthaj Arafat, "Current Sex Role Conceptions and Conflicts" (unpublished paper, City College of the City University of New York, 1974); Ann P. Parelius, "Emerging Sex Role Attitudes, Expectations, and Strains among College Women" (paper presented at the meeting of the Society for the Study of Social Problems, Montreal, 1974).

4   Yorburg and Arafat, "Current Sex Role Conceptions."

5   Parelius, "Emerging Sex Role Attitudes"; May Ahdab Yehia, "Attitudes toward Women's Work Commitment: Changes from 1964–1974" (Ph.D. diss., Wayne State University, 1976).

6   Constantina Safilios-Rothschild, "Dual Linkages between the Occupational and Family Systems: A Macrosociological Analysis," *Signs: Journal of Women in Culture and Society* 1, no. 3, pt. 2 (1976): 51–60.

7   Safilios-Rothschild, "Dual Linkages."

8   Kahne and Kohen, "Economic Perspectives."

9   *World of Work Report* 1, no. 1 (March 1976).

10 Safilios-Rothschild, *Women and Social Policy*, p. 57.

11 Beatrice Dinerman, "Sex Discrimination in Academia," *Journal of Higher Education* 42 (1971): 253–64.

12 Eva Ruth Kashket et al., "Status of Women Microbiologists," *Science* 183 (1974): 488–94.

13 Safilios-Rothschild, *Women and Social Policy*, pp. 65–66.

14   Lawrence Simpson, "A Myth Is Better than a Miss: Men Get the Edge in Academic Employment," *College and University Business,* February 1970, pp. 72–73; Benson Rosen and T. Jerdee, "Effects of Applicant's Sex and Difficulty of Job on Evaluation of Candidates for Managerial Positions," *Journal of Applied Psychology* 59 (1974): 511–12.

15   Yorburg and Arafat, "Current Sex Role Conceptions."

16   E. A. Cecil, R. J. Paul, and R. P. Olins, "Perceived Importance of Selected Variables Used to Evaluate Male and Female Job Applicants," *Personnel Psychology* 26 (1973): 397–404.

17   Rosen and Jerdee, "Effects of Applicant's Sex"; B. M. Bass et al., "Male Managers' Attitudes toward Working Women," *American Behavioral Scientist* 15 (1971): 221–36; Randi Hagen and A. Kahn, "Discrimination against Competent Women" (unpublished paper, Iowa State University, 1974); James R. Terborg and Daniel L. Ilgen, "A Theoretical Approach to Sex Discrimination in Traditionally Masculine Occuptions" (paper presented at the American Psychological Association meeting, New Orleans, 1974); and V. E. Schein, "The Relationship between Sex Role Stereotypes and Requisite Management Characteristics," *Journal of Applied Psychology* 57 (1973): 95–100.

18   Bass et al., "Male Managers' Attitudes."

19   Terborg and Ilgen, "A Theoretical Approach to Sex Discrimination."

20   Ibid.

21   H. H. Kelley, "Attribution Theory in Social Psychology," in *Nebraska Symposium on Motivation,* ed. D. Levine (Lincoln: University of Nebraska, Department of Psychology, 1967).

22   Terborg and Ilgen, "A Theoretical Approach to Sex Discrimination"; Cynthia F. Epstein, *The Woman Lawyer* (Chicago: University of Chicago Press, 1974).

23   John Miller, Sanford Labovitz, and L. Fry, "Differences in the Organizational Experiences of Women and Men: Resources, Vested Interests, and Discrimination" (paper presented at the American Sociological Association meeting, Montreal, 1974).

24   Hagen and Kahn, "Discrimination against Competent Women."

25   Joan Acker and Donald R. Van Houten, "Differential Recruitment and Control: The Sex Structuring of Organizations," *Administrative Science Quarterly* 19 (1974): 211–20.

Index

DATE DUE

7. 24. '80	APR 25 '90
10. 23. '80	JUN 13 '90
11. 13. '80	DEC 0 2 1995
4. 02. '81	
6. 11. '81	
5. 20. '82	
7. 15. '82	
7. 29. '82	
3. 03. '83	
11. 17. '83	
2. 09. '84	
ret. 2/26	
11. 22. '84	
6. 14. '85	
10 ▸ 4. '87	
12. 07. '88	